Monetary Economics

Monetary Economics

Karl Brunner and Allan H. Meltzer

Basil Blackwell

First published 1989

Basil Blackwell Ltd
108 Cowley Road, Oxford, OX4 1JF, UK

Basil Blackwell Inc.
432 Park Avenue South, Suite 1503
New York, NY 10016, USA

British Library Cataloguing in Publication Data

Brunner, Karl, 1916–
   Monetary economics.
   1. Monetary systems. Theories
   I. Title II. Meltzer, Allan H. (Allan Harold), 1928–
332.4'01

   ISBN 0-631-16335-2

Library of Congress Cataloging in Publication Data

Brunner, Karl, 1916–
   Monetary economics/Karl Brunner and Allan H. Meltzer.
    p.   cm.
   Includes index.
   ISBN 0-631-16335-2
   1. Money -- United States. 2. Monetary policy -- United States.
3. Fiscal policy -- United States. 4. Money. 5. Monetary policy.
6. Fiscal policy. I. Meltzer, Allan H. II. Title.
HG501.B75 1989
332.4'973 – dc19

88-24341
CIP

Typeset in 10 on 12pt Times
by Colset Private Limited, Singapore
Printed in Great Britain by Bookcraft Ltd., Bath, Avon

To Rosmarie, Marilyn, and the children

Contents

Introduction

Karl Brunner and Allan H. Meltzer

The papers selected for this collection span more than 20 years, from 1964 to 1986. This period covers a major portion of the years of our long collaboration, and the pieces are a representative sample of our joint work. Our earliest efforts focused on the development of money supply theory, the role of credit markets and intermediaries, and the integration of money supply into the theory of asset markets. We extended our analysis to incorporate the demand for money and, later, to interactions between asset markets and the real sector. Our work on asset markets, output, and their interrelation is in the tradition of static, general equilibrium theory. With the emergence of dynamic, rational expectations models, we developed a rational expectations model for an economy, subject to permanent and transitory shocks, in which information is used efficiently but prices are not fully responsive to all ongoing shocks.

For us, economics is a policy science. One of our earliest joint efforts was a study of the way in which the Federal Reserve operates in financial markets. We have continued that interest throughout our collaboration. Several of the papers included here consider policy issues. There is a survey of the development of the macroeconomic analysis of fiscal policy and a comparison of the variability experienced by countries operating under fixed and fluctuating exchange rates. Our interest in institutions and the role of information led us to consider the benefits arising from the use of a medium of exchange, money.

Although the volume is a representative sample of our work, there are some differences. The papers in this volume strike a different balance between theory and empirical studies. And there is less explicit attention to the political economy of policy institutions and policymaking than is found particularly in our current work.

The papers are reprinted largely as they were written. We have found little reason to change our arguments or to make other substantive changes. Typographical errors have been corrected.

Federal Reserve Policymaking

The volume starts with one of our earliest joint efforts, part of a study prepared for the Committee on Banking and Currency of the House of Representatives. The study arose out of a concern by the committee chairman, Representative Wright Patman, about the implementation and conduct of monetary policy. At the time, Chairman Patman believed that the problems arose in the dealer market for government securities. We persuaded him that the problems lay elsewhere. The result was a three-chapter study of monetary policymaking.

The chapter published here examines in some detail the conception guiding the decisions and actions of the Federal Reserve. We believe that to understand the strategy and tactical arrangements used by the Federal Reserve authorities, we have to understand their conception of the relevant aspects of the monetary process, since their conception and beliefs guide their actions and their interpretation of events and observations.

At the time, very little attention was given to such matters either in the press or in the professional literature. Most textbooks repeated the descriptive material found in *Purposes and Functions of the Federal Reserve System*, prepared by the Federal Reserve staff. This material paid little attention to the way in which actions by the Federal Reserve were presumed to influence money, credit, interest rates, and economic activity or to the way in which the Federal Reserve used information about markets or the economy to guide policy.[1] Minutes of meetings were not published. There was very little in the public record about the principles that guided action. To fill this gap, we relied on interviews with officials, their printed speeches and comments, and the record of their actions.

In an earlier period, Federal Reserve officials and economists had worked to develop a framework for policy. The origins of this framework reach back to the 1920s and reflect the influence of Benjamin Strong, Governor of the Federal Reserve Bank of New York, and of Federal Reserve economists, Randolph Burgess and Winfield Riefler. Experience during the steep 1920-1 recession, and Congressional reaction to the rise in interest rates in 1920, encouraged the belief within the Federal Reserve that discount rate changes are a relatively slow and blunt instrument for controlling borrowing and domestic credit expansion.

Strong, Riefler, and Burgess shifted emphasis from the discount rate to open market operations as a means of controlling borrowing. The basis for this change appears to have been observations showing that bank borrowing,

---

[1]This situation changed markedly. Since the late 1960s professional economists have carefully monitored Federal Reserve actions. Federal Reserve officials discuss their methods and procedures, and academic economists analyze their statements and procedures.

and thus borrowed reserves, were negatively correlated with open market purchases. The effect of open market transactions on total reserves was attenuated by changes in member bank borrowing. According to Strong, Riefler, and Burgess, policy operations were not attenuated; the negative correlation showed that the Fed was able to drive the member banks to borrow or repay.

The Fed settled on bank borrowing as the link between Federal Reserve actions and the money supply process. Borrowing occurred despite the "reluctance" of banks to borrow, independent of any costs and returns. To the Fed, this implied that lower bank borrowing would be translated into accelerated asset expansion by banks and lower interest rates. Larger bank borrowing was said to have the opposite effect.

Events thoroughly contradicted this conception during the 1930s. Subsequent observations, particularly the accumulation of excess reserves at banks, modified the Fed's views. The free reserve doctrine appeared as a generalization of the reluctant bank borrowing notion. Free reserves, defined as excess reserves minus member bank borrowing, replaced member bank borrowing as the crucial nexus of the money supply process. Larger free reserves were presumed to accelerate banks' asset expansion and lower free reserves to moderate expansion or induce contraction. Borrowed reserves and non-borrowed reserves had entirely different, indeed opposite, effects on the money supply process. Increases in borrowed reserves are contractive whereas increases in non-borrowed reserves exert an expansive effect.

The free reserve doctrine dominated the Federal Reserve's vision of the money supply process into the 1960s. As seen by Chairman Martin, the central bank served as regulator and guardian of the nation's credit flows. Money and monetary processes played no role in this vision; the emphasis was on credit and interest rates, particularly short-term rates. Arthur F. Burns, who succeeded Martin as Chairman, fitted well into this tradition. His collected essays (1969) address the importance of credit and credit flows and give little attention to monetary processes.

The free reserve doctrine was always subject to some reservations within the Federal Reserve System. In our interviews, some Governors relied on metaphors that were not entirely consistent with the free reserve doctrine. Objections to the doctrine based on good, elementary economic analysis could also be found. Since the basic vision was spelled out in fragments and isolated pieces, there were ambiguities and possibly inconsistent aspects in the frameworks used by individual members.

At the time of our study, we recognized a possible transition to a new framework of analysis. The change was complete by the early 1970s. The free reserve doctrine was replaced by an approach centered on the demand for money and the Federal funds rate. Further modifications occurred by the late 1970s and the early 1980s.

Despite this evolution of the strategic conception and tactical procedures, residues of the free reserve doctrine remained. Chairman Volcker always considered increases in borrowed reserves to be contractive in contrast to increases in non-borrowed reserves which are expansive. Lombra and Kara-mouzis (1988) find some surviving ingredients of the free reserve doctrine in recent years.

An understanding of the free reserve conception clarified some aspects of the Fed's policy procedures, particularly the target and indicator problems. The target problem involves the choice of a short-range or intermediate target to guide the execution of monetary policy. The indicator problem, in contrast, involves the choice of a scale allowing comparisons of the stance adopted by monetary policy. The free reserve conception immediately suggested to the Fed that free reserves be used both as target and indicator. In the former role, free reserves were used to instruct the New York Federal Reserve Bank about the conduct of monetary policy. In the latter function, larger free reserves were interpreted as expressions of an "easier policy" and lower free reserves as a "tighter policy." Evidence of the use of free reserves as an indicator of the stance of monetary policy is clearly revealed in our study by the correlation between the level of free reserves observed and the FOMC's assessment and recommendations for "ease" or "tightness" reported in the published *Record of Policy Actions.*

The problem of optimal choice of targets and indicators arises under conditions of uncertainty about the state of the economy and uncertain knowledge about its structure. The staff of the Federal Reserve, faced with the problem of guiding and monitoring the implementation of policy, chose free reserves and later the Federal funds rate, total reserves, non-borrowed reserves and other variables as targets or indicators. Academic economists have generally ignored these problems by assuming either that they possess reliable information that they do not have or by pretending that the structure of the economy is represented by a highly corroborated econometric model. A rational policy procedure must recognize the uncertain state of our knowledge. Recognition of this uncertainty requires recognition of the target and indicator problems.

The Federal Reserve authorities could not avoid the problem. Their uncritical commitment to the free reserve notion, however, prevented a rational choice of an adequate target and indicator. It can be easily demonstrated that wrong choices can mislead policymakers. The Fed's choice of indicator led the Fed to make serious misjudgments about its policy on many occasions. This happened both in the 1930s and in the postwar years. Our study investigates this problem in some depth and concludes that the Fed's rhetoric expressed by interpretations of its policy (as "easy" or "tight", or more or less expansionary) is often negatively associated with its actions. Policy would be described as expansionary, when the Fed undertook actions that reduced money and bank credit, e.g. in 1960; the Fed engaged in expansionary actions, but asserted that it followed a tight policy, e.g. in 1950. Monetary growth was generally procyclical, rising faster in economic expansions than in contractions. Our study reveals that the reason for these misinterpretations is that the level of free reserves is a poor indicator of the Fed's actual behavior. The use of an inappropriate indicator explains in large part the Fed's failure to respond properly to evolving events in 1930 and subsequent years. The same misconception led the Fed to double reserve requirements in 1936/7 and thus initiate the second or third largest recession of this century at a time when the country had not fully recovered from the Great Depression. The price of misjudgment resulting from systematic misinterpretations was very high indeed.

At the time of our study there was much discussion about the monetary policy lag – the lag between an event and the response to the event of policy actions expressed by some credit or monetary magnitude. The recognition lag, measuring the lag between the event and its recognition by the policy-makers, is one component of the total policy lag. The study considers the quality of the Fed's recognition of critical turning points, based on assessments explicitly made at the time and published in the *Record of Policy Actions*.

The result was surprising. We found that the recognition lag was remarkably short and would be very hard to reduce. We also noticed that the vagueness of the discussion at meetings of the Federal Open Market Committee (FOMC) and the corresponding vagueness of the directive issued to the New York Federal Reserve Bank had the effect of granting substantial autonomy to the manager who implements the policy. The directive required interpretation on the part of the manager and could not be unambiguously translated into specific actions. Despite the ambiguity, the actions of the account manager were rarely criticized by the members of the FOMC. When criticisms were made, members of the committee would disagree about whether their instructions had been followed. As a result the manager had considerable discretion, and he appears to have used his own judgment at times.

Re-reading the study after 24 years, we find several ideas which have moved to the center of our analysis. These include the effect of pervasive uncertainty, and most particularly monetary uncertainty, on the level and behavior of interest rates. Our earlier study also develops in some detail the comparative role of perceived permanent and transitory shocks in portfolio managers' decisions and banks' reserve adjustments. This theme returns in a later paper, jointly authored with Alex Cukierman and included in this volume, where we explore the implications of uncertain inferences about the nature and composition of shocks for decision-makers' behavior. The relation of this inference problem to the problems of pricing and monetary policy in economies with comparatively inflexible prices is treated in our recent work (Brunner and Meltzer, 1989).

Our study of Federal Reserve policymaking relied on some of the work on the nature of money supply processes that had been a theme of our research pursued since the late 1950s. A review of the literature indicated that, at the time, economists did not have a coherent analysis of the simultaneous determination of money stock, bank credit and interest rates on asset markets. Textbooks offered at most a formular inherited from the 1920s which described the magnitude of credit expansion in response to surplus reserves. This formula had little relation to economic analysis, i.e., to the analysis of behavior responding to costs and returns. Moreover, the formula did not take into account interactions on asset markets. The initial surplus reserves remained unrelated to any observable term.

We explored different approaches at the time. We were motivated less by abstract generality and elegance than by an interest in developing an analytic approach linking money, credit and interest rates to central bank behavior that offered definite propositions. We were particularly concerned to develop an analysis which would allow us to integrate institutional arrangements into the analysis.

The second and third papers included here represent some of the initial steps in our endeavor. The final form, guiding our subsequent work, was completed about 1970 and appears in this volume. (See Chapter 4 and also Brunner and Meltzer, 1988b).

Money Supply Theory

Chapter 2, "A Credit Market Theory of the Money Supply and an Explanation of Two Puzzles in US Monetary Policy," (1966) explicitly addresses the basic theme maintained in our subsequent papers on money supply. Money stock and bank credit emerge from the joint interaction of the monetary authorities, banks and the public. The analysis provides a framework which determines the relative importance of public, banks and central banks for the movement of money stock and bank credit. The analysis also centered on the interaction of financial markets, including the credit markets typically neglected in IS/LM analysis.

As the title suggests, "A Credit Market Theory . . ." directs attention to the role of the credit markets and intermediation in the money supply process. The model has separate loan and bond markets. The banks lend to the public and hold a bond portfolio. On the loan market, interest rates adjust the public's desired loan liability portfolio and the banks' stock supply of loans. In the bond market, the banks' and the public's demand for bonds confronts a given stock. Banks allocate their assets among reserves, loans, and bonds in response to relevant costs and returns. The public responds to similar incentives. The credit market system determines, jointly with some other relations connecting the credit markets with the banks' and the Federal

Reserves' balance sheets, the interest rates on bonds and loans, the money stock, and the volume of bank credit. A money demand function is not incorporated in the analysis. The equilibrium is, therefore, a partial equilibrium of the asset markets reflecting decisions about intermediation and allocation of the banks' portfolios but neglecting feedbacks from the market for real assets. In particular, the price of real assets is implicitly held constant throughout the argument. This procedure brings out that the demand for money is not the dominant determinant of money stock and monetary growth, contrary to many assertions made by the Federal Reserve and by research economists.

The analysis shows, also, that credit market shocks have very different consequences for the monetary system. The same is true for shocks to the demand for money (Brunner and Meltzer, 1988a), a conclusion that is particularly visible when we compare a monetary with an interest rate strategy. The two credit markets also respond differently to perceived permanent or transitory shocks. This follows from the underlying rationale, based on comparative information costs, that justifies the differentiation into two markets. The analysis developed in the paper moreover throws light on several issues. The joint interaction between money and credit reveals that the two magnitudes behave differently over the business cycle and respond differently to the underlying determinants of the system. The analysis explains variations in the ratio of money stock to bank credit as a consequence of different responses to changes in policy and in the behavior of banks and the public.

In the years after World War II, the profession had a lively discussion of the merits or problems associated with the Fed's rigid interest rate control policy. This policy, imposed by the Treasury, was generally described as "an engine of inflation." The US economy experienced both inflation and deflation under the policy, however. "A Credit Market Theory . . ." shows that a policy of interest rate control can have inflationary or deflationary consequences depending on the prevailing fiscal policy. A persistent large deficit that increases the outstanding stock of bonds combined with an obligation on a central bank to maintain interest rates (or a major segment of interest rates) at a low level, is sufficient to generate monetary expansion. This situation prevailed during the war. But the fiscal stance changed at the end of the war. A budget surplus replaced the deficit, and the stock of securities outstanding fell. Interest rates drifted down. The policy of maintaining fixed interest rates required a decline in the monetary base, lowering monetary growth. In later work, we explored further the effects of fiscal policy on money and money growth and the long-run consequences of budget finance.

The third paper, "Liquidity Traps for Money, Bank Credit, and Interest Rates," arose as a by-product of our endeavor to analyze the money supply process. Many economists, following a suggestion by Keynes, asserted that a liquidity trap disconnected monetary policy from any possible effect on economic activity during the 1930s. Monetary policy was likened to "pushing on a string," capable of inducing contractions but not expansions. This and other metaphors prevailed over analysis.

There were many different "traps." Some referred to properties of the demand for money, others to properties of the banks' demand for reserves and still others to properties of the bank credit market. We found in the literature "absolute," asymptotic, total or partial traps. They all shared in common the notion that under various conditions in the financial markets, monetary policy was impotent. For some traps, impotence arises because the monetary authority cannot change the money stock. In the most familiar version of this trap, excess reserves accumulate in the banking system. In other cases, the money stock can increase without limit but without any effect on output, prices, or interest rates.

Without systematic integration into a coherent analysis of monetary processes, these assertions remain isolated impressions. The ruling paradigm represented by the IS/LM framework cannot accommodate these ideas. More fundamentally, it suffers from a basic flaw. It either postulates that money substitutes only with "bonds," or alternatively that money substitutes over the whole range of assets, with bonds and real assets occurring as perfect substitutes. This is sometimes meant literally, but it can be interpreted as a constraint on the application of the analysis. In the latter case, the analysis applies only to states of affairs exhibiting comparatively small movements in the relative conditions between bonds and real assets. Thus, the implicit structure of the IS/LM framework either eliminates a wide range of experiences from consideration under one interpretation, or must be rejected as empirically untenable under the other interpretations. The structure of the paradigm also makes it inapplicable to many problems (Brunner and Meltzer, 1975, 1989).

Considerations of this kind led us to develop analyses of money supply and of the transmission process in which assets are imperfect substitutes. A model with three assets – money, bonds or financial assets, and real assets – has the minimum number of assets for analysis of intermediation.

The "Liquidity Trap" paper differs from the preceding paper in two major respects. First, the credit market is aggregated; loans and securities are combined in the banks' portfolio. A subsequent paper, not included in this volume, shows that aggregation does not affect the qualitative results (Brunner, 1976). Second, the analysis presents a complete equilibrium of the asset markets with full interaction between the credit and money markets. The paper starts with a partial equilibrium framework for the credit markets, however; there is no demand function for money. A demand for money is introduced to examine the money market – credit market interaction. The analysis uses a somewhat truncated balance sheet of the banking system and a correspondingly truncated measure of bank credit. Even so, the previous results concerning the relative movements of money supply and bank credit are confirmed. Bank credit moves more responsively to underlying changes than the money supply. Later work showed that this pattern is strengthened for a more comprehensive measure of bank credit.

We distinguish six types of liquidity traps and list the set of sufficient and necessary conditions for each trap. The results are unambiguous. Pushing on strings may be a problem, but liquidity traps seem poorly founded in analysis and evidence. The interaction between the asset markets assures us that, under the conditions prevailing in the 1930s, monetary policy was not disconnected from the real sector. More generally, the requirements for the various liquidity traps are not satisfied.

Markets for Assets and Output

By 1970, we had extended the asset market analysis in a small general equilibrium model that included a real sector and interaction between the real sector and the financial sector. Subsequent work developed the analysis further, particularly the treatment of fiscal policy and the financing of fiscal deficits. A relatively final formulation was reached in our 1974 paper, "An Aggregative Theory for a Closed Economy," presented at a conference on "Monetarism" at Brown University. This paper appears as Chapter 4 in this volume.

Some minor changes are introduced in the description of asset markets. The rate of interest on non-financial assets, used in the preceding paper, is replaced by the nominal price of real assets and the expected real return on real assets. The latter depands on real income with an elasticity that varies with transitory and permanent changes in income. The interest rate and asset price level are the principal links between the financial markets and the output market. The system satisfies basic homogeneity properties.

To approximate the dynamics of the system we use a sequence of three equilibrium positions. Short-run equilibrium determines the current state of the economy. It represents the solution of the system for given stock variables (monetary base, stock of government securities and the stock of real capital), price expectations and fiscal policy (real expenditures, tax parameters). The short-run equilibrium reflects the response of prices and output to interaction between the output and asset markets. The government budget position depends on prices and output. These changes induce further changes in the stocks of financial assets – base money and bonds – issued to finance the deficit. The changes in financial assets modify the short-run equilibrium position.

The paper considers an intermediate equilibrium represented by a solution for given price expectation, stock of real capital, fiscal policy and a balanced budget constraint. A "final" equilibrium position reflects the gradual adjustment of money wages and expected prices to the evolution of the current state represented by the shifting short-run equilibrium. The "final" equilibrium satisfies one more constraint than the intermediate run equilibrium: output must coincide with normal output. The analysis concentrates attention on the monetary transmission mechanism and fiscal policy but does not incorporate a long-run equilibrium describing a steady state with an endogenous capital stock.

Leading Keynesians (Paul Samuelson and James Tobin among others) use the IS/LM framework to describe the analytic difference between Keynesian and monetarist analysis. They claim that the difference depends on assumptions about the size of the interest elasticity of the demand for money. Our analysis shows that this characterization depends on the IS/LM model. Once we broaden the range of subsittution among assets by incorporating a credit market, the results obtained from an IS/LM analysis no longer hold. The enlarged range of transmission of monetary impulses to the real sector depends on the *comparative* magnitudes of interest elasticities on the credit and money market, irrespective of the size of the interest elasticity of the demand for money.[2]

The relation between the short- and intermediate-run opens an interesting issue. An unbalanced budget continuously modifies the short-run position and consequently the size of the budget deficit or surplus and the stocks of government debt and monetary base. The issue arises as to whether the process unleashed by deficit (or surplus) financing is stable, i.e., whether the process converges to a balanced budget. Our analysis implies that convergence is assured if a minimum portion of the deficit is financed with an expansion of base money, provided (1) the tax schedule is progressive and (2) taxes depend on current income or (3) fiscal policy fixes nominal expenditures. The short-run equilibrium then converges to an intermediate-run financial stock equilibrium. A deficit financed entirely by bonds can be unstable, however. Stringent auxiliary constraints are required to avoid instability. Without such constraints, budget balance can only be achieved by resetting the fiscal policy variables, expenditures or tax rates.

A related issue is the long-run interrelation between monetary and fiscal policies. A long-run non-inflationary monetary policy requires constraints on the size of the deficit. Large deficits may require either an inflationary monetary policy for eventual budget balance or a change in fiscal policy.

The transmission of monetary and fiscal policy is dominated by substitu-

---

[2]Comparison with IS/LM requires some careful distinction. We refer to the standard IS/LM system understood in the sense of a structural model. This must be distinguished from a pair of IS and LM relations derived by partial solutions from a larger system containing an income and interest rate variable. This semi-reduced version exhibits properties very different from the structural version. We note among other aspects that the random term operating on the demand for money cannot be interpreted as a shock to money. The term is a function of random shocks operating on all the asset market relations in the system.

tion processes and a corresponding play of relative prices among assets and between assets and output. The wealth effect has a minor role in the transmission mechanism. The emphasis on wealth effects usually occurs where money is the only asset (Patinkin, 1965) or in a model with an emasculated substitution process.

Our paper written with Alex Cukierman, "Money and Economic Activity, Inventories and Business Cycles," Chapter 5, explores a different approach. The paper attempts to address explicitly several issues neglected in previous work. To reduce complexity, we omit the credit market and replace capital by inventories.

It is generally understood that some form of incomplete information is a necessary condition for short-run monetary non-neutrality. The paper combines a particular specification of the problem of acquiring information with comparatively inflexible prices and rational expectations based on a (partial) micro foundation. The analysis is developed within the context of general equilibrium analysis.

The information structure differs from the familiar Lucas–Phelps procedure. In their work, the inference problem arises because agents cannot separate current allocative and global influences on prices. The reason is that, by assumption, global information is acquired with a lag.

We introduce an additional inference problem which we believe is more relevant–uncertainty about the temporal dimension of underlying shocks. People respond differently to (more or less) permanent and to (more or less) transitory shocks. People do not know the composition of ongoing shocks, although they know the stochastic process generating the shocks. The main idea is specified as an augmented random walk incorporating both transitory and permanent shocks.

Agents exploit all available information, using suitable inference procedures to develop a perception of the shocks they face. This perception, while correct on average, is not correct in general. In the presence of prices preset for the period, misperception offers leverage for monetary variables to affect real variables.

A micro foundation provides an underpinning for price-setting. Producers use all available information about permanent market conditions to set prices, but they ignore transitory changes in market conditions; inventories buffer the transitory shocks. Firms are assumed to confront a kinked demand curve with the kink at the price they set.[3]

At the beginning of a period, producers set prices and output in response to their perception of the period's permanent state. Since the perceived state is a function of the expected permanent shocks, transitory shocks and

---

[3]We do not explain the kink in the demand curve. An alternative approach to price-setting behavior is suggested in Brunner and Meltzer (1989).

misperceptions cause actual values to deviate from expected values. Financial markets and inventories absorb the discrepancy. At the start of the next period, producers reset prices and output. The changes in inventory and in financial markets affect their plans. The most recent shock induces them to revise their beliefs about permanent and transitory changes. Thus, the unplanned changes in inventories and the change in the expected permanent shock influence next period's output and price decisions, and the effect of the shocks and the rational, but erroneous, inferences influences future values. The average length of time before full adjustment to a shock depends on the relative variances of the permanent and transitory shocks.

Prices are not fully flexible; they do not reflect, and do not adjust to, all ongoing shocks at the time of the shock. Adjustment is distributed temporally. Yet, contrary to a common claim, the analysis does not require disequilibrium. It requires different kinds of equilibrium.

Prices and output are determined each period by the expected permanent shock and inherited inventories. The output market reaches a short-run equilibrium that depends on actual shocks, inherited inventories, and given output and price decisions. The money market adjusts to an equilibrium that reflects actual shocks and depends on perceived permanent values of the shocks. Further, each period the system determines an expected equilibrium path. This path characterizes the movement of the system holding the expected permanent shock constant at its current level. All the variables except inventories achieve their expected permanent values along this path. The dynamics of the path arise from the fact that, in general, initial inventories do not satisfy the conditions for full stock equilibrium – a state in which all variables are at the permanent values determined by the expected permanent shock. The equilibrium system is consistent in the sense that the equilibrium path of inventory adjustment converges to the expected stock equilibrium. No transversatility condition is required. The structure of the model assures this result.

Various adjustment lags or costs have been used to explain the persistence of output responses to nominal shocks. The inventory adjustment process assures persistence in our case. This is not the only mechanism yielding the result. The very nature of the inference problem itself contributes to persistence. Although the unconditional expectations of market transactions are unbiased with serially uncorrelated errors, we show that this does not preclude serial correlations of errors for finite samples. Such correlation may arise whenever the permanent component of the shock changes by a comparatively large amount. Price setters will perceive part of the change as a transitory event; the precise distribution depends on the past history of shocks. Prices do not adjust fully to the shock, so inventories and output change. Since it takes time to learn that a large, permanent shock has occurred, errors can be serially correlated for a time. An econometrician, looking back on the data, can find evidence of inefficiency but, at the time, people base their actions on all the available information. Looking back, they recognize that they underestimated the size of the shock.

It is generally accepted that real wages move less than unemployment. Hall (1977, 1980) interpreted this observation as evidence in support of a "disequilibrium analysis." Our analysis denies this interpretation by reproducing the observed pattern in an equilibrium analysis. Suppliers and demanders on the labor market always achieve their optimal positions. However unemployment dominates the movement of real wages.

The Use of Money

For decades, the existence of money has been not just an unsettled issue but a topic not discussed. The issue became more clearly focused following the development of general equilibrium models based on Arrow–Debreu foundations. The reason is that there is no role for money in an Arrow–Debreu world. The use of money does not raise efficiency and welfare.

The problem is not unique to money. In an Arrow–Debreu world, there is no reason for most of the social institutions that we observe. Clearly, explanations of social institutions, including money, must move beyond this analytic scheme. To explain why institutions arise and persist, we must relax the assumption of full information and zero transaction costs.

We began to discuss this problem early in the 1960s. By the end of the decade, we had written "The Uses of Money: Money in a Theory of an Exchange Economy." The paper emphasizes the role of incomplete information and transaction costs. Money offers a social device that simultaneously lowers uncertainty for market transactors and allows a more efficient use of resources.

The basic idea of our analysis can be expressed as follows. Transactors confront a distribution of information costs over types of goods and people. The distribution does not shift erratically from one person to the next. There are similarities in the distributions as perceived by different transactors. The cost of exchange, measured in welfare terms, varies widely depending on the choice of goods offered in exchange.

The costs associated with any potentially tradeable object guide the choice of transaction chains. These chains are the sequences of transactions by which an individual transactor converts his initial endowment into his preferred basket of goods. Costs are mainly costs of acquiring information about the properties of the goods and costs of transacting.

Transactors concentrate on the lower cost chains. The similarity among cost distributions assures some similarity among individual transaction chains. Moreover, involvement in exchange operations increases information capital and spreads information among individuals. Eventually some dominant transaction chains emerge with a minimum of intermediate steps. The objects used in these optimal transaction chains form the social group's money. Thus, money consists of any objects generally and regularly used as a medium of exchange.

A peculiar feature of a monetary economy is the existence of a small subset of objects which are used dominantly to execute transactions. Exchange operations are not costless; money lowers the costs of such operations. The social productivity of money arises from the opportunity to lower transaction costs and save resources. Individuals can also lower exchange costs by investing in the acquisition of information. The choice of a minimum cost transaction chain, i.e., the use of money, lowers the need for such investment for any given exchange operation.

Lower costs of exchange operations also permit markets to expand and increase the opportunity for exchange. Extending markets encourages the division of labor. The social gain from using money arises from the saving in exchange and information costs realized by means of this social institution.

Money serves other functions. It may be used as a store of value. That function is not a uniquely monetary function. Any durable tradeable object can be used as a store of value.

The analysis explains the persistent use of money in large inflations and deflations. Hyperinflation raises the cost of holding money to a comparatively high level. If the social productivity of money is high, people continue to use money as a medium of exchange despite the holding cost. Some other devices may appear, but since the cost of establishing a new money is high, previous money remains in circulation. At some point, an increasing number of transactors may use other devices in transactions. This means that the cost of the traditional transaction chain has risen so much that individuals are induced to search for alternative transaction chains. If this happens, the most efficient solution is to have the government substitute new money for old. For a successful exchange, government must reduce the rate of inflation.

Large deflations raise the private cost of using money by increasing the gain from holding money. The paper helps to explain the emergence of incentives to search for new money. An increased demand to hold money encourages the search.

Two Independent Efforts

Our collaborative work encompassed much of our professional activity. Even when we have published independently, we often had lengthy discussions of the topic or of the specific paper. After 30 years of close collaboration and lengthy discussions, it is often difficult to separate the source of ideas, and we do not try. The last two papers in the volume reproduce work published independently in recent years.

We began work on fiscal policy in the 1960s and have maintained our interest from that time. Brunner's paper, "Fiscal Policy in Macro-Theory: A Survey and Evaluation," was written for a conference honoring the late Homer Jones of the Federal Reserve Bank of St Louis. The paper shows the evolution of professional discussion of fiscal policy during the past 25 years.

The paper begins with a re-examination of the discussions in the mid-1960s between Keynesians and monetarists about the role of fiscal policy in macroeconomics; it concentrates on the nature of the arguments and the adequacy of the tests for the issues raised.

A principal issue was the relevance or irrelevance of money for nominal income. Keynesian analysis does not require that money is irrelevant, as is now generally recognized. Much of the work carried out in the Keynesian tradition treated money as irrelevant, however.[4] The relevance of fiscal policy actions was a related issue. Though initially not at the center of the discussion, the size and reliability of responses of economic activity to fiscal actions became a major theme.

Looking back on the discussion after several decades, it seems to us that the discussion encouraged Keynesians to accept that monetary actions affect output, employment and prices. Some monetarists recognized the nominal and real effects of fiscal policy, as shown by several papers in this volume. An incidental result of the discussion is clarification of the meaning of "Keynesian theory." Textbook literature and linguistic use often convey the impression that "Keynesian theory" offers a single, well formulated hypothesis. The discussion showed that there is a wide class of hypotheses with substantial variations in their implications. The re-examination also showed that the empirical assessments presented at the time were appropriate relative to the problem explicitly under consideration. Much of the criticism arose because the critics misinterpreted the central issue in the tests.

These early controversies appear in retrospect to be of almost pastoral simplicity when compared with the contemporary state of fiscal policy analysis. The original issues were comparatively narrow. The range of issues in the controversy has expanded substantially in the past ten years. Although there had been some early discussion of the neutrality of bond-financed deficits, non-neutrality of a bond-financed deficit was rarely questioned until the middle 1970s. Opinion differed about the magnitude and duration of the effects on output, and the Keynesian–monetarist controversy probably increased skepticism about the durability and reliability of the responses to fiscal action.

---

[4]The paper develops this claim.

In recent years, some have argued in the professional literature that larger deficits are contractive and smaller deficits expansionary. Such discussions remain very much in the nature of analytic exercises. More serious and interesting is Barro's assault on the conventional position. Barro's (1974) careful analysis argues that bond-financed and tax-financed expenditures are equivalent. This implies that variations in the financing of the deficit do not affect the real sector. The ensuing discussion qualified this result. Tax distortions can change the result. Various risk elements and patterns of redistribution suspend Barro's equivalence. Our analysis, developed in some of the papers in this volume, implies that the consequences of a non-neutral, bond-financed deficit remain at a marginal level for purposes of shorter-run analysis. This seems consistent with the tenuous and somewhat inconclusive state of the evidence.

The role of fiscal policy has been thoroughly reconsidered by the new classical macroeconomics. Expenditures and (distorting) taxes modify the price level, output and interest rate. Some versions (Barro, 1984) attribute larger effects on output to permanent than to transitory changes in government expenditures. In all cases, the multiplier effects remains modest, however. Unlike Keynesian analysis, the size of the expenditure multiplier depends on various supply side responses. These responses contribute substantially to the multiplier reaction. This contrasts with the Keynesian emphasis on aggregate demand and neglect of aggregate supply.

The survey of fiscal policy comments on a major gap in macroanalysis of fiscal policy. Typically, the government is treated as a sink-hole for privately produced goods. Martin Bailey (1962) attempted to break this pattern by considering the government sector as a productive sector. Inputs are acquired from the private sector to produce a mixture of outputs. Property rights analysis teaches that this production process differs from private production processes. The effect of such processes and the effect of their output on consumption, investment and private production remains an open, neglected and unresolved problem.

Early discussion of fiscal policy neglected long-run effects. This changed during the 1970s, and an active discussion has continued since that time. A main conclusion is that, if the real rate of interest exceeds the normal growth rate of output, a constant basic deficit (excluding interest payments) increases the ratio of debt to national income without bound. Sargent and Wallace (1981) show that a stage will be reached when the consequences of the rising debt ratio induce government to replace debt finance with inflationary finance. Inflation allows the government to prevent a further rise or even lower the debt ratio. This result establishes the long-run interdependence of monetary and fiscal policy. Monetary control requires fiscal control; a long-run non-inflationary policy requires adequate fiscal control of the budget. This implication reinforces the result obtained in "An Aggregative Theory . . ." There we show that dynamic stability cannot be assured when the stock of debt rises relative to the money stock.

The analysis of debt and money remains incomplete. The mechanism inducing inflationary finance has not been worked out. The paper also shows that a stable debt finance process (real rate of interest less than the normal rate of growth) does not remove the problem. Equilibrium is achieved at values of the debt ratio probably inducing inflationary finance. Recent experience in South America and Israel seems to confirm this conjecture (Helpman and Leiderman, 1988).

Our approach to understanding economic fluctuations distinguishes the propagation or transmission problem from the impulse problem. The alternative, a totally endogenous process, may be metaphysically appealing, but it seems an inferior choice for empirical research. During the 1960s we accepted a simple impulse hypothesis that seemed consistent with much of the empirical evidence at the time – the dominance of monetary impulses. We did not deny the occurrence of real impulses but we treated real impulses as of second order compared to the monetary impulses. This hypothesis seemed consistent with the prevailing institutional arrangement, the Bretton Woods system, with considerable autonomy at the Federal Reserve.

The end of the Bretton Woods system and the oil shocks of the 1970s caused us to re-examine the hypothesis and, eventually, to abandon monetary dominance. We classified impulses as: (1) nominal or real, (2) allocative or aggregative, (3) permanent or transitory.

Meltzer's study, the last paper in the volume, examines the nature of shocks affecting the price level, output, and money in Japan and the United States under fixed and fluctuating exchange rates. Meltzer uses a Kalman filter, with Bayesian adaptation, to forecast expected values of prices, output, money and velocity and to disaggregate shocks into three types. There are transitory shocks to the level, permanent shocks to the level (transitory to the rate of growth) and permanent shocks to the growth rate. The data suggest that most shocks are either permanent shocks to the level or permanent shocks to the growth rate. The data also suggest that the growth rate is stochastic. These results reinforce some of the conclusions obtained by Nelson and Plosser (1982) and by Stulz and Wasserfallen (1985) with different data and statistical procedures. Transitory shocks to the price level, the main shocks explaining fluctuations in output in the Lucas analysis, appear to be insignificant. Unlike earlier studies, however, the filter suggests that the business cycle is mainly composed of transitory shocks to the rate of change (i.e., permanent shocks to the level).

Much public discussion suggests that the fluctuating exchange rate regime has increased variability in prices and output. The paper compares experience in two countries under the fixed and fluctuating exchange rate regimes. The evidence suggests that, in Japan and the United States, unanticipated changes in prices and output did not increase. In later work Meltzer (1986) finds similar evidence for other major economies.

For Japan, the variances of actual and forecast values of prices and output and the variance of forecast errors declined under fluctuating rates and declined further after the Bank of Japan announced targets for money. Similar declines are not found for the United States. A plausible explanation for the difference is that Japan, freed of the fixed exchange rate constraint, was able to increase the credibility of its anti-inflationary policy and reduce variability and uncertainty. The US was not much constrained by the fixed exchange rate system. Policy, and uncertainty about the future, changed little after the Bretton Woods system ended. These findings suggest that credible annoucements can reduce variability and uncertainty.

If currency substitution dominated exchange rate changes, shocks to monetary velocity in the two countries would be related. The paper shows that there is no systematic relation between shocks to velocity in the two countries and no evidence of systematic responses of exchange rate changes to velocity shocks or of velocity shocks to exchange rate changes.

The pattern of shocks appears to have differed under the two regimes. Under fixed exchange rates, shocks to the US money stock affect Japan's money stock and, thus, Japanese output. Shocks to US GNP affect both the US money stock and Japan's GDP. Under fluctuating exchange rates, the study finds no relation between shocks to money in the two countries. Shocks to money in each country affect that country's output. The findings are consistent with an important role for monetary shocks. They are inconsistent with a theory in which real shocks are interrelated or in which monetary shocks are mainly the result of prior shocks to nominal or real output.

References

Bailey, M. 1962. *National Income and the Price Level*. New York: McGraw Hill.

Barro, R. J. 1974. Are government bonds net wealth? *Journal of Political Economy* 82, 1095–117.

—— 1984. *Macroeconomics*. New York: Wiley.

Brunner, K. 1976. The money supply process in open economies with interdependent security markets: The case of imperfect substitutability. In *Bank Credit, Money and Inflation in Open Economies*, ed. M. Fratianni and K. Tavernier (supplement to *Kredit und Kapital*).

—— and A. H. Meltzer 1975. Fiscal policy, inflation and the price level. Paper presented at an international conference on monetary problems in Helsinki, Finland, August.

—— 1988a. Money and credit in the monetary transmission process. *American Economic Review* 78 (May), 446–51.

—— 1988b. Money supply In *Handbook of Monetary Economics*, ed. Friedman, B. M. and F. H. Hahn, Amsterdam: North Holland.

—— 1989. Money and the Economy: Issues in Monetary Analysis. The 1987 Raffaele Mattioli Lectures, Cambridge: Cambridge University Press, 1989.

Burns, A. F. 1969. *The Business Cycle in a Changing World*. New York: Columbia University Press.

Hall, R. E. 1977. Expectation errors, unemployment and wage inflation. Manuscript, Center for Advanced Study in the Behavioral Sciences, September.

—— 1980. Labor supply and aggregate fluctuations. *Carnegie-Rochester Conference Series on Public Policy* 12, 7–33.

Helpman, E. and Leiderman, L. 1988. Stabilization in high inflation countries: Analytical foundations and recent experience. *Carnegie-Rochester Conference Series on Public Policy* 28, 9–84.

Karamouzis, N. and R. Lombra 1988. Federal reserve policymaking: an overview and analysis of the policy process. Paper presented at the Carnegie-Rochester Conference on Public Policy, Spring.

Meltzer, A. H. 1986. Size, persistence and interrelation of nominal and real shocks: Some evidence from four countries. *Journal of Monetary Economics* 17, 161–94, January.

Nelson, C. R. and Plosser, C. I. 1982. Trends and random walks in macroeconomic time series: Some evidence and implications. *Journal of Monetary Economics* 10(2), 139–62.

Patinkin, D. 1965. *Money, Interest and Prices*, 2nd edn. New York: Harper & Row.

Sargent, T. J. and Wallace, N. 1981. Some unpleasant monetarist arithmetic. *Federal Reserve Bank of Minneapolis Quarterly Review* 5, 1–17.

Stulz, R. and W. Wasserfallen 1985. Macroeconomic time series, business cycles and macroeconomic policies. *Carnegie-Rochester Conference Series on Public Policy* 22, 9–54.

1

The Federal Reserves Attachment to the Free Reserve Concept

Karl Brunner and Allan H. Meltzer

1 Evidence from Published Statements

Letter of Transmittal

Hon. Wright Patman
Chairman, House Banking and Currency Committee
House of Representatives, Washington, DC

Dear Mr. Chairman
The material transmitted herewith represents the second part of a three-part study, "An Analysis of Federal Reserve Monetary Policymaking," that is being prepared for the committee. These chapters attempt to develop in more detail the nature of the conception that guides Federal Reserve actions, the position of free reserves in their analysis, and the relevance of the modified free reserve conception as an explanation of changes in money and credit.

In the subcommittee print of February 10, "Some General Features of the Federal Reserve's Approach to Policy," we discussed some of the diverse and often disconnected strands that play a prominent role in policy discussions by spokesmen and officials of the System. We found that one recurrent theme appears to occupy a dominant position in their notions about the monetary process: the asserted relation between the level of free reserves and the rate of credit expansion. While this relation has by no means been developed into a coherent frame for analysis of the monetary process, the persistent references suggest that it occupies a central position in the Federal Reserve's analysis.

This paper was presented to the US Subcommittee on Domestic Finance, Committee on Banking and Currency, House of Representatives, 88th Congress, Second Session, on May 7, 1964.

Section 1, "The Federal Reserve's Attachment to the Free Reserve Concept: Evidence From Published Statements," develops the meaning of the free reserve doctrine as it is used within the System. Three separable roles are assigned to free reserves. First, and most important, free reserves are regarded as an important causal factor affecting credit expansion and contraction. Second, free reserves are used as an indicator of a given monetary situation. Third, they are used as a target of Federal Reserve policy. Much of the confusion engendered by the contemporaneous denials and explicit affirmations of the role of free reserves results from the three uses of the term. For example, the use of free reserves as a target may be denied without affecting the role of free reserves as the centerpiece of the causal mechanism used by the Federal Reserve.

This section indicates that the free reserve conception evolved out of an older notion developed most coherently by Riefler in the twenties. The character of this evolution is of particular importance, since many of the notions that formed a part of older views continue to dominate current thinking, long after their rationale has disappeared. Moreover, the discussion of the evolving notions helps to explicate some of the actions of the Federal Reserve in the thirties and forties. For example, the severely deflationary action of the mid-thirties, the doubling of reserve requirements, was appraised by the Federal Reserve in terms of the dominant Riefler notion. Had this notion been well founded, and applicable to the then current events, the doubling of reserve requirements would not have had severely deflationary consequences. But the notion was inapplicable and incorrect. Increased unemployment and a reduction in the pace of economic activity ensued.

Dramatic events, like the doubling of reserve requirements in the thirties, do not take place at frequent intervals. But they serve to indicate the importance of a validated conception of the monetary mechanism and to illustrate the costs to society resulting from the application of invalid, untested theories.

The remainder of section 1 presents evidence from published Federal Reserve statements and from the as yet unpublished responses, by the members of the Board of Governors and the presidents of the Reserve Banks, to a series of questions posed in connection with this study. The recent modifications of the doctrine, associated with the recognition that the demands for free reserves play a role in the monetary process, are discussed. We find that the recognition of demand factors has introduced important additional elements into the Federal Reserve's analysis.

A major conclusion of the section is that many of the new notions that have been introduced conflict with older views. These conflicts remain unresolved within the Federal Reserve. Had the Federal Reserve attempted to develop and test their conception, many such conflicts would be recognized, and resolved on the basis of evidence; analysis and understanding would be improved, and the foundations of monetary policy making would be strengthened. The failure of the Federal Reserve to carry out systematic appraisals of the mechanism that has been entrusted to their control perpetuates incorrect and poorly developed views, and renders monetary policy less useful as a tool of economic policy.

In contrast to section 1 that looks at the evidence from the professed views of officials and spokesmen, section 2 concentrates principally on the actions taken by the Federal Reserve. We noted in chapter II that the Federal Reserve has an extremely short-run policy focus, that actions are taken in response to weekly, daily, and even hourly events on the financial markets. Section 2 builds on the earlier discussion and reveals the way in which concentration on short-run occurrences and the absence of systematic analysis leads to a substantial grant of authority to the Manager of the System Open Market Account.

A principal piece of supporting evidence for our view of the position of the Manager, his reliance on free reserves as an indicator, and his use of free reserves as a target, is of particular importance. A comparison of decisions by the Federal Open Market Committee with the recorded movement of free reserves indicates that the level of free reserves quite often moved decisively in advance of a decision by the Open Market Committee to "ease" or "restrain." The observed pattern strongly supports our interpretation that the absence of a systematic framework and the concentration on extremely short-run market events has resulted in a substantial grant of authority to the Manager. At major turning points, in the post-Accord period, it has often been the Manager's action that reversed the direction of policy. This action was then ratified at a meeting of the Federal Open Market Committee. Contrary to published statements by officials of the System, the Manager appears to occupy a major policymaking role.

Our appraisal of the Federal Reserve's record at post-Accord turning points in economic activity suggests that, in this respect, the Federal Reserve has compiled a good, even excellent record. They have been alert and sensitive to a variety of indicators, and they have made timely and appropriate judgments about the pace of economic activity. We contend that in the present state of knowledge, it would be difficult to improve upon their record in this respect.

However, recognition of the turning points in the pace of economic activity must be accompanied by appropriate action to alter the money supply, if discretionary monetary policy is to have an appropriate countercyclical influence. The Federal Reserve does not directly control the stocks of money or credit. Without a valid conception of the relation between their actions and the stock of money and credit, the usefulness of their judgment of the timing of turning points in economic activity is diminished. Unless appropriate action is taken, our economy does not benefit from their timely recognition of the turning point.

The type of action that is taken depends on the conception of the monetary process that is held. If that conception is seriously deficient, it is quite likely that correct judgment of turning points will not be accompanied by action appropriate to reduce unemployment or to prevent inflation. Section 3, "The Relation of Free Reserves to Changes in Money and Credit," therefore provides some evidence on the validity of the modified free reserves conception.

The evidence is quite clear. The modified free reserves mechanism bears almost no relation to changes in the stock of bank credit or money. Indeed, the relation is so poor that it raises questions about the usefulness of Federal Reserve policy as a means of controlling money or credit. Judged in terms of the Federal Reserve conception, an overwhelming proportion of observed changes in money and credit are outside the control of the Federal Reserve. If their view of the monetary mechanism were the only admissible view, we would be forced to concede that monetary policy is little more than a futile exercise.

Karl Brunner
Allan H. Meltzer

One of the dominant Federal Reserve conceptions centers on the role of free reserves in the monetary process. This idea has had an important influence on assessments made by the Federal Reserve authorities and on the policies applied in concrete situations. We contend that the Federal Reserve has viewed, and continues to view, free reserves as an element playing a causal role of central importance in the monetary process and simultaneously supplying a useful summary measure of "ease and restraint." Detailed evidence is presented in this and a subsequent section in support of our contention.

The evidence presented in this section comes almost exclusively from the statements made by members of the Board of Governors, the FOMC,[1] and their staffs. It would be useful, perhaps, to supplement these statements by indications of the importance attached to free reserves, both as an index and as a causal factor, by Members of the Congress, the banking community, the academic profession and others. But to do so seems beyond the scope of this inquiry and adds little direct evidence to the point. In the following section, a second type of evidence will be presented, evidence from the record of policy actions and the actual movements of the level of free reserves in the postwar period.

Free reserves are defined as the difference between measured excess reserves and member bank borrowings. They are the volume of measured excess reserves not borrowed from the Federal Reserve. To obtain the volume of free reserves, the amount of required reserves and the amount of member bank borrowing are subtracted from total reserves.

---

[1]The FOMC refers to the Federal Open Market Committee. This Committee determines major aspects of monetary policy, in particular the Federal Reserve's open market policy.

In the context of the dominant notion to be considered, the level of free reserves is viewed as a causal factor affecting the rate at which commercial banks adjust their portfolios of earning assets. An increase in free reserves is expected to accelerate the expansion rate of bank portfolios; i.e., to increase the rate at which banks acquire earning assets or decrease the rate at which they unload securities and/or compress outstanding loans. A decline in free reserves, on the other hand, is expected to retard the expansion rate; either the rate of acquisition will be lower or portfolios contract. A systematic association thus links the level of free reserves with the rate of change of the commercial banks' portfolio of earning assets.

The association of free reserves with the banks' asset expansion, combined with the causal role assigned to free reserves, influenced the choice of free reserves as an index of the monetary situation – a summary measure indicating relative "ease" or "restraint." According to the Federal Reserve's notion, policy actions and other events modify the monetary process to the extent that they change the prevailing level of free reserves. Open market operations immediately change total reserves and free reserves by the same amount. Banks respond by modifying the adjustment rate of their portfolios. As a result, required reserves and borrowing change, and the initial impact of open market operations on free reserves is attenuated. However, free reserves do not return to their initial level even after the impulse triggered by open market operations has been fully absorbed.

Changes in reserve requirements immediately change the volume of required reserves relative to an unchanged volume of total reserves. There is no direct effect on borrowings from Federal Reserve Banks. Thus there is an instantaneous change in free reserves that affects the banks' portfolio adjustment. Subsequently, part of the initial change in free reserves is absorbed, via the gradual shift in required reserves associated with changes in deposits induced by the portfolio adjustments.

The effect of other events, gold flows, currency flows, a redistribution of the public's deposits between demand and time accounts, the division of the Treasury's balances between holdings at Federal Reserve Banks or on tax and loan accounts at commercial banks, etc., can be traced in a similar manner. A necessary and sufficient condition for all these events to exert an influence on the money supply and credit markets is the existence of an immediate impact on the level of free reserves. This, in essence, is the foundation of the free reserve conception of the monetary process.

1.1 Genesis and Development of the Free Reserve Conception of Monetary Processes

A short description of genesis and development of the "free reserve doctrine" seems appropriate before we discuss the evidence supporting our contention about the dominant role of this "doctrine" among Federal

Reserve views (see Meigs 1962, Ch. 2). This description focuses attention on the behavior patterns and operating problems that stimulated the development of the free reserve doctrine. Recent emergence of important modifications will also be noted. However these modifications of the free reserve doctrine have neither been systematically developed nor absorbed into a coherent view. Conceivably, these new elements will lead, in the future, to a reassessment of the Federal Reserve's viewpoint about the role and significance of free reserves.

The origins of the free reserve "doctrine" may be traced to the discovery of open market operations. Such operations emerged in the early twenties as a result of the Reserve's Banks' endeavor to bolster their revenues with suitable earning assets. The Federal Reserve authorities rapidly realized that open market operations immediately affect the commercial banks' reserve position. Purchases inject additional reserves, and sales siphon off available reserves. Open market operations thus appeared to offer an excellent opportunity to modify the commercial banks' positions in the direction and extent desired by the Federal Reserve authorities. But the gradually accumulating observations concerning the commercial banks' reserve and borrowing behavior slowly dispelled this belief. Open market operations typically induced a response in bank borrowing from the Federal Reserve Banks which seriously mitigated the impact of open market operations on the total volume of reserves. Purchases generated a repayment of outstanding loans and sales "forced banks into the central bank" and induced an increased volume of borrowing. Open market operations were systematically associated with offsetting variations in the banks' borrowing from the Federal Reserve Banks.

The banks' behavior almost annihilated any potential effect of open market operations on the volume of bank reserves in the twenties.[2] But the composition of reserves between borrowed and unborrowed reserves

---

[2]Two regressions were computed in order to appraise the order of magnitude and significance of compensating variations in the Federal Reserve's "discounts and advances," denoted by A for the period of the 1920s. The regressions relate first differences of A between adjacent months or corresponding months of adjacent years with similar first differences of the adjusted base B^a. The latter magnitude is equal to the base minus discounts and advances. It is thus equal to the sum constituted by the Federal Reserve's portfolio of securities including float, the Treasury's gold stock net of Treasury cash, Treasury currency outstanding, the negative value of Treasury deposits and foreign deposits at Federal Reserve Banks, and some other minor accounts including "other deposits" at Federal Reserve Banks. The result of the regressions are collected below:

$$\Delta A_{t,\,t-1} = 0.0086 - 0.8742 \Delta B^a_{\,t,\,t-1}$$
$$\quad (0.0070)\ (0.0962)$$
$$\quad R^2 = 0.3697$$
$$\Delta A_{t,\,t-12} = 0.1057 - 1.1729 \Delta B^a_{\,t,\,t-12}$$
$$\quad (0.0357)\ (0.0830)$$
$$\quad R^2 = 0.6059$$

changed decisively. Open market sales by the Federal Reserve gave rise to increased borrowing by member banks that approximately restored total reserves. Excess reserves were small during the period and exhibited negligible variations. Hence variations in bank indebtedness were practically equivalent to variations in free reserves. (Of course the values of free reserves and member bank indebtedness moved in opposite directions as would be expected from the definition of free reserves and the relatively unchanging value of excess reserves.)

Under the circumstances of the period, the volume of bank reserves did not appear to play any important role in the transmission of the impulses set off by open market operations. Students of monetary policy were seemingly forced to recognize the futility of open market operations or to search for an alternative route transmitting the impact generated by open market operations.

1.2 Riefler's Contribution to the Analysis

The behavior patterns summarized above appeared to hint at an alternative route which was explored in a pathbreaking study of our monetary system by W. Riefler (1930). This alternative view made variations in banks' indebtedness the focal point of the money supply and credit market process. But Riefler fully realized that bank indebtedness could only assume an important role in explaining the effective transmission of Federal Reserve policy if the banks had little control over the volume of their indebtedness to the Reserve Banks. In the early part of his book, therefore, he devoted much attention to the rationale for member bank borrowing. Two hypotheses are considered, a profit hypothesis and a "needs and reluctance" hypothesis. The alternative views may be summarized in his own words:

> The most obvious theory is that member banks, on the whole, borrow at the Reserve Banks when it is profitable to do so and repay their indebtedness as soon as the operation proves costly. The cost of borrowing at the Reserve Banks, accordingly, is held to be the determining factor in the relation between Reserve Bank operations to money rates, and the discount rate policy adopted by the Reserve Banks to be the most important factor in making Reserve Bank policy effective in the money markets. At the other extreme, there is the theory that member banks borrow at Reserve Banks only in case of

where

$$\Delta A_{t,t-1} = A_t - A_{t-1}; \ \Delta B^a_{t,t-1} = B^a_t - B^a_{t-1}$$
$$\Delta A_{t,t-12} = A_t - A_{t-12}; \ \Delta B^a_{t,t-12} = B^a_t - B^a_{t-12}$$

Sample period: January 1918 to December 1929.

necessity and endeavor to repay their borrowing as soon as possible. According to this theory the fact of borrowing in and of itself – the necessity imposed by circumstances on member banks for restoring to the resources of Reserve Banks – is a more important factor in the money market than the discount rate . . . and open market operations . . . contribute more directly to the effectiveness of Reserve Bank credit policy than changes in discount rate. (Riefler, 1930, pp. 19–20)

After the sketch of the two theories, Riefler discusses the implications of the profit theory and notes that under this theory interest rates on the open market should be close to the discount rate, with only minor or transitory deviations.[3] A confrontation of this conclusion with observable rate behavior on short-term open markets leads Riefler to reject the profit theory.

We may easily concede the pertinent facts and admit that the open market rates diverged markedly and persistently from the discount rate. On the other hand, the behavior of the acceptance market was consistent with the implication of the profit theory as formulated by Riefler; i.e., the pertinent market rates followed closely and deviated only little from the Federal Reserve's acceptance rate.[4]

Riefler concludes his appraisal of the rival conceptions concerning the process generating the banks' indebtedness to Federal Reserve Banks with a decision in favor of the "needs and reluctance" theory of bank borrowing:

There is little question, on the whole, that the first of the two theories outlined above, covering the relation of Reserve Bank rates to money

---

[3]"If member bank borrowing has been governed primarily by motives of profit during this period, money rates would have been dominated by the discount rates charged by the Reserve Banks. Particularly would this have been true of rates in the short-term open markets where member banks can lend freely and withdraw funds entirely on their own volition without regard to the results of their actions on future lending operations. As member banks had plenty of eligible paper on which to borrow at the Reserve Banks during most of this period, there was nothing to prevent them from 'scalping' a profit out of the open market whenever rates in those markets were above discount rates. If member bank borrowing had actually been governed by the profit motive in this manner, offers of additional funds in the short-term open markets would have been so plentiful whenever opportunity presented itself that rates in those markets could never have risen far above discount rates, so long as eligible paper continued available in ample supply. Nor could rates in the short-term open markets have fallen much below discount rates so long as an appreciable volume of member bank borrowing at the Reserve Banks represented indebtedness incurred under the profit motive, since member banks would have withdrawn funds from the short-term open markets to repay indebtedness at the Reserve Banks whenever continued borrowing became unprofitable, and rates in those markets could not have fallen much below discount rates until member banks had liquidated a considerable proportion of their indebtedness" (Riefler, 1930, pp. 20–1).

[4]"The relationship which this theory (i.e., the 'profit theory') envisages between the discount rates of the Reserve Banks, on the one hand, and the money rates in the short-term open markets, on the other, is essentially that which prevailed in the acceptance market in this country" (Riefler, 1930, chapter 2, p. 21).

rates in the money markets, applies to the rates at which acceptances sell in the open market. It does not, however, as might be expected, apply with anything approaching the same precision to rates in other short-term markets which have varied widely from discount rates . . . it is impossible to explain the movements of money rates in the open market and the levels which they have occupied during recent years by the movements and levels of discount rates at the Reserve Banks alone. (Riefler, 1930, pp. 23, 25)

Then his main conclusion with respect to the two alternatives:

The functioning of the Reserve Banks in the money market must, therefore, be considered from the point of view of the theory that changes in the volume of member bank borrowing exert a more important influence on rates than do changes in discount rate. (Riefler, 1930, p. 25)

In the remainder of his book, Riefler developed an analysis of the monetary process connecting Federal Reserve operations with the money supply and the behavior of the banks and the public. Though incomplete and deficient in several important respects and dominated by very short-run considerations, his analysis was an extremely useful and important beginning. Unfortunately the theory construction that he began has not been completed by others. Instead, several of the notions that he introduced were uncritically accepted by the Federal Reserve and have continued to appear in their discussions despite their inconsistency with other elements that have been introduced. Of particular interest in the light of later developments is the emphasis placed on the expansion or contraction of bank credit in response to changes in the volume of member bank borrowing at the Reserve Banks. While we make no attempt to present the theory in detail consideration of his central idea is a useful introduction to later discussions by Federal Reserve officials.

Riefler's theory contains four major elements. The first, and by far the most important, seeks to explain the relation of market rates of interest and the volume of bank indebtedness. Larger bank indebtedness and a higher discount rate are said to raise the prevailing market rates; smaller indebtedness and lower discount rates depress market rates. "(T)he volume of member bank indebtedness at the Reserve Banks at any given time is one of the most important single monetary factors in the level of money rates, and . . . the prospect of increase or decrease in the indebtedness is one of the most important single factors in the rate outlook" (Riefler, 1930, pp. 27, 124). Open market operations by the central bank were at the root of the rate changes since, under the "needs and reluctance" notion, member banks borrowed when open market operations reduced member bank reserves and repaid borrowing when the central bank increased reserves. Riefler stated the point as follows:

(F)luctuations of money rates in the short-term open markets should be governed by corresponding fluctuations in the aggregate volume of member bank indebtedness at the Reserve Banks, increased borrowing there being reflected in a rise of money market rates and decreased borrowing in a decline of rates in these markets. This would be expected because . . . member banks do not borrow in order to increase their loans, but rather endeavor to contract their loans in order to repay their indebtedness.[5]

A second element concerns the public's response to the changes in market rates initiated by the Reserve Banks. Higher interest rates were said to reduce the demand for bank credit either directly or indirectly because the public sold fewer securities to the banks. Lower rates expanded the quantity of bank credit demanded. Given the volume of bank indebtedness to the Reserve Banks, the "quality evaluation" of loan applications by commercial banks and the public's behavior determined the volume of earning assets held by banks and the total deposit liabilities.

The volume of acceptances held by the Reserve Banks was the third main element. The Federal Reserve set a rate at which it was willing to buy acceptances. When market rates rose relative to the acceptance rate, banks sold acceptances to the Reserve Banks and total reserves increased. The Federal Reserve's portfolio of acceptances thus was determined by the prevailing market conditions and the acceptance rate.

The last main building block introduced by Riefler is designed to explain the variations in member bank indebtedness. The amount of indebtedness is shown to be equal to required reserves plus currency held by the public minus the Federal Reserve's holdings of Government securities and float, minus the gold stock net of Treasury cash, minus Treasury currency outstanding, plus Treasury and foreign deposits at the Federal Reserve Banks, plus "other deposits" and "other accounts" on the balance sheet of the Federal Reserve Banks. For Riefler this relationship is not simply a balance sheet identity from the consolidated Federal Reserve statement. It reveals a causal relation that determines the volume of member bank borrowing. Banks have no desire to borrow from the Reserve Banks; variations in the pressure to borrow emanate from changes in the elements described. When "favourable" circumstances permit – e.g., when the currency flows into the

---

[5]Idem. Other references augment the clues about the central relation visualized by Riefler. For example, he writes ". . . changes in this indebtedness appear to be the initiating force in corresponding changes in money rates. It is this relationship apparently which has given to Reserve Bank operations in the open market that peculiar efficacy for control over the money market, which must be written more fully than it has been written into Reserve banking theory . . . Induced through open market operations, changes in the volume of member bank indebtedness have been used since 1922 both to tighten and to ease the money markets, independently of changes in discount rates."

banks from the public, when there is a gold inflow or an open market operation, etc. – the banks follow their fundamental disposition, viz., they reduce indebtedness.

The four building blocks jointly operate to determine the response of the monetary system to the policy actions taken by the Federal Reserve authorities. The transmission of typical policy actions to the credit markets and the money supply may be traced with the aid of Riefler's framework. Open market purchases lower the banks' indebtedness dollar for dollar; lower indebtedness induces banks to lower the yields on money markets; the public responds with a larger supply of earning assets to banks; the banks' asset portfolio and deposit liabilities expand. Open market purchases thus expand "bank credit" and the money supply and lower the interest rates on the credit markets.

Riefler's exposition of central banking theory thus made the volume of member bank borrowing completely unresponsive to any direct influence of interest rates. Only to the extent that these rates operated on currency flows, gold movements, or the other balance sheet items listed above could they alter the amount of borrowing. This view carried over, in part at least, to the initial formulation of the free reserves doctrine.

Riefler is rather vague about the role of the discount rate in the process. At times he seems to suggest that the discount rate has no effect on the environment described by the four building blocks. Other suggestions hint that the discount rate operates independently of changes in bank indebtedness but not independent of the existence of borrowed reserves by the banks. Also missing from the Riefler discussion is any consideration of variations in the volume of excess reserves held by banks. As we have noted, fluctuations in excess reserves were relatively small during the twenties, and this may account for the lack of attention. Finally, a reading of Riefler's book shows that his discussion is dominated by concern with extremely short-run money market considerations. This emphasis has an important bearing on his acceptance of the "reluctance" theory of bank indebtedness that occupies a vital position in his analysis.

1.3 Burgess' Views

Shortly after Riefler's book, a revised edition of Burgess' well-known study appeared (1936). Burgess accepted most of the Riefler formulation of the monetary process and added a slightly more explicit treatment of the role of the rediscount rate. Like Riefler, he notes the close correspondence between the behavior of money market rates and the volume of indebtedness. He explains this association in terms of the banks' reluctance to borrow or to remain in debt.

> When the member banks find themselves continuously in debt at the Reserve Banks, they take steps to pay off their indebtedness. They tend

to sell securities, call loans, and restrict their purchases of commercial paper and other investments. The consequence is that when a large number of member banks are in debt, money generally becomes firmer, commercial paper sells rapidly, and rates increase. Conversely, when most of the member banks are out of debt at the Reserve Banks, they are in a position to invest their funds; and money rates, including commercial paper rates, become easier. This relationship rests largely on the unwillingness of banks to remain in debt at the Federal Reserve Banks. (Burgess, 1936, p. 220)

The central feature of Riefler's discussion – that Federal Reserve policy operates on the monetary system by inducing variations in member bank indebtedness – is repeated by Burgess (1936, pp. 236, 238). In addition, Burgess recognizes the operation of discount rate policy as a separate element in the process that is reinforced by open market operations.

The effectiveness of purchases and sales of Government securities as an instrument of policy lies usually in their influence on the indebtedness of member banks at the Reserve Banks. Purchases enabled member banks to pay off loans and thus tend to make money easier; sales lead banks to borrow more heavily and thus tend to make money firmer. Government security transactions supplement and enforce discount policy. (1936, p. 253)

Elsewhere, after commenting on the principle of open market operations along the lines described by Riefler, Burgess notes:

It can thus be seen that buying and selling [by the Reserve Banks] is not only an independent influence on the credit situation, but may and often has been used as a means of preparing for discount rate changes and making them more effective. (p. 238)

Variations in the rediscount rates were seen as an independent influence on "bank credit." Such influences operated in conjunction with open market policy. When open market operations reduced reserves, banks borrowed from the Reserve Banks, as Riefler had described. Open market operations were effective in changing interest rates and could be reinforced by fiat changes in the rediscount rate that made increased bank indebtedness more or less expensive and contributed to the variation of market rates.

The explicit recognition of the discount rate as a separate influence on market interest rates and on member bank borrowing might have stimulated further interest in the influence of costs and yields on banks' reserve positions and an analysis of the demand by banks for reserves. But the Riefler-Burgess conception was dominated by the "reluctance theory" of bank borrowing, and this further step was not taken. As a result, the role of "excess reserves" and the growth of such reserves during the thirties could not be interpreted in the prevailing Federal Reserve view.

1.4 Goldenweiser's Views

The persistence of the viewpoint explored by both Riefler and Burgess is clearly revealed by Goldenweiser's (1941) article. The major change is in the direction of weakening the description of the causal connection between open market operations, bank indebtedness, and "credit expansion" and increased emphasis on the bankers' "frame of mind."

> . . . When the System wishes to ease credit conditions . . . it purchased Government securities in the open market and simultaneously reduced the discount rate at the Reserve Banks. It thus provided member banks with reserve funds to reduce their indebtedness at the Reserve Banks and also made such indebtedness as remained less burdensome to the member banks. This policy was intended to put member banks in a position and a frame of mind to be more liberal in extending credit. (Goldenweiser, 1941, p. 400)

Like Burgess, Goldenweiser is more explicit than Riefler about the role of discount rates in the central relation. Discount rate changes appear to affect market rates of interest by an amount that depends directly on the volume of bank indebtedness. This view is particularly interesting in view of later suggestions that the primary effect of changing the discount rate was the psychological impact associated with the announcement of the change.

Goldenweiser also stressed an important implication of the Riefler–Burgess conception which explains the Federal Reserve's policy in 1936–7. The absence of excess reserves and the existence of bank indebtedness are presented as necessary conditions for monetary policy to be effective. According to the Riefler–Burgess notion the evaporation of bank indebtedness during the 1930s broke the chain linking the Federal Reserve with the credit markets and the money supply.[6] Restoration of an effectively working monetary policy thus required that "contact be reestablished with the market." Reestablishment of contact meant the potential emergence of bank indebtedness and the disappearance of large excess reserves. The drastic increase in reserve requirements arranged in the late summer of 1936 and the early months of 1937 seemed ideally designed, under the ruling notion developed by Riefler–Burgess and carried on by Goldenweiser, to render monetary policy more potent without exerting any deflationary damage. Goldenweiser asserted with particular emphasis that this dramatic jump

---

[6]"After the autumn of 1933 these instruments (i.e., the discount rate and open market operation) were not usable, because the banks were out of debt and had a large volume of excess reserves. The banks were therefore largely independent of the Federal Reserve System's traditional method of credit regulation" (Goldenweiser, 1941, p. 391). "A necessary condition for the effectiveness of such a policy (i.e., of encouraging credit expansion) is that the volume of excess reserves at the disposal of member banks be limited" (Ibid., p. 400).

in reserve requirements "was not a reversal of the policy of monetary ease pursued since the beginning of the depression . . . The Board's action was precautionary in character and placed the system in a position where an injurious credit expansion, if it should occur, could be controlled by open market operations and discount rate policy" (Goldenweiser, 1941, p. 410).

Goldenweiser thus explicitly indicated that accumulating excess reserves and vanishing bank indebtedness broke a crucial link of the monetary process and rendered policy incapable of coping with potential problems.[7] Under the Riefler–Burgess conception excess reserves have no role to play in the monetary process. They are inconsistent with this view of the monetary mechanism. It is therefore intriguing to note that the emergence of excess reserves was immediately interpreted to mean a breakdown of policy mechanisms and not a denial or falsification of the Riefler–Burgess conception, that denies the existence of excess reserves.

The exclusion of excess reserves from systematic consideration was closely associated with the involuntary and imposed character attributed by the Federal Reserve to bank indebtedness. The implicit denial of any systematic response of the volume of bank indebtedness to market conditions was extended to cover excess reserves. It was therefore consistent for the Federal Reserve authorities to consider excess reserves throughout the thirties as a redundant surplus of no use and of no function in the monetary process. But excess reserves persisted and still exist, particularly among country banks.

The persistent occurrence of excess reserves must have slowly eroded the old version of the Riefler–Burgess conception. We find it difficult to obtain clear evidence of the gradual transformation of this dominant view into a notion emphasizing the central position of free reserves. This transformation must have occurred during the late 1940s or early 1950s.[8] In the new view excess reserves were treated as an extension of bank indebtedness, a magnitude offsetting the retarding influence of member bank borrowing. Free reserves assumed the position and role which originally had been assigned to bank indebtedness. The free reserve conception thus emanated as a result of an adjustment in the central building block of the Riefler–Burgess view of the monetary process.

Additional modifications occurred in the late 1950s. It should be noted, however, that while there are periodic changes in the prevailing views, the

---

[7]In passing we note two points. One, the concern with the possible problem of inflation appears to have dominated the concern for the existing problem of underutilization of resources. Two, those who continue to assert that monetary policy in recession is analogous to "pushing on a string" should be aware that the origin of this view is the Riefler–Burgess notion that denied any influence of interest rates on member bank borrowing or excess reserves and any relevance to the demand by banks for reserves.

[8]Irving Auerbach of the Federal Reserve Bank of New York is often given credit for the development of the free reserves concept.

basic conception is almost never completely formulated and has never been subjected to a searching appraisal or even to the discursive arguments that Riefler provided for his views. No doubt, such an appraisal would show that the broad movements of interest rates and excess reserves during the 1930s are consistent with many of the transformations that have been made in the old notions. But this gain in empirical relevance is bought at a high cost; viz., it would be impossible to justify the Federal Reserve's policy in 1936–7 with the modified free reserve conception. The Federal Reserve authorities apparently never realized this implication of their evolving notions that substituted free reserves in place of bank indebtedness as a central magnitude in the causal process. Such unawareness is a typical symptom of the unsystematic and essentially impressionistic nature of their discourse concerning these problems. A clear and definite grasp of pertinent implications can only be obtained by tracing the conception as a whole in a coherent, systematic manner. The interactions of the distinct blocks composing the whole process must be carefully followed in order to fully understand the patterns implied by a given framework. To date, the Federal Reserve has not done this.

1.5 The Causal Position of Free Reserves: Free Reserves as an Index of a Monetary Situation and Free Reserves as a Policy Target

To understand the role of free reserves in Federal Reserve discussions, it is important to separate three distinct meanings assigned to the term. Each of these meanings involves the use of the term in a different way, with markedly different connotations. It is symptomatic of the manner in which the Federal Reserve discusses the monetary mechanism that the three uses of the term are not distinguished. Thus, when there is an occasional denial or affirmation of the importance of free reserves, it is not made clear which of the three uses of free reserves is involved, and we can only judge from the context. As we shall note, this has encouraged needless confusion about the status of the free reserve conception and its importance in Federal Reserve thinking.

One meaning of free reserves has to do with the causal role assigned to the concept. Previous sections have presented the broad outlines of the causal connection that was said to exist between free reserves and interest rates, or changes in bank credit in the later evolution of Riefler's notions. A second meaning gives to free reserves the function of indicating changes in the prevailing monetary situation, particularly modifications of the Federal Reserve's policy posture. Sustained movements productive of large differences in the level of free reserves usually have been interpreted to indicate more or less "ease" or "restraint" in the monetary system. Closely associated with the signal or indicator function, often assigned to free reserves by Federal Reserve officials, is the third use of the term. This is the target function or the practice of incorporating some particular range of free reserves as a guideline for monetary policy.

The occurrence of free reserves as a policy *target* is heavily dependent on the assumption, implicit in the free reserves conception, that free reserves play a central role in the causal process linking policy actions with the behavior of the credit markets and the money supply. But this conception of the monetary process does not imply the use of free reserves as a policy target. Thus it is quite consistent with the continued adherence to the free reserves conception that other targets may replace free reserves. As we shall see, the choice of an alternative target provides no information that permits us to conclude that the Federal Reserve has rejected the conception of monetary processes centered on the causal role of free reserves. Neither does the use of some other target necessarily indicate that free reserves have been abandoned as a signal of changes in the monetary situation. However, abandonment of the causal connection between free reserves and changes in bank credit would destroy any basis for the indicator or target functions often assigned to free reserves.

Before discussing the use of free reserves as an indicator and/or target of policy actions, it is useful to consider the large variations in free reserves that have occurred since 1946. Since 1955 the monthly average has moved between $500 million and minus $500 million.

For reasons that have been cited and are inherent in the definition, the Federal Reserve cannot control the volume of free reserves on a daily or weekly basis up to the last dollar. Banks and the public can affect the value of free reserves by borrowing or repaying borrowing, converting demand deposits into time deposits, or depositing and withdrawing currency. These operations cause changes in required or total reserves. Other factors such as float, movements of the Treasury balance between commercial banks and Federal Reserve Banks, etc., introduce changes in the volume of free reserves available on any given day. Movements of deposits from Reserve city banks to country banks also change the volume of free reserves since reserve requirements for country banks are lower than for Reserve city banks.[9] As a result of movements of deposits into country banks, fewer reserves are classed as required reserves, more reserves are measured as excess reserves, and free reserves are larger. Movements of deposits in the opposite direction reduce free reserves.

The Federal Reserve is principally concerned with extremely short-run market influences, but it cannot hope to anticipate with precision all of the movements occurring each day or week. It can and does make projections designed to offset some or all of the anticipated changes. But it must be satisfied with a level of free reserves that is subject to daily and weekly variation.

The amount of variation that must be accepted has been reduced in recent years. Better information, improved coordination with the Treasury, and

---

[9]At the time member banks were classified into reserve city banks (New York, Chicago), reserve city banks (major other cities) and country banks (the remainder). The highest reserve requirements were imposed on reserve city banks, the lowest on country banks.

elimination of the higher reserve requirement for central Reserve city banks have all contributed to the reduction in weekly fluctuations. Most of the week-to-week changes in free reserves in 1962 were less than $50 million. Ten years earlier, week-to-week changes of $100 or $200 million were not uncommon.

1.6 Free Reserves as a Policy Target

The Federal Open Market Committee at times specifies a range for the value of free reserves. At other times, they may specify some other criterion or a set of criteria. These alternative criteria are often vague, e.g., concepts such as "tone" or "feel" may be used. The Manager of the System Open Market Account must then translate these statements into an operative concept, i.e., into a range of free reserves or some other magnitude that he will attempt to maintain. Quite often it is a range of free reserves that is chosen.

The choice of free reserves as the manager's target is very likely to emerge under the circumstances. The account manager's position on the credit market is similar to the position of the commercial banks' money desk men in important respects. Both appraise events in the context of a single bank's frame, and both focus on extremely short-run occurrences. The operational duties imposed on both the account manager and the money desk men channel their views in the direction mentioned.[10] Free reserves provide the manager with a concept that is analogous to the "money (or Federal funds) position" that plays a dominant role as a target for the money desk men. Variations in free reserves consistently tend to play a major role in the account manager's considerations. And these same considerations will frequently lead the FOMC to incorporate levels or ranges of free reserves among the policy targets, or will influence the account manager to translate other policy targets into a range of free reserves that he attempts to maintain.

We do not contend that free reserves are the only or most important policy target of the Federal Reserve authorities. As we noted, the acceptance of the free reserve doctrine as a conception about the structure of monetary processes, the choice of free reserves as a specific signal or indicator of monetary situations, and the choice of free reserves as a policy target are distinct and only partly dependent issues. The dependence of these issues is quite asymmetrical in the sense that rejection of the free reserve doctrine would effectively remove free reserves both as indicator and policy target, whereas acceptance of the doctrine does not entail the other choices, except by a purely nonlogical connection. The use of other policy targets, accompanied by a modified or fading emphasis on free reserve targets, is perfectly com-

---

[10]The money desk men are responsible for short-run adjustments in the banks' portfolios and reserve positions.

patible with the recognition that free reserves play a causal role in the monetary mechanism and are also used as an indicator of "the degree of ease."

The modification and adjustment of the policy targets, however, poses some problems not fully or explicitly appreciated by the Federal Reserve authorities. A close control over some market rates would preclude a close control over free reserves, unless the discount rate and the reserve requirement ratios are continuously adjusted to evolving circumstances similar to the FOMC's open market operations. But to the extent that requirement ratios and the discount rate are maintained at certain levels, the close control of some interest rates near a target level implies abandonment of free reserves as a closely controlled target. One goal must be sacrificed, in part at least, to the other. For example, in the pre-Accord period, when interest rates were pegged from above to prevent bonds from selling below par, some control of free reserves was lost. Most recently, when bill yields have been pegged from below to prevent a decline in short-term money market rates, some of the control of free reserves has been lost again.

When the Federal Reserve withdraws reserves from the banks through open market operations to maintain a given bill yield, total reserves decline. Some reduction in free reserves will result either because member banks borrow additional reserves to restore some of the reserves removed, or because there is not an equal concomitant reduction in required reserves through a decline in demand deposits or a shift of demand to time deposits. Pegging bill yields is therefore inconsistent with tight control of the level of free reserves.

The pegging of short-term rates in recent years has changed the role of free reserves as a policy target. But that does not mean that they have not remained an important indicator or measure of ease and restraint. An illustration of the effect of choosing bill yields as a guide to policy is contained in a graph accompanying an article by the present Manager of the Open Market Account (Stone, 1963). The graph is entitled "Free Reserves fluctuated from week to week while Short-Term Rates moved narrowly."

The graph shows the effect of choosing bill yields and rejecting free reserves as the primary target of Federal Reserve policy. We have seen that a necessary condition for the choice of free reserves as an indicator and target is the belief that a high level of free reserves induces a rapid rate of credit expansion and that persistently low levels decelerate credit expansion. By choosing the bill yield as policy target, the Federal Reserve surrenders some control of the level of free reserves. The primary instrument becomes the bill yield; the level of free reserves must be adjusted to maintain the bill yield at or near some minimum level.

The choice of Treasury bill yields as a primary target of System policy is one indication that the goals of System policy have changed. The goal is now related to the so-called balance-of-payments problem. The Federal Reserve has adopted the position that the difference between domestic and foreign (especially European and Canadian) short-term interest rates is an important source of the outflow of gold. To reduce the outflow of gold, domestic short-term interest rates are pegged from below.

It is indicative of the absence of analysis as a base for Federal Reserve policymaking that the choice of the new instrument and the new policy have not been supported by any detailed study that confirms or even strongly suggests that short-term capital movements are highly sensitive to interest rate differentials. This does not mean that the relationship does not exist. Some indirect evidence from general economics supports the relation, but no direct evidence has been adduced thus far that confirms a close and sensitive response of short-term capital to differentials in short-term interest rates. Nevertheless, the new policy and the new target appear to have supplanted free reserves and the goal of achieving ease or restraint; i.e., full employment and price stability.

The adoption of a new policy and a new target does not imply that free reserves have been rejected as a *measure* or indicator of ease and restraint. Rather it suggests that domestic expansion has been relegated to a position of lower priority. We may state with the aid of current and past euphemisms, that the "discipline of the balance of payments" has been accepted in place of the policy of "leaning against the wind."

Does the modified free reserve doctrine continue to measure ease and restraint? We suggest that the bulk of the evidence supports the view that it does. The choice of a new target of System policy is important, because it indicates a change in the aims of policy. If domestic expansion will be encouraged by the System only to the extent that the constraints on short-term interest rates permit, then the use of free reserves as a target has been suspended, while the causal role of free reserves is not affected.

This is not the first time in recent years that the System has used an instrument other than free reserves as a target. During the period in which Chairman Martin and others continued to refer to free reserves as an indicator of ease and restraint, other targets were mentioned at times in the "Record of Policy Actions." For example, at the meeting of May 27, 1958, the manager's targets were "to maintain the current posture of monetary ease, without further depressing Treasury bill rates" (Record of Policy Actions, 1958). At other times, particularly during Treasury offerings, the manager is told to "maintain an even keel."

Numerous other targets have been used. At the meeting of December 19, 1961, a principal target of short-run policy was the level of "available reserves." This measures the "net change in total reserves after allowing for reserves provided or absorbed to offset seasonal factors and changes in Treasury tax and loan balances at member banks."[11] References to total reserves,

---

[11]See Noyes, 1963, p. 148. Noyes was Director of the Division of Research and Statistics, Board of Governors at the time.

unborrowed reserves, and a variety of other instruments are found also. At other times, no specific credit market target is mentioned.

1.7 The Indicator Function of Free Reserves

The importance of random elements in the volume of free reserves implies that a single policy target specified in terms of free reserves does not assure even approximate control of free reserves in the shortest run. Moreover, banks do not respond immediately to variations in the volume of free reserves according to the best explications of the free reserve conception. The very short run, or instantaneous, relation between free reserves and "credit expansion" is, therefore, admittedly loose. A longer policy horizon lowers the relative importance of the random components and raises the extent to which the level of free reserves can be controlled. These differences between the Federal Reserve's ability to control the short- and longer-run variations in free reserves are of importance for a discussion of free reserves as an indicator or signal of changing monetary conditions.

Day-to-day variations in free reserves are relatively large. Banks receiving increased reserves may hold them for a day or more, or lend them in the Federal funds market rather than purchase securities or reduce loan rates to stimulate borrowing. That is, banks may interpret the inflow of reserves as "transitory," the result of a "defensive" operation when the Federal Reserve had in mind a "sustained" change in a reserves, a "dynamic" operation or a combination of the two. Similarly, losses of reserves may be treated as "transitory" rather than "sustained" by the banks and thus lead to borrowing in the Federal funds market. For this reason the Federal funds rate and the movements of Federal funds become additional indicators of the effect of policy operations.[12]

Experiments with the reported free reserve totals suggest that a 3-week moving average of total free reserves provides a relatively reliable indicator of Federal Reserve policy. We will consider the evidence in more detail in section 2. It is pointed out here to suggest that there may be a lag of several weeks between a change in the range of free reserves and an evaluation of the change as a sustained change by the market.

Several bankers have indicated to us that their staffs perform similar smoothing operations to obtain a moving average of weekly reported free

---

[12]During the 1950s the Federal Reserve began to describe its operations in terms of dynamic and defensive maneuvers. Defensive operations are designed to offset transitory or permanent influences modifying banks' reserve position at times when policymakers wish to maintain a prevailing stance on the money markets. Dynamic operations are directed to change this stance. A good description of this policy may be found in Robert V. Roosa "Interest Rates and the Central Bank," in: *Money, Trade and Economic Growth*, prepared in honor of John Williams, New York: Macmillan, 1951, pp. 270–95.

reserves. Three weeks is often used as the period of the moving average. It is probably not a coincidence that the 3-week moving average permits observers to isolate the periods between meetings of the FOMC. In any case, it suggests that bankers and other interested observers of Federal Reserve policy may not respond immediately to a change in the level of free reserves by increasing or decreasing their outstanding loans and investments. Much may depend on the size of the change in free reserves, the rate on Federal funds, the discount rate, the rate on Treasury bills, and the direction in which these rates move. These and other signs are carefully watched for clues to infer the composition of the changes experienced. The response of banks to variations in reserve positions substantially depends on their interpretation of these changes. Modifications of reserve positions interpreted as only transitory will not induce the portfolio adjustments typically associated with changes in reserve positions deemed to be persistent and systematic.

From the viewpoint of the banks' money desk men or the Federal Reserve System's account manager the central building block of the free reserve conception – connecting free reserves to "bank credit" expansion – seems most natural and rather obvious. Continuous exposure to the daily variations in reserve positions and the associated portfolio adjustments seems to support the relationship. But the reader is once more cautioned against such impressionistic evidence that contributes little to the discriminating evaluation of accustomed beliefs. Less subjective procedures will be used in section 3 to examine the central core of the free reserves conception and will lead us to reject it. Such rejection immediately invalidates both the causal role and the signal or indicator function attributed to free reserves.

At the present we consider an essentially logical issue, viz., the appropriateness of assigning an indicator character to free reserves *in the context of the free reserve conception*. We are thus not questioning, at the moment, the empirical relevance of this conception. We accept it for the moment and question the signal and indicator function attributed to free reserves by the Federal Reserve authorities.

The logical issue cannot be settled by a direct critical examination of statements made by the Federal Reserve authorities. Their pronouncements are usually too vague to permit a searching analysis without first translating them into a more coherent and definite analytical context. Our appraisal of the compatibility of the indicator character with the free reserve conception is therefore based on a specific translation which we undertook for the examination of this question and related issues. Once more we emphasize that there is no guarantee that our explanation of the Federal Reserve's notion is "correct." It is offered as a substitute for the product never supplied by the Federal Reserve authorities. Its comparative adequacy, however, can be judged by the extent to which typical Federal Reserve statements can be successfully subsumed by our analysis.

The explicit construction of the Federal Reserve's free reserve notions yields a remarkable result. It turns out that free reserves could rationally serve as a signal or indicator in the manner used by the Federal Reserve only if we possess detailed and reliable information about crucial links in the monetary process that are presently beyond our disposal. The required information must be sufficient to separate the strands composing the observable behavior of free reserves. In particular, the component attributable to policy actions should be separated from the influences on free reserves emanating from the economy via the public's asset supply to banks. But in our present situation, i.e., in the absence of sufficiently detailed and reliable information concerning the structure of the monetary process, no useful indicator function can be rationally assigned to free reserves on the basis of the free reserve conception. Indeed, it can be shown that even large variations in free reserves cannot be safely interpreted as modifications of relative "ease" or "tightness" with the usual connotations of accelerated or decelerated rates of "credit expansion." Moreover, even if all the required information were available, other elements (to be explained in section 4) supply a simpler and more useful indicator of the prevailing monetary situation and the Federal Federal Reserve's posture.

Detailed analysis thus exhibits the inadequacy of assigning free reserves an indicator function, even if the central causal role of free reserves is acknowledged. Under these circumstances, how can we explain the attention focused on free reserves by the Federal Reserve authorities? The answer must be found in the piecemeal nature and uncoordinated character of the Federal Reserve's conception. The Federal Reserve apparently never viewed the simultaneous operation and interaction of all the building blocks. Emphasis was placed on the central block, relating market rates, or more recently, the banks' portfolio adjustment with free reserves and the discount rate. The other building blocks were vaguely disregarded.

Attention limited to the single relation emphasizing the causal role of free reserves generated a view of free reserves as a summary measure of the monetary situation. The relevant feedbacks and interactions generated by the other relations constituting the monetary process were neglected, although many of them were a part of the Riefler tradition. The Federal Reserve's procedure may be likened to an explanation of price and output in terms of supply only, disregarding that price and output emerge from the joint interaction of demand and supply forces.

1.8 Evidence from Published Statements

Our discussion has recognized three separable aspects in the Federal Reserve's view of free reserves, viz.: (1) the recognition of their central position in the transmission of monetary impulses, (2) their acceptance as a summary measure of a monetary situation, the signal or indicator function, and (3) their use at times as a target for monetary policy. Two statements made in 1958 provide a relatively clear exposition of the free reserve doctrine as seen by the Federal Reserve.[13] The article published by the Federal Reserve Bank of New York appears, on superficial reading, to be a criticism of "the free reserves doctrine." But careful reading yields a different result. A causal role of central importance is explicitly recognized, and a qualified indicator function is acknowledged.

The qualifications that are introduced take the form of explicit recognition that other elements shape the banks' portfolio adjustments *jointly* with the volume of free reserves. The joint operation of free reserves and other elements at times modifies the interpretation that can be placed on the effect of a particular level of free reserves on the banks' behavior. For example, "while excess reserves have been fairly stable, free reserves have moved over a wide range, marking out the major swings between monetary ease and restraint." An important qualification is introduced to explain why a given level of free reserves does not always mean the same thing. Country banks are willing to hold larger excess reserves than money market banks. The accrual of free reserves at money market banks is expected, in general, to have a different effect on portfolio adjustments than a corresponding accrual at country banks.

Other qualifying factors must be considered. "At times when banks have, for example, higher ratios of loans to deposits, or of long-term to short-term loans (measures of liquidity), they may be *less* responsive to higher levels of free reserves." However, the report notes that the qualifications are not denials of the role of free reserves; they simply indicate that the process of influencing "credit" is not instantaneous. For example, note the following:

When free reserves are *held for some time* at a relatively high level, member banks will not only continue to make loans available to their customers – and probably *more readily available* than at lower levels of free reserves – but they are also likely to seek out new investment opportunities aggressively . . . It is in this way, through the pressure of an enlarged supply of bank funds seeking investment against a reduced demand for bank credit, that there is a tendency for a high level of free reserves to be associated with falling interest rates, increased liquidity in the banking system, expansion of credit, and growth in the money supply.

After a discussion of the effects of a reduction in free reserves the New York Bank adds the following indication that it is the level and not the rate of change of free reserves that influences credit expansion.

(E)asing or restraining effects are related primarily to the *level of free*

---

[13]The significance and limitations of free reserves (1958) and Riefler (1958). The former will be referred to as "New York Bank"; the latter as "Riefler." [Emphasis has been added.]

reserves that is being maintained and are not dependent on continuing further changes in that level. To be sure, as noted above, a given magnitude of free reserves may induce different degrees of ease at different times, depending on a variety of influences. But in maintaining whatever *degree of ease or restraint has been achieved* under the conditions prevailing at any particular time, *it is not necessary for free reserves* or net borrowed reserves to *rise continuously* to higher and higher levels, as has sometimes been supposed.

On occasion one may encounter passages that seem to deprecate the causal role or the indicator function of free reserves. The New York Bank article refers to the "loose fit of any specific level of free reserves to any degree of credit ease or restraint . . ." We have considered earlier the way in which random variations impose a "loose fit" in the very short run. But the formulation also refers to the modification of the free reserves doctrine mentioned toward the end of the last section. Other elements supplement free reserves as causal factors operating to shape the banks' rate of portfolio adjustment. The report suggests that "consideration must be given to the distribution of bank assets among loans and investments of varying degrees of liquidity, the size and composition of bank liabilities, and the level and structure of interest rates." Other factors may be mentioned on other occasions. A perusal of Federal Reserve pronouncements supplies ample evidence that the range of arguments in the central relation was extended beyond free reserves and discount rate, but the nature of the extension remains ambiguous.

Nevertheless, the conclusion is quite clear. "For all its limitations, the free reserves concept *remains a useful guide* to the interpretation of credit policy." A very similar conclusion with many fewer qualifications is reached in the Riefler article:

"Federal Reserve operations also affect the prices and yields of Government securities *because they change the volume of free reserves available* to member banks." Indeed, Riefler's discussion of Federal Reserve operations provides an indication of their beliefs about the quantitative impact of any change in reserves.

> For example, if, as general analysis suggests, something like seven-eighths of the effect of an open market operation on the availability of funds in the market represents the effect of that operation on bank reserve positions . . . while only one-eighth reflects the fact that bills were simultaneously put into or withdrawn from the market, it follows that a comparable change in the level of net free reserves *from whatever cause* ultimately *should affect the general credit situation* and interest rates to roughly the same extent as the open market operation or within seven-eighths of the same extent.

The above remarks pertain to the recognition of free reserves both as an indicator of current policy ("marking out the major swings") and as a target of policy ("held for some time," "the level of free reserves that is being maintained"). Riefler also introduces some qualifications about the interpretations of free reserves as a measure of "ease and restraint." To remove doubt that statements published in 1958 are applicable to the interpretation of current policy operations, more recent quotations are provided. These indicate that the free reserve concept has played a major role during the past five years.

One very clear set of statements appears as a part of the answers that the Federal Reserve gave to questions asked by the Commission on Money and Credit. Under the heading "Operating Guides and Procedures," we are told:

"The figure of 'free reserves' or its negative counterpart 'net borrowed reserves' provides a convenient and significant working *measure* of the posture of policy at the time . . . It is also a device that is better adapted than its components taken separately for estimating and projecting the net impact of regular variations in factors affecting reserves.

"The general level of free reserves prevailing over a long period of time may be viewed as an indicator of the degree of restraint or ease that exists in the money market."[14] The writer elaborates on some qualifications that must be made. "The particular level of free reserves that may be needed to *achieve the objectives of policy* may vary from time to time depending on changing economic conditions." Recognition is given to the possible changes in required and borrowed reserves.[15]

Further recognition of the causal position of free reserves is given (p. 8) in the statement "The Federal Reserve restrains (or encourages) bank credit expansion by reducing (or increasing) the banks' primary liquidity." The latter term is defined (p. 6) as follows: "Primary bank liquidity relates to the net reserve position of commercial banks." These remarks clearly indicate that the policy of the Federal Reserve is to operate on the level of free reserves in order to effect an increase or decrease in the rate of credit expansion. However, qualifications or modifications are shortly introduced (p. 9).

"The significance at any given time of net borrowed reserves (or free reserves) as a factor tending to restrain (or encourage) bank credit expansion depends on at least five things: (1) the magnitude of free reserves (or net borrowed reserves); (2) the level of short-term money rates relative to Federal Reserve discount rates; (3) the vigor of actual current demands for bank credit; (4) the existing level of total bank liquidity; and (5) the variations among different classes and groups of banks with respect to the conditions just named."

---

[14]Commission on Money and Credit, 1963, pp. 19–20. [Italics have been added here and in the following quotations.]

[15]Ibid., p. 20. The page numbers in the text that follows refer to the Federal Reserve's answer to the Commission on Money and Credit.

The last quotation, reportedly written by Woodlief Thomas of the staff of the Board of Governors (Noyes, 1963, p. 147), makes quite explicit the role of free reserves as a causal entity of central importance and as a measure or indicator of policy. It should be noted that few of these statements suggest that only free reserves influence that rate of credit expansion. But all of the statements assign an important role to free reserves as a measure of credit policy and as a magnitude to be modified by policy action in order to achieve desired changes in credit markets or the money supply.

Additional testimony to this effect appeared in an article by Young and Yager (1960). Their statement assigns a primary role to free reserves and omits many of the qualifications.

> [T]hese mechanical aspects of monetary regulations find their summary in the movement of net reserve positions of the banks. This quantity, in effect, may be thought of as the *rudder* by means of which the monetary ship is made to 'lean against the winds' . . . Since operations to increase or decrease the System's portfolio are undertaken to change the direction of the rudder – that is to influence the net reserve position of the banking system on the basis of either short- or longer-term considerations or both . . .

The evidence that free reserves have been used as both a measure and, in their causal role, as an instrument of policy is relatively clear. However, one final quotation is introduced to establish (1) that the interpretation of free reserves as an indicator of policy has been suggested within the last several months and (2) that our interpretation of Federal Reserve views is confirmed by statements of their staff (Federal Reserve Bulletin, 1963, pp. 891, 893). In particular they state that increased borrowing by member banks has a contractive effect on the stock of credit or its rate of adjustment.

"One of the most sensitive measures of the day-to-day interaction of monetary policy and market forces is the so-called net reserve position of banks. This measure is computed by subtracting member bank borrowing at the Federal Reserve from excess reserves." A *"persistent change in net reserve positions* over a period of several weeks *often indicates a basic shift in the credit climate."*

> In fact such market conditions are likely to stimulate growth in total bank reserves by increasing the willingness of member banks to borrow from the Federal Reserve. However, if a rise in total reserves is composed largely of borrowed reserves, it is less likely to be sustainable than if it is composed mainly of nonborrowed reserves. Member bank borrowing at Federal Reserve Banks is generally regarded as a temporary source of reserves both by the borrowing bank and by the Federal Reserve officials who administer discount operations. This transitory or emergency nature of borrowed reserves, . . . tends to limit the volume of credit that can be supported by such reserves.

These statements, as a group, are sufficiently clear that no summary is required. Our interpretations and some criticism have already been made in an earlier section. Additional indications of the attachment of the Board of Governors, the Federal Open Market Committee, and their staffs to the free reserves concept are readily available, however.[16]

1.8.1 Some Clues Suggesting Recent Developments of the Free Reserve Conception

Recently, a series of statements with somewhat different import have been made. These statements are somewhat difficult to interpret; they may indicate a change of views in the System, or they may reflect existing dissents or discussions. Some people within the System apparently reject the level of free reserves as an indicator and question the causal role customarily assigned to free reserves. Despite the very recent statement of the Manager of the System Open Market Account describing policy operations in 1962 in terms of the modified free reserves doctrine, there is some evidence that the usefulness of the free reserve concept is not accepted throughout the System.

1.8.2 Clues from Published Statements

A recent publication of the Federal Reserve Bank of Atlanta asks rhetorically what the Federal Reserve System controls. The answer given is clearly not free reserves but total reserves. It is total reserves that influence the expansion and contraction of "bank credit."[17]

Lest some doubt remain that the free reserves conception is being reconsidered by some officials, the article discusses excess reserves and borrowings as indicators of policy. It rejects these measures largely for the usual reason that the distribution of excess reserves and borrowing is important. Free reserves are then discussed. The report stresses that "they are greatly overrated as a barometer of credit availability. In fact, focusing on free reserves

---

[16](1) Martin, 1963. See especially p. 124. (2) Rouse, 1961, p. 34. (3) Martin, ibid., p. 95, pp. 96–7. (4) Stone, 1963, p. 431: "Indicative of the mildness of the shift in emphasis toward less ease in June, weekly average free reserves most often moved in a range of about $350 million to $500 million from mid-June to mid-December . . . Continuing attention was paid to free reserves, but not to the extent of pursuing particular free reserve levels at the expense of wide swings in the general tone of the money market." Other factors are then mentioned. They are (a) the location of reserves, (b) the availability of Federal funds, (c) dealer financing needs, (d) trends in short-term rates, (e) the pattern of capital market developments, (f) credit expansion, and (g) growth in the money supply. (5) Various meetings of the Federal Open Market Committee reported in "The Record of Policy Actions" in Annual Report of the Board of Governors of the Federal Reserve System. See for examples the reports of the meetings on July 11, 1961, Mar. 25, 1959, and Aug. 19. 1958.

[17]"What it does come close to controlling are the reserves of banks that are members of the Federal Reserve System . . . A greater volume of reserves enables banks to expand credit. Thus, the relationship between reserves and bank credit is close, although changes in one are not always accompanied by corresponding changes in the other" Brandt, 1963, p. 1.

can be misleading. . . . Failing as a sure sign of credit availability, free reserves are also faulty as a measure of the intensity of credit demand. Moreover, they are not usually very indicative of actual bank credit trends" (Brandt, 1963, p. 4).

On other recent occasions, Federal Reserve spokesmen have assigned only the shortest run significance to levels of free reserves, and longer run significance to total reserves. Such statements suggest a modification, but not a rejection, of the free reserves conception. They can be reasonably interpreted in the context of a coherently formulated free reserve conception that explicitly traces the interaction of the relations composing the monetary process. The affirmation of the longer run significance of total reserves does not necessarily reveal a disposition to reject the free reserves conception. More likely it suggests that some of the building blocks described earlier, that had been discarded, are now explicitly considered and acknowledged as relevant.

A more fundamental attack on the free reserves doctrine was mentioned earlier. The statement "use of the term 'excess reserves' to indicate a supply of readily available funds or unused lending power is probably misleading" attacks the root of the free reserves concept as an indicator of potential expansion. It substitutes the view that "a relatively high average level of excess reserves that persists for several months does not necessarily indicate that there is an expansive force on bank credit and money; instead it may reflect a weak credit demand, low interest rates, or an increased desire for liquidity by bankers" (Federal Reserve Bank of St. Louis, 1963, p. 15). The banks' demand for cash assets or reserves is thus introduced as an influence on the rate of expansion of money and credit and interpreted as a response to the prevailing level of interest rates. As suggested above, this position is inconsistent with the analysis based on free reserves and the use of free reserves as an indicator of "ease and restraint."

The admission of a systematic response to prevailing interest rates in the banks' cash asset position is not a minor adjustment of prevailing views. It is a major break with the Riefler–Burgess tradition that assigned a nonvolitional character to banks' indebtedness and later to free reserves. The abandonment of this position is a rejection of the causal role and the indicator function assigned to free reserves by the Federal Reserve authorities. The discovery of banks' demand for free reserves by the Federal Reserve authorities must lead eventually to a fundamental readjustment of the Federal Reserve's conception of the monetary process. Such a readjustment will involve a radical break with an accumulated heritage of views and pronouncements assessing monetary situations and guiding monetary policy.

1.8.3 Clues from Answers to Questionnaires

These signs of dissension or disagreement within the Federal Reserve System suggested that there may be serious questioning of the causal role and indicator function assigned to free reserves. To obtain more information, a questionnaire was sent to each president of the 12 Reserve Banks and to each member of the Board of Governors. The presidents and the Board members both answered the questionnaire as a group and indicated substantial agreement within each group.[18]

What do their answers indicate? Questions II, V, and VII in effect asked the FOMC members to explain the substantive content of "ease" and "restraint," to describe the monetary mechanism, to specify the role of free reserves in the monetary process and the meaning that they assign to changes in the level of free reserves. Question III asked that the analysis be applied to a particular context, the year 1962. The responses to these questions are extremely helpful in clarifying the state of the Federal Reserve's thinking. Moreover, the answers provide evidence of disagreement between the two groups, since important differences of emphasis appear. These differences suggest the emergence of a "conceptual interregnum." The free reserve doctrine is no longer accepted by all as the primary block in the analysis. The answers provided multiply the signs that the inherited doctrine is being reconsidered. But the answers also reveal quite clearly that the reconsideration has not proceeded far enough to provide a firmer foundation for monetary policy or a more appropriate analysis of the monetary situation. Residues of the free reserve doctrine, emanating from the Riefler–Burgess tradition, continue to hold a prominent place in the Federal Reserve conception.

The 12 presidents indicate that free reserves are one of the indicators but usually not the most important indicator of "credit conditions" even in the very short run. Short-term market interest rates are important in relation to the discount rate (II).[19] All of these factors are summarized in the statement that appears to define changes in the degree of ease as "an availability of reserves relative to the economy's demand for credit" (V).

Levels of free reserves above $500 million have occurred in periods of ease since the "Accord." But the degree of ease is not the same each time the level of free reserve rises above $500 million because there is no unique association between free reserves of $500 million or more and a particular level of borrowing, short-term interest rates, or credit expansion (II.4). The demand for reserves must also be considered (II.2 and V.2). In fact it is total reserves, not free reserves, that is "relevant from a longer term point of view" (II.2).

The Board of Governors notes that "ease" and "restraint" are relative terms. They must be interpreted in the light of the demand for reserves by banks. "Interaction between the supply of and demand for free reserves gets

---

[18]The questionnaires with the replies were published in 1964 by the Committee on Banking and Currency, House of Representatives, 88th Congress, 2nd Session.

[19]Roman numerals appearing in the text refer to the numbers of the questions in the appendix to the original publication, when the answers have been paraphrased or quoted. If a particular subsection is paraphrased or quoted, the reference is given as II.3.

reflected in the rate of expansion in total required reserves." The distribution of free reserves is at times an important indicator of short-run behavior of the monetary system (II.1). "The level of free reserves is . . . an *indicator* of the degree of ease or restraint if interpreted in the light of prevailing demand conditions" (II.2; italic in the original). But the most important fact is the demand and supply for loanable funds.

The principal supply factor subject to Federal Reserve policy is said to be the supply of total reserves. This is reflected in the level of free reserves, on the supply side, but must be judged relative to the demand for free reserves. The latter shows primarily changes in the desired borrowing of member banks since the desired excess reserve position of member banks "changes only infrequently" (II.2 and II.1).

Measurement of the demand for free reserves cannot be precise. But the factors influencing the demand are provided "by changes in bank loans, especially business loans, and by the level of interest rates on short-term securities and the Federal funds rate and their relationship to the discount rate." The context suggests that other, unnamed factors might be important also (VII).

The Board appears to place substantially greater influence on the level of free reserves than do the Reserve Bank presidents. Both emphasize a number of other factors, that modify the "free reserves doctrine," but the presidents seem to suggest that free reserves are a relatively poor indicator of short-term policy and that total reserves are better both as a target and as an indicator of policy. Both groups seem to agree that if free reserves are used as an indicator of policy, the following must be used to interpret the meaning of the level of free reserves:

1 The rate of expansion of bank loans and investments, the rate of expansion of bank loans, or both;
2 The Treasury bill rate relative to the rediscount rate;
3 The Federal funds rate relative to the rediscount rate;
4 The distribution of free reserves, an important factor in the very short run only. To these the presidents would add "tone" or "feel."

There is substantial agreement in the two statements that free reserves are generally not the target of monetary policy. At times free reserves may be used for this purpose. But a variety of other measures and concepts are also used from time to time. This topic will be considered in a later section when we discuss the procedures at the FOMC meetings and the information that is given to the Manager.

Both groups recognize that "ease" and "restraint" are relative matters. Both define these concepts in terms of demand and supply. For the presidents, it is the demand for credit relative to the supply of reserves; for the members of the Board, it is the demand for and supply of loanable funds that determines the prevailing degree of ease and restraint. But this is probably more a difference in wording than in content. The supply of loanable funds is influenced by the supply of reserves. It is in this way that monetary policy is said to operate.

A part of the mechanism underlying and responding to monetary operations is described by both groups. The 12 presidents separate the effects of changes in the supply of reserves from those associated with the demand for reserves by banks, although they suggest that the mechanism is similar in both cases. Central to the discussion of ease is the implicit assumption of a small short-run response by business borrowers to a reduction in interest rates occurring as a result of increases in reserves (V.1). No evidence has been provided to support this contention, but it is assumed to be a basic feature of the process. As a result banks restore and increase their earning assets by buying securities. This reduces interest rates and adds to the stock of money. The 12 presidents seem to recognize that the rate of monetary expansion or contraction may differ from cycle to cycle even if the rate of credit expansion or contraction is the same (V).

The major point of interest that seems to emerge from the discussion is that the stock of credit or its rate of change is the focus of policy. Money is said to respond to an unspecified and complex set of other factors (V.1). A part of any increase in reserves stemming from open market purchases will be used to advance credit (VII). Indeed this is true of any increase in non-borrowed reserves. Borrowed reserves apparently are not used to support or increase credit according to the 12 presidents.

The Board's reply explicitly lists the ways in which banks will use reserves in periods of ease following periods of restraint. The details differ slightly, and the discussion is less informative, but the conclusions are approximately the same as the presidents' (V). The effect of time deposit rates and rates of interest paid by savings and loan associations are explicitly recognized as important factors that influence the rate of monetary expansion and the distribution of deposit balances between demand and time deposits.

These statements, when read in detail, seem to suggest that some earlier criticisms of Federal Reserve pronouncements made in this report are not applicable to the present FOMC. Both the presidents and the Board of Governors appear to be aware of the differences in the rates of credit and monetary expansion and even appear to explain the differences in these rates in a manner somewhat similar to the analysis presented in a previous section. Weaknesses in the free reserve concept are more or less implicitly acknowledged and the demand for reserves by banks is introduced as an important influence in the process, difficult to measure, but nonetheless capable of being approximated by reference to observable market entities. Among the important influences affecting the demand for reserves, short-term interest rates relative to the discount rate appear to be prominent. Thus despite the many earlier indications to the contrary, the replies suggest that the Federal Reserve has abandoned, perhaps recently, much of the previous analysis of the monetary process that has been criticized here.

But some disturbing elements remain. Recall that a basic feature of the free reserves concept is the view that borrowing by member banks exerts a restrictive effect on the expansion process and that repayments of borrowing have an expansive effect. This interpretation of borrowing remains as an anachronism. Moreover, the emphasis is still on the rate of credit expansion, not on the rate of monetary expansion. "Monetary policy is concerned with the overall availability of credit." Although it is recognized that credit expansion does not mean the same thing when the rate of monetary expansion is slow as when it is fast, "credit" – not money – is regarded as the factor transmitting System policy to the economy. This means that if credit is expanding at a rapid rate, ease is occurring, *even if the money supply is reduced.* The answers to some specific questions make this clear.

1.8.4 Policy in Some Specific Contexts

The questionnaire asked about some specific policy situations, 1949 and 1961. The answers provide strong evidence that the "credit" view remains dominant. The reformulation of "ease" and "restraint" in terms of the inter-action of the demand for and supply of reserves or free reserves has not been systematically absorbed. The analysis that plays a prominent role in response to more general questions is nowhere in evidence when specific questions were answered.

During 1949, a year of recession, the money supply declined. From the end of June 1948 to the end of June 1949, the stock of money decreased by more than $1 billion. For the calendar year 1949, the decline was smaller, less than one-half billion dollars. During the early months of the recession in 1957, the stock of money fell at the rate of 2.7 percent per annum. In 1961, a year of recovery, the money supply grew at about 2.6 percent per annum. The members of the FOMC were asked to explain these differences in rates of change in question I.6.

The Board of Governors replied that they were following "an active countercyclical monetary policy in both years," i.e., 1949 and 1961. The fact that the stock of money did not increase during the year of recession but did increase in the year of recovery was due apparently to other forces. The 12 presidents stated that "if the Federal Reserve were to attempt to force an increase in the money supply at a faster rate than the public was willing to add to its cash balances at prevailing price levels, the result would be rising prices and aggravation of the balance-of-payments situation rather than pro-motion of sustainable economic growth."

The Board characterized policy in 1949 and 1961 as "stimulative." This assessment follows if one accepts the inherited notions composing the "free reserve doctrine," described in previous sections. Toward the middle of 1949 free reserves moved from a level of approximately $600 million to a level of approximately $800 million. Again in 1961 free reserves would be interpreted to reflect a "stimulative policy." The radical difference in the behavior of the money supply observed during the recession of 1949 and the upswing of 1961 is therefore attributed to the operation of "other factors." "Among the most important of these factors are the economy's demands for bank credit, public preferences for holding liquid assets in particular forms, and the incentives for banks to make loans and purchase investments." But the Board's answer supplies no clues or reference to explanations of *how* these other factors operate to affect the money supply. No information is given about the relevance of these "other factors" in the money supply process.

Our own analysis of the two periods yields a different result. The difference in the behavior of the money stock in the two periods is dominated by the difference in the Federal Reserve's policy behavior. The monetary base published by the St. Louis Federal Reserve Bank shows a negative growth rate of about − $500 million during most of 1949; in 1961 the growth rate was positive and rapidly accelerating.

Monetary policy was thus strongly stimulative in 1961 and strongly deflationary in 1949. The differential behavior of the money supply thus reflects the difference in the policy pursued by the Federal Reserve authorities. "Other factors" do not explain the deflationary policy pursued in the 1949 recession. Indeed, some relevant "other factors" helped to offset the deflationary consequences of the Federal Reserve's behavior in that year. Foremost among these factors is the public's reallocation of its "payment money" between currency and checking deposits.

The decline in the money supply in 1949 was not the result of "other factors" compensating a properly "stimulative policy." Neither did it reflect the working of a substantial lag between policy actions and the responses of the monetary system. The decline in the money supply reflected the policy pursued by the Federal Reserve authorities. There simply was no "stimulative policy" during the recession of 1949.

The presidents' answer indicates that an increase in the money supply beyond the volume desired by the public would only raise prices and aggravate the balance-of-payments deficit. The last point of course has no bearing for 1949. But the central portion of the presidents' answer appears to deny any effect of increases in the money supply on real output. The effect would be completely exhausted by rising prices. The answer provides, of course, no analysis or evidence supporting the contention that an increase in the money supply during a recession only raises prices without raising real income. To our knowledge no analysis has been performed by the Federal Reserve in order to present a reasonable case for this contention. A mass of contrary evidence suggests the opposite conclusion.

Question III asked the FOMC to interpret some published statements by the present Manager of the System Open Market Account. It was asserted that policy has shifted toward "slightly less ease" in 1962. Our observations indicate that free reserves declined with little noticeable effect on the stock of money and credit or on interest rates. The replies of the Board of Governors and the 12 presidents were similar except for one point. Both agreed that policy contributed to expansion in 1962, that the policy of "slightly less ease" was reflected in money market rates, particularly on Treasury bills and Federal funds, and that it was not clear that "credit" was restricted. The presidents add that they did not intend to restrict credit but *only* to increase interest rates. This appears to deny any effect of increased interest rates on the demand for loans, a position that is inconsistent with their explanation of the operation of monetary policy by inducing changes in interest rates.

What are the facts about interest rates and free reserves in 1962? The monthly averages of daily figures for particular months are shown in Table 1.1:

Table 1.1   Federal funds rates and free reserves for selected months of 1961–1962

Month	Federal funds rate in %	Free reserves in millions $
December 1961	2.35	419
January 1962	2.15	546
March 1962	2.84	379
June 1962	2.68	391
July 1962	2.70	440
August 1962	2.92	439
November 1962	2.94	473
December 1962	2.92	268

Federal funds rates increased strongly from January to March. Thereafter, they fluctuated in a rather narrow range. When the System allegedly shifted toward "slightly less ease" in mid-June, there is almost no sign of an increase in the Federal funds rate, and there is a rise in free reserves on a month-to-month basis. It was not until August that the Federal funds rate rose above the rate prevailing in March. Thereafter it fell slightly, rose in November, and was the same in December as in August to five decimal places. In late December, when the System again shifted to "slightly less ease," free reserves fell noticeably. But that is the only indication of slightly less ease in the monthly figures.

Treasury bill yields were higher in December than in several previous months. But the peak for the year occurred in July, and yields were lower at the end of the year than in the middle. The same is true in general for 6-month bills, 1-year bills, longer term Government bonds, and municipal bonds. Moreover, the annual rate of change of the money supply was one of the largest for any 6-month period since late 1951, 6 percent in the latter part of 1962 against minus 0.9 percent in the early part of 1962.[20] Aside from the

[20]The rates of change of the money supply are reported in Federal Reserve Bank of St. Louis, 1961, 1963b.

change in free reserves in December, it is difficult to find any indication of "slightly less ease" in the information which the Federal Reserve replies referred.

One last answer should be mentioned. Question IV asked both groups to explain what was meant by an "even keel." References to the "even keel" policy are not uncommon in System statements, but we had not been able to find any explanation of what was supposed to remain "even." The presidents replied that maintaining an "even keel" meant that no action would be taken that would alter conditions in the financial markets before, during and shortly after Treasury financing operations. A minor policy shift might be undertaken. The Board of Governors' reply was slightly more explicit. There are no changes in rediscount rates, reserve requirements or reserves, and money market conditions large enough to cause a change in expectations. We interpret this to mean that there are no "dynamic" operations.

The presidents add that free reserves would not be kept constant. Some effort would be made to keep them in a range. But, it is added, free reserves are a highly imperfect indicator of market atmosphere (IV.3.). Emphasis is on "reserve availability," in a context that seems to suggest that total reserves, less the reserves required to support Treasury deposits, are taken as the reserve guideline. However, "every market situation is unique" and no general conclusions can be drawn (IV.1).

The Board of Governors do not so clearly deny the relevance of free reserves as a market indicator. Instead, they repeat that constant free reserves are not inconsistent with an unchanged monetary position. This suggests that some operations on free reserves may be attempted.

At first glance it is difficult to reconcile these differing replies to specific questions. How can a single committee have differing interpretations of the meaning of policy? How can a particular measure mean slightly different things to different groups serving on the same committee and making policy decisions? The answer must be that policy directives are made in relatively broad form and that specific meanings have not been assigned or agreed upon. Consideration of the available information on the procedures of the FOMC suggest that this is the case. After a summary of the evidence in this section, we will return to that discussion.

1.8.5 Summary: The Modified Free Reserves Doctrine
The evidence from the statements submitted by the members of the FOMC is subject to a number of interpretations, particularly when read in the light of earlier statements and of applications of their conceptions to particular events. It seems clear that no attempt has been made to write down an explicit statement of the mechanism that relates the actions of the Board of Governors and the FOMC to the stock of money or credit, and to investigate how much can be explained by the particular mechanism. Even if one firmly believes that "judgment" is the most important element in decisionmaking,

it does not follow that facts and evidence are useless. Even "judgment" must be shown to be relevant.

Yet there is little or no evidence provided that shows or denies that a particular measure of reserves, perhaps augmented by some measures of interest rates, has a clear and definite relationship to the stock of credit or money or to some other magnitude. Evidence of this kind would seem to be a prerequisite for policy and for the belief that a certain conception is valid as well as the belief that a particular measure of reserves is more useful than certain other measures. Without analysis and detailed evaluation of the evidence, it is extremely difficult to improve understanding of the mechanism connecting monetary policy with the economy.

For these reasons, we attempt to set down in explicit form the mechanism that seems to emerge from the statements quoted. Enough has been said to indicate that there are areas of disagreement within the FOMC, that at times some factors are considered to be more important than others. But unless detailed evidence is used to support these assertions, there is little chance that monetary policy operations can be improved, that the "degree of control" can be increased. Moreover, the statements quoted above generally do not deny that free reserves are an indicator and, at times, a target of policy. Generally, they suggest that free reserves are only one of the elements that must be used. It is for that reason that the conception is referred to here as "the modified free reserves doctrine."

We believe that the free reserves concept is regarded as one of the crucial links in the so-called credit mechanism or the money supply process. To represent the view that a particular level of free reserves does not always bear the same relation to the rate of change of credit, three interest rates are explicitly mentioned as modifying factors. These are the rate on Federal funds, the rate on Treasury bills, and the discount rate. But the references usually suggest that two of these rates, the Treasury bill rate and the Federal funds rate, must be measured relative to the third interest rate, the discount rate. Thus, it is not the absolute yield on Treasury bills or Federal funds that matters; these interest rates must be judged relative to the prevailing discount rate. In the very short run, the distribution of free reserves is said to be of importance also. In addition, some ambiguous fringe elements remain, their position unresolved in Federal Reserve thinking.

The core of the many and often divergent statements of the Federal Reserve may be summarized as follows:

1   Given the prevailing economic conditions, the demand for and supply of reserves can be expressed in terms of the level and distribution of free reserves, and the two measures of relative yields. These factors are influenced by monetary policy and in fact, dependent, at least in part, directly on policy operations.

2   The rate of expansion of bank credit is dependent, at least in part, on the way in which monetary policy operations influence the factors affecting

the demand for and supply of reserves. The rate of credit expansion is dependent on monetary policy also, but indirectly rather than directly. The intervening relations are the measures used to summarize the demand for and supply of reserves.

3 Recent pronouncements of the Federal Reserve authorities do not deny or reject the inherited free reserves conception. Instead, they compound the confusion by introducing new notions that contradict the old in important respects. But the older ingredients remain, and the inconsistencies are not resolved. Among the most fruitful of the "new ideas" is the recognition that bank indebtedness and the prevailing level of excess reserves result from systematic choices made by bankers in response to prevailing market conditions. But the older conception, emphasizing an alternative view of these entities as elements imposed on the banking system, remains. There is no evidence that this conflict has been recognized. If the Federal Reserve attempted to develop a coherent and useful conception, the conflict would become apparent. More important, it is doubtful that the new conception has reached the policymaking bodies.

The dependence of the rate of expansion of bank credit in the short run on the level and distribution of free reserves and relative interest rates does not imply an absence of other influences. There may be changes that arise by chance, e.g., errors in the interpretation of Federal Reserve policy, predominantly local influences that do not balance out nationally, and other random events. Moreover, there may be lags in the effect of some of these factors on the rate of expansion of bank credit or other influences that have not been mentioned in their statements. No amount of private speculation and guessing can substitute for a critical examination of the extent to which the rate of expansion of bank credit or of money has been influenced by the factors summarized above. Only after the attempt has been made to examine the evidence in relation to the presumed mechanism can we intelligently accept, reject, or modify the conception.

The heart of our intended criticism of the Federal Reserve System is that we have found no evidence which suggests that any detailed tests or systematic evaluations have been performed. This has had three important results:

1 It has prevented a clear formulation of the relation between monetary policy and the rate of credit expansion that can be used as a guide to future policy operations;
2 It has prevented any thorough internal evaluation of the success and failures of past policy action as a guide to improved understanding of the process and the avoidance of future errors;
3 It has given Congress and the public very little real understanding of the power or lack of power of monetary policy as a means of promoting employment and price stability.

Does the modified free reserves doctrine permit the Federal Reserve to predict the rate of expansion of bank credit? Has it worked well in the past? Can it be relied on in the future? How much room must be left for judgment or "feel" in the short run or in the long run? Does it work best in expansion or in contraction? Does monetary policy merely "push on strings" as has been asserted? Is one measure of reserves a better indicator of the impact of policy than another?

Useful answers to these and other questions are not obtained by intuition or by unsupported judgment. Analysis and evidence are required, but before such evidence can be usefully appraised, the conception must be specified clearly. If our interpretation of the Federal Reserve's view of the monetary process is incorrect or deficient, our test of the presumed conception will be inapplicable or irrelevant. If this is the case, we ask only: What is the Federal Reserve's view of the monetary mechanism and where is the analysis and the evidence to support it?

2 Evidence from Announced Changes in Policy

Another source of information bearing on the use of the doctrine that is centered on free reserves comes from the "Record of Policy Actions" published in the Annual Reports of the Board of Governors. These records contain indications of the policy that was agreed upon at the meeting of the FOMC. If the indicated changes in policy are quickly reflected in the prevailing level of free reserves, this would suggest that free reserves are used as either a target or indicator of policy. If there is no clear relation between changes in the level of free reserves and changes in announced policy, the evidence that free reserves are a target or indicator of policy is weaker.

It might appear that this second source of evidence is redundant. Did not the previous section conclude that the "modified free reserves doctrine" is a formulation of the conception that is used by the Federal Reserve? While the question is answered in the affirmative, it does not resolve the issue. The statements that we have quoted come mainly from the remarks of the staff and the members of the Board of Governors and the FOMC. It is the Manager of the System Open Market Account who carries out the policy. The evidence in this section is presented to indicate the way in which he interprets the policy decision made at the FOMC meeting. An indication of his interpretations of the policy decision can be observed by comparing movements of free reserves with changes in FOMC policy. A systematic association of policy changes and changes in free reserves would support our contention about the role of free reserves in the Federal Reserve's policy conception.

To evaluate the evidence in this section, it is helpful to understand the relationship between the Manager and the FOMC. Unfortunately, the detailed records of the FOMC meetings are not released,[21] so we must rely on the condensed information that is made available and occasional comments about procedure made in System publications and at congressional hearings. From these we can attempt to assess how much discretion is left to the Manager in the choice of targets and indicators or in the magnitude of open market operations. Before presenting the evidence relating free reserves to the Record of Policy Actions, we discuss the role of the Manager and the control over his operations exercised by the FOMC.

2.1 The FOMC and the Manager

The Manager is not a member of the FOMC. He has no vote in the policy-making process, but he has an important voice in the deliberations. He briefs the members and other participants about the details of System operations and the factors affecting reserves in advance of each meeting. He provides a detailed weekly summary of operations, and a less detailed daily summary, to each of the presidents and each member of the Board of Governors. He brings the information up to date at each meeting of the FOMC in a written and verbal statement. He provides and discusses the estimates of the short-run movements of float, Treasury balances, currency, etc., that are deemed to be important between meetings of the FOMC. With the members of the staff of the Board of Governors, who describe the prevailing domestic and international economic climate, he provides the essential background information that is relevant to the decision taken.

Each member of the FOMC and each president, whether currently a member of the Committee or not, has the opportunity to express his views about past policy and desirable future policy. The Manager makes notes for his future guidance. His notes, a statement of consensus, a rather vague directive and an unofficial set of notes taken by the staff of the Board of Governors are the written guidelines available to the Manager between meetings. By the time of the next meeting, currently at the end of three weeks, the notes taken by the staff of the Board of Governors are summarized in a report that is published as a part of the annual Record of Policy Actions. Such records do the Manager little good. He must rely on the more informal documents.

The participants in the discussion offer a rich variety of suggestions and criteria. There is no official format for statements. Even if there is agreement about the direction of policy, there may be disagreement about the method of bringing about greater "ease or restraint" or the size of the desired change. One participant may conclude that greater restraint should occur

---

[21]The record is now made available after a delay.

and may mention an amount or range of amounts by which total reserves should be reduced. Another may clarify his statement by suggesting a range of free reserves, lower than the range prevailing, as an indication of the increased degree of tightness. Still a third may indicate an increase in Treasury bill rates or a level of such rates that would in his judgment represent the desired increase in "restraint." A fourth participant may summarize his position in terms of "tone" or "feel" of the money market.

There are 19 participants at the meeting. There is little or no apparent attempt, at most of the meetings, to summarize the statements of the participants in terms of an objective. (Occasionally, as indicated in the preceding section, a specific target is named, for example, free reserves, bill yields, or total reserves.) Instead, a "directive" is issued or reissued to the Federal Reserve Bank of New York, as the agent for the System, and a statement of consensus is made to summarize the discussion. We consider each of these in turn.

2.1.1 The Directive

This formal document has been a curious admixture of detailed restrictions and broad policy goals. In the immediate postwar period and until mid-June 1955, the directive was addressed to an executive committee of the FOMC. The most common form contained an instruction to "provide for the credit needs of commerce and business" or "to relate the supply of funds in the market to the needs of commerce and business." This was the "a" part of paragraph 1. It referred to the seasonal aspects of the problem. The "b" of the paragraph contained a broad indication of economic or monetary policy. For example, the Executive Committee and later the Federal Reserve Bank of New York would be directed to "maintain orderly markets," "prevent disorderly markets," "avoid deflationary tendencies," "avoid deflationary tendencies without encouraging a renewal of inflationary developments," or some similar generality.

In contrast, the remainder of the directive contained very explicit statements. The Executive Committee or the Federal Reserve Bank was told that they could buy or sell in amounts that would change the holdings in the System account by at most a specified number of dollars, that they could only hold a specified dollar amount of Treasury certificates of indebtedness issued directly to the Reserve Banks, that they could exchange directly with the Treasury only a specific amount of securities for gold certificates. During much of the period, agreement was reached that only short-term securities with specific maximum maturity would be used in regular operations, the so-called "bills only" policy.

The "b" clause of paragraph 1 was sufficiently broad that in many years it was possible to change the policy without changing the directive. The converse was also true. At times, the directive would be changed, but it would be noted in the Record of Policy Actions that there was no change in policy.

One example of the former type occurred in 1950–2. A new directive was adopted at the meeting of August 18, 1950. Thereafter, in the words of the Committee, the directive issued was "in the same form" as the directive issued at the previous meeting. This phrase reappears from meeting to meeting until late in 1952. Even the famed "Accord" did not require a change in the form of the directive. At times during the period, the Record refers to the need for greater "restraint"; at other meetings, the Committee expresses satisfaction with the degree of "restraint" and states that more restriction is unnecessary; at the meeting of August 18, 1950, strong language was used in the statement accompanying the directive to indicate that the FOMC and the Board "are prepared to use all the means at their command to restrain further expansion of bank credit." At times the policy is described as one of "neutrality." Conversely, the report in 1957 notes that "four changes in the wording of the directive of the Open Market Committee were made during 1957 . . . The January 8 and March 5 changes continued policies . . . in effect . . ."

The most recently published directives, for the year 1962, are somewhat less vague. They provide a more detailed statement of the framework in which the Manager must operate. For example, it was not uncommon in 1962 for the FOMC to add a paragraph indicating how the policy should be implemented. Phrases such as "provide moderate reserve expansion," "avoid downward pressure on interest rates," "foster a moderately firm tone in the money market," or "offset the seasonal easing of Treasury bill rates" have been added to the directive.

One wonders why it is desirable to make very explicit statements about purchases of gold certificates from the Treasury or the use of bills only and very vague statements about the objectives of monetary policy. One wonders, also, why it is possible to indicate a very clear direction at times and no clear direction at other times. For example, the directive of the meeting of December 19, 1961, contained the comparatively explicit statement that the Manager should provide a "somewhat slower rate of increase in total reserves than during the recent months. Operations shall place emphasis on continuance of the 3-month Treasury bill rate at close to the top of the range recently prevailing. No overt action shall be taken to reduce unduly the supply of reserves or to bring about a rise in interest rates." If the Committee at times can issue a clear statement of the specific intent of policy, why must it be vague at other times?

2.1.2 The Consensus

Part of the answer to the question lies in the role of the consensus. At almost every meeting of the FOMC, a statement of consensus, that is not part of the directive, is attached to the Record. This statement summarizes the views of the Committee. After each participant expresses his views, the Chairman indicates the direction of policy – more or less "ease or restraint" or no change in direction. The statement of consensus and accompanying remarks provide a direction for policy until the next meeting. Only on rare occasions does the "consensus" take note of a specific target like reserves or bill yields. More often it takes refuge in vague phrases to indicate the direction of change in policy, if any.

The most obvious reason for the vague directive and the rather broadly stated consensus has already been noted. There is incomplete agreement about the immediate target of monetary policy. This decision is left to the Manager because agreement about a desire for "greater ease or restraint" does not mean that there has been agreement about the exact meaning of the policy. If, as we are told by the 12 presidents (II.1, last paragraph) a variety of indicators are used, it is not unlikely that the Manager is left relatively free to choose the immediate target or measure that seems correct to him. To return to an earlier example, when the various members or participants use total reserves, market interest rates, free reserves, and perhaps "tone" as their indicators of desired policy, it may be impossible for the Manager to satisfy all of them. Meeting the interest rate goal suggested by one participant may increase total or free reserves by more or less than some other member thinks desirable. Under such circumstances, it is difficult for the presidents and Governors to reprimand or criticize the actions taken.[22]

Furthermore, the Committee is concerned with day-to-day operations. Errors in float projections, shifts in the Treasury balance, and numerous other short-term changes can and apparently are used to explain deviations from the policy desired by a particular member or members. (For a recent example, see the report of the meeting of January 1962.)

If the Committee cannot or does not agree upon a specific increase or decrease in reserves or some other target, and if it does not agree upon any specific target, it is left for the Manager to decide whether the actions that he takes are appropriate in the light of the general policy statement or consensus. This provides a large measure of autonomy for the Manager that is further encouraged by the reference to numerous and possibly divergent indicators with which participants amplify their statements. It is not uncommon for total reserves and bill yields to move in the same direction for several days. Which criteria does the Manager follow if both have been used by the Committee members as indicators of desired tightness? The choice must be made by the Manager. If five or six different criteria are used, the discretion left to the Manager is enlarged.

In practice, some devices have been developed to exercise a measure of control over the autonomy of the Manager in carrying out the consensus. Each morning there is a telephone conversation between the trading desk at

---

[22]A former Manager of long duration reports that he was never asked to explain his action in terms of the specific statements of the Committee and that he was never blamed for failures to carry out instructions. See Rouse, 1961, pp. 31–2.

the New York Bank, the Board of Governors staff in Washington, and one Reserve bank president. The Manager, or one of his principal assistants, outlines the plans for the day. The members or staff of the Board of Governors or the president of some Reserve Bank can question the decision of the Manager and the extent to which it fits within the framework of the directive and the consensus. But the Manager can always point to a large number of market occurrences that indicate to him that the decision is an appropriate interpretation of the sense of the last meeting. If there is no clear, tested conception of the process by which open market operations, interest rates, and other observable market phenomena affect the desired portfolios of banks and the public and no clear statement of FOMC objectives, only unanalyzed judgment can be used to interpret the events that the market is recording and their relation to the FOMC's consensus. Responsible men often differ in their personal judgments. It would be surprising if the views of the Manager, who has the responsibility for the final decision, did not generally prevail.

Other devices used to inform the committee members; e.g., a telegram outlining the telephone discussion for those who did not participate, suffer the same weaknesses. Ultimately, the Chairman or a member of the FOMC must either accept the judgment of the Manager, attempt to modify it, or substitute his judgment for the opinion of the Manager. There is no record of the number of times that such differences have occurred or have been appealed to the Chairman of the Board of Governors, but it would be surprising if the Chairman interfered frequently to reverse or alter the daily decisions of the Manager.

A clear goal for monetary policy has recently been formulated, the maintenance of a particular short-term interest rate. The members of the Committee are consequently in a better position to judge the actions of the Manager. In essence, the Committee has taken a longer-run view of policy operations. On the basis of a belief – largely unsupported by detailed examination of direct evidence – that higher short-term interest rates in the United States will reduce the gold outflow, they attempt to maintain a particular interest rate. The administrative effect of this policy is to instruct the Manager that whatever "defensive" operations are taken daily must be tailored to the longer-run policy of maintaining the Treasury bill rate. Any member who wishes to judge the actions of the Manager need only look at the bill rate prevailing in the market to see whether or not the primary goal is being achieved.

Very similar procedures could be followed in principle if a particular rate of monetary or credit expansion is taken as the desired goal of monetary policy. But to do so requires an understanding of the precise effect of changes in reserves on the rate of monetary or credit expansion. This requires an explanation of the behavior of the stock of money or credit that usefully predicts future movements with reasonable accuracy. Until there is internal agreement within the FOMC on the relevance and utility of a particular conception of monetary mechanisms, there can be no agreement about the change in some measure of reserves required to achieve a particular long-range goal. We believe that it is primarily because understanding of the monetary process has not been developed that the FOMC has been concerned with the day-to-day operations in the past and the Manager has developed a large measure of autonomy.

Our understanding that the Manager has exercised substantial autonomy in the past is supported by evidence. The same evidence also suggests that during much of the postwar period, the Manager interpreted the directive and the consensus in terms of a level or range of free reserves. That is, he operated in the market to achieve short- and long-range objectives by altering the level of free reserves. We turn to consider the evidence.

2.1.3 Policy Objectives and Free Reserve Levels

Each author of this report independently read relevant portions of the Record of Policy Actions for each meeting of the Federal Open Market Committee from 1946 through 1962. Since the language is often vague, a question of judgment is involved at times as to whether or not there is a minor adjustment of policy. At other times, the signal is quite clear. Using a scale ranging from +1 (decisive easing) to −1 (decisive tightening), we recorded our independent judgments of the meaning of the directive, the consensus, and the accompanying remarks. We then compared these judgments and arrived at our own consensus about the interpretation of the "Record of Policy Actions" for each meeting.[23] At times, the Record indicated no change in open market policy but referred instead to actions taken by the Board of Governors. These actions – changes in reserve requirements, in discount rates, in preferential buying rates for particular securities – were of importance particularly in the pre-Accord period.

A 3-week moving average of the level of total free reserves was computed. This eliminated some of the extremely short-run fluctuations and permitted a clearer indication of the timing of changes in level. Without reference to our previous dating of changes in the announced policy of the FOMC, we dated the changes in the level (or direction of change) of the 3-week moving average of total free reserves. The two series were then compared to indicate the relation of announced policy changes to changes in free reserves. For the period 1946–51, open market operations were used primarily to control bond prices. The analysis of policy operations for these years will be considered when we discuss the rationale and the results of changes in reserve requirements in a later section.

[23]These judgments differed at times, but they never went in opposite directions. At most, one of us felt that there was no change while the other interpreted the wording to mean a slight change in ease or restraint. By re-reading the report for the relevant meeting, a consensus was reached.

During the years 1951–62, we recorded 163 meetings of the FOMC including special meetings called for a variety of purposes. At 76 meetings, we recorded a change in policy. All changes are not of the same importance. For example, some of the policy changes are given a scale value of 1/8. This value is used to note a minor modification that is indicated by a statement such as "doubts should be resolved on the side of ease during a period of Treasury financing" or "any deviation should be on the side of less restraint." But at times, such minor changes are of importance since they may be an initial indication of a reversal of policy.

In keeping with the extremely short-run orientation of the FOMC, most policy decisions are made for the period between meetings. Thus our scaling of the magnitude of policy changes refers only to the change from the previous meeting and cannot be interpreted as an indicator of the absolute level of free reserves. The desired policy holds for a period of three weeks under present arrangements. If unexpected events occur, a special meeting may be held, often by telephone, and members of the Committee may decide on a new policy or a new directive. Like the regular meetings, the special meetings generally make decisions that are relative to the prevailing policy and are not absolute. Even when a specific criterion is mentioned, e.g., a particular range of free reserves, the decision must be understood as an agreement that holds only until renewed or modified at the next meeting of the FOMC.

Several questions can be considered using the moving average of free reserves and our scaling or index of policy actions. First, how promptly did the FOMC recognize changes in economic events and respond to them according to the scale that we have developed? Second, how promptly were these actions reflected in the moving average of free reserves? We have already noted that there are more than 70 indicated changes in the direction or magnitude of policy operations. There are a similar number of identified changes in the moving average of free reserves. Many of these are, as noted, minor movements. We will consider, first, the more important movements revealed by the record of Federal Reserve action at or near turning points of economic activity.

2.1.4 The FOMC and Free Reserves at Post-Accord Turning Points

The National Bureau of Economic Research provides a record of cyclical turning points that shows the month in which the economy is judged to have moved from expansion into contraction, or vice-versa.[24] In the post-Accord period, six turning points have been noted. A brief history of the record of Federal Reserve policy decisions and the movement of free reserves is provided for each turning point. To indicate the decision taken, we will present a quotation or summary statement taken from the published Record of Policy

---

[24]This record, like our index of policy action, is based on judgment. As an alternative, the monthly index of industrial production could be used for this purpose. At times the latter would produce slightly different findings about the speed of response of the FOMC.

Actions for the meeting before, during and/or after the turning point. If the direction of policy did not change at any of these meetings, the date and quotation are given for the first meeting or meetings at which a desired reversal of policy was indicated.

Information is also given for the movement of free reserves during the period. It should be noted that our 3-week moving average is not centered in the middle week. The average for the 3-week period is given the date on which the period ended. This was done to assure that the changes in the level of free reserves would not be reflected in the moving average earlier than they occurred. They may have occurred earlier, and in cases where the exact dating is of some consequence for later discussion, information is also given for the unadjusted weekly level of free reserves.

Peak dated July 1953   Last meeting of the FOMC before the peak, June 11:

> Decision: "It was the view of the Committee . . . that policy should be one of aggressively supplying reserves to the market." (Scale of the decision: +1)

First meeting of the FOMC after the peak, September 24:

> Decision: "Further easing would be needed to assure ready availability of credit." (Scale: $+\frac{1}{2}$)

Movement of free reserves during the period: The moving average had remained between −$500 and −$700 million since February. In the week ending May 27, the moving average rose $200 million. Free reserves continued to rise for several weeks and became positive in the week ending June 10, i.e., *before* the change in policy had been decided upon at the FOMC meeting. From late June until late July, the moving average remained in a narrow range around +$500 million. During August there was a sharp decline, but in the week ending September 23, the moving average of free reserves increased by $200 million to +$267 million. Again the change occurred *before* the FOMC meeting.

Trough dated August 1954   Last meeting of the FOMC before the trough, June 23:

> Decision: A reduction in reserve requirements was to be partially com-pensated by open market operations. The net effect was further ease. (Scale: $+\frac{1}{4}$)

First meeting of the FOMC after the trough, September 22:

> Decision: " . . . Resolve doubt on the side of ease . . ." (Scale: $+\frac{1}{8}$)

First meeting announcing a clear change in policy, December 7:

> Decision: "A reexamination of the policy of 'active ease' . . . led the Committee to the conclusion that the developing economic situation

did not warrant continuing as active a program of supplying reserves as had been followed during the preceding year . . ." (Scale: $-\frac{1}{2}$)

Movement of free reserves during the period: The moving average remained between +$500 and +$700 million from March 24 through June 16. In the week ending June 23, the moving average increased to approximately $740 million and remained between $650 and $800 million until the week ending November 24. In the week ending December 1, the moving average declined by $250 million to $541 million. Both of the changes noted in this period occurred *before* the meeting of the FOMC.

Peak dated July 1957   Last meeting before the peak, June 18:

Decision: ". . . a firm policy of restraint should be continued for the present . . ." (Scale: 0)

Two meetings in the peak month, July 9 and 30:

Decision on July 9: ". . . to maintain but not to increase the existing degree of pressure . . ."

Decision, July 30: ". . . To keep the banking system under substantial pressure . . ." (Scale of these decisions: 0)

First meeting after the peak, August 20:

Decision: ". . . the System account would have flexibility in providing reserves . . ." (Scale: $\frac{1}{8}$ (also $\frac{1}{8}$ for meeting September 10)) ". . . doubts would be resolved on the side of less rather than greater restraint."

First meeting announcing a clear change in policy, October 22:

Decision: ". . . although general policy was not to be changed appreciably, it would tend on the easier side from where it had been in recent weeks." (Scale: $+\frac{1}{4}$)

Movement of free reserves during the period: For several months prior to July 24, the moving average of free reserves remained between −$400 and −$600 million. In the last week of July and the first week of August, the moving average increased sharply but then returned to the range −$400 to −$525 million until the week ending October 16. During the week ending October 23, the moving average of free reserves rose $180 million to the level −$321 million. It remained in the range of −$200 to −$350 million until December 11. Either the level of free reserves moved in advance of the meeting of October 22, or a sufficient volume of free reserves was supplied on the day following the meeting of the FOMC to raise the 3-week moving average.

No clear indications of the August 20 and September 10 decisions are observable. Two additional indications of an easier policy were made at the meetings of November 12 and December 3. The moving average of free reserves fails to record any significant response to these changes. However, there is a response to the modification of the directive at the meeting of December 17. Free reserves respond in the week ending December 18, gradually moving toward a positive level and ultimately to the range +$450 to +$550 million in mid-March 1958.

Trough dated April 1958   Last meeting before the trough, March 25:

> Decision: ". . . operations in the System account should be directed toward maintaining a slightly larger volume of free reserves and money market conditions slightly easier . . ."   (Scale: $+\frac{1}{4}$)

Meeting during the month of the trough, April 15:

> Decision: "Easing" was "contemplated" in the form of lower discount rates and reserve requirements.   (Scale: $+\frac{1}{4}$)

First meeting after the trough, May 6:

> Decision: ". . . the prevailing policy of ease should be continued . . ." (Scale: 0)

First meeting indicating a slight change of policy, May 27:

> Decision: ". . . maintain the current posture of monetary policy without further depressing Treasury bill rates . . ."   (Scale: $-\frac{1}{8}$)

First recognition of a major change in policy direction, August 19 (on July 29 a smaller policy change was indicated also):

> Decision, July 29: "Absorb redundant reserves generated by emergency purchases of securities."   (Scale: $-\frac{1}{4}$)

> Decision, August 19: "that the rate of expansion in the money supply . . . should be tempered and that operations for the System Open Market Account should move in the direction of lower free reserves . . ."   (Scale: $-\frac{1}{2}$)

Movement of free reserves during the period: The level $450 to $550 million that had been reached in mid-March was retained throughout the spring. Neither the moving average nor the unadjusted weekly data show any significant effect of the decisions taken at the meetings on March 25 and April 15. The meeting of July 8 indicated no change in policy, but free reserves moved up slightly in the week ending July 9, perhaps for seasonal or holiday reasons. The range of $540 to $600 million was maintained until the week ending August 6. The decision taken at a special meeting on July 18, to ease the money market in response to the "disorderly conditions," has very little effect on the moving average.

The first sign of change toward a policy of increased restraint appears in the moving average of free reserves in the week ending August 13. Once again this change *precedes* the decision to restrict the rate of growth of the money supply that was made at the meeting of August 19.

Between the week ending August 13 and the week ending September 17, the moving average declined steadily to a range between $50 and $125 million. No further indications of policy change or increased restraint are noted at the FOMC meetings until December 2 and December 16 when a desire for further tightening is recorded. As if in anticipation of these decisions, the level of free reserves began to fall in the week ending November 26, became negative in the week ending December 3, and remained in the range 0 to −$100 million until mid-March 1959.

Peak dated May 1960   Last meeting before peak, April 12:

Decision: "the consensus favored easing further the reserve position of member banks." (Scale: $+\frac{1}{2}$)

Meetings during the month of the peak, May 3 and 24:

Decisions taken: (May 3) ". . . moving moderately in the direction of increasing the supply of reserves available to the banking system." (Scale: $+\frac{1}{4}$) (May 24) "The consensus favored . . . a further supply of reserves . . ." (Scale: $+\frac{1}{2}$)

First meeting after the peak, June 14:

Decision: ". . . any deviation should be on the side of ease . . ." (Scale: $+\frac{1}{8}$)

First recognition of a major change in policy direction, March 1 (taken in advance of the peak):

Decision: "The Committee concluded that it would be appropriate to supply reserves to the banking system somewhat more readily." This was characterized as a policy of "moderately less restraint." (Scale: $+\frac{1}{4}$)

Movement of free reserves during the period: In early June 1959, the moving average of free reserves fell below −$370 million and remained below that level, with the exception of two weeks in late January, until the week ending March 2, 1960. During most of this period, average free reserves were below −$450 million. Concurrent with, or in advance of, the meeting of the FOMC on March 1, the moving average rose until it reached the range −$100 to −$225 million where it remained from March 23 to May 17. The decision to ease further taken at the meeting of April 12 has no perceptible influence on the moving average. During the weeks ending April 6, 13, and 20, free reserves are near the top of the range indicated. There is some slight increase in the following two weeks and a further increase following the meeting on May 3. In advance of the decision on May 24, free reserves rose during the week ending on that date and remained between 0 and +$200 million during most of the summer.

Trough dated February 1961 Last meeting before the trough, January 24:

Decision: ". . . there should be no change in the existing degree of monetary ease . . ." Close attention to the bill rate was urged for balance-of-payments reasons. (Scale: $-\frac{1}{8}$)

Meeting during month of the trough, February 7:

Decision: "The consensus of the Committee favored no change in open market policy . . ." (Scale: 0)

First meeting after the trough, March 7:

Decision: "The consensus of the Committee was that the existing monetary policy of ease should be followed . . ." (Scale: 0)

First post-trough decision for a minor policy change, August 22:

Decision: The consensus favored continuing the policy of early August "when a confluence of market factors contrived to produce more firmness than had otherwise been the case." (Scale: $-\frac{1}{8}$)

First post-trough decision for a significant change in policy, December 19:

Decision: ". . . no substantial change from recent policies was called for . . . a somewhat slower rate of increase in total reserves than during recent months . . ." (Scale: $-\frac{1}{4}$)

Movement of free reserves during the period: In December 1960 and January 1961, the moving average remained in the range +$650 to +$750 million. During the first week of February, the average fell $125 million to $609 million, most likely reversing a seasonal increment in reserves during the late fall. Thereafter, the average remained between $450 and $600 million throughout the year 1961 with very minor exceptions. There is no indication of a move toward lower free reserves following the meeting of August 22. Indeed free reserves rose in the week ending August 23, by $63 million from the lower level that had prevailed in advance of the meeting. The lower level of early August was not regained until October.

The desired increase in tightness indicated by the decision made in late December is reflected in the average free reserves for the week ending January 3, 1962. Thereafter free reserves returned to the approximate range in which they had been, $450 to $600 million. However, free reserves are generally high or rising in January as currency flows back to the banks. The failure of the average to rise may be an indication of the move to a tighter policy.

The record at turning points in economic activity is summarized in Table 1.2.

Table 1.2 A summary of policy actions and movements of free reserves at post-Accord turning points

Date of turning point (NBER) (month)	First indication of		Change in the moving average of free reserves (week ending)
	Any change in the direction of policy (day)	Major change in policy (day)	
July 1953	June 11	June 11	May 27
August 1954	Dec. 7	Dec. 7	Dec. 1
July 1957	Aug. 20	Oct. 22	Oct. 23
April 1958	May 27	Aug. 19	Aug. 13
May 1960	Feb. 9	Mar. 1	Mar. 2
February 1961	Jan. 24, 1961, or Aug. 22	Dec. 19	Jan. 3, 1962

Table 1.3 Scaling of the Policy for 1962

Date of meeting	Magnitude of desired change	Quotation or paraphrase of the Record
Mar. 6	$+ \frac{1}{8}$	The majority favored no change, but "promote further expansion of bank credit."
Mar. 27	$+ \frac{1}{4}$	Slightly more expansion in reserve avaliability than had developed.
June 19	$- \frac{1}{4}$	"Avoid redundant reserves." "Slightly less easy policy indicated."
Dec. 18	$- \frac{1}{4}$	A somewhat less easy policy was favored by the majority to firm Treasury bill rates.

Before commenting upon some important issues and questions that arise from this discussion, we will present some additional evidence of the relation of free reserves to the desired policy changes published in the Record of Policy Actions.

2.1.5 The FOMC and Free Reserves in 1962–1963
Our earlier discussion of the targets and indicators of Federal Reserve policy suggested that policy actions in 1962 were reflected in the movement of free reserves despite the attention paid to the level of Treasury bill yields as a target of policy action. A careful reading of the Record of Policy Actions and the changes in the moving average of free reserves for the year largely confirms our earlier statement. Moreover, it provides additional indication of the importance of the level of free reserves in the management of the System Open Market Account.

Our index of policy indicates one minor and three more important changes in desired policy recorded in the reports of the meetings of the FOMC. These

Table 1.4   Free reserve ranges during 1962 and early 1963

Date(s)	Range of the level of free reserves (million dollars)
Week ending–	
Feb. 7	504
Feb. 14 to Mar. 14	425 to 450
Mar. 21 to May 16	375 to 425
May 23 to June 13	440 to 490
June 20 to July 4	360 to 390
July 11 to Dec. 5	400 to 450
Dec. 12 to Jan. 30, 1963	300 to 375
Feb. 6, 1963 to March 1963	280 to 315

changes are shown in table 1.3. All other meetings of the FOMC produced no change in desired policy and are scaled 0.[25]

The moving average of free reserves remained in a very narrow range during most of the year. Certain changes in level are discernible however and are recorded in table 1.4.

The data in the two tables suggest that the level of free reserves was not reduced in response to either indication by the Committee of a slight desire to ease. Instead, a movement toward a lower free reserve level occurred between the two decisions to ease. However, both desired changes toward tighter money markets are reflected in the level of free reserves in advance of the meeting of the FOMC at which the decision was made. The change in June was reversed partially in July, and the moving average of free reserves remained in very narrow bounds during the next five months.

The Record of Policy Actions for 1963 is not yet available. Nevertheless, for the first months, the moving average of free reserves suggests that a movement toward increased restraint occurred in early February. Perusal of the unadjusted data suggests that an additional desired policy change toward increased restraint was made about the middle of May.

2.2   Appraisal of The Post-Accord Record of Policy Actions

Three principal conclusions about the record of FOMC actions during the post-Accord period emerge from the data. A discussion of each of these permits additional appraisal of the policymaking procedures of the FOMC and the Federal Reserve's understanding of the monetary mechanism. We will

[25]The meeting of October 23 indicates seasonal easing to be accomplished by a reduction in time deposit reserve requirements by the Board.

consider in turn (1) the timing of decisions at turning points or speed of response of the FOMC, (2) the autonomy of the Manager, and (3) the meaning of the findings for the role of free reserves in the Federal Reserve's view of the monetary mechanism.

2.2.1 The Timing of Policy Changes

The FOMC's record at post-Accord turning points, summarized in table 1.2, is most impressive. Much of the academic criticism of the Federal Reserve has suggested that the FOMC or the Board is slow to respond to changes in economic indicators. Our appraisal of the evidence suggests the opposite. In particular, when economic activity has reached a peak and discretionary policy should move toward "ease," the FOMC has been quick to recognize the need for a change in policy. Indeed, our index or scaling of the Record of Policy Actions suggests that the Federal Reserve indicated a desire to reverse the direction of policy in advance of the peak recorded by the National Bureau at two of the three postwar peaks.

We submit that this record is remarkably good. It should be recalled that the turning points recorded by the National Bureau are chosen with hindsight. But the desired direction of monetary policy must be made by considering the detail of present and past events and by attempting to assess the near-term future. The record at peaks suggests an extremely competent assessment of economic data by the staff and the use of excellent judgment by the Committee.

Some writers have presented an alternative interpretation of a part of this record. It has been suggested that the reversal of policy in 1953 was accidental, a response to the "disorderly conditions" that had developed in the bond market. We do not believe that detailed examination of the record supports this conclusion. First, the level of free reserves began to increase before the development of disorderly markets in June. The unadjusted weekly data for free reserves record an increase in the level of free reserves of more than $400 million in the week ending May 20. The moving average of free reserves places the change in policy a week later. In any case, the change was initiated before there was any indication of difficulty with the newly issued 3¼-percent bonds. Second, the increase in the moving average of free reserves during the "disorderly period" was reversed, while the earlier change was not. In early August, the moving average of free reserves returned to the range in which it had been in early June and remained between −$100 and +$100 million in every week from August 5 to September 16. Thereafter, free reserves increased perhaps in anticipation of the decision by the FOMC at the meeting on September 24. Third, the response to the disorderly markets in July 1958 proceeded in a rather similar way. In 1953, the unadjusted data show that almost $750 million of additional free reserves was supplied during the 2-week period June 10 to 24. The newly created reserves were withdrawn by early August as noted above. In

July 1958, the System was maintaining a policy described as "ease" and had not yet indicated a desire for any significant increase in "restraint." Nevertheless, the unadjusted weekly data show that only $250 million was supplied temporarily and withdrawn within two weeks. The System acted with greater restraint, and reversed more quickly in 1958, but, in both "disorderly markets," the previously existing level of free reserves was restored. Later additional policy actions were taken. It is difficult to understand why a temporary increase in reserves should ease the banking system in one case but not in the other. But that conclusion seems implicit in the argument of those who regard the prompt response by the FOMC to the developing recession in 1953 as a fortunate accident. Finally, the FOMC showed again in 1960 that it was capable of recognizing a deceleration in the pace of economic activity before the cyclical peak was reached.

Table 1.2 also suggests that the lag between the trough and the indicated desire to tighten is longer than the lag between the peak and the indicated desire to ease. More importantly, the table suggests that these lags are comparatively short. The latter conclusion is directly opposed to the finding of Brown, Solow, Ando, and Kareken, in a study prepared for the Commission on Money and Credit. The difference between the findings here and findings of Brown et al. arises from a difference in measurement procedure associated with different conceptions about the monetary process. Our procedure is related to the dominant notion guiding the Federal Reserve's evaluations and policy actions. Brown et al. select some maximally achievable stock of bank credit as an index of modifications in monetary policy. The lag in the appropriate motion of this index behind cyclical turning points is then interpreted to measure the Federal Reserve's "recognition lag," its habitual lag in recognizing changing economic circumstances. But the lag measured by Brown et al. permits an alternative interpretation which denies the significant occurrence of a recognition lag, at least for the peak. We have already submitted evidence indicating a recognition lag not longer than the period required for purely "technological" reasons to collect and prepare the necessary information. This period is substantially shorter than the lag estimated by Brown et al. We do not question the existence or the relevance of the lag obtained by Brown et al., but we do contend that it is not attributable to a lag in recognition. The lag observed by Brown et al. is the natural outcome of policy actions based on a misconception about the structure of the monetary process. In case of an onsetting recession the Federal Reserve observes the rapid upsurge of free reserves and feels that it has pursued a "stimulative policy." It has rapidly become aware of the change in circumstances and adjusted the prevailing policy posture according to its own conceptions. But guidance based on the free reserve doctrine frequently leads the Federal Reserve authorities into a position where they believe that a countercyclical monetary policy is underway, while for many months almost no relevant action is taken. Consider, for example, open market purchases intended by the Federal Reserve to "ease reserve positions" and thus exert an expansionary effect. Suppose that the injected reserve funds are used to repay borrowings. Total reserves are therefore unchanged, and Brown et al. would indicate no change in Federal Reserve policy, although the FOMC, judging policy actions in terms of the modified free reserve doctrine, would believe that it had moved toward "ease." While we have indicated that the modified free reserve doctrine is a defective tool, we have suggested quite strongly that it is the doctrine that the FOMC uses. However correct or incorrect the views propounded by Brown et al., one cannot measure the lag in recognition according to a theory which does not guide actual policy-making. For this reason, the measurement of the lag between turning points and Federal Reserve recognition and action should not be measured by the rate of change of maximum bank credit. The findings of Brown et al. simply indicate again one of the problems with the free reserve (or modified free reserve) doctrine.[26]

The fact that the lag in changing policy at troughs is longer than the lag at peaks does not necessarily indicate a slower recognition of recoveries. It is doubtful that more rapid movement toward "restraint" would be desirable from the viewpoint of either the FOMC or the economy. There is always the danger that a more rapid reversal of policy at the trough – "tightening" faster – would smother the incipient recovery. Since the FOMC and the staffs of the Federal Reserve have not attempted to appraise carefully the relation of monetary policy to the stock of money and the pace of economic activity, they have no information about the length of the lag between their decisions and their effects on money and national income. Still, it would appear to the outside observer that the Federal Reserve authorities assume the lag to be very short. This assumption is at least consistent with the quick reversals in policy direction which may be observed on occasion. The Record of Policy Action for the period 1955–7 is most instructive in this respect.

Several reversals of policy were made during that period since the judgment of the FOMC indicated that the economy may have reversed direction. The year 1956 is particularly interesting in this regard. There were ten major changes or minor adjustments in policy at the 18 meetings held. Only a few of

---

[26]Brown et al. recognize in their appendix the problem raised here. They dismiss free reserves for a reason analogous to the one mentioned in the text. This seems to miss the point. The lag between recognition and action may be very short. But if the theory or doctrine used by the FOMC has little relation to the rate of change of the stock of credit or money or to the maximum stock of bank credit, criticism should be directed toward the theory and not toward the length of time that the FOMC takes to recognize changes in the pace of economic activity or turning points.

For further evidence of the problem raised by inappropriate judgment of its actions by the FOMC, see our discussion in Brunner and Meltzer, 1964 of the differences in average monthly changes in money and "credit" during economic expansion and contraction.

these changes are considered here to indicate the frequency of some major policy revisions that the FOMC desired to institute.

January 24: "a shift in emphasis seemed desirable" "some relaxation of restraint appropriate in the near future." (Scale: $+\frac{1}{2}$)

March 27: "The supplementary clause which was introduced in January 24, was eliminated" "instructions to take into account deflationary tendencies . . . not consistent with the existing situation." (Scale: $-\frac{1}{2}$)

May 23: "the Committee agreed that during the immediate future additional reserves should be supplied to take care . . . of growth needs." The qualifying phrase deleted from the instructions in March 27 was reintroduced. (Scale: $+\frac{1}{2}$)

August 7: The qualifying phrase reintroduced on May 23 was deleted. Instructions required that attention be directed toward inflationary developments. (Scale: $-\frac{1}{2}$)

In the space of eight months the desired direction of policy changed at least four times. For the many reversals of policy in 1956 to have an important bearing on the pace of activity three conditions must be satisfied: (1) the Federal Reserve's control mechanism must operate with very short lags; (2) the money supply must respond rapidly to changes in the level of free reserves; and (3) the pace of economic activity must respond very quickly to changes in the stock of money. But if the control mechanism operates only slowly on the level of economic activity, these frequent reversals in the direction of policy have no justification. The inclination to reverse policy direction easily and rapidly is likely to generate uncertainty and raise interest rates comparatively.

When the turning point did occur in the summer of 1957, the Federal Reserve moved more slowly than it had at the start of the earlier or later postwar recession. There was recognition that the economy had been "moving sidewise" for several months, but more than three months passed before there was a major change in desired policy. It is not unlikely that the experience of 1956, and the judgment by members of the Committee that their response to the events of 1956 had contributed to "inflationary pressures" in 1957, delayed action at this turning point. The record indicates that one member of the Board of Governors opposed all movements toward ease at FOMC meetings until December and opposed a reduction in the discount rate in November because of his fear of "inflation."

The lesson from this experience seems to be that the FOMC has had a good – and perhaps excellent – record in judging the timing of post-Accord turning points. Whether or not its judgments between turning points have been appropriate depends on the relevance of the modified free reserves doctrine. This is not solely a judgmental matter; it is one that requires detailed appraisal of evidence. Some information on that question will be presented shortly. We will reopen the question at that point.

2.2.2 The Autonomy of the Manager

The timing of the responses of free reserves shown in table 1.2, and the discussion in the text about the movement of free reserves at or near cyclical turning points, suggested quite strongly that the free reserve levels often change in advance of meetings of the FOMC. Additional evidence often pointing in the same direction is provided at times of other policy changes or modifications. Some of the policy actions in 1956 have been indicated in the preceding section. Changes in free reserve levels around these dates are considered here, using the 3-week moving average to date changes in level:

1 The decision of January 24: The moving average remained in the range −$350 to −$500 million in the fall of 1955. It rose to −$192 million in the week ending December 28 and to −$50 million in the first 2 weeks of January. Following the FOMC meeting indicating a desire for further ease, the free reserve level began to decline. If there was any movement toward ease, it appears in advance of the meeting, not after, if judged by the moving average of free reserves.

2 The decision of March 27: A decision was made to tighten. The moving average indicates a reduction of $140 million from the level prevailing in the previous two weeks. This reduction came in the week ending March 28 and returned free reserves to the level existing in mid-December. Again the Manager appears to have moved in advance of the FOMC decision.

3 The decision of May 23: A movement toward greater ease was indicated at the meeting. The moving average had remained between −$450 and −$600 million from late March until the time of the meeting. Free reserves increased slightly in the week of the meeting, but did not leave the prevailing range until the week ending June 6, when they rose to −$364 million. Thereafter they continued to rise for several weeks until they attained the range −$100 to −$200 million where they remained until early August. This policy change is not reflected in the moving average until after the meeting of the FOMC.

4 The decision of August 7: The FOMC instructed the Manager to increase restraint. The moving average responded rather promptly, but again the response came after the meeting. In the week ending August 8, there is a slight fall in the level, but free reserves remain in the previous range. In the following week, ending August 15, the moving average fell $125 million. We interpret this response as one that occurred after the meeting, although it could be an advance indication of the decision taken at the meeting on August 21 that called for additional restraint.

At two of the four meetings in 1956, at five of the six turning points shown in table 1.2, as well as at other times, the moving average of free reserves appears to have changed direction in advance of the decision by the FOMC. Moreover, the close correspondence between changes in the moving average of free reserves and the decisions of the FOMC is unlikely to reflect the operation of chance factors or solely the behavior of the banks and the public. Instead the relation between decisions of the FOMC and the changes in the moving average suggest that free reserves are an important part of the control mechanism used by the Federal Reserve.

Most important, the evidence suggests that the Manager has much wider latitude for policy operations than has generally been conceded. We have noted that he is largely responsible for the day-to-day operations that are an important part of open market operations. And we have seen that an important analyst of System operations, R. V. Roosa (1951), has concluded that the "dynamic" or policy operations "emerge from the day's confusion as a dominating force." But only by examining the evidence of the relation of FOMC decisions to the movement of free reserves has it been possible to observe that the FOMC often ratifies a decision that has already been made rather than directing policy operations.

If there is no clear guide to policy operations and no clear understanding of the relation of policy operations to the rate of change of the stock of money and credit, it becomes extremely difficult for members of the Committee to make independent judgments about the state of the market or to interpret the prevailing policy. While our evidence does not indicate that the Manager is making the policy decisions, it does suggest that frequently someone or some group other than the full Committee is making policy decisions that Congress has entrusted to the Federal Open Market Committee.

2.2.3 Free Reserves as an Indicator of Desired Ease and Restraint

The evidence on the relation of policy decisions to changes in the moving average of free reserves bears out the conclusions of the lengthy discussion on the Federal Reserve view of the monetary mechanism. We contended that there is no single, unified, consistent view that can be characterized as the Federal Reserve view. But we noted also that many of the statements made are consistent with our interpretation that free reserves are regarded by the Federal Reserve as a major element in the monetary mechanism.

Consideration of the details of policy operations in this section provide strong confirmation of the importance of free reserves in the Federal Reserve's policy operations. Although there may be many different and changing interpretations of the usefulness of particular indicators within the FOMC, there is a single Manager. We have now found that there is a strong indication that his actions are more than a reflection of the policy views of the Committee. Often the reverse is true; the Manager permits or encourages changes in the level of free reserves, and the Committee often ratifies his prior decision.

However useful it may be for the Committee to change the guides to desired policy or to refer to a variety of targets and indicators in their discussion, it is extremely difficult for the Manager to continually readjust his operations to a new target or indicator every few weeks. Market events do not have the same interpretation in terms of all of the criteria that are proposed. In self-defense the Manager must choose and retain a particular criterion or set of criteria by which he can judge the effect of his operations. He then translates the vague and often changing suggestions of the Committee into the framework that is useful to him in his operations. Moreover, it is the Manager who furnishes the principal information on the "tone" of the money market to the Committee. It is not difficult to understand, therefore, why the Committee is often in the position in which it can do little more than ratify his prior judgments. Since the FOMC as a group does not have any explicit criteria or analytic frame for independent judgment, it is not clear that they are aware of the autonomy exercised by the Manager.[27]

Thus it occurs that the Manager is relatively free to make adjustments in policy in advance of the FOMC meetings or to avoid adjustments judged to be desirable by the Committee. Since both Managers have testified about the importance of free reserves in their view of the mechanism, little doubt remains about the importance of free reserves in the actual operations of the System.[28]

2.2.4 Summary

We have found that the moving average of free reserves is often an adequate guide to System policy and that movements in the level of free reserves are often made in anticipation of decisions of the FOMC.[29] But at other times, we have found that changes in desired policy are not noticeably reflected in the level of free reserves. Small changes in emphasis; e.g., modifications characterized by the statement "resolve doubts on the side of ease," are rarely observable in the moving average. We must conclude that either (1) these small changes are eliminated along with many other random variations when the moving average is constructed, (2) that free reserves are not used to effect these small changes; e.g., only the distribution of reserves is affected, or (3) that the Manager ignores some of the instructions given by the

[27]The procedures described do help to explain why the Committee does not "blame the Manager for mistakes or alter his judgment about the state of the market." See the testimony of the former Manager on this point in Rouse, 1961 pp. 31–2.

[28]See the statement by Robert Rouse, ibid., p. 34, discussing the relation of free reserves to the rate of change of bank credit and suggesting the importance of free reserves in his understanding of the monetary mechanism. See also the statement in Stone, 1963. As we have indicated above, Stone's discussion of policy changes is largely in terms of the free reserve concept.

[29]We have found only one writer who has noted that the level of free reserves often moves in advance of policy decisions. Cf. Ahearn, 1963, p. 218–n.6. It is not clear from Ahearn's discussion whether he is referring to discount policy only or to open market policy as well. In any case, he offers very little evidence in support of his finding.

Committee. In view of large week-to-week changes in unadjusted free reserves and the relatively wide range of values for the moving average that characterizes a particular policy, it is likely that the first or second interpretation is correct.

More troublesome for our interpretation is the absence of changes in the level of free reserves when somewhat larger changes in policy are directed. For example, we noted that the level of free reserves shows little change toward ease either before or after the meetings of March 25 and April 15, 1958, or March 27, 1962. Our index gives each of these statements a value of ¼. On the basis of our analysis, we cannot reach a firm conclusion about these counter-examples.

Nevertheless, the detailed examination of System policy seems to indicate that the timing of many of the major changes in monetary policy actions in the post-Accord period can be observed using the moving average of free reserves. Moreover, the evidence suggests that the FOMC moves rather quickly at times of change in the direction of economic activity. In current academic parlance, the "inside lag" in monetary policy appears to be extremely short. On two of the three occasions when the economy turned toward recession, the "recognition lag" was negative; when the economy turned toward recovery, the "recognition lag" was longer, averaging three to four months. But this longer lag is most likely a reflection of the desire on the part of the FOMC to avoid stifling an incipient recovery. The "action lag" – the length of time that it takes for decisions to be carried out – is at most zero and often negative, if we choose the moving average of free reserves as the measure of System policy. We conclude, therefore, that the System's post-Accord record of recognizing and acting at turning points can only be regarded as splendid.

The size of the response by the System and the speed with which the change in free reserves affects the rate of change in money and credit have not yet been considered. Recognition and action at turning points are undoubtedly important. But it is also important to take action in terms of the best available instruments that an understanding of the monetary mechanism can provide. We turn, therefore, to consider the relation of free reserves and the "modified free reserves mechanism" to the rate of change of money and credit.

3 The Relation of Free Reserves to Changes in Money and Credit

Analysis of the effectiveness of monetary policy can be divided into three subtopics: (1) The timing of the recognition of the need for policy changes and the decision to act; (2) the choice of appropriate action to influence promptly the stock of money and credit; and (3) the effect of changes in money and credit on the pace of economic activity. We have seen that the post-Accord decisions of the FOMC have been timed commendably and that action has often been taken by the manager in advance of the Committee's decision to act. But effective monetary policy depends also on the extent to which the action taken by the Federal Reserve is capable of altering the stock of money in the appropriate direction. This in turn depends on an understanding of the mechanism relating policy actions to the stock of money; i.e., on the use of an appropriate concept as a measure and indicator of monetary policy.

Much of the discussion in the earlier sections attempted to describe the prevailing Federal Reserve view of the monetary mechanism. Evidence was presented to support the contention that the dominant notion guiding the Federal Reserve in the post-Accord period has been centered on the role of free reserves as a measure of the impact of policy. Examination of the details of policy operations, supported by statements of the managers and other officials, indicates that free reserves are used as a target and signal of policy as well. We have called this view of the monetary mechanism the "modified free reserves doctrine," since at times there is clear recognition in official statements that the effect of a particular level or range of free reserves is modified by prevailing interest rates and by the distribution of free reserves among classes of banks. In this chapter evidence bearing on the relation of free reserves and the modified free reserves mechanism to the stocks of money and credit is presented.

Two principal sources of evidence will be considered. The first, based on the findings of Meigs' (1962) study, considers the effect of interest rates and open market operations on the demand for free reserves and the rate of change of deposits. These findings are concerned with the evidence for a position that some Federal Reserve spokesmen seem to have accepted – that the supply or level of free reserves must be considered in relation to the banks' desired holdings. A second set of findings was developed as a part of the present study. These seek to isolate the effects of interest rates and the level of distribution of free reserves on three measures of money and credit – demand deposits plus currency held by the public, total deposits plus currency held by the public, and total loans and investments of member banks.

The evidence presented confirms in large part some assertions made earlier in this study that the Federal Reserve has failed to develop a useful working knowledge of the monetary mechanism. After 50 years, the System's degree of control over changes in the stock of money or credit, judged in terms of the modified free reserves doctrine, is so pitifully small that retention of free reserves as an important measure or indicator of policy appears to be completely unwarranted.

3.1 The Demand for Free Reserves by Banks

Meigs' book began as a study of the factors determining the money supply (pp. 3, 66). But he did not develop an explanation of the money supply. The closest he came was to consider some possible determinants of the rate of change of demand deposits. His preliminary results led him to investigate the relation between the ratio of free reserves to deposits, interest rates, and the rate of change of unborrowed reserves (p. 66). In the process, he broke important new ground in our understanding of the monetary process by developing and testing a theory of the demand for free reserves by banks.

Meigs' results on this topic can be summarized succinctly. Three of his findings are of particular interest. First, he found that open market operations had only a small positive direct effect on the demand for free reserves. This effect is observable within the month in which the operation is conducted. Experiments with lags suggested that the direct response of desired free reserves to open market operations was substantially stronger in the month following the operation, but the effect remained relatively small withal. Second, the yield on Treasury bills appeared to have a much more important influence on the desired level of free reserves than the direct effect of open market operations. An increase in Treasury bill yields was accompanied by a reduction in the desired level of free reserves. The effect of lagged Treasury bill yields on the demand for free reserves was in the same direction as current yields, but in general the lagged relation was no stronger. Third, Meigs was able to explain by far the larger part of the month-to-month change in the ratio of free reserves to deposits by the proximate determinants of the demand for and supply of free reserves.

We have seen that the Riefler–Burgess view of policy operations, from which the simple free reserves notion appears to have emanated, considered the direct effect of open market operations on reserves to be largely offset by changes in member bank borrowings. It was through such changes in the proportion or volume of borrowed reserves that monetary policy was said to be made effective.

It was previously indicated that during the twenties variations in member bank borrowing and changes in the adjusted base (dominated by the gold stock, Treasury currency and the Federal Reserve banks' portfolio of Government securities) were closely correlated. A dollar change in the adjusted base was associated on the average with a dollar change in the opposite direction of member bank borrowing. This pattern vanished in the thirties and has not reappeared. Even the fifties, though exhibiting substantial variations in the volume of member bank borrowing, show no significant correlation between these variations and changes in the adjusted base. Thus, open market operations immediately modified the supply of free reserves in the postwar period by changing the banks' volume of reserves and excess reserves.

Meigs' investigations reveal, on the other hand, a comparatively small direct effect of open-market operations on the bank's desired level of free reserves. This magnitude appears to respond most decisively to changes in prevailing interest rates. Variations in credit market conditions, expressed by a spectrum of interest rates, induce banks to adjust their reserve position. Open market operations (or other events affecting the magnitude of the adjusted base) thus immediately create a divergence between the banks' desired and actual free reserve position. This divergence triggers a process involving readjustments in the banks' balance sheets and generates modifications in both the money stock and interest rates. The variations in interest rates form an essential part of this process, induced by the banks' endeavor to adjust their actual reserve position to their desired position. This endeavor generates losses in free reserves, via changes in required reserves and currency flows. These losses occur in response to deposit liabilities created or destroyed during the process. Desired free reserve positions respond to the changes in interest rates that accompany the process and also contribute to the elimination of the difference between actual and desired free reserves.

Meigs' investigations suggest a view of the monetary process radically different from the Riefler–Burgess heritage. Our previous discussion emphasized the peculiar character attributed to member bank borrowing and free reserves under the Riefler–Burgess notions and the subsequent evolution of the free reserve conception. Free reserves were typically visualized as a magnitude emerging from a process imposed on banks and independent of any choice behavior on the part of banks. The analysis developed by Meigs, supported by his statistical results, strongly emphasizes the neglected volitional aspects of free reserves. Banks are shown to hold free reserves in response to market conditions.

It follows from Meigs' analysis and results that banks adjust their asset portfolios in response to prevailing levels of free reserves relative to their *desired volume of free reserves*. Some of the answers provided in the context of the questionnaires to which the Governors and Presidents responded reveal a partial acknowledgement of Meigs' and similar results. Such acknowledgement is a decisive break with past Federal Reserve conceptions, in particular with the Riefler–Burgess heritage. Numerous policy statements and evaluations made in the past, and repeated in the questionnaire, are inconsistent with the acknowledgement that banks modify their desired free reserve position in response to market conditions.

Meigs' analysis and results also bear significantly on the Federal Reserve's use of various "liquidity measures." Such measures have no meaning by themselves but must be interpreted within an appropriate conception. The Federal Reserve's conceptions bearing on "liquidity" and "liquidity measures" are inconsistent with the best validated portions of economic theory and seriously challenged by Meigs' results. It is worth noting (1) that the evidence in Meigs' study supports the argument made earlier and (2) that the

Federal Reserve's use of "liquidity measures" is an indication of their failure to fully understand the meaning of a demand by banks for free reserves. Despite the important role that has been assigned to the demand for free reserves in the responses of the presidents and the governors, the evidence suggests that they have not drawn the logical conclusions with respect to "liquidity" and the monetary mechanism.

3.2 The Percentage Change in Deposits Resulting from the Interaction of the Demand for and Supply of Free Reserves

We have noted above that Meigs did not fully develop and test a theory of the relation of free reserves to the money supply. Nevertheless, his findings, about the effect of interest rates, free reserves, and open market operations on the monthly change in deposits, provide important information about the inadequacy of the Federal Reserve's conception. Some of Meigs' findings are summarized here:

1   Meigs constructed a comparatively simple explanation of the monthly percentage change in bank deposits in terms of the interaction of the supply of and demand for free reserves. He was able to account for two-thirds of the variability of the percentage change of bank deposits for the period 1947–58 in terms of his framework.[30] His results suggest that one-third of the variations in the rate of change of demand deposits is outside the control of the Federal Reserve. Since the currency component of the money supply is excluded from consideration in Meigs' study, we can reach no firm conclusions as yet about the meaning of these findings for the rate of change of the money supply.

2   Free reserves have a *negative* effect on the monthly percent change in demand deposits in Meigs' formulation. The higher the ratio of free reserves to demand deposits, the lower the percent change in deposits, holding interest rates and open market operations unchanged. This implication was strongly supported by the evidence, a finding that flatly contradicts the Federal Reserve's interpretation of free reserves as an indicator of "ease" and "restraint." A rise in free reserves means an increase in measured excess reserves of the banking system or a fall in member bank borrowing. Thus a decline in borrowing is associated with a reduction in the percentage change in demand deposits; an increase in member bank borrowing *raises* the percentage change in demand deposits. Increased member bank borrowing adds to the total reserves of the banking system and contributes to the growth of demand deposits. Moreover, a rise in excess reserves relative to deposits appears to reduce the percentage increase in demand deposits. The Federal

---

[30]Meigs, 1962, p. 96, equation T 7. To obtain this explanatory power, Meigs allowed for a separate effect of the interest rate ratio in each month. If this separate, monthly seasonal is neglected, the explanatory power is reduced to 48 percent. See equation T 9, p. 96.

Reserve's interpretation of free reserves is directly contrary to these findings. The evidence suggests that their conception is incorrect.

3   The effect of an increase in the percentage of unborrowed reserves (open market operations), like the increase in borrowed reserves, has an expansive effect on the rate at which demand deposits increase. But the direct effect of open market operations is relatively small in each of Meigs' equations. We have noted above that spokesmen for the Federal Reserve often refer to a six or seven dollar expansion of the amount of deposits per dollar of increased reserves (Riefler, 1958). Meigs' results suggest that the appropriate value of the reserve multiplier is smaller; a 1-percent change in unborrowed reserves is associated with at most a ½-percent change in the rate of change of demand deposits for given interest rates. Under the conditions prevailing in recent years, Meigs' results suggest that an open market operation had a multiple effect on the change in demand deposits, but the multiplier is between 2.5 and 3, not 6 or 7.

These examples of the evidence available from Meigs' study raise broader questions about the Federal Reserve's conception of the monetary process. Meigs' finds that the direct effect of open market operations on changes in the ratio of free reserves to deposits is much smaller than the indirect effect through interest rates. This raises doubts about the Federal Reserve's rationale for attaching significance to random and often self-reversing changes in float, Treasury balances, etc.

Clearly, more needs to be known about the effect on interest rates of changes in the supply of reserves and the timing and magnitude of the effect of changes in Treasury bill rates on other interest rates. Then a firmer conclusion can be drawn as to whether many of the "defensive" operations are stabilizing rather than destabilizing. Preliminary evidence presented earlier on the variability of monthly changes in the supply of money and the stock of bank credit suggests that these "defensive" operations may be the source of increased instability in the stock of money. Additional evidence on this subject comes from the computation of the monthly changes in the money supply, currency plus demand deposits. The simple correlation of the change in one month with the change in the following or preceding month is negative (−0.20). This suggests the interpretation that an increase in the money supply this month will more likely than not be followed by a decrease in the next month. A similar result is found for monthly changes in bank credit. It is difficult to find any rationale for such variability. By smoothing the extreme variability in bank reserve positions, the Federal Reserve seems to contribute to the variability of money supply and bank credit changes. It is difficult to judge, in the present state of knowledge, the effect of such short-run variability in the financial variables on the pace of economic activity. But there has been no analysis or supporting evidence adduced to suggest that the variability contributes to economic stability.

If variations in float or Treasury balances affect individual banks adversely, there is no reason why open market operations must be used to offset these temporary disturbances. Banks that are under temporary pressure can, if they desire, pay a price to obtain reserves temporarily in the Federal funds market. If no sales of Federal funds are offered at a price less than or equal to the discount rate, banks can borrow from the Federal Reserve banks, i.e., use the discount or collateral loan facilities of the Reserve banks. This may require a change in the Federal Reserve's long-cherished notions about borrowing, although it would seem to be in keeping with the spirit of the original Federal Reserve Act to permit banks to borrow for these short-term purposes. In any case, it is difficult to understand why the Federal Reserve is willing to supply reserves through open market operations that it might be unwilling to supply through the discount window, since borrowed reserves and unborrowed affect the money supply in a similar way.

3.3 Money, Credit, and the Modified Free Reserves Doctrine

By asking and answering a number of questions and suggesting some interpretations of the evidence, we can assess the usefulness of free reserves as an indicator of a monetary position and the relevance of the modified free reserves doctrine. The questions that will be asked concentrate primarily on the relation between interest rates, free reserves, the modified free reserves mechanism, money, and bank credit. The answers to the questions are given in terms of computed coefficients of determination. This computation permits us to measure relations between magnitudes and to express the percentage or fraction of yearly or monthly variation in one magnitude that accompanies, i.e., occurs jointly with, another magnitude.

It should be noted that the coefficient of determination gives no indication of cause or effect. If we find that the coefficient of determination between interest rates and free reserves is relatively large, for example, we cannot judge from this observation alone whether changes in free reserves caused changes in interest rates or whether interest rates caused changes in free reserves. All that we can infer from the given observation is the extent to which the two moved together or in opposite directions, perhaps under the influence of a common causal factor. But the observation of such correlations yields support for conceptions asserting a systematic (or causal) association between the magnitudes under consideration. Further observations may be gathered in order to discriminate more sharply between different conceptions compatible with the given gross correlation.

The coefficient of determination between monthly free reserves and the yield on Treasury bills is 0.42 for the 170 months from November 1948 to December 1962. Furthermore, the correlation between the two is negative. These observations support the contention that desired free reserves rapidly adjust to the prevailing volume of free reserves and depend on market conditions. The observed correlation indicates that, under this conception, 42 percent of the variation observed in free reserves during the period is explainable by the concomitant variation in interest rates. Since the correlation is negative, we infer, in addition, that large positive levels of free reserves are associated with low yields on Treasury bills.

These data suggest that there is a closer relation between the level of free reserves and the Treasury bill yield than between the level of free reserves and changes in the stock of money or credit that are considered below. This is similar to the finding of Meigs' study. But, we should note, in passing, that the addition of the years 1959–62 to the data that Meigs used has increased the correlation between free reserves and Treasury bill yields. A possible explanation for the increased coefficient of determination is that the relation may be stronger in times of high interest rates than in periods of low interest rates.

To go beyond the simple facts provided by the coefficients of determination requires detailed tests of alternative theories about the monetary mechanism. Here we are interested only in the presentation and interpretation of some elementary facts bearing on the adequacy of prevalent Federal Reserve notions (theories) about the factors influencing the supply of money and bank credit.

The measure that we have chosen, the coefficient of determination, must be between zero and one. The closer that the computed value of this measure comes to one, the closer the correspondence in the movements of the magnitudes under consideration. Conversely, when the computed coefficient of determination is near zero, there is no evidence of any systematic relation between the magnitudes, and there is no indication of any influence running from one to the other. Thus, if we find that the coefficient of variation between free reserves and total reserves is very close to 1, it might make very little difference which of these measures was used in the explanation of the monetary mechanism or interpretation of the events in the money market. Of course, the two might be closely related while neither has a close relation to changes in money and credit.

In addition to the questions and answers about the relation of one monetary factor to another, we will use the coefficient of determination to evaluate the combined effects of a series of separate factors operating jointly on a particular measure of monetary change. For example, we can consider the combined effects on the change in bank credit on (1) the level of free reserves, (2) the distribution of free reserves among classes of banks, and (3) interest rates. The extent to which the positions or levels of these three factors contribute jointly to an explanation of the change in bank credit will be measured by the computed coefficient of determination. The following questions and answers present the evidence on the Federal Reserve's conception of the monetary mechanism in terms of these computed coefficients.

Question 1. Is the monthly change in the supply of money or in member bank loans and investments closely related to the monthly average level of free reserves?

Table 1.5   Measures of the relationship between monthly average free reserves and monthly changes in money supply and member bank credit outstanding, November 1948 to December 1962[a]

Item	Months of contraction in the economy[b]	Months of expansion in the economy[c]	All months
Monthly change in currency plus demand deposits	0.02	0.14	0.04
Monthly change in currency plus total deposits	0	0.06	0.04
Monthly change in total loans and investments in member banks	0.01	0.02	0.03

[a] Figures in the table are coefficients of determination.
[b] 16 months from National Bureau peaks to troughs during the period November 1948 to February 1961.
[c] 108 months from National Bureau troughs to peaks during the period October 1949 through May 1960.

Answer. No. There is almost no evidence of a relation between the level of free reserves and changes in money and credit. The coefficients of determination in table 1.5 suggest that the level of free reserves has almost no influence on the change in money supply or member bank credit and vice versa. There is a slight indication that the relation is stronger during periods of expansion than during periods of contraction in the economy. This is particularly true for the monthly change in demand deposits plus currency.

Question 2. Is the relatively poor explanation evidenced by the values shown in table 1.5 largely a reflection of extremely short-run money market variations? Wouldn't an average of free reserves taken over a period longer than a month show a substantially stronger relation?

Answer. No. We recall that the 3-week moving average of free reserves was a useful indicator of changes in the direction of Federal Open Market Committee policy. It was sufficiently smooth for major swings in desired policy to be revealed. The monthly averages of free reserves are less erratic than the weekly moving averages. They also mark out clearly the changes in desired Federal Reserve policy. The more appropriate interpretation seems to be that free reserve levels tell almost nothing about the changes in money and bank credit.

Annual moving averages of free reserves were used to provide more evidence on this point. Much of the short-run variation that remained in the monthly data was eliminated by the use of annual data. Seasonal variations in money and credit were eliminated by comparing free reserves to annual percentage rates of change from one month to the corresponding month in the following year. The explanatory power of the relation between free

Table 1.6   Measures of the relationship between annual moving averages of free reserves and annual percentage rates of change in money and credit, November 1948 to December 1962

	Coefficient of determination		
Item	Using annual average of free reserves (1)	Using (1) and distribution of free reserves by bank class (2)	Using (2) and Treasury bill yields (3)
Annual percent rate of change in demand deposits plus currency	0.08	0.33	0.45
Annual percent rate of change of total deposits plus currency	0.03	0.24	0.42
Annual percent rate of change of total loans and investments of member banks	0.08	0.29	0.34

reserves and changes in money and credit improved very little when annual data were used.

Allowing for the distribution of free reserves among classes of banks and allowing for the role of Treasury bill yields as additional explanatory factors did improve the annual results quite a bit. But the best explanation was for the annual percentage rate of change of money, demand deposits plus currency held by the public, and not for total bank credit that is so much emphasized in Federal Reserve discussions of the monetary mechanism. These results are shown in table 1.6.

Question 3. Do measures of the distribution of free reserves and interest rates have a similar effect in improving the explanatory power for *monthly* changes in money and bank credit?

Answer. No. For the 170 monthly changes in bank credit and money between November 1948 and December 1962, there is almost no improvement when we allow for the distribution of free reserves between classes of banks, the yield on Treasury bills, and/or the ratio of Treasury bill yields to the prevailing rediscount rate. This is shown in table 1.7.

Question 4. Do the data in the last column of table 1.7 provide evidence about the modified free reserves doctrine as an explanation of monthly changes in money and credit?

Answer. Yes. The evidence in column (3) suggests that the modified free reserves doctrine provides almost no explanation of monthly changes in money or credit.

Question 5. Does the relatively weak relation for both monthly changes

Table 1.7   Measures of the relationship between monthly changes in money and credit and the level and distribution of free reserves and interest rates, November 1948 to December 1962

| | Coefficients of determination | | |
| | Using free reserves and their distribution | Using (1) and Treasury bill rates | Using (1) and the ratio of Treasury bill rates to rediscount rates |
Item	(1)	(2)	(3)
Monthly change in currency plus demand deposits	0.04	0.05	0.05
Monthly change in currency plus total deposits	0.07	0.10	0.07
Monthly change in total loans and investments of member banks	0.05	0.06	0.06

in money and monthly changes in bank credit suggest that while neither is closely related to free reserves, changes in money and credit are closely related to each other?

Answer. No. Changes in money and credit have a monthly coefficient of determination of 0.01 when money is measured as demand deposits plus currency. These data indicate that there is no support whatsoever for the position that monetary expansion and credit expansion are one and the same, as the Federal Reserve spokesmen have maintained.

Question 6. Is the relatively weak support for the modified free reserves doctrine and the relation of free reserves to changes in money and credit partly explained by the relatively low interest rates of the pre-Accord period and the early post-Accord period?

Answer. Yes, there is some support for this interpretation from the evidence on changes in the stock of money. For changes in the stock of credit, the evidence suggests the opposite conclusion as shown in table 1.8. But the explanatory power remains small. Moreover, there is very little evidence of any steady direction of change in either the stock of money or credit. The correlation between the successive changes in the money supply in adjacent months is small and negative. The same is true for monthly changes in bank credit as noted earlier. Despite the fact that both of these changes have been positive on the average over the 14-year period, an increase in money or credit in one month is not a reliable indication that there will be an increase in the following month.

It should be noted also that the monthly variation in free reserves has been smaller in the past few years than in the years of the early fifties when swings in free reserves of more than $500 million were more frequent. Accompany-

Table 1.8 Measures of the relationship between monthly changes[a] in money and credit and the level and distribution of free reserves and interest rates, 3 postwar periods

	Coefficients of determination		
	Using free reserves and their distribution	Using (1) and Treasury bill rates	Using (1) and the ratio of Treasury bill rates to rediscount rate
Item	(1)	(2)	(3)
	November 1948 to July 1953		
Monthly change in currency plus demand deposits	0.05	0.08	0.08
Monthly change in currency plus total deposits	0.10	0.16	0.15
Monthly change in total loans and investments of member banks	0.24	0.24	0.25
	July 1953 to July 1957		
Monthly change in currency plus demand deposits	0.14	0.20	0.14
Monthly change in currency plus total deposits	0.09	0.09	0.09
Monthly change in total loans and investments of member banks	0.05	0.06	0.28
	July 1957 to May 1960		
Monthly change in currency plus demand deposits	0.32	0.32	0.41
Monthly change in currency plus total deposits	0.36	0.37	0.37
Monthly change in total loans and investments of member banks	0.10	0.11	0.10

[a] Using monthly percentage rates of change gives very similar results.

ing the greater stability in the level of free reserves, there has been a growth in the number of banks participating actively in the Federal funds market. These changes in market conditions, or arrangements, probably help to account for the steady improvement in the relation between free reserves and changes in money supply and in the influence of the modified free reserves mechanism on changes in the money stock. But, of course, this explanation cannot account for the very poor relation between free reserves and bank credit that we observe from July 1957 to May 1960.

Question 7. Is there any additional evidence that the factors included as part of the modified free reserves doctrine have different effects in

Table 1.9 Measures of the relationship between monthly changes[a] in money and credit and the level and distribution of free reserves and interest rates in months of expanding and contracting economic activity

	Coefficients of determination		
	Using free reserves and their distribution	Using (1) and Treasury bill rates	Using (1) and the ratio of Treasury bill rates to rediscount rate
Item	(1)	(2)	(3)
	46 months from peak to trough		
Monthly change in currency plus demand deposits	0.06	0.06	0.10
Monthly change in currency plus total deposits	0.12	0.17	0.18
Monthly change in total loans and investments of member banks	0.02	0.02	0.08
	108 months from trough to peak		
Monthly change in currency plus demand deposits	0.14	0.21	0.15
Monthly change in currency plus total deposits	0.07	0.10	0.07
Monthly change in total loans and investments of member banks	0.04	0.05	0.04

[a] Using monthly percentage rates of change gives very similar results.

periods of relatively low interest rates and economic activity and periods of relatively high interest rates and economic activity?

Answer. Yes; the evidence in table 1.9 suggests this conclusion for the changes in currency plus demand deposits. Interest rates were higher on the average in 108 months from trough to peak than in the 46 months from peak to trough. The modified free reserve doctrine is a better explanation of changes in the stock of money in months from trough to peak. We have noted earlier that the level of free reserves was more closely related to interest rates in recent months when interest rates have been higher on the average.

This circumstance might explain the relative improvement in the relation between the level and distribution of free reserves and changes in money supply during the 108 months from peak to trough (col. 1).

Data for the three periods shown in table 1.8 suggest that the association between changes in the money stock and free reserves is stronger in high interest rate periods than in periods of comparatively low interest rates. The average level of interest rates rises from period to period as we move down the table and the explanatory power measured in columns 1, 2, and 3 rises also. But the improvement in explanatory power holds only for changes in the stock of money; it does not appear when we consider changes in member bank credit.

Table 1.9 again indicates that the improvement in the explanatory power of the modified free reserves doctrine in periods of comparatively high interest rates applies to changes in the stock of money but not to changes in the stock of credit. Reasons for the Federal Reserves attachment to, and emphasis on, credit cannot be obtained from the evidence that we have examined. None of the evidence gives any indication that there is a reliable association between free reserves, or the modified free reserves mechanism, and the change in bank credit.

Question 8. Do the findings suggest that further modifications and tests of the Federal Reserve explanation of the monetary mechanism, centered on the free reserves doctrine, would be useful?

Answer. We can never be certain that additional modifications would not improve the explanatory power. One can only try. But the accumulated evidence falsifies so many of the features of the Federal Reserve conception that time can more usefully be spent developing an alternative explanation that avoids these errors.

Question 9. Do the poor results obtained necessarily indicate the irrelevance of a conception inherited from the Riefler–Burgess tradition and centered on the free reserve mechanism?

Answer. No. Such results might be obtained under a coherently formulated free reserve conception if the adjustment of the banks' portfolio of earning assets is very rapid. In particular, little association between the variations in money stock or bank portfolios and free reserves would remain in monthly data, if the adjustment process is concentrated within a month. Under such circumstances the central relation of the Federal Reserve's conception, associating "credit-expansion" and free reserves, would operate significantly only in the shortest run and could not be detected in the monthly data used here. But in this case some other problems arise.

If this formulation of the free reserve conception is advanced, free reserves must be abandoned as an indicator of a monetary situation and as a target of monetary policy. The interaction of the relation centered on free reserves with other pertinent relations, constituting the structure of a rapidly adjusting process, implies that free reserves cannot be interpreted as an indicator or used as a target by the Federal Reserve authorities. Furthermore, other implications of the reformulated free reserve conception can be shown to be seriously incompatible with validated portions of economic analysis. Thus either the central relation of the Federal Reserve conception is seriously invalidated by the observations presented, or a reformulated conception, compatible with the data in tables 1.5 to 1.9, is incompatible with the burden placed on free reserves as an indicator and target by the Federal Reserve authorities.

3.4 Summary and Conclusion

The chapters discussing and analyzing the Federal Reserve conception of the monetary mechanism are now complete. We noted some of the logical and factual errors that mar the Federal Reserve's understanding of the mechanism. And we looked at some of the reasons for these errors – particularly their extremely short-run orientation, their concern with daily or weekly defensive operations, their tendency to view the banking system as analogous to a single bank. We noted repeatedly that if the Federal Reserve had looked seriously at the evidence, they would not persist in repeating these errors.

Sections 1 and 2 attempted to demonstrate that particular factors, summarized in the modified free reserve doctrine, have dominated the prevailing Federal Reserve view. Inconsistencies, qualifications, and modifications that appear from time to time made this task laborious and difficult. But the evidence from the "Record of Policy Actions" and the repeated references to the same factors suggested quite strongly that the modified free reserve doctrine comes reasonably close to a statement of some of their dominant views. In arriving at this judgment, we noted that the absence of a clear, generally accepted statement of the mechanism, the concern with hourly, daily, and weekly money market changes, and the emphasis on "defensive" operations contributed to a substantial grant of authority to the Manager of the System Open Market Account.

In this section, some of the evidence on the Federal Reserve's conception of the mechanism controlling the stock of money has been assessed. We found that the relation between Federal Reserve policy and the change in money and credit is quite poor judging from the monthly and annual data used in our tests.

A new question arises, therefore: Does it really matter very much what the Federal Reserve does? By far the larger part of the monthly and annual changes in money and credit seems to be outside their control, judged by their conception of the mechanism.

The proviso of the last sentence is the crux of the matter. If the Federal Reserve's conception of the monetary process, centered on the position of free reserves, were the only admissible view, we would have to concede that monetary policy is little more than a futile exercise. But alternative conceptions of the monetary mechanism have been formulated, and it is essential to consider them before accepting such a negative conclusion. It should be noted, therefore, that our analysis does not suggest the futility of monetary policy but only supports our contention about the failure of the Federal Reserve to develop a coherent, validated conception.

The failure of the Federal Reserve to develop a useful conception of the monetary mechanism does not mean that one cannot be developed.

References

Ahearn, D. A. 1963. *Federal Reserve Policy Reappraised*. New York: Columbia University Press, p. 218, n.6.

Ando, A., E. C. Brown, J. Karaken, and R. M. Solow. 1963. Lags in fiscal and monetary policy. In Commission on Money and Credit, *Stabilization Policies*. Englewood Cliffs, NJ: Prentice-Hall, pp. 1–163.

Brandt, H. 1963. Controlling reserves. *Monthly Review of the Federal Reserve Bank of Atlanta*, September, p. 1.

Brunner, K. and A. H. Meltzer. 1964. *Some General Features of the Federal Reserve's Approach to Policy*. Subcommittee on Domestic Finance, House Committee on Banking and Currency, 88th Congress, 2nd session. February 10th, 1964. Washington: Government Printing Office.

Burgess, W. R. 1936. *The Reserve Banks and the Money Market*. New York: Harper and Bros, rev. edn.

Commission on Money and Credit. 1963. *The Federal Reserve and the Treasury*. Englewood Cliffs, NJ: Prentice-Hall.

Federal Reserve Bank of St. Louis. 1961. *"Excess Reserves" Review*, October.

—— 1963a. *"Excess Reserves" Review*, April, p. 15,

—— 1963b. *"Excess Reserves" Review*, August.

Federal Reserve Bulletin. 1963. Measures of member bank reserves, July.

Goldenweiser, E. A. 1941. Instruments of Federal Reserve policy. In *Banking Studies*. Washington: Board of Governors of the Federal Reserve System.

Martin, W. McC. 1963. Statements to Congress: Monetary policy and the economy. *Federal Reserve Bulletin*, February.

Meigs, A. J. 1962. *Free Reserves and the Money Supply*. Chicago: University of Chicago Press, ch. 2.

Noyes, G. 1963. Short-run objectives of monetary policy. *Review of Economics and Statistics*, supplement, February.

Record of Policy Actions, 1958. *Annual Report of the Board of Governors for the Year 1958*.

Riefler, W. W. 1930. *Money Rates and Money Markets in the United States*. New York: Harper and Bros.

—— 1958. Open market operations in long-term securities. *Federal Reserve Bulletin*, November.

Roosa, R. V. 1951. Interest rates and the central bank. *In Money, Trade and Economic Growth*, Essays in Honor of John H. Williams. New York: Macmillan, pp. 270–95.

Rouse, R. G. 1961. *Review of the Annual Report for 1960*. Joint Economic Committee, Washington, p. 34.

The significance and limitations of free reserves. 1958. *Monthly Review of the Federal Reserve Bank of New York*, November.

Stone, R. W. 1963. Federal Reserve open market operations in 1962. *Federal Reserve Bulletin*, April, p. 431.

Young, R. A. and C. A. Yager. 1960. The economics of bills preferable. *Quarterly Journal of Economics*, August, 359.

2

A Credit Market Theory of the Money Supply and an Explanation of Two Puzzles in US Monetary Policy

Karl Brunner and Allan H. Meltzer

Federal Reserve policy in the early postwar years has frequently been described as an "engine of inflation."[1] Continuation of the wartime policy of supporting the government bond market required the central bank to absorb securities sold by the private sector. Given the large stock of government securities left as a residue of wartime finance, the expectation that the support policy would lead to inflation was quite reasonable. The puzzling feature about the period is that substantial inflation did not occur. Instead, the growth rates of the money supply and of the monetary base collapsed shortly after the end of World War II. By 1949, the economy had moved to a position in which the policy problem was one of removing recession and deflation. Despite the continuation of the support policy, prices in 1949 were falling, not rising.

If the support policy prevented the Federal Reserve from achieving an effective counter-cyclical monetary policy, it seems reasonable to expect counter-cyclical policy to have emerged once the support policy ended. The famed "accord" with the Treasury in March 1951 terminated the agreement to maintain a fixed "pattern of yields" on government securities. But it did not usher in a period of markedly counter-cyclical policy. The expansion of the money supply in 1951 was larger than it had been in any of the preceding four years. In the decade following the accord the monetary base and the money supply generally moved in a pro-cyclical rather than a counter-

This paper appeared in T. Bagiotti (ed.), *Investigations in Economic Theory and Methodology*, Essays in Honor of Marco Fanno. Padova, Italy: Cedam, 1966, vol. 2, pp. 151–76. Reprinted with permission. Helpful discussion with Armen A. Alchian and Milton Friedman is acknowledged gratefully.

[1]One statement of the Federal Reserve's interpretation is contained in Joint Committee on the Economic Report, 1952, part 1, p. 357.

cyclical direction. This pro-cyclical pattern is the most puzzling aspect of US monetary policy in the post-accord years.

Attempts to explain the Federal Reserve's behavior frequently suggest that there is a delay in recognizing the appropriate time for policy changes or "recognition lag" (Metzler, 1948; Ando et al., 1963). On the surface, this line of argument appears quite plausible. Unfortunately, it is not supported by an examination of the timing of Federal Reserve decisions. A comparison of post-accord policy decisions with cyclical turning points reveals an impressive ability to recognize turning points rapidly.[2]

Thus observations invalidate the standard conclusion about the support policy, deny the policymaker's confident assertion of a systematic, counter-cyclical policy and reject the attempt to salvage the counter-cyclical flavor of policy through the medium of a recognition lag. But then the two major puzzles remain. How can we explain the collapse of the growth rates of the base and the money supply under the rigid support policy? In the absence of a recognition lag, how can we explain the pro-cyclical pattern in monetary policy and the divergences between professed and actual policy?

In this paper we expand a theory of the money supply presented elsewhere[3] to incorporate an analysis of bank earning assets. The extended theory describes the joint determination of money, bank credit – loans and investments of commercial banks – and some interest rates on the bank credit market. The solutions combine the behavior of the banks and the public with the constraints imposed by monetary policy. They thus provide a framework for analyzing the two most puzzling features of postwar monetary policy in the US.

1 The General Framework

The Federal Reserve sets the reserve requirement ratios and the proportion of vault cash of member banks to be counted as required reserves, decides on its portfolio of government securities, announces the discount rate, regulates the discount window, and classifies member banks. The Treasury plays a minor role through the administration of its cash balances. Commercial banks respond to their environment by allocating total assets between cash assets and earning assets, distributing earning assets between loans and investments, and borrowing or repaying indebtedness. These decisions determine the relative size of four items on the asset side of the consolidated

---

[2]See the *Record of Policy Actions* published in the Annual Report of the Federal Reserve and the discussion in Brunner and Meltzer, 1964a, b.

[3]See Brunner and Meltzer, 1964b. The present paper is based on an expansion of the non-linear hypothesis on pp. 248–56.

balance sheet of the banking sector: loans, investments, borrowed and unborrowed reserves.

The public confronts the banks on the loan market with a supply of loans and interacts with the banks on the securities market. Moreover, the public's allocation of money balances between currency and demand deposits and the partition of total deposits between demand and time account exert a significant effect on monetary and credit magnitudes. Like the banks' allocation decisions, the public's demand and supply behavior (with the exception of its currency demand) is shaped by the movement of interest rates on the bank credit market.

Policy decisions and some of the market responses just discussed can be summarized by five parameters and a policy variable. In this section, we present a compact statement of the underlying theory and, in the following section, summarize the broad outline of the money–bank credit process in a diagram. The simultaneous solution for money, bank credit and interest rates on the credit market is suppressed for this purpose. The restriction is removed in a later section where the effects on interest rates are more explicitly stated.

1.1 The Adjusted Monetary Base

By consolidating the government sector accounts, the Federal Reserve's balance sheet and the monetary accounts of the Treasury, a statement of sources and uses of the monetary base is obtained. This statement includes member bank borrowing, an endogenous variable determined jointly with interest rates, money and bank credit. The monetary base net of member bank borrowing – the adjusted base, B^a – is taken as an exogenous variable. Equation (2.1) expresses the adjusted base in terms of its uses.

$$B^a = R_u + C_p \qquad\qquad (2.1)$$

where R_u is total unborrowed reserves of all commercial banks and C_p is currency held by the public. The adjusted base occupies a central position in the analysis that follows since it summarizes the operations of the monetary authority during periods of unchanged reserve requirement ratios and rediscount rates.[4]

---

[4] The source components of the base include policy, predetermined and stochastic variables. The gold stock and Treasury currency are predetermined relative to the current money supply process and are, therefore, taken as exogenous magnitudes. Treasury cash is treated as exogenous also, since it is under the control of the fiscal authorities. Reserve Bank credit net of borrowing includes a policy variable – the Federal Reserve's portfolio of securities – and a stochastic variable, float. The latter is related to the volume of bank debits and is affected somewhat by the current money supply process. Nevertheless, the base is taken as an exogenous variable since the

1.2 Two Behavior Parameters for Commercial Banks

The reserve ratio r describes the banks' division of total assets between earning assets and reserves. The latter consists of vault cash and deposits at Federal Reserve banks. The parameter is measured by the ratio of total reserves to the banking system's total deposits (including Treasury deposits). The reserve ratio is effectively explained by the average requirement ratios against demand and time deposits, the level and expected variability of interest rates, and the banks' anticipation with respect to the average value and the variability of currency flows. We omit a detailed statement of the hypothesis for the reserve ratio and simply write eqn (2.2):

$$r = r(r^d, r^t, i_G, \rho, i_L; \pi_1) \tag{2.2}$$

where r^d and r^t designate the average requirement ratios against demand and time deposits; i_G denotes the average yield on government securities, i_L an index of loan-rates, and ρ is the discount rate. The parameter π_1 combines the omitted determinants. The derivatives of r with respect to r^d, r^t and ρ are positive; the derivatives are negative, with respect to the two market rates of interest.

The borrowing ratio, b, expresses the banks' partition of total reserves between borrowed and unborrowed reserves. This behavior parameter is measured by the ratio of total bank borrowings from Federal Reserve banks to the banks' total deposits. It is explained in eqn (2.3).

$$b = b(i_G, i_L, \rho; \pi_2). \tag{2.3}$$

The borrowing ratio responds positively to the market rates of interest and negatively to the discount rate. As before, the parameter π_2 reminds us of omitted factors that have played a sizeable role on occasion (e.g., the tax treatment of borrowing costs).

1.3 One Parameter for the Treasury

The Treasury holds deposits at both Federal Reserve and commercial banks. Treasury deposits at the Federal Reserve are included among the sources of the base. Tax and loan accounts at commercial banks are described for present purposes by a parameter, d, the ratio of Treasury deposits at commercial banks to the public's demand deposits. This parameter is assumed to be the result of tax and spending decisions by the Congress, cash management practices of the Treasury, etc., so that d may be taken as exogenous.

---

uses of the base, eqn (2.1) of the text, are the total monetary issue of the central bank and can be controlled completely.

For a more complete description of the sources and uses of the base, see Brunner and Meltzer, 1964a, pp. 9–12.

1.4 Two Behavior Parameters for the Public

The public's decision to hold some proportion of their demand deposits as currency is expressed by k. The allocation of money balances between currency and demand deposits has at times played a decisive role in the monetary process. An adequate explanation of the short-term behavior of k is badly needed. But, at the moment, there is no reliable hypothesis for this purpose. Since our concern here is with the relation of interest rates, money and bank credit and there is no evidence that k is dependent on interest rates, k is taken as a datum that influences – but is not influenced by – current monetary processes.

The ratio of time to demand deposits, t, is dependent on the current monetary process. The time deposit ratio appears to be highly sensitive to the rate paid on time deposits (i_t), to the yields on Treasury bills and on longer-term securities. In addition, the ratio responds positively to the public's real wealth, w. Equation (2.4) states the relation.

$$t = t(i_t, i_G, i_L, w). \tag{2.4}$$

The derivatives with respect to i_t and w are positive; the others are negative. Competitive pressure between banks generates a delayed response of i_t to the two market determined rates. A more detailed analysis would also include yield and "quality" changes in saving and loan association shares.

2 The Stock of Bank Credit: A First Approach

A relatively simple solution for the stock of bank credit can be obtained if the effects of interest rates and the public's behavior on the credit markets are ignored temporarily. The underlying system can be compressed into four equations represented in the four panels of Figure 2.1.

The banks' balance sheet together with the definition of the reserve and borrowing ratio implies the following relation between the banks' desired stock of earning assets E_b and the volume of unborrowed reserves R_u:

$$E_b = \frac{1 - (r - b)}{r - b} \cdot R_u \tag{2.5}$$

The line in the first quadrant of figure 2.1 corresponds to this relation. The slope of the line is expressed as a rational function of the parameters r and b occurring in eqn (2.5). It follows that changes of requirement ratios, the discount rate and market rates of interest modify the slope and thus rotate the line around the origin.

Equation (2.5) associates "bank credit" with the volume of unborrowed reserves by means of the reserve and borrowing ratios, two parameters characterizing bank behavior. According to eqn (2.1) the supply of

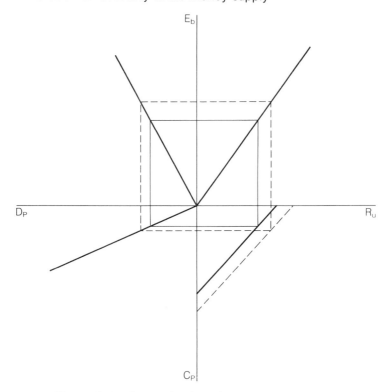

Figure 2.1   Determination of money and credit.

unborrowed reserves depends on the adjusted base and the public's absorption of currency. This is expressed in the fourth quadrant of figure 2.1. The position of the line depends on the magnitude of the adjusted base. This magnitude is measured by the intercepts on the two axis. Every point of the line indicates a possible partition of the base between unborrowed reserves of banks, and the public's currency holdings. Every change in the adjusted base, whatever its origin, involves a parallel shift of the line in the fourth quadrant.

The supply of unborrowed reserves has been linked to the public's currency holdings. The latter are associated, according to our discussion in a previous section, to the banks' supply of demand deposits. The currency ratio k establishes this association, which is appropriately expressed by the line in the third quadrant of figure 2.1. The slope of the line measured with respect to the horizontal axis is equal to the currency ratio k. Any rotation of the line around the origin thus reveals a change in the public's desired currency ratio.

Our last building block links demand deposits with "bank credit." Demand deposits, (D_p) are generated through the acquisition of earning assets. While it has become customary to think of this relation as a fixed proportion, our analysis denies that the ratio of demand deposits to earning assets is constant. It implies instead that the slope of the line in the second quadrant is dependent on the parameters d, t, r, and b introduced earlier and hence on interest rates, the rediscount rate and the requirement ratios. The line associates demand deposits and bank credit and may be expressed by the formula

$$D_p = \frac{1}{(1 + t + d)[1 - (r - b)]} \cdot E_b \qquad (2.5a)$$

The diagram may be used to trace the general direction of the response in E_b to variations in the underlying variables or parameters. The solid line connecting points in the four quadrants shows a (partial) equilibrium position of the monetary system and cuts off unique values for E_b, D_p, C_p and R_u. Any increase in the adjusted base, e.g., an open market purchase, a gold inflow, etc. shifts the line in quadrant IV away from the origin. The new box, shown by the dotted line in figure 2.1, contains the old box. Each of the monetary variables is increased.

The precise effects of policy operations depend on the values of the parameters. For example, economy in the use of currency, represented by a flatter line in quadrant III, produces larger responses in E_b and D_p for a given increase in the base. Increases in the time deposit ratio alter the slopes in the first and second quadrants. The larger the t ratio, the larger the response of bank credit relative to the response of demand deposits. Increases in the ceiling interest rate on time deposits, when a large proportion of banks have reached the prevailing ceiling, raise the time deposit ratio and rotate the line in quadrant II to the right. Reductions in the reserve requirement ratios have an effect similar to increases in the ceiling rate.

Other policy changes or institutional rearrangements can be investigated using the simple framework. Each such change can be shown to alter the ratio between the banks' demand for earning assets and the adjusted base. In a later section, we will return to consider this ratio in more detail. Before doing so, it is desirable to remove the assumption of constant interest rates and to introduce relations summarizing the behavior of the public on the credit market.

3 A Description of the Credit Market

Policy actions affect the money supply and bank credit via two distinct channels. An open market purchase increases the base and lowers interest rates. The effect of a change in the base is suggested in figure 2.1 above. Analysis of the second channel – the response of money and bank credit to changes in market interest rates – requires some discussion of the bank credit market. In this section, our argument is extended to cover the second channel. The response of money and bank credit to policy variables operating through the two channels is combined in the following section.

Bank credit is divided into its components, loans and investments. This division reflects the substantially higher marginal cost of acquiring information about loans, a cost that has important consequences for the adjustment of bank portfolios.[5] Let L_b and I_b denote the aggregate desired loan and investment (or securities) portfolios of commercial banks. We postulate that I_b and L_b are proportional to total demand, time and Treasury deposits $(D+T)$ with proportionality factors, α_1 and α_2, dependent on interest rates and the ratio of actual to expected income, y/y_e. Thus[6]

$$I_b = \alpha_1(D+T); \tag{2.6}$$

$$L_b = \alpha_2(D+T) \tag{2.7}$$

where

$$\alpha_1 = \alpha_1(i_G, i_L, y/y_e) \; \alpha_{11} > 0 > \alpha_{12}; \alpha_{13} < 0$$

and

$$\alpha_2 = \alpha_2(i_G, i_L, y/y_e) \; \alpha_{21} < 0 < \alpha_{22}; \alpha_{23} > 0$$

The restrictions imposed on the parameters α_1 and α_2 are not completely independent. The balance sheet of commercial banks implies that the four parameters used to characterize bank behavior are constrained by a linear relation,

$$r + \alpha_1 + \alpha_2 = 1 + b.$$

This relation and the derivatives of the reserve ratio (r) and borrowing ratio (b), introduced earlier, imply that the direct derivatives of the α_1 are numerically larger than the respective cross derivatives, i.e., $\alpha_{11} > |\alpha_{21}|$ and $\alpha_{22} > |\alpha_{12}|$. An increase in i_G ir in i_L, other rates remaining unchanged, alters the portfolio composition of the banking system. However, the division of earning assets between loans and investments has been assumed to be independent of the discount rate. The balance sheet constraint therefore implies that the derivatives of the reserve ratio and the borrowing ratio with respect to the discount rate are numerically equal but of opposite sign. From these constraints it follows also that $\alpha_{13} = -\alpha_{23}$, i.e.,

$$\frac{\partial \alpha_1}{\partial(y/y_e)} = \frac{-\partial \alpha_2}{\partial(y/y_e)} \, .$$

Changes in the index of transitory income (y/y_e) affect the allocation of earning assets between loans and investments but do not alter the distribu-

---

[5]For a more detailed discussion of the loan portfolio see Hester, 1962.
[6]α_{11} is the partial derivative of α_1 with respect to i_G; α_{12} is the partial of α_1 with respect to i_L.

tion of total assets between cash and earning assets. The existence of earning assets with very low transaction and information costs is crucial to this result.

The public's behavior on the bank credit market is represented by eqn (2.8), the public's stock demand for securities (I_p), and eqn (2.9) the supply of loans to commercial banks (L_p). These variables are assumed to depend on prevailing interest rates, the index of transitory income and on expected nominal income, Y_e, a measure of the current value of wealth.[7]

$$I_p = s_1 (i_G, i_L, y/y_e, Y_e); s_{11}>0>s_{12}; s_{13} \geq 0 < s_{14} \tag{2.8}$$

$$L_p = s_2 (i_G, i_L, y/y_e, Y_e); s_{21}>0>s_{22}; s_{23}<0<s_{24} \tag{2.9}$$

Interaction between the public and the banks on the credit market proximately determines the two interest rates, i_G and i_L, and distributes the outstanding stock of debt (S) between the two sectors. The credit market is thus described by the two equations

$$I_b + I_p = S \text{ and } L_b = L_p.$$

After the appropriate substitution in eqns (2.6) and (2.7), the credit market eqns can be rewritten in terms of the exogenous and predetermined variables.

$$a_1 (i_G, i_L, y/y_e, r^d, r^t, k, \rho) B^a + s_1 (i_G, i_L, y/y_e, Y_e) = S$$

$$a_2 (i_G, i_L, y/y_e, r^d, r^t, k, \rho) B^a = s_2 (i_G, i_L, y/y_e, Y_e)$$

The parameters a_1 and a_2 depend on interest rates and the index of transitory income by construction, since they are proportional to α_1 and α_2 of eqns (2.6) and (2.7).[8] They also depend on the reserve requirement ratios, the rediscount rate and the currency ratio and on the variables that enter as arguments of the reserve, borrowing and time deposit ratios.

The influence of monetary and fiscal policies on credit market interest rates can be obtained from the two equations. Monetary policy operates either through the parameters a_1 and a_2 or by changing the adjusted base. The history of fiscal policy is reflected in the outstanding stock of securities held by the banks and public, S. The response of i_G and i_L to each of the policy

---

[7]Separation of the effects of changes in prices and real wealth is ignored. A more detailed analysis than is provided here would require some statement about the separate effects of these variables as well as the response of the public's desired indebtedness to anticipated and unanticipated price changes, changes in the real yield on real capital, etc. Introduction of these additional variables would increase the complexity of our analysis without altering the conclusions in any important way. For similar reasons, no explicit attention is given to the separation of financial intermediaries from the rest of the public.

[8]Specifically,

$$a_i = \alpha_i \left[\frac{1 + t + d}{(r-b)(1+t+d) + k} \right]$$

variables, expressed as an elasticity, is shown in table A.1 of the appendix. The restrictions imposed on the various equations prove to be sufficient to determine a unique sign for each of the elasticities.

Among the implications obtained from the elasticities, three are of particular interest. First, variations in the volume of outstanding securities induce a larger response in the yield on securities than on loan rates. This is a consequence of the restriction which makes the cross derivatives smaller than the direct derivatives. A sale of debt to the banks or the public, e.g., the financing of a deficit, raises both securities and loan rates but increases the former relative to the latter. Second, the elasticities of the two interest rates with respect to the stock supply of debt are not constant. In particular, they appear to depend positively on the proportion of the debt held by the public. Thus deficits financed primarily by the sale of new issues to the public are likely to increase the responsiveness of i_G and i_L to debt operations. Third, open market operations exert a more pronounced effect on interest rates than other changes in the base or fiscal policy operations. An open market operation is characterized by the conditions $dS = -dB^a$. Hence, the response of interest rates to central bank purchases and sales is given by the expression

$$\left[\epsilon(i_j, B^a) - \epsilon(i_j, S)\frac{B^a}{S} \right] \frac{dB^a}{B^a}$$

where $\epsilon(i_j, B^a)$ and $\epsilon(i_j, S)$ are the elasticities of a particular interest rate with respect to the adjusted base and the stock of outstanding debt. Since the bracketed expression exceeds each of its components in numerical value, the effect on interest rates of an open market purchase by the Federal Reserve exceeds the effect of any equivalent change in one of the other sources of the base or of an equivalent volume of debt retirement by the Treasury. The magnified effect of an open market operation is the result of the simultaneous change in the demand for and supply of interest-bearing debt.

4   The Determination of Bank Credit and Money

The solutions for interest rates on the credit market implicitly define an equilibrium stock of money and bank credit. This may be recognized formally by inserting the interest rates determined by the credit market equations into the relations defining I_b and L_b. The sum of the two stocks, E_b, is the volume of bank credit net of Treasury deposits at commercial banks. By a simple rearrangement of the relations shown in figure 2.1 earlier, the money supply, currency and demand deposits, is obtained also. This is expressed in eqn (2.10).

$$M = \beta E_b \qquad (2.10)$$

The ratio β will be referred to as the issuing quotient, the amount of money issued by the monetary system per dollar of earning assets. The discussion of figure 2.1 has already indicated that the issuing quotient is not a constant. It depends on the ratios r, b, k, and t. But, unlike the analysis in figure 2.1 where interest rates were held constant, β depends on interest rates and the rediscount rate as well. Specifically, β responds positively to changes in the reserve requirement ratios, the currency ratio and the rediscount rate, whereas it reacts negatively to changes in market interest rates. The precise way in which the ratios affect β is shown in footnote 10 below.

The analysis underlying figure 2.1 can now be extended to combine the effects of policy variables and interest rates on the stocks of money and bank credit. Part a of figure 2.2 describes the (proximate) determination of the loan portfolio and the loan rate. The position of the two schedules depends,

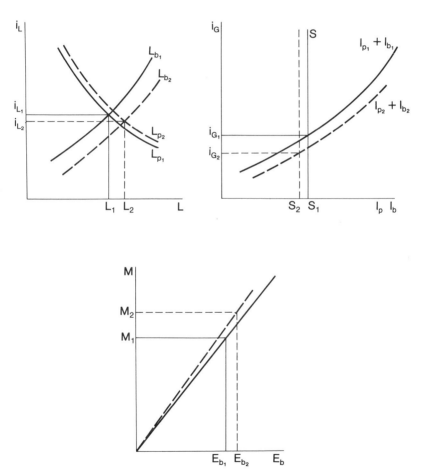

Figure 2.2   The effect of an open-market purchase; (a) The loan market; (b) The securities market; (c) The issuing quotient.

of course, on the securities yield as well as on the other variables of the L_b and L_p functions. The securities market is described in part b. The stock supply, taken as a given magnitude in the present analysis, must be absorbed into the portfolios of the banks and the public. Their combined demands, I_p and I_b, depend on the loan rate, policy variables, and other arguments previously introduced. The equilibrium stock of bank credit resulting from the interaction of the banks and the public on the two markets is shown on the horizontal axis of panel c. Corresponding to each equilibrium stock of bank credit and a particular value of the issuing quotient, there is an equilibrium money supply. The slope of the line in figure 2.2c is the issuing quotient. The money supply can be read on the vertical axis.

Solid lines on the diagram are used to indicate an initial position. We will consider in turn three changes which disturb this equilibrium: an open market purchase, a reduction in reserve requirement ratios, and an increase in the public's demand for loans. Dotted lines have been used to indicate the position attained after the effects of the open market purchase on the credit market have been achieved.

Open market purchases raise the base and consequently expand the banks' demand for loans and securities, shifting L_b and I_b to the right and reducing interest rates on the loan and securities markets. In panel b, the decline in interest rates is magnified by the reduction in the stock supply of securities by the amount of the open market purchase. Securities are redistributed between the banks and the public in response to the changes in loan and securities rates, and the public's supply of loans to banks increases slightly. The interplay between the two markets continues until the rates i_{G2} and i_{L2} are established. At these rates, the outstanding volume of loans is L_2 and the banks hold an amount of securities equal to I_{b2}. The sum of these items is the increased stock of bank credit, E_{b2}, in panel c.

However, since interest rates fall, the issuing quotient increases and the line in panel c rotates to the left. The total response of the money supply is thus made up of two components. One expresses changes which are directly proportional to the change in bank credit; the other results from the operation of interest rates on the issuing quotient. In the particular case considered, the change is larger for money than for bank credit. More generally, the analysis suggests that the elasticity of the money supply with respect to open market operations exceeds the corresponding c'asticity for bank credit.[9] This is a consequence of the smaller interest elasticity for the money supply than for bank credit.

Let us now consider the effect of an increase in the public's supply of loans to commercial banks, L_p. Interest rates rise on both markets. Since the reduc-

[9]Relative rates of change in money and bank credit differ substantially at different phases of the cycle. The hypothesis explains the mechanism generating these differences.

tion in the banks' securities portfolio is smaller than the increase in loans, total bank credit expands just as it did in response to an open market purchase. This time, however, the effect on the money supply (panel *c*) is not amplified by an increase in the issuing quotient. Instead, the issuing quotient falls, since interest rates have increased, and the line in panel *c* rotates to the right. The effect on the money supply of an expanded stock of bank credit remains positive but is less than proportional to the change in bank credit.

The opposite result is obtained if the initial change is assumed to be an increase in the public's demand for securities, I_p. Interest rates fall in response to the increased demand for the given stock of debt. The issuing quotient rotates to the left, and the money supply rises by more than the proportion indicated by the initial value of β.

Our argument may be summarized as follows: Credit market changes that induce changes in interest rates in the opposite direction affect the money supply more than bank credit. Open market operations, other changes in the base, or changes in the demand for securities have this effect. Variations in loan demand or in the stock of securities induce movements of interest rates in the same direction. Consequently, these variations have a larger effect on bank credit than on money.

What is the effect of the public's currency behavior and of other policy instruments on money and credit? Analysis suggests that there are partially compensating influences on the issuing quotient. A reduction in the reserve requirement ratios or in the rediscount rate induces an increase in the banks' portfolio and lowers interest rates in panels *a* and *b*. In panel *c*, the effect is the same as in the case of an open market purchase. Money and bank credit expand along the existing issuing quotient, and the issuing quotient rotates to the left, increasing the rate of monetary expansion. But now there is an additional effect. The issuing quotient depends, by construction, on the reserve requirement ratios, the discount rate, etc. Reductions in the reserve requirement ratios and in the discount rate cause the line to rotate to the right, offsetting, at least in part, the movement induced by the decline in interest rates.

The diagrams do not yield information about the net effect of policies that change both interest rates and other components of the issuing quotient. However, solutions for the money supply and bank credit in terms of the policy variables and the parameters can be obtained from the preceding analysis. The volume of bank credit, E, and the stock of money, M, are expressed in the equations below as the product of a multiplier and the adjusted base. Parentheses are used to indicate the dependence of the multipliers on the interest rates, the rediscount rate and the parameters introduced earlier.[10]

---

[10]In these equations,

$$m = \frac{1 + k}{(r-b)\,(1+t+d) + k} \quad \text{and} \quad a = \frac{(1+t+d)\,[1-(r-b)]}{(r-b)\,(1+t+d) + k}$$

$$M = m(\ )B^a; E = a(\ )B^a$$

In some previous work, we have demonstrated that the interest elasticity of the monetary multiplier is less than the interest elasticity of the bank credit multiplier and that both elasticities are positive (Brunner and Meltzer, 1968). By combining the interest elasticities of the two multipliers with the response of the multipliers to changes in the reserve requirement ratios (or other parameters), some information about the direction of change in the issuing quotient can be obtained. The elasticities of the money supply and bank credit with respect to policy variables have been collected in table A.2 of the appendix. Items 3 and 4 of the table show the responses to the reserve requirement ratios and other parameters. Each response is expressed as a combination of the simple response in the money or bank credit multiplier and the modification introduced by the operation of the interest mechanism.

The simple or direct responses of the multipliers are negative. While these elasticities are attenuated by the interest mechanism, the direction of change in money and credit is not reversed. Both money and bank credit are affected negatively by changes in the requirement ratios, the rediscount rate and the currency ratio.

To obtain the direction of change in the issuing quotient, β, the elasticies have been rearranged in table A.2. The effect on β is equal to the difference between the responses in M and in E. This difference is shown on line 5 of the table. The hypothesis implies, as the discussion of figure 2.2 suggested, that changes in the base have a larger effect on money than on bank credit. This suggests that other policy operations also have larger effects on money than on bank credit and that the issuing quotient increases when the reserve requirement ratios or the discount rate are reduced. However, the second component on line 5 is the difference between the direct elasticities of the credit and money multipliers. Both are negative, but the asset elasticity is numerically larger than the monetary elasticity. Thus the second term on line 5 affects the issuing quotient in the direction opposite to the first. On balance, the issuing quotient moves very little. It follows that bank credit is comparatively more sensitive to requirement and discount policy than to variations in the base.

Additional inspection of table A.2 shows three distinct patterns, one for the base, one for the parameters operating directly on the multipliers and one for the variables that work neither through the base nor the multipliers. In the absence of the interest mechanism, the elasticities of money and credit with respect to the base would be unity. The interest mechanism attenuates

---

Hence, the issuing quotient, β, is

$$\frac{m}{a} = \frac{1 + k}{(1+t+d)\,[1-(r-b)]}$$

the size of these elasticities and makes the elasticity larger for the money supply than for bank credit. In our discussion of the effect of changes in reserve requirement ratios, we noted that the interest mechanism also reduced the elasticity of money and credit with respect to policies operating through the multipliers. These elasticities are approximately equal for money and credit and are substantially smaller than the elasticities with respect to the base.

The third pattern in table A.2 is exemplified by the elasticities with respect to the outstanding stock of securities, but similar solutions are obtained for variables like expected income, Y_e, which do not operate through the base or the multiplier. Bank credit is more responsive to these variables than the money supply, but both elasticities are substantially smaller than the elasticities with respect to the base. The reason is that each is multiplied by the interest elasticity of the appropriate multiplier. Preliminary investigations suggest that these interest elasticities are substantially below one-half. It follows that variations in the public's demand for loans or the government's fiscal policy exert a comparatively small effect on the volume of bank credit and money.

Additional implications of credit market behavior and their influence on the money supply can be obtained from the hypothesis. Analysis of the effects of interest rates on the time deposit ratio, for example, furnishes a useful clarification of some developments in the United States during recent years. More detailed consideration of the response of money and bank credit to changes in the currency ratio reveals the precise effects of increases in the demand for currency that are important for understanding US monetary history. Discussion of these problems has been deferred, however, to permit more detailed examination of two puzzling features of recent monetary history.

5 Money Stock and Interest Rates under the Support Program: Explanation of the First Puzzle

Detailed concern about stable interest rates was not an alien commitment imposed on the Federal Reserve by the Treasury. Monetary policy had been greatly influenced by such concern at least since 1937. The constraint imposed in 1942, however, formalized the obligation and removed discretionary authority from the Federal Reserve for almost ten years. The accord of March 1951 ended the Federal Reserve's obligation to maintain particular yields on Treasury securities.

There are two quite distinct phases during the support period. Both the money supply and the adjusted base grew at a rapid rate during the war, while in the postwar period both exhibited sharply declining growth rates which became negative for a time in 1948–9. Both accelerated in the second half of 1950 following the outbreak of the Korean War. Thus the support policy appears to have been "an engine of inflation" during both wars but not during the postwar readjustment.

Many of the consequences of the support policy can be investigated within the framework developed in previous sections. Some modification is required, however, since the support policy imposes a constraint on the operation of the credit market. This constraint takes the form of an inequality. If the market-determined rate on government securities is higher than the ceiling rate set by the authorities, the ceiling rate is effective. The yield on government securities remains at the ceiling and is, therefore, a predetermined variable. The adjusted base becomes an endogenous variable determined by the support policy and the operation of the monetary system.[11] If the market-determined yield of government securities is less than the ceiling rate, the patterns discussed in the preceding sections apply. The base remains exogenous and the credit market elasticities shown in tables A.1 and A.2 are applicable.

Even if the interest rates had been substantially below the ceiling rates at the start of the war, they would not have remained there. The large budget deficit increased the upward pressure on interest rates generated by expanding income and a higher currency ratio. Increases in the reserve requirement ratios, under these circumstances, would not abate inflationary pressure, since such increases would accelerate the approach of i_G to the ceiling rate. However, increases in the base would operate to keep interest rates below the ceiling.

The initial choice of the ceiling rate, the large budget deficit, and the increased demand for currency made the constraint operative early in the war. The system was transformed to one in which the ceiling rate was effective and the responses were altered. Some of the elasticities that are of interest have been collected in table A.3 of the appendix.

Much of the war was financed by government deficits. The table shows that the elasticity of the base with respect to the debt (line 1) is positive. The larger the debt, the greater is the increase in the base. Moreover, this elasticity contains the ratio of total outstanding securities to the banks' holdings of securities, S/S_b. Sales of debt to the public rather than to the banks, therefore, raised this elasticity. Whatever anti-inflationary effect was achieved by

---

[11]The formal properties of the system do not require that the base becomes endogenous. Any of the exogenous variables – S, r^d, r^t, etc – would satisfy the formal requirement. The choice of the adjusted base results from supplementary considerations. Had S been chosen, fiscal policy would become dependent. The budget would have to be continuously readjusted. During part of the period, "tap" securities permitted the private sector to call forth issues of government debt. But the public was given no means of reducing the deficit. Under the circumstances, the base seems a more likely choice than S. Similar considerations apply to the reserve requirement ratios. The choice of these variables or the rediscount rate would require their continuous adjustment or violation of the constraint.

such sales through reduction in the public's propensity to spend was offset, at least in part, by the increased elasticity of the base.

In the absence of a support policy, increases in the desired currency ratio, the discount rate and reserve ratios lower the money supply and have no effect on the base. The support policy substantially changed the monetary effect of changes in these parameters. The increased wartime demand for currency raised both the base and the money supply, but raised the former more than the latter. Discount policy was adjusted to the support program. The discount rate was maintained at a relatively low level and preferential borrowing rates were introduced. These served to reduce the growth rate of the base. Their elimination early in the postwar period and the subsequent increase in the discount rates worked in the opposite direction. Under the support policy, increases in the discount rate have a slightly expansive effect on the base and the money supply.

Required reserve ratios were changed several times during the period. In 1942, the average ratio was lowered slightly. Had the support policy not been in effect, the reduction would have lowered interest rates on the loan market. Under the support policy, they had no direct effect an loan rates; instead, they had the effect of reducing the growth rate of the base. Postwar increases in the reserve requirement ratios, of course, had the opposite effect. It is not surprising, therefore, to find that the contractive effect of each of the increases in reserve requirement ratios in 1948 was rather rapidly offset by increases in the base.[12]

The principal explanations of the inflationary experience during the early years of the support policy are given by the behavior of the currency ratio and the budget deficit. Both increased substantially during the war. Minor reductions in the average requirement ratio or introduction of a preferential lending rate on securities had only a slight effect in the opposite direction, an effect that was far from sufficient to reverse the expansion in the money supply.

The same variables – Treasury deficit and currency ratio – explain the puzzling features of postwar monetary policy. Shortly after the war, the deficit was replaced by a substantial surplus, and the currency ratio fell sharply. Each of these induced a decline in the growth rate of the base and the money supply. The budget surplus and the decline in the currency ratio pushed market rates to the ceiling rate and thus permitted the Federal Reserve to decelerate the monetary base. Given the Federal Reserve's traditional concern for "orderly money market conditions," deceleration of the base was a response to the absence of pressure from market rates on the ceiling rate.

---

[12]For a more detailed discussion of the timing and magnitude of the offsetting movements in the base, see Brunner and Meltzer, 1964b, p. 66.

The return to an inflationary monetary policy after the start of the Korean War can be explained in much the same way. The budget surplus was replaced by a deficit, and the downward adjustment of the currency ratio was completed. The slack in the system disappeared, so that the base was pulled up by the renewed market pressures. The Federal Reserve continued to respond to these pressures until fears of inflation encouraged them to demand and eventually to exercise renewed authority.

6   A Brief Digression on Recent Policy

Recent monetary history has produced a mirror image of the constrained system just discussed. Treasury and Federal Reserve concern for the balance of payments position and the outflow of gold encouraged them to seek policies that would prevent interest rates from falling. Despite substantial unemployment in 1961, expansionary monetary policy was regarded as inappropriate. Domestic expansion was to be achieved by fiscal policy. According to Federal Reserve descriptions, their policy would seek to improve the balance of payments positions by slightly increasing monetary restraint.

We accept the description of fiscal policy. The characterization of monetary policy, however, is quite misleading. From 1962 to 1965, the monetary base grew at the fastest rate since World War II. Moreover, this growth rate was achieved by the expansion of the Federal Reserve's portfolio of securities. Never before has the Federal Reserve engineered a growth rate of similar size and duration in peacetime. Yet, the yield on government securities has not declined.

The key to an understanding of recent monetary experience is provided by the constraint on interest rates. The ceiling on interest rates imposed during the war has been replaced by a floor. The constraint, therefore, works in the opposite direction. If the market-determined rate is above the floor, the constraint is inoperative, and the elasticities of interest rates are those shown in table A.1. Whenever the market rate becomes less than the minimum rate, the base must be reduced, or some other policy must be introduced, to raise interest rates. If the base becomes endogenous, the constraint becomes effective and the elasticities in table A.3 are again applicable.

Without the substantial tax reduction and the resulting increase in the deficit, sustained expansion of the base would have been inconsistent with the floor on interest rates. Fiscal policy, therefore, permitted an expansionary monetary policy of record proportion. By increasing the upward pressure on interest rates, fiscal policy permitted the base to expand while the floor on interest rates was maintained.

The currency ratio and the public's demand for loans contributed to the admissible rate of expansion in the base. The currency ratio has increased persistently since 1961, and banks have expanded their loan portfolios substantially during the period. Both movements operated to raise interest rates and thereby permitted an acceleration of the growth rate of the base.

7 The Divergence of Actual from Stated Policy: Explanation of the Second Puzzle

A second puzzling feature of US monetary policy is the frequent divergence between the policies pursued by the Federal Reserve and their interpretation of these actions. The period since 1962 provides an excellent example. Policies have been described as "less easy" despite acceleration of bank credit, of the Federal Reserve's securities portfolio and the monetary base.

An explanation of the divergence between actual and stated policy requires some understanding of the various roles assigned to free reserves in the Federal Reserve's view of the monetary mechanism and the role that is implicit in the theory developed here.[13] The Federal Reserve has assigned an important, causal position to free reserves – excess reserves minus member bank borrowing – since the 1920s. High levels of free reserves are said to induce low interest rates, expansion of bank credit, and conversely. In this role, free reserves are viewed as the center of the mechanism connecting monetary policy to the stocks of money and bank credit. On occasion, free reserves are used also as the target of monetary policy. Open market operations are conducted so that free reserves are kept at a prescribed level or within a specified range. In their third role, free reserves are taken as an indicator of monetary policy and of the position of the bank credit market. Movements of free reserves are interpreted as changes in the extent of "money market pressure." A reduction in free reserves is interpreted as a sign of increased pressure on the banks and a slowing of the rate of credit expansion. Higher levels of free reserves are viewed as an indication of an "easier" policy, one designed to expand the pace of economic activity; lower free reserve levels are treated as a sign of "tighter" policy.

Our analysis denies that there is a close association between levels of free reserves and the direction of monetary policy. It suggests that there is no unique association between movements of free reserves and changes in the rate of monetary or credit expansion. The role of free reserves is implicit in the analysis that has been presented. The desired reserve ratio, r, and the desired borrowing ratio, b, were introduced in an earlier section. The reserve ratio includes the ratio of excess reserves to total deposits, e, as one com-

---

[13]While there is not a uniform "Federal Reserve view" accepted by all members of the Federal Open Market Committee, there is a strong tendency to discuss or analyze the monetary situation in terms of free reserves. For more detail on this and related points, see Brunner and Meltzer, 1964a. See also Meigs, 1962 and Dewald, 1963.

ponent. The difference between the desired excess reserve and borrowing ratios, $e-b$, is the desired free reserve ratio. The dependence of e and b on interest rates and the discount rate determines a corresponding dependence for the free reserve ratio. The interest elasticity of the free reserve ratio is negative and appears to be substantially greater than unity.

A solution for the level of free reserves, denoted F, may be obtained from the equations of the system. The equation below expresses this solution as the product of the adjusted base, B^a, and a proportionality factor, Θ. Parentheses are used to indicate that Θ is not a constant but depends on the ratios r, b, t, and k and hence on interest rates, the discount rate, the reserve requirement ratios, etc.

$$F = \Theta(\ )B^a$$

The desired level of free reserves has been drawn as a function of the yield on securities, i_G, in figure 2.3. The curve has a negative slope. Its position depends on the base and the parameters included in Θ. Given the values of the base and the parameters, there exists a value of i_G for which $\Theta = 0$ and hence $F = 0$. At higher rates Θ and F become increasingly negative and at lower rates increasingly positive. Changes in the base, in the loan rate, in the ceiling rate on time deposits, and in the other parameters change the position of the free reserve relation in a manner determined by the above equation.

The diagram clarifies the effect of monetary policy and other events on the volume of free reserves. The solid line is the initial position of the free reserves function. An open market operation expands the base and the stock of bank credit. (See figure 2.2 for the effect on loans and investments and the

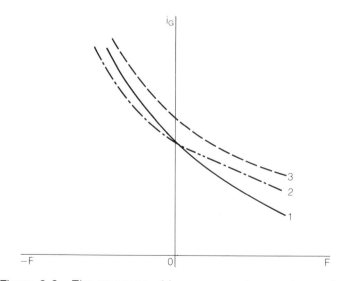

Figure 2.3   The response of free reserves to monetary policy.

credit markets). The free reserve curve rotates around its intersection point on the i_G axis as a result of the increase in the base. The slope becomes flatter as shown by curve 2 of the diagram. The reduction in loan rates resulting from the expansion of bank credit, however, shifts the curve up and to the right. The new curve, labelled 3 in the diagram, is flatter and has a higher intersection point on the i_G axis. The volume of free reserves in the banking system is higher after the open market operation. Similar results are obtained when other sources of the base expand. Open market sales, or other reductions in the base, reduce the volume of free reserves.

Reduction in the reserve requirement ratios or the discount rate raise the free reserve level. Both policy actions lower interest rates since they induce increases in L_b and I_b. Furthermore, these policies alter the value of Θ and raise the position of the curve in figure 2.3. The upward shift of the curve is thus the result of two forces: the direct effect on Θ of the lower requirement ratios or lower rediscount rate, and of the lower interest rate on the loan market.

Fiscal policies exert an effect on the volume of free reserves opposite to the effect of monetary policies. Sales of government securities to finance a deficit raise interest rates on the securities market. The higher rates on securities spill over to the loan market. Free reserves therefore fall for two reasons. First, increases in i_G involve a movement along the curve in figure 2.3 in the direction of higher values of i_G. Second, higher loan rates shift the curve to the left and thus lower the intersection point. On the other hand, a Treasury surplus used to retire outstanding debt raises the free reserve level.

Thus changes in the level of free reserves are not necessarily an indication of changes in monetary policy. They may result from fiscal policies. Moreover, monetary and fiscal policies are not the only influences on free reserves. All of the variables in the public's loan and securities demand functions affect the level of free reserves.[14] These variables enter as determinants of interest rates on the credit market. The relatively high interest elasticity of free reserves suggests that their effect on free reserves is not negligible.

The frequent divergence between actual and alleged policy can be traced to two sources: (1) the Federal Reserve's inappropriate choice of free reserves as an indicator, and (2) the sensitivity of free reserves to the operation of non-policy variables. In particular, free reserves respond substantially to changes in the factors affecting the public's loan-demand or stock demand for securities. Suppose that the public's supply of loans to banks, L_p, shifts in response to forces arising from the income process. If, for some reason, L_p

---

[14]This statement applies to the money supply and bank credit as well. But there are substantial differences in the effect on money, bank credit and free reserves. These differences depend primarily on the interest elasticities of M, E, and F. The effect of changes in the loans or securities demand on money and bank credit are damped by an interest elasticity substantially below unity. The interest elasticity of free reserves appears to be above unity.

declines relative to L_b, interest rates decline and free reserves increase. The Federal Reserve interprets this as an increase in "ease." In our framework, the increased free reserves are viewed as a part of the financial adjustment. If the base and policy parameters have not changed, monetary policy has not changed.

Or, assume that the growth rate of the base falls substantially as it did in 1952-3 and in 1958-9. The retardation in L_b and I_b is gradually distributed through the economy. Interest rates rise and free reserves fall markedly. The Federal Reserve correctly infers that policy is more restrictive. But after a lag of several quarters, economic activity reaches a peak and starts to decline. The public's supply of loans falls relative to the banks' demand and may even be reduced. Interest rates fall and the level of free reserves rises. Interpretations of policy based on the level of free reserves suggest that policy has become easier. The Federal Reserve may respond by further reducing the growth rate of the base through open market sales. Such interpretations are incorrect and delay appropriate action, since the Federal Reserve is convinced by the free reserve indicator that appropriate action has been taken.

The lag between turning points in economic activity and changes in Federal Reserve policy has recently been studied by Kareken and Solow (1963). They attribute the delay at turning points to a "recognition lag" and suggest that the Federal Reserve is slow to act at turning points. But if the Federal Reserve interprets increases in free reserves as an indication of easier policy, movements in bank credit or maximum earning assets are not a useful measure of the timing of policy changes. The misinterpretation of the rising (or falling) volume of free reserves induces a fall (rise) in the growth rate of the base and hence in money and bank credit. This occurs even if there is speedy recognition of turning points and cannot be attributed to a long delay in recognition of the need for action.

Appendix 2.1

Table A.1   Elasticities of interest rates with respect to policy variables: $\epsilon(x, y)$ denotes the elasticity of x with respect to y

$$\epsilon(i_G, B^a) = \frac{-\epsilon(a_2, i_L) + \epsilon(a_1, i_L) + \epsilon(s_1, i_L) + \epsilon(s_2, i_L)}{\Delta} < 0$$

$$\epsilon(i_L, B^a) = \frac{-\epsilon(a_1, i_G) + \epsilon(a_2, i_G) - \epsilon(s_1, i_G) - \epsilon(s_2, i_G)}{\Delta} < 0$$

$$\epsilon(i_G, S) = \frac{\epsilon(a_2, i_L) - \epsilon(s_2, i_L)}{\Delta} \cdot \frac{S}{S - S_p} > 0$$

$$\epsilon(i_L, S) = -\frac{\epsilon(a_2, i_G) - \epsilon(s_2, i_G)}{\Delta} \cdot \frac{S}{S - S_p} > 0$$

$$\Delta = \left[\epsilon(a_1, i_G) + \epsilon(s_1, i_G) \frac{S_p}{S - S_p} \right] [\epsilon(a_2, i_L) - \epsilon(s_2, i_L)]$$

$$- [\epsilon(a_2, i_L) - \epsilon(s_2, i_L)] \left[\epsilon(a_2, i_G) - \epsilon(s_2, i_G) \frac{S_p}{S - S_p} \right]$$

S_p = Stock of securities held by the public
a_1 = Banks' demand function for securities
a_2 = Banks' demand function for loan assets
s_1 = Public's demand function for securities
s_2 = Public's demand for loans from the banks
i_G = Interest rate on securities
i_L = Interest rate on loans

Table A.2   Elasticities of the money supply and bank credit

1. $\epsilon(M, B^a) = 1 + \epsilon(m, i_G) \epsilon(i_G, B^a) + \epsilon(m, i_L) \epsilon(i_L, B^a) < 1$

2. $\epsilon(E, B^a) = 1 + \epsilon(a, i_G) \epsilon(i_G, B^a) + \epsilon(a, i_L) \epsilon(i_L, B^a) < \epsilon(M, B^a)$

3. $\epsilon(M, x) = \epsilon(m, x) + \epsilon(m, i_G) \epsilon(i_G, x) + \epsilon(m, i_L) \epsilon(i_L, x) > \epsilon(m, x) < 0$

4. $\epsilon(E, x) = \epsilon(a, x) + \epsilon(a, i_G) \epsilon(i_G, x) + \epsilon(a, i_L) \epsilon(i_L, x) > \epsilon(a, x) < 0$

   for $x = r^d, r^t, \rho, k$;
   Note: $\epsilon(a, x) < \epsilon(m, x) < 0$

5. $\epsilon(m, x) - \epsilon(a, x) + [\epsilon(m, i_g) - \epsilon(a, i_g)] \epsilon(i_g, x) + [\epsilon(m, i_L) - \epsilon(a, i_L)] \epsilon(i_L, x)$

6. $\epsilon(M, S) = \epsilon(m, i_G) \epsilon(i_G, S) + \epsilon(m, i_L) \epsilon(i_L, S) > 0$

7. $\epsilon(E, S) = \epsilon(a, i_G) \epsilon(i_G, S) + \epsilon(a, i_L) \epsilon(i_L, S) > \epsilon(M, S)$

m = monetary multiplier
a = asset-multiplier
Both were defined in note 10

Table A.3   Elasticities of the base and the loan rate under an effective support policy

1. $\epsilon(B^a, S) = \dfrac{\epsilon(a_2, i_L) - \epsilon(s_2, i_L)}{[\epsilon(a_2, i_L) - \epsilon(s_2, i_L)] - [\epsilon(a_1, i_L) - \epsilon(s_1, i_L)]} \dfrac{S}{S - S_p} > 0$

2. $\epsilon(B^a, x) = - \epsilon(a_1, x) > 0$ since $\epsilon(a_1, x) = \epsilon(a_2, x)$
   for $x = r^d, r^t, \rho, k$

3. $\epsilon(i_L, S) = \dfrac{1}{\Delta} \dfrac{S}{S - S_p} > 0$

4. $\epsilon(i_L, x) = \dfrac{\epsilon(a_1, x) - \epsilon(a_2, x)}{\Delta} = 0$

5. $\epsilon(i_L, c) = \dfrac{\epsilon(a_1, i_G) + \epsilon(s_1, i_G) \dfrac{S_p}{S - S_p} - \epsilon(a_2, i_G) + \epsilon(s_2, i_G)}{\Delta} > 0$

Symbols are given at the bottom of table A.1
c = ceiling rate

References

Ando, A., E. C. Brown, J. Kareken and R. M. Solow. 1963. Lags in monetary policy. In *Stabilization Policies*. Englewood Cliffs, NJ: Prentice-Hall for the Commission on Money and Credit.

Brunner, K. and A. H. Meltzer. 1964a. *The Federal Reserve's Attachment to the Free Reserve Concept*. Washington: House Committee on Banking and Currency, pp. 37–47.

—— 1964b. *An Alternative Approach to the Monetary Mechanism*. Washington: House Committee on Banking and Currency, pp. 119–25.

—— 1964c. Some further investigations of demand and supply functions for money. *Journal of Finance*, May.

—— 1968. Liquidity traps for money, bank credit, and interest rates. *Journal of Political Economy* 76, 1–37.

Dewald, W. 1963. Free reserves, total reserves and monetary control. *Journal of Political Economy*, April.

Hester, D. 1962. *Empirical Examination of the Commercial Bank Loan Offer Function*. Yale Economic Essays.

Joint Committee on the Economic Report. 1952. *Monetary Policy and the Management of the Public Debt*. Washington: the Committee, part I, p. 357.

Meigs, A. J. 1962. *Free Reserves and the Money Supply*. Chicago: University of Chicago Press.

Metzler, L. 1948. Three lags in the circular flow of income. In *Employment and Public Policy: Essays in Honor of Alvin Hansen*. New York: W. W. Norton.

3

Liquidity Traps for Money, Bank Credit, and Interest Rates

Karl Brunner and Allan H. Meltzer

Few conclusions about economic events have been repeated as frequently or have had as much influence on economists' attitudes toward monetary policy as the assertion that the monetary system of the thirties was "caught in a liquidity trap." Empirical studies of the public's demand for money and the banks' demand for earning assets seemed to support the assertion about a trap and the closely related conclusion that monetary policy had no effect on output, employment, and prices during at least some part of the thirties.[1] Conclusions about the occurrence of a trap and the ineffectiveness of monetary policy were reinforced by central bankers' statements that likened monetary policy to "pushing on a string."[2] Taken together, the empirical evidence and the central bankers' interpretations convinced many economists that some form of a trap had existed (Keynes, 1936, p. 207; Fellner, 1948, pp. 81–3, 91–3; Villard, 1948, pp. 324, 334, 345; Shaw, 1950, pp. 283–5).[3]

There are a number of reasons for re-examining these conclusions and reopening the discussion of liquidity traps. First, recent empirical studies of the demand for money by Bronfenbrenner and Mayer (1960), Brunner and Meltzer (1963), and Meltzer (1963*a*) contradict the earlier finding that there was a "trap" in the public's demand for money during the thirties. Second,

This paper appeared in Journal of Political Economy 76 (Jan.–Feb.). Chicago: University of Chicago Press, 1968, pp. 1–37. Reprinted with permission. We acknowledge especially the detailed comments of Milton Friedman and Peter Frost on earlier drafts.
[1] On the trap in the demand for money, see Tobin (1947); for the trap in the banks' demand for earning assets, see Horwich (1963). The statement in the text might be modified to take account of the Pigou effect, but, as the Pigou effect is generally assumed to operate slowly and to be of little short-run significance, we will ignore it until the conclusion of the paper.

[2] One excellent example is the statement of Marriner Eccles before the House Banking and Currency Committee; part of the statement is reproduced in n.20 below.

[3] Some of the writers cited, Keynes (1936) in particular, did not regard a liquidity trap as an event that was likely to occur. For an early statement denying the implications of a trap, see Warburton (1950).

both the behavior of interest rates and the responses of the banking system to the doubling of reserve-requirement ratios in 1936–7 are inconsistent with an explanation based on some form of trap. Interest rates rose after the doubling of reserve-requirement ratios but declined to lower levels thereafter. Banks, attempting to restore their excess-reserve positions, reduced earning assets and the money supply in the process. The decline in long-term interest rates after 1938 contradicts the statement that interest rates reached a "floor"; the reduction of earning assets and the increase in excess reserves are difficult to reconcile with the notion that banks regarded excess reserves as a redundant surplus. Third, an alternative interpretation of the behavior of the banking system in the late thirties has been offered. This interpretation attributes the banks' large accumulation of excess reserves to inept and inappropriate Federal Reserve policies which shifted the relation between desired excess reserves and interest rates (Friedman and Schwartz, 1963; Brunner and Meltzer, 1964a, 1964b; Brunner, 1965; Frost, 1966).

Traps have been said to affect interest rates, the banks' demand for excess reserves, the public's supply of loans to commercial banks, and the public's demand for money.[4] Although each of these traps is said to prevent monetary policy from affecting output, employment, and prices, no attempt has been made to establish that conclusion for each of the traps. In most cases, the argument has not proceeded beyond the statement of an assumption that one or another elasticity is at an extreme value – zero or infinity.[5] Such assumptions may be insufficient for the conclusion that monetary policy becomes powerless or may conflict with other implications of monetary policy. It is desirable, therefore, to investigate the conditions for and implications of various liquidity traps as a part of the theory of money.

In this paper, we extend our recent work on the money supply (Brunner and Meltzer, 1964c, 1966) to discuss the interaction of money supply, bank credit, and interest rates. The following section outlines a theory of the

[4]Statements about the various traps are frequently not carefully separated. An example that is typical of the treatment in many textbooks is provided by Maisel (1957, pp. 457–8): "Even if money is expanded in a contraction, it may not be a powerful enough weapon to end a deflation. There may be a credit deadlock. Banks have in the past carried large excess reserves for long periods without expanding the money supply . . . If demand was lacking for other reasons, prospective borrowers would not borrow even if rates were cheap. A minimum interest rate will exist because of precautionary and institutional reasons. At this rate, investment may not be forthcoming.

"On the other hand, at some degree of liquidity people will probably spend . . . This point, however, may require improbable additions to the money supply." A more succinct statement is contained in Burstein (1963, p. 378).

[5]This is less true of the traps in the demand for money than for the traps affecting the banking system. See Modigliani (1944) or Klein (1947). For an indication that the traps have generally been stated in terms of elasticities, see Bronfenbrenner and Mayer (1963), Fellner (1948, p. 81), and Shaw (1950, pp. 285 and 325).

monetary process, more fully developed in the appendixes, and uses the theory to explain differences in the cyclical behavior of money and bank credit. We then derive necessary and sufficient conditions for most of the liquidity traps that have been mentioned in the literature and separate the traps into (1) those that are incompatible with the theory and must be rejected if the theory is correct and (2) those that depend on the sign or size of particular parameters. A discussion of some empirical findings and a conclusion complete the paper.

1   The Interaction of Money Supply, Bank Credit, and Interest Rates

Changes in the money supply and bank credit are used extensively as measures or indicators of the direction of monetary policy. Since money and bank credit often move in opposite directions or change at different rates, the two measures provide different information about the direction of policy.[6] Policy has been relatively more expansive during postwar recessions than during expansions when it is judged by changes in bank credit; it has been relatively more expansive during postwar periods of rising economic activity than during recessions when judged by changes in the stock of money. Although differences in the movements of money and bank credit appear to be systematic, no attempt has been made to link the two indicators in a theory of the money-supply process or to explain their divergent rates of change. This section outlines a framework that combines the banks' demand for earning assets (bank credit), the public's supply of earning assets to banks, the money supply, interest rates, and the monetary-policy variables. We use the theory to discuss a number of liquidity traps in the following section.

Three variables are used to summarize monetary policy: the weighted-average reserve-requirement ratio, the rediscount rate, and the adjusted monetary base – currency plus reserves minus member-bank borrowing from the Federal Reserve.[7] Allocation decisions of the banks and the public in response to interest rates, policy, and other variables proximately determine the equilibrium stocks of money and bank credit. The framework

---

[6]From the start of the Federal Reserve System to the end of World War II, the money supply expanded at a much greater rate than bank credit, so that the ratio of bank credit to money supply declined by 50 percent. From 1946 to 1964 this ratio moved in the opposite direction and rose by 50 percent, so that during the first 50 years of the Federal Reserve the ratio of bank credit to money supply declined by only 25 percent. During postwar half-cycles, the ratio of bank credit to money has generally fallen or grown less rapidly during periods of recovery and expansion and risen or grown more rapidly during cyclical recessions.

[7]The principal sources of changes in the adjusted base are open-market operations and gold flows. The sources of the base are described in appendix 3.2.

suggests some reasons for the observed differences in the short-run move-ments of the money supply and bank credit and in the information provided by some of the monetary variables that have been used frequently as indi-cators of the direction of monetary policy. Appendix 3.2 contains a more complete statement of the hypothesis and the underlying assumptions; a glossary of symbols is provided in appendix 3.1.

1.1 The Supply of Money and the Banks' Demand for Earning Assets[8]

Equations (3.1) and (3.2) express the quantity of money supplied (M_1 = currency and demand deposits) and the quantity of earning assets demanded by banks (E_b) as the product of the adjusted base (B^a) and a multiplier, m_1 or a. The multipliers are assumed to depend on an index of interest rates (i_e) representing yields on loans, government securities, and other earning assets included in the banks' portfolios; on the reserve-requirement ratios (r^d); and on other entities discussed in Appendix 3.2.

$$M_1 = m_1(i_e, r^d, \ldots)B^a. \tag{3.1}$$

$$E_b = a(i_e, r^d, \ldots)B^a. \tag{3.2}$$

Policy variables affect money and bank credit in two distinct ways, one direct, the other indirect. The direct effect of monetary policy is either (1) a change in the monetary (m_1) and earning-asset (a) multipliers resulting from a change in the reserve-requirement ratio or in the rediscount rate or (2) the change in the base due to open-market operations. The indirect effect is the change in m_1 and in a induced by the change in interest rates that results from the change in policy (that is, from the open-market operation, the change in a reserve-requirement ratio, etc.).

Interest rates are assumed to change the monetary and asset multipliers through three relations expressing desired ratios. (1) The ratio of desired excess reserves to total deposits is assumed to depend on market interest rates and on the rediscount rate. (2) A similar dependence is assumed for the ratio of the desired volume of member-bank borrowing to total deposits. The excess-reserve and borrowing ratios have been combined in a single ratio, the desired-free-reserve ratio, denoted f. (3) The index of market interest rates, the interest rates paid by banks on time deposits, and other variables (see appendix 3.2) affect the public's allocation of deposits between time and demand accounts. The ratio of time to demand deposits, t, summarizes this allocation. The dependence of the multipliers on interest rates results from

---

[8]This subsection is a brief restatement of the argument in appendix 3.2. The interested reader should refer to the appendix for a more complete definition of the multipliers and a more com-plete statement of the effect of policy changes on the stocks of money and bank credit.

their dependence on the f and t ratios and from the dependence of f and t on interest rates.[9]

If policy operations, changes in interest rates, and changes in other components of the monetary and asset multipliers (see appendix 3.2) had an equal effect on both multipliers, the ratio of bank credit to money, denoted β, would be constant. The differences in the size and direction of changes in bank credit and money discussed above indicate, however, that the ratio β varies over time. Since eqns (3.1) and (3.2) are multiplicative, they can be written in logarithmic form. After differentiation, differences in the rates of change E and M_1 can be expressed as differences in the elasticities of the multipliers with respect to the variables on which the multipliers depend. The effect of interest rates and other factors[10] on the difference in the relative rates of change of M_1 and E is shown in eqn (3.3), where $\epsilon(a, i_e)$ and $\epsilon(m_1, i_e)$ are the elasticities of the multipliers with respect to interest rates and $\epsilon(a, x)$ and $\epsilon(m_1, x)$ are elasticities of the multipliers with respect to other entities on which the multipliers depend. (The multipliers are discussed more fully below.)

$$\frac{dE}{E} - \frac{dM}{M} = [\epsilon(a, i_e) - \epsilon(m_1, i_e)]\frac{di_e}{i_e} + [\epsilon(a, x) - \epsilon(m_1, x)]\frac{dx}{x},$$

(3.3)

where $\epsilon(a, i_e) - \epsilon(m_1, i_e) = \epsilon(\beta, i_e)$. For the present, $\epsilon(\beta, i_e)$ is assumed to be positive. In the discussion of liquidity traps below, we will consider the implications of positive, negative, and zero values for this sum of elasticities.

1.2 Equilibrium on the Bank-Credit Market

Equilibrium on the market for bank credit requires that the volume of earning assets demanded by banks is matched by the volume of earning assets supplied to banks. The latter quantity (E_p) is the nominal value of loans

---

[9]The details of the f and t relations and assumptions about signs of derivatives are given in appendix 3.2, eqns (A2) and (A5). The position of f and t in the monetary and asset multipliers is shown in eqns (A6)–(A8), and the response of the multipliers to changes in f and t is given by eqns (A9)–(A13). A more complete discussion of the effect of interest rates on the multipliers appears in the text of a later section and in n. 28 below.

[10]Two problems that require further discussion are ignored at this point. (a) We will show below that the use of elasticities rather than derivatives has little if any bearing on the conclusions that we reach in this section or on the conclusions about liquidity traps in the following section. (b) Several variables on which the multipliers depend – the reserve-requirement ratios, the rediscount rate, etc. – are summarized by a variable, x, in eqn (3.3) of the text and are discussed more fully at eqn (3.5) of the text below. The hypothesis in appendix 3.2 implies that the elasticities of m_1 and a with respect to x are not uniformly proportional. Interest rates and some of the determinants included in x modify the comparative growth rates of bank credit and money.

obtained from banks and of the stock of government bonds sold to banks. In the process by which equilibrium is established, the outstanding stock of government securities is absorbed into the portfolios of the banks and the public; bank loans are extended or repaid; and interest rates are adjusted on bank loans, government securities, and other financial assets traded on the bank-credit market. A summary description of this process, encompassing a wide range of the public's financial behavior, is introduced as eqn (3.4).

$$E_p = s \left(i_e, \frac{Y}{Y_p}, \frac{W}{P_a}, p, n, i_o \right) ; \qquad (3.4)$$

$$s_1 < 0; \; s_2, \, s_3, \, s_4, \, s_5, \, s_6 > 0.$$

The sign of the derivative of the stock-supply function with respect to each of the arguments is stated below the equation. Numbers are used to refer to the position of the variable in the equation. The symbols E_p and i_e have been introduced above. The other symbols are used to represent the index of transitory income, Y/Y_p; the real stock of non-human wealth, including the stock of government debt outstanding, W/P_a; a price index, p, of current output; the yield on real capital, n; and an index of rates on financial assets not traded on the bank-credit market, for example, corporate bonds, i_o.[11]

From the bank-credit-market equations and the market-equilibrium condition, $E_p = E_b$, we can solve for i_e and for the equilibrium stock of bank credit, E. These equilibrium values depend, of course, on (1) the variables that enter the stock-supply equation, assumed to be predetermined relative to the bank-credit-market process; (2) the components of the earning-asset multiplier, a, such as the currency ratio and the reserve-requirement ratios; and (3) the adjusted monetary base. Once interest rates and the value of β are determined, the money stock is determined also.

Before proceeding to an algebraic statement of the solution on the bank-credit market and some implications of the hypothesis, the discussion to this point is summarized in a diagram. We will, then, relax the assumptions about the signs of the elasticities of the E_b, E_p, and β functions with respect to interest rates and consider the conditions for a number of liquidity traps. Figures 3.1 and 3.2 depict the simultaneous determination of the money supply (M_1), a value of the index of interest rates (i_e), and the stock of bank credit (E). The lines labeled E_b and E_p represent the banks' demand for earning assets, described by eqn (3.2), and the public's supply of assets to banks, eqn (3.4). The ratio of bank credit to money, β, is graphed on the right-hand panels.

---

[11]Strictly speaking, the condition $E_p = E_b$ requires that E_p be defined as the supply of earning assets net of Treasury deposits and net worth. The dependence of E_p on real wealth and prices separately should not suggest "money illusion" in the E_p function. We have written the equation in the most general way, since the analysis in this paper does not require more detailed discussion of the equation or assumptions about the homogeneity of the function.

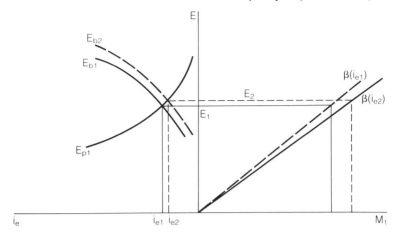

Figure 3.1   Change in equilibrium position after expansionary monetary policy. Solid lines show original positions, dashed lines new positions.

In figure 3.1, the bank-credit-market equilibrium is disturbed by expansive monetary policy, for example, an increase in the base or the reduction of a reserve-requirement ratio. Expansive policies increase the banks' demand for earning assets from the solid line E_{b1} to the dotted line E_{b2} and reduce interest rates on the bank-credit market. Interest rates fall from i_{e1} to i_{e2}, and the stock of bank credit rises from E_1 to E_2. Since $\epsilon(\beta, i_e)$ is assumed to be positive, β falls in response to the fall in interest rates, and the money supply rises by a larger percentage than bank credit to reach the new (partial) equilibrium position shown by the broken lines. The magnitude, but not the direction, of the change in β depends on the specific policy variable that is used to expand money and bank credit. A 1 percent change in B^a induces a larger change in the E_b curve and in i_e than a 1 percent change in a reserve-requirement ratio.

In figure 3.2 the public's supply of earning assets to banks is assumed to increase in response to a technological change that raises the yield on real capital. Such a change makes the public desire to borrow more from banks at each interest rate and/or to hold a smaller proportion of the outstanding stock of government securities. The E_p function shifts to the left along the E_b curve, raising interest rates to i_{e2} and the bank credit to E_2. This time the β line rotates to the left, since interest rates have increased, and the money supply expands relatively less than bank credit.

The diagrams suggest the importance of carefully interpreting the meaning of changes in M, E, and i_e. Expansive monetary policies induce a fall in interest rates and in β, the ratio of bank credit to money; increases in the public's supply of earning assets raise i_e and the ratio E/M_1. However, interest rates on the bank-credit market generally rise in periods of economic expansion and fall during recessions. We have noted elsewhere (Brunner and

Meltzer, 1964*b*) that changes in the base are procyclical rather than counter-cyclical on the average. If changes in the base had a dominant effect on i_e, i_e would fall in periods of economic expansion and rise in recessions, just the opposite of the observed movements.[12] On the other hand, if changes in i_e dominated the movements of E/M_1, the ratio would rise with i_e in expansions and fall in recessions, opposite to the observed movements of the ratio.

This discussion of interest rates and of the observed changes in policy variables suggests that the use of changes in interest rates as a measure of the current or recent direction of monetary policy is misleading. By interpreting the rise in interest rates as an indication of contractive policy, the policy-maker ignores the procyclical movements of the policy variables and attri-butes the rise in interest rates to policy action, rather than to the change in E_p resulting from variables (other than interest rates) in the E_p function. The growth rate of the money supply corresponds more closely to the growth rate of the policy variables than the growth rate of bank credit or changes in interest rates and more clearly reflects the procyclical movements of the policy variables. For this reason, the growth rate of the money supply is a better indicator of policy operations than changes in interest rates or the growth rate of bank credit, two variables often used as indicators by eco-nomists and policymakers (see Brunner and Meltzer, 1967).

1.3 Solutions for Interest Rates, Money, and Bank Credit

An explicit statement of the equilibrium condition underlying the diagrams is introduced in eqn (3.5). The equation shows that equilibrium on the bank-credit market depends on the factors listed above – interest rates, the variables other than interest rates in the public's asset-supply function, the adjusted base, and the variables on which the bank-credit multiplier, a, depends. The last group includes several symbols not previously discussed: r^d and r^t, the weighted-average reserve-requirement ratios for demand and time deposits; the currency ratio, k; and the rediscount rate, ρ.

$$a(i_e, r^d, r^t, k, \rho)B^a = s\left(i_e, \frac{Y}{Y_p}, \frac{W}{P_a}, p, n, i_o\right). \qquad (3.5)$$

Equation (3.5) may be solved for the index of interest rates on bank earn-ing assets (i_e).[13] Some of the responses of i_e to policy and other variables are

---

[12]The conclusion in the text must be qualified slightly. The effects of a procyclical policy are superimposed on movements of the β ratio generated by the components of the monetary and asset multipliers discussed in appendix 3.2. A pronounced procyclical policy remains visible in the accelerations or decelerations of the movements of the β ratio induced by other factors.

[13]Solutions for the components of the index i_e depend on other relations. For example, the solution for one component may be obtained from the demand and supply equations for loans, a second from the term structure of interest rates, etc. For more detailed discussion of the port-

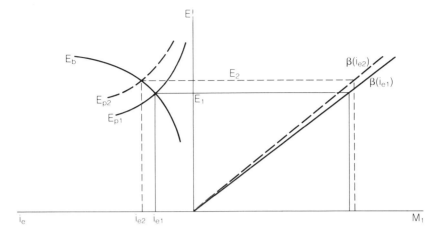

Figure 3.2   Change in equilibrium position after increase in the yield on real capital. Solid lines show original positions, dashed lines new positions.

expressed as elasticities in table 3.1. The details of the derivations are given in appendix 3.3.

The assumptions introduced earlier imply that each elasticity has a unique sign.[14] An increase in the base lowers i_e by an amount that depends inversely on the response of the banks and the public to interest rates. The larger the response of the banks' free-reserve ratio to interest rates, the larger is $\epsilon(a, i_e)$. And the larger $\epsilon(a, i_e)$ or the absolute value of $\epsilon(s, i_e)$ the smaller the response in interest rates to variations in the base or any of the other variables.

Table 3.1   Elasticities of the interest rate i_e with respect to some determinants of the volume of bank credit

$$\epsilon(i_e, B^a) = \frac{-1}{\epsilon(a, i_e) - \epsilon(s, i_e)} < 0 \qquad \epsilon(i_e, i_0) = \frac{\epsilon(s, i_0)}{\epsilon(a, i_e) - \epsilon(s, i_e)} > 0$$

$$\epsilon(i_e, r^d) = \frac{-\epsilon(a, r^d)}{\epsilon(a, i_e) - \epsilon(s, i_e)} > 0 \qquad \epsilon(i_e, n) = \frac{\epsilon(s, n)}{\epsilon(a, i_e) - \epsilon(s, i_e)} > 0$$

---

folio behavior of banks, see Hester (1962); for a discussion of the term structure of interest rates, see Meiselman (1962). We have discussed the determination of the components of i_e in more detail (Brunner and Meltzer, 1966).

[14]Evaluation of the rational expressions that are components of the numerators suggests the following order condition:

$$-\epsilon(i_e, B^a) > \epsilon(i_e, k) > \epsilon(i_e, r^d) > \epsilon(i_e, r^r).$$

See eqns (A14) and (A15) of appendix 3.2 for the components of the numerators.

A preliminary conclusion about one type of liquidity trap can be drawn from a discussion of the elasticities in table 3.1 by relaxing our previous assumptions about the slopes of the E_p and E_b functions. Suppose that, in some period, i_e was unaffected by monetary policy, that is, the denominator of $\epsilon(i_e, B^a)$ approached infinity, so that the effect of open-market operations or other policy changes on i_e approached zero. In this case, interest rates on the bank-credit market and other financial interest rates are unrelated, since $\epsilon(i_e, i_o)$ must approach zero also. A significant positive correlation between yields (i_e) on assets that banks traditionally buy (government bonds) and those that banks do not generally buy (corporate bonds) would be inconsistent with this type of liquidity trap under our hypothesis. In fact, the yields are positively correlated during the period in which the trap is most often said to have occurred, so the data support our hypothesis about the slopes of E_p and E_b and deny the existence of a trap of this kind.[15]

To analyze other liquidity traps that affect the supply and the demand functions for money or bank credit, we require a solution relating the money supply to interest rates and to the determinants of the equilibrium stock of bank credit. Equation (3.1) expressed the dependence of the money multiplier, m_1, on i_e. If the solution for i_e from eqn (3.5) is substituted in eqn (3.1), the money supply becomes dependent on the variables in the E_p and E_b equations. The solution for the money supply then expresses the interaction of the money supply, bank credit, and interest rates on the bank-credit market. It is the analytic foundation for the solution pictured on the right side of figures 3.1 and 3.2. The equilibrium solution for the money supply plus time deposits, M_2, is obtained in the same way. The procedure used to obtain these solutions is described more fully in appendix 3.3.

The elasticities of the monetary variables – M_1, M_2, E – with respect to each of the predetermined variables of the money–bank-credit process are derived from the solution equations. Some of these elasticities are shown in table 3.2. Each contains a factor $q_j(j=1,2,3)$ defined at the bottom of table 3.2 and obtained as a part of the solution process just described. The components of the q_j are interest elasticities of the monetary and asset multipliers and of the public's supply of assets to banks. (See sec. B of appendix 3.3 for the derivation of the q_j.)

A brief explanation will clarify the role of the q_j. If an open-market opera-

[15]Monthly interest-rate data from January, 1935, to December, 1939, were used for the correlations. The simple correlation between long-term government bonds and corporate bonds is 0.74 for the period. The partial correlation between the two yields given the bill rate is 0.70. Bill rates have a simple correlation of 0.46 with corporate bonds and 0.78 with long-term government bonds. Partial-correlation coefficients for bill yields were not computed. These results can be compared to the correlations using annual data for 1919–41 and 1952–8. From the annual data, the correlation between government bonds and corporate bonds is 0.91, the correlation between bills and government bonds is 0.81; and between bills and corporate bonds it is 0.85.

Table 3.2   Some elasticities of the monetary variables with respect to some variables of the money-credit process

With respect to	Elasticity of		
	M_1	M_2	E
B^a	$1 - q_1$	$1 - q_2$	$1 - q_3$
r^d	$\epsilon(m_1, r^d)(1 - q_1\alpha)$	$\epsilon(m_2, r^d)(1 - q_2\alpha)$	$\epsilon(a, r^d)(1 - q_3)$
n	$\epsilon(s, n)q_1$	$\epsilon(s, n)q_2$	$\epsilon(s, n)q_3$
i_0	$\epsilon(s, i_0)q_1$	$\epsilon(s, i_0)q_2$	$\epsilon(s, i_0)q_3$

Definitions of the q_j and α:

$$q_1 = \frac{\epsilon(m_1, i_e)}{\epsilon(a, i_e) - \epsilon(s, i_e)}; \quad q_2 = \frac{\epsilon(m_2, i_e)}{\epsilon(a, i_e) - \epsilon(s, i_e)}; \quad q_3 = \frac{\epsilon(a, i_e)}{\epsilon(a, i_e) - \epsilon(s, i_e)}; \quad \alpha = \frac{m_2}{a} > 1.$$

The interpretation of the q_j is discussed in the text below.

tion had no effect on interest rates, the monetary multipliers (m_1, m_2, and a) would be unaffected by open-market operations, the q_j would be zero, and the elasticity of each of the monetary variables (M_1, M_2, and E) with respect to the base would be unity. Since open-market operations affect interest rates and since the multipliers depend on interest rates, there is a feedback through interest rates to the monetary and asset multipliers and to E_p. Hence there is a feedback to M_1, M_2, and E. If the q_j are between zero and one, the feedback reduces the response of the monetary variables to changes in the policy variables, and the elasticities with respect to the base fall from 1 to $1-q_j$. At values of $q_j = 1$, changes in the base have no effect on money and bank credit.

The values of the q_j, therefore, have an important role in our discussion of several types of liquidity traps. By assuming that the $q_j = 0$, we can examine the implications of the type of liquidity trap under which monetary policy affects the stocks of money and bank credit (but not via interest rates); by assuming that all (or some) of the $q_j = 1$, we can investigate the implications of a trap under which changes in the base affect i_e but not the stocks of money and/or bank credit.[16]

[16]Some additional points should be noted: (a) The denominators of the q_1 are equal to $-\epsilon(i_e, B^a)$ and hence are positive by previous assumption. (b) Until these assumptions are modified below, q_3 is assumed to be a proper fraction. (c) Previous assumptions that determined the direction in which the β line in figures 3.1 and 3.2 rotated make $q_3 > q_1$ but do not make q_1 positive. This subject will be discussed in the following section. (d) Values of the q_j greater than unity imply that open-market purchases reduced the monetary variables and that open-market sales increase them.

2   The Conditions for Various Liquidity Traps

Although there is widespread agreement that monetary policy lost "effectiveness" in the thirties, substantial disagreement exists about the reason for the change. Some type of liquidity trap is often suggested as an explanation, but there is little agreement about the type of trap that is said to have occurred. Two main lines of argument are advanced: one asserts that a trap occurred in the demand for money; the second suggests that a trap operated within the banking system either because the banks desired to hold excess reserves and were unwilling to lend or because the public was unwilling to borrow. Agreement appears to be limited to the propositions that interest rates reached – or approached – a "floor" at which some interest elasticity became – or approached – zero or infinity and that monetary policy became powerless to restore full employment (see US Congress, 1935; Klein, 1947; Tobin, 1947; Fellner, 1948; Villard, 1948; and Horwich, 1963).

In this section we consider some of the traps that have been suggested. To analyze the many different statements about the effect of traps, we separate the traps into categories called "absolute" or "asymptotic," "complete" or "partial." If some elasticity is assumed to approach, but not reach, a critical value, the trap is called "asymptotic"; if the critical value is reached, the trap is "absolute." Traps for the money supply or bank credit are said to be "complete" if money or bank credit does not respond to any policy action. "Partial" traps occur if some policy actions become ineffective while others remain capable of inducing changes in the monetary variables. Various combinations are possible; for example, a complete or partial trap may be either absolute or asymptotic.

If the money supply and bank credit responded identically to changes in the policy variables, a trap for one of the monetary variables would, of course, imply a trap for the other. The equality of response of money and bank credit to policy operations is often described as a consequence of the balance sheet of the banking system. Money and credit are regarded as "two sides of a coin."[17] Yet our earlier analysis of the ratio of bank credit to money, β, showed that changes in policy and in predetermined variables induce changes in interest rates and in β. The analysis of this section shows that the equality of relative responses of bank credit and money to policy variables is a part of the necessary and sufficient conditions for some versions of the trap. A denial of the conditions required for equality of the relative responses of the monetary variables is often sufficient, therefore, to deny particular types of liquidity traps.

---

[17]See the response to a written question submitted to Federal Reserve officials (US Congress, 1961) and the discussion of this subject in Brunner and Meltzer (1964b).

While the discussion cannot rule out or even consider all possible traps, it suggests strongly that a trap is most unlikely to occur if our hypothesis is true. The truth of the hypothesis is assumed provisionally throughout this section, and all of the standard slope properties in appendixes 3.2 and 3.3 are assumed to remain operative unless explicitly repealed. Empirical support for the theory is presented in a later section.

2.1 Absolute Traps for Interest Rates, Money, and Bank Credit

Necessary and sufficient conditions for six absolute liquidity traps are listed in table 3.3. Four of the traps are rejected because they conflict with some part of the theory developed in the appendixes and discussed in the previous section. One cannot be rejected without empirical evidence. And one pair of partial traps (row 6) is in an intermediate position; some sets of conditions that imply these traps conflict with the theory; others require empirical evidence. After discussing the six absolute traps, we will consider some asymptotic traps briefly.

When discussing the elasticities in table 3.1, we showed that a trap for interest rates, proximately determined on the bank-credit market, cannot be

Table 3.3   Summary of the principal absolute liquidity traps

Type of trap	Necessary and sufficient condition	Conclusion	Reason
1 Interest rate on bank-credit market	$\epsilon(i_e, B^a) = 0$	Reject	Impossible. $\epsilon(i_e, B^a)$ can approach but not equal zero
2 Complete monetary	$q_1 = q_2 = q_3 = \alpha = 1$	Reject	Definition of α; $\alpha = 1$ if and only if the base equals zero
3 Complete money supply	$q_1 = \alpha = 1$	Reject	Definition of α
4 Complete bank credit	$\epsilon(s, i_e) = 0$	Obtain empirical evidence	Condition is contrary to assumption of "standard" slope properties but does not involve any other contradiction
5 Demand for money	$\epsilon(i^*, B^a) = 0$ and $\epsilon(i^*, r^d) = 0$	Reject	Definition of α. See Table 4 and text
6 Base trap for both money and bank credit or for money alone	$q_1 = q_3 = 1$ or $q_1 = 1$	Reject or obtain empirical evidence	Several sets of assumptions considered; some cases rejected; others depend on particular signs for parameters

absolute, since $\epsilon(i_e, B^a)$ cannot equal zero (table 3.3, row 1). The reason is that the elasticities of the E_p and E_b functions are not infinite.[18] In principle, these elasticities may *approach* infinity and cause $\epsilon(i_e, B^a)$ to *approach* zero. The data for the thirties, however, deny that this occurred, since the evidence suggests that interest rates on assets purchased by banks remained correlated with interest rates on other financial assets, contrary to the implication of this trap.

The denial of a trap for interest rates on bank earning assets shows that some interest rates can always be reduced by expansive policy action. Rejection of this trap denies that interest rates reached an absolute "floor" in the thirties, a conclusion that is common to most of the assertions that some type of trap existed. These conclusions do not depend on the choice of a particular interest rate or on the assumption of constant elasticities. The same conclusions are reached if the analysis is stated in terms of slopes: the derivative of i_e with respect to B^a cannot possibly be zero in a banking system that holds earning assets.[19]

However, the fact that interest rates can always be reduced by expansive monetary policy does not establish that such policies must expand bank credit and the money supply. Row 2 of table 3.3 shows a necessary and sufficient condition for a trap affecting all of the monetary variables, the complete monetary trap. If the monetary system is in this trap, the monetary authority can do nothing to increase or decrease the stocks of money and bank credit; M_1, M_2 and E do not respond to any change in the policy variables. In principle, the complete monetary trap could occur if the decrease in i_e resulting from an expansive policy induced banks to hold as excess reserves all of the increase in the adjusted base or in excess reserves brought about by the expansive policy.[20]

---

[18]In n.22 below, we consider some consequences of assuming that the E_b curve *became* horizontal. These cases may represent more fully some commonly held views about the liquidity traps.

[19]The derivative of i with respect to B^a, obtained from eqn 3.5, is

$$i_{B^a} = \frac{-a}{a_i B^a - s_i},$$

where a_i and s_i are partial derivatives of the banks' demand and the public's supply functions for earning assets with respect to i_e and where a is the bank-credit multiplier. A necessary and sufficient condition for a zero value of i_{B^a} is a zero value for the bank-credit multiplier, a. This implies that banks hold earning assets in an amount no larger than their capital.

Of course, the slope can *approach* zero if the denominator of i_{B^a} approaches infinity. But the conditions under which this would occur also make $\epsilon(i_e, B^a) \to 0$, so little if any difference in the conclusion about the interest-rate trap results from the use of derivatives rather than elasticities.

[20]This seems to have been the situation that Chairman Eccles had in mind when he testified that, even if currency was used to purchase government bonds from the public, there would be no increase in the money supply or in bank credit.

The necessary and sufficient conditions for the complete monetary trap imply that the responses of the monetary variables to changes in the policy variables are equal, since all the responses are zero. A subset of these conditions ($q_1 = q_2 = q_3$ and $\alpha = 1$) makes the response of money and bank credit to changes in each of the variables in table 3.2 equal, contrary to the argument of the previous section suggesting that the responses are unequal.

The conditions for the complete monetary trap and for the equality of the relative responses of the monetary variables to policy and other variables require that the monetary base equal zero. There is no other condition under which α, the ratio of M_2/E, equals unity.[21] The complete monetary trap involves a contradiction with one of the basic conditions for a monetary system and is, therefore, rejected. Monetary policy can always increase at least one of the monetary variables.

Since α cannot equal unity, the complete money-supply trap (row 3) and a similar trap for M_2 are rejected also. The denial of an absolute trap for the money supply means that either an increase in the base or the lowering of a reserve-requirement ratio, or both, will increase the money supply. At worst, $q_1 = 1$ or $q_1 = 1/\alpha$. Hence, one of three conclusions must be accepted (see table 3.2): (1) The direct response of M_1 to changes in B^a is never completely offset by the effect of changes in interest rates, that is, $q_1^{\cdot} < 1$; (2) the response of M_1 to changes in the reserve-requirement ratios (and in the rediscount rate) is not completely offset by changes in interest rates, $q_1 < 1/\alpha$; (3) or the money supply responds to all policy variables. In short, a trap for the money supply can, at most, be one of the partial traps discussed below. Here we note (1) that monetary policy never is reduced to a completely powerless act as suggested in the metaphor about "pushing on strings" and (2) that our conclusions do not require any specific assumption about the level of interest rates or the size of policy operations.

We have now established that expansive monetary policy always reduces some interest rate and expands the money supply. The conclusion can be extended to show that expansive policies always increase bank credit. A bank-credit trap is impossible, within our framework, if our earlier assumption about the slope of the E_p function is maintained. Inspection of table 3.2

MR. CROSS: Why not pay off all government bonds and get rid of paying any interest – because that would be inflation itself?

GOVERNOR ECCLES: Here is what would happen: . . . such action would simply increase the reserves of the banking system by the amount of government bonds which were purchased with currency. The currency would go out, if it was $10 billion or $20 billion or $3 billion, whatever amount the government paid out in currency to retire its bonds; but the currency would immediately go into the banks and from the banks into the Federal Reserve banks . . . and you would have additional reserves, additional excess reserves . . . (US Congress, 1935, p. 321).

[21]$E = D_p + T - (R-A) = M_2 - B^a = (m_2-1)B^a$. The bank-credit multiplier, a, equals $m_2 - 1$ by definition. The ratio $\alpha(=m_2/a)$ must, therefore, be greater than unity if B^a is not zero.

indicates that the necessary and sufficient condition for a complete bank-credit trap ($q_3 = 1$) is met if and only if $\epsilon(s, i_e)$ is zero. This condition means that there are no partial traps for bank credit. Either bank credit responds to all policy variables or to none of them.

However, there is an important difference between the argument used to reject the bank-credit trap and the arguments that reject liquidity traps for interest rates and the money supply. The latter traps are inconsistent with observations or with a positive value of the monetary base. Rejection of the bank-credit trap depends on an assumption that may not be accepted by proponents of a trap, namely, that the volume of earning assets supplied to banks remained dependent on interest rates. Proponents of liquidity traps generally assert that the standard slope properties did not apply in the depression of the thirties. Hence, we will not conclude that the bank-credit trap is rejected until empirical evidence is presented to support the assumption that $\epsilon(s, i_e)$ remained negative.

Nevertheless, we can dispose of some statements that are made about a bank credit trap. For example, it is often suggested that the failure of banks to reduce interest rates, or their willingness to hold as excess reserves any and all additions to reserves, is evidence for a trap of this kind. Our analysis shows that the existence of an absolute bank-credit trap does not depend on assumptions about the behavior of banks[22] or on the usual assertion that the public becomes extremely sensitive to small changes in market interest rates. In fact, a bank-credit trap requires that the public becomes completely insensitive to the level of interest rates when borrowing or selling securities to banks, so a trap of this kind does not imply a trap in the demand function for money or the existence of a "floor" to interest rates. On the contrary, the conditions for a bank-credit trap and the condition usually suggested as requirements for a trap in the demand function for money are completely opposed.

2.2 An Absolute Trap in the Demand for Money

An absolute trap in the demand function for money prevents monetary policy from reducing market interest rates below a minimum level. If the

---

[22]An alternative hypothesis in which the absolute bank-credit trap depends on the behavior of banks can be developed. The crucial assumption is a switching rule that makes the bank's demand for excess reserves "horizontal" at some interest rate. Our investigation of this approach leads to the following conclusions: (a) There is a zero correlation between i_e and i_o, a conclusion denied by evidence. (b) Bank credit and money do not change as a result of any change, positive or negative, in reserve-requirement ratios, a conclusion denied by the response of the monetary system in 1936–7. (c) An increase in the ratio of currency to demand deposits *raises* the money supply, a conclusion denied by the movement in the money supply in 1929–33 or following other banking panics.

minimum level of interest rate is above the rate required for a full-employment equilibrium of investment and saving, monetary policy is said to be powerless to increase output, employment, and the price level by lowering market interest rates.

We have shown elsewhere that the interest elasticity of the demand for money – estimated from any one of a number of alternative demand functions – did not become extremely large in the thirties.[23] This evidence suggests that a money-demand trap did not occur. However, in the regression equations a particular interest rate was chosen to represent the influence of "interest rates" on the demand for money. It is important to show that the empirical findings hold quite generally and that they do not depend on the choice of a particular interest rate. To do so, the solution for M_1, E, and i_e on the bank-credit market is extended to include the determination of the quantity of money demanded (D) and two interest rates, i_e and i_o. If both i_e and i_o are unaffected by monetary policy, or if the effect on the quantity of money demanded of changes in one index rate is exactly offset by changes in the other, then it is impossible for monetary policy to create any excess supply or demand for money; there is an absolute trap in the demand for money.

Simultaneous solutions of i_e and i_o are obtained from the credit-market (E_p and E_b) and money (M_1 and D) equations. To simplify the presentation, the solutions for i_e and i_o have been combined in a weighted average, i^*, with weights that depend on the interest elasticities of the demand for money.[24] The elasticities of i^* with respect to monetary policy variables, shown in table 3.4, are weighted averages of the elasticities of i_e and i_o, as shown at the bottom of the table. A necessary and sufficient condition for a money-

---

[23]See Brunner and Meltzer (1963), where distributions of the interest elasticities of velocity equations of the "Keynesian" and "wealth adjustment" type are given in the appendix. See also Meltzer (1963b).

[24]Since the demand function for money is now included in the system, the solutions for i_e or $\epsilon(i_e, B^a)$ differ from those given above. The solutions for $\epsilon(i_e, B^a)$ and $\epsilon(i_o, B^a)$ in table 3.4 are obtained from the matrix of elasticities in this footnote. The first row of the matrix is obtained from the equilibrium condition $E_p = E_b$, the second row from the equilibrium condition $M_1 = D$. The solutions for $\epsilon(i_e, B^a)$ and $\epsilon(i_o, B^a)$ –

$$\begin{vmatrix} \epsilon(a, i_e) - \epsilon(s, i_e) & -\epsilon(s, i_o) \\ \epsilon(m_1, i_e) - \epsilon(D, i_e) & -\epsilon(D, i_o) \end{vmatrix}$$

– are then combined in a weighted-average elasticity $\epsilon(i^*, B^a)$ by assuming that

$$\log i^* = w_1 \log i_e + (1 - w_1)\log i_o,$$

where

$$w_1 = \frac{\epsilon(D, i_e)}{\epsilon(D, i_e) + \epsilon(D, i_o)}$$

and $\epsilon(D, i_e)$ and $\epsilon(D, i_o)$ are interest elasticities of the demand for money. The results and some definitions are shown at the bottom of table 3.4. Similar procedures are used to obtain $\epsilon(i^*, r^d)$.

Table 3.4   The elasticity of i^* with respect to B^a and r^d

$$\epsilon(i^*, B^a) = \frac{-\epsilon(D, i_e)\epsilon(S, i_0) + \epsilon(D, i_0)(q_1 - 1)[\epsilon(a, i_e) - \epsilon(S, i_e)]}{[\epsilon(D, i_e) + \epsilon(D, i_0)]Z} < 0,$$

and

$$\epsilon(i^*, r^d) = \frac{\epsilon(m_1, r^d)\{\epsilon(D, i_0)(q_1\alpha - 1)[\epsilon(a, i_e) - \epsilon(S, i_e)] - \epsilon(D, i_e)\epsilon(S, i_0)\}}{[\epsilon(D, i_e) + \epsilon(D, i_0)]Z} > 0,$$

where Z is the determinant of the matrix in n. 24 and

$$Z = \epsilon(S, i_0)[\epsilon(m_1, i_e) - \epsilon(D, i_e)] - \epsilon(S, i_0)[\epsilon(a, i_e) - \epsilon(S, i_e)] > 0,$$

$$\epsilon(i^*, B^a) = \frac{\epsilon(D, i_e)}{\epsilon(D, i_e) + \epsilon(D, i_0)}\, \epsilon(i_0, B^a) + \frac{\epsilon(D, i_0)}{\epsilon(D, i_e) + (D, i_0)}\, \epsilon(i_e, B^a),$$

$$\epsilon(i_e, B^a) = \frac{\epsilon(D, i_0) - \epsilon(S, i_0)}{Z},$$

$$\epsilon(i_0, B^a) = \frac{\epsilon(m_1, i_e) - \epsilon(D, i_e) - \epsilon(a, i_e) + \epsilon(S, i_e)}{Z},$$

and $\epsilon(D, i)$ is an interest elasticity of the demand for money.

demand trap is that i^* is invariant with respect to changes in all monetary-policy variables[25] – B^a, r^d, etc. – as suggested in table 3.3, row 5.

An absolute trap in the demand for money is impossible. This is shown by examination of the only conditions that we have found that make both $\epsilon(i^*, B^a)$ and $\epsilon(i^*, r^d)$ equal zero, namely, that $q_1 = 1 = \alpha$ *and* that either $\epsilon(S, i_0)$ or $\epsilon(D, i_e)$ equals zero while other components remain bounded. These conditions contain a contradiction, since we have shown previously that α cannot equal unity. Moreover, neither set of conditions implies that there is a "horizontal" portion, or trap, in the demand curve for money; the traps depend on an inability to increase the money supply by policy opera-tions ($q_1 = 1 = \alpha$) and a D or E_p curve that is *vertical* with respect to one of the two interest rates. All other assumptions that make the numerator of the elasticities of i^* equal zero make the denominators equal zero also, imply that the money–bank-credit process is indeterminate, and also make the demand function for money vertical. Since these implications have no eco-nomic meaning, the conditions that imply them can be safely disregarded. It follows that there is always some policy action that reduces i^*.

Since interest rates can always be reduced and the money supply can always be increased, there cannot be an absolute liquidity trap in the demand

---

[25]Since the conditions that make $\epsilon(i^*, r^d) = 0$ apply to $\epsilon(i^*, r')$ and $\epsilon(i^*, \rho)$, the analysis applies to these policy variables as well.

for money. Someone must hold the increased supply of money at the lower interest rates, so the quantity of money demanded must increase. Again, none of these conclusions depends on the use of elasticities in the analysis. Similar results are obtained using derivatives.

2.3 Summary and Further Extension of the Theory

We have now shown that the theory of the money–bank-credit process precludes the possibility of absolute traps for interest rates and money. A trap for the stock of bank credit can occur if and only if the public is assumed to be totally insensitive to the level of interest rates when demanding and repaying loans or when selling government securities to banks. But even if there is a bank-credit trap, monetary policy remains capable of creating an excess supply of money, lowering interest rates, and thereby inducing changes in output, employment, and prices.

However, we have not shown that open-market operations or other changes in B^a have an expansive effect, only that there is always some policy action that expands the money supply and lowers interest rates. Table 3.4 shows that, if $q_1 = q_3 = 1$ and if $\epsilon(D, i_e)$ or $\epsilon(s, i_o)$ is zero, the monetary system is in a partial trap, "the base trap." Changes in the base have no effect on the money supply, bank credit, or i^*, and the monetary authority must then *raise* the reserve-requirement ratios or the rediscount rate to increase the money supply and lower i^*.[26] Moreover, the analysis has concentrated on absolute traps. Assumptions that make the various elasticities approach, but not reach, zero or infinity have not been considered. These traps will be discussed briefly after we have analyzed the conditions that imply a base trap.

The components of the interest elasticities of the monetary (m_1) and asset (a) multipliers are of particular importance for the discussion of the base trap and the asymptotic traps that follows. These components were introduced earlier as part of the discussion of β. Interest rates were described there as operating on m_1, and a through the free-reserve (f) and time-deposit (t) ratios. Equations (3.6) and (3.7) below express the interest elasticities of m_1 and a as linear combinations of the interest elasticities of the f and t ratios weighted by the elasticities of the monetary and asset multipliers with respect to f and t. Equations (A9)–(A12) of appendix 3.2 indicate that the latter elasticities are the source of the difference in the interest elasticities of the monetary and asset multipliers.

The first combination of elasticities in eqns (3.6) and (3.7) shows the effect of interest rates on m_1, and a through the free-reserve ratio, f. The partial

---

[26]The reason is that both $\epsilon(M_1, r^d)$ in table 3.3 and $\epsilon(i^*, r^d)$ in table 3.4 change sign as a result of the assumptions in the text. This peculiar conclusion suggests that q_1 is always substantially less than unity and that there is never a base trap for the money supply. For conv .nience, we will hereafter omit the subscript on i unless it is required for clarity.

derivative of f with respect to i is negative by assumption, but the sign of the partial interest elasticity of the free-reserve ratio, $\epsilon(f, i)$, depends on the sign of f. When the free-reserve ratio is positive, $\epsilon(f, i)$ is negative, and vice versa. But $\epsilon(f, i)$ always appears multiplied by the elasticity of the monetary or asset multiplier with respect to f. These elasticities, $\epsilon(m_1, f)$ and $\epsilon(a, f)$ also have signs that are opposites of the signs of f, so that the first product in the interest elasticities of the monetary and asset multipliers is always positive.

$$\epsilon(m_1, i) = \epsilon(m_1, f)\epsilon(f, i) + \epsilon(m_1, t)[\epsilon(t, i^t)\epsilon(i^t, i) + \epsilon(t, i)]; \qquad (3.6)$$

$$\epsilon(a, i) = \epsilon(a, f)\epsilon(f, i) + \epsilon(a, t)[\epsilon(t, i^t)\epsilon(i^t, i) + \epsilon(t, i)]. \qquad (3.7)$$

The second combination of elasticities in eqns (3.6) and (3.7) describes the effect of interest rates operating through the time-deposit ratio. The public's desired ratio of time to demand deposits, t, is assumed to depend on the interest rate paid on time deposits, i^t, on interest rates on alternative assets, i; and on other variables. (See eqn (A5), appendix 3.2.) A change in i is assumed to affect the time-deposit ratio in three ways. (1) A rise in i reduces the t ratio, that is, $\delta t/\delta i$ is assumed to be negative. (2) The rate i^t paid by banks on time deposits is partially dependent on i. Competition among banks or between banks and non-bank financial institutions induces a positive response in i^t to changes in i; $\delta i^t/\delta i$ is assumed to be positive. (3) The partial derivative of the t ratio with respect to i^t is assumed to be positive also.[27] The combined effect of interest rates on the t ratio is expressed in the bracketed partial elasticities obtained from these partial derivatives. The sum of the bracketed elasticities will be positive if the product of the first two exceeds the third in absolute value.[28]

[27]Some support for these assumptions may be found in two recent studies, Christ (1963) and Feige (1964). Both studies suggest that the net effect of interest rates on the time-deposit ratio is probably positive, a conclusion that is suggested also by our own earlier work (Brunner and Meltzer, 1964c) on demand functions for money and for money plus time deposits.
   One additional comment about these assumptions may forestall possible misinterpretation. The derivative $\delta i^t/\delta i$ is, of course, bounded by the ceiling rate. Through most of our history, ceiling rates have not been applicable. Recent experience suggests that the ceiling rate is increased when the ceiling becomes effective at a large proportion of the banks.
[28]In the discussion of the β line, $\epsilon(a, i)$ was assumed to be positive. This assumption is almost certain to be correct if the bracketed interest elasticity of the time-deposit ratio is positive. (See n. 27). If the bracketed interest elasticity of the time-deposit ratio is negative, the interest elasticity of the monetary multiplier is positive. If the bracketed elasticity is positive, $\epsilon(m_1, i)$ depends on the relative magnitude of its two components.
   The reason for the possible ambiguity about the signs of $\epsilon(m_1, i)$ and $\epsilon(a, i)$ is that the response of the monetary multiplier to a change in the t ratio, $\epsilon(m_1, t)$ is most likely negative, while the corresponding elasticity of the earning-asset multiplier, $\epsilon(a, t)$ is almost certain to be positive. See eqns (A10) and (A12) of appendix 3.2.
   Standard economic theory suggests that the sum of the elasticities is positive, since that is equivalent to assuming that the direct elasticity is larger than the cross-elasticity and that $\epsilon(i^t, i)$ is approximately unity in the long run. This is the reason for our assumption in a previous section that $\epsilon(a, i)$ and $\epsilon(\beta, i)$ are positive.

2.4 Base Traps

The base traps for the money supply or for both the money supply and bank credit are the last of the absolute traps listed in table 3.3. These traps eliminate the possibility of increasing M_1, or both E and M_1, by open-market operations or other changes in B^a. To discuss these traps, first we assume that $q_1 = q_3$, the necessary and sufficient condition for equal responses of M_1 and E to changes in B^a (see table 3.2), and then we derive the conditions that satisfy the equality. We next assume that $\epsilon(s, i) = 0$, so that $q_1 = q_3 = 1$, and there is a base trap for M_1 and E. The necessary and sufficient condition for a base trap affecting the money supply only ($q_1 = 1$) is then obtained by modifying the assumptions slightly.

Since the denominators of q_1 and q_3 are identical, $q_1 = q_3$ if and only if $\epsilon(m_1, i) = \epsilon(a, i)$. A more useful statement of this equation is obtained by expressing $\epsilon(a, f)$ and $\epsilon(a, t)$ of eqn (3.7) in terms of $\epsilon(m_1, f)$ and $\epsilon(m_1, t)$ of eqn (3.6). Equations (A11) and (A12) of appendix 3.2 permit the substitutions to be made. The difference $\epsilon(a, i) - \epsilon(m_1, i) = 0$ is then given by eqn (3.8), the necessary and sufficient condition for $q_1 = q_3$.

$$(\alpha-1)\left\{\epsilon(m_1, i) + \frac{t}{\Delta}\left[\epsilon(t, i')\epsilon(i', i) + \epsilon(t, i)\right]\right\} = 0, \tag{3.8}$$

where Δ is the denominator of the monetary and asset multipliers and all other parameters have been introduced previously.

Two alternative solutions satisfy eqn (3.8). The first, $\alpha = 1$, is impossible if the monetary base is not zero. Only the set of conditions which make the bracketed expression equal zero requires investigation. Suitable transformation of eqn (3.8) yields[29]

$$\frac{(\delta f/\delta i)i}{\epsilon(t, i')\epsilon(i', i) + \epsilon(t, i)} \cong \frac{(1 - f)t}{1 + t}. \tag{3.9}$$

The right side of (3.9) is positive. Since $\delta f/\delta i$ is negative, the sum of the interest elasticities of the time-deposit ratio must be negative also. Any other sign is logically inconsistent with $q_1 = q_3$ under the hypothesis.

The necessary and sufficient conditions for the equality of q_1 and q_3 are

[29]Eqn (3.6) is substituted into eqn (3.8), and terms are rearranged as follows:

$$\epsilon(m_1, f)\epsilon(f, i) = \left[-\epsilon(m_1, t) - \frac{t}{\Delta}\right][\epsilon(t, i')\epsilon(i', i) + \epsilon(t, i)].$$

Substitution of eqn (A10) from appendix 3.2 shows that

$$-\epsilon(m_1, t) - \frac{t}{\Delta} = \frac{t}{\Delta}[\tau r^t + f + v - 1].$$

Eqn (A9) is substituted for $\epsilon(m_1, f)$. The small terms τr^t, v, and d are ignored in the approximate equality shown in the text as eqn (3.9).

extremely difficult to satisfy. An empirical finding that the sum of the interest elasticities of the time-deposit ratio is non-negative disposes of any base trap and of the equality of elasticities of money and bank credit with respect to the base. A finding that the sum of the interest elasticities of the t ratio is negative does not assure that $q_1 = q_3$. More restrictive conditions are required, namely, that eqn (3.9) is satisfied by the values of i, f, t, etc.

To summarize, the joint base trap for money and bank credit can occur if and only if three conditions are met. First, $\epsilon(s, i)$ must be zero. Second, the sum of the interest elasticities of the time-deposit ratio must be negative. Third, both the derivative and the elasticities on the left of eqn (3.9) must be bounded. If all these conditions are satisfied, the money supply is unaffected by open-market operations, and bank credit is unchanged by any policy action.

By changing one assumption, we can obtain the conditions under which there is a base trap for the money supply while bank credit responds, at least slightly, to all policy variables. Assume that $\epsilon(s, i)$ is negative, so that q_3 is less than one. Then all of the other conditions above, plus the assumption that $\epsilon(m, i) = \epsilon(a, i) - \epsilon(s, i)$, impose the base trap on the money supply only. A pair of values for f and t can then be found to satisfy an equation similar to (3.9) under the alternative assumption. The values of f and t in this case will, of course, differ from those required for the joint base trap. But even if the modified eqn (3.9) is satisfied, the money supply continues to respond to changes in the reserve-requirement ratios and in the rediscount rate.

It is logically possible – but very unlikely – that the stated conditions for the base traps are satisfied by the money–bank-credit relations. We noted earlier that $\epsilon(s, i) = 0$ (or approximately so) is a peculiar requirement for a trap, since it implies that the public is willing to borrow the same amount (or sell the same volume of securities to banks) whatever the prevailing interest rates on the bank-credit market. This assumption is difficult to reconcile with the assumption that the public responds to interest rates, albeit negatively, in adjusting its desired ratio of time to demand deposits. Furthermore, the restriction imposed by the requirement that eqn (3.9) must hold continuously makes the base traps very fragile. The problem is that an open-market operation raises the excess- or free-reserve ratio. As f rises, the ratio on the right of eqn (3.9) falls. For the base traps to remain, the terms on the left of eqn (3.9) must change also to maintain the approximate equality.[30]

---

[30] A continuous accumulation of excess reserves in the banking system would eventually break the base trap for the money supply, for bank credit, or for both. As f rises toward unity, $\tau r^t + f + v$ (see n. 29) becomes greater than unity, and the interest elasticities of the monetary and asset multipliers become unequal. Of course, f cannot approach unity unless required-reserve ratios are reduced. But the reductions in required-reserve ratios expand the money supply, a point that is reaffirmed in the text just below.

It should be noted that a zero value for i does not satisfy eqn (3.9). If the denominator is zero,

The base traps do not imply that interest rates or the demand for money is trapped. Changes in all policy variables continue to affect i_e (see table 3.1), and changes in the reserve-requirement ratios or the rediscount rate induce changes in the money supply, in i^*, and in the quantity of money demanded. However, the responses of i^* and M_1 to r^d, r^t, or ρ are reversed. To expand M_1 and lower i^*, r^d, r^t, or ρ must be increased. But such actions raise i_e and thus cause i^* and i_e to move in opposite directions, contrary to observations. These peculiar implications cast doubt on the likely occurrence of a base trap. Data for the thirties reinforce these doubts, since the increase in the reserve-requirement ratios lowered the money supply. Moreover, the time-deposit ratio rose during the thirties when interest rates rose and fell when interest rates fell, contrary to the assumption that the sum of the bracketed interest elasticities of the t ratio is negative. Data for other periods, for example, following the recent changes in Regulation Q, furnish additional evidence suggesting a positive value for the sum of these interest elasticities. Such observations constitute a prima facie case against the base trap. Consideration of more detailed evidence must await parameter estimates. Some are provided after a brief discussion of "asymptotic traps."

2.5 Asymptotic Traps

While the responses of the money supply or interest rates to monetary policy operations never become zero, it is often suggested that they may become so small that the monetary authority could acquire all financial assets without having a noticeable effect on output, employment, or prices. This problem is discussed by Patinkin (1965, pp. 349–54). A review of the literature cited in previous sections suggests that many other writers failed to distinguish carefully between asymptotic traps and the absolute traps discussed earlier. It is important, therefore, to consider some cases in which various elasticities (or slopes) converge to zero or infinity and to show that some of the asymptotic traps are impossible while others require values of particular elasticities that are inconsistent with available evidence.

Many of the absolute traps were rejected because α – the ratio of M_2/E – must be greater than unity. Rising excess or free reserves raise α, so the accumulation of excess reserves by the banking system in the thirties does not negate the arguments used to reject the absolute traps and does not suggest that these traps hold in the limit. Moreover, eqn (3.9) shows that a rising free-reserve ratio does not imply that open-market operations become ineffective. Additional assumptions must be made about $\delta f/\delta i$, the

---

there is an indeterminacy; if the denominator is non-zero, f must equal 1. Excess reserves must be equal to total deposits, a condition that has never occurred. Note that a zero value of i means that *all* interest rates on all bank earning assets are zero.

sum of the interest elasticities of the time-deposit ratio and $\epsilon(s, i_e)$. In short, the convergence of the interest elasticity of the free-reserve ratio to minus infinity and the accumulation of excess reserves by the banking system do not imply that the money supply becomes independent of monetary policy.[31]

The critical assumptions for the monetary system are that the elasticities of D_m and either m_1 or a with respect to all interest rates converge to plus or minus infinity together. These assumptions are sufficient to make the responses of interest rates to all policy variables approach zero as shown by the elasticities of i^* in table 3.4. (The much simpler assumption, that either $\epsilon(a, i_e)$ or $-\epsilon(s, i_e)$ approaches infinity, implies that the effect of policy on i_e approaches zero in the simpler case presented in table 3.1.) Although monetary policy remains an effective means of expanding the supply of money and the banks' demand for earning assets, the increases in M_1 and E are absorbed by the public and the banks, respectively, without a noticeable reduction in any interest rate.

A summary of the more important conditions for the various asymptotic traps appears in the following section along with estimates of the values of critical parameters. Before considering the evidence obtained from these estimates, it is useful to recall some of the findings presented earlier. First, interest rates included in the indexes i_e and i_o remained correlated during the thirties, contrary to the assumptions above, which imply that they were uncorrelated. Second, interest rates on long-term securities generally did not reach their lowest levels until the early or middle forties. The decline in long-term interest rates during and after the late thirties is inconsistent with the implication that i_e and i_o reached a "floor." Third, the estimated interest elasticity of the demand for money in the thirties is smaller in absolute value than the estimate for the period 1900–1958, as noted in Meltzer (1963a, p. 242). These findings are incompatible with the conditions required for the various traps.

---

[31]Necessary and sufficient conditions for some asymptotic traps can be derived using eqns (3.6) and (3.7). Two sets of assumptions make q_3 approach unity and q_1 approach $1/\alpha$ so that there is a complete, asymptotic trap for bank credit and a trap for M_1 for changes in the reserve-requirement ratios and the rediscount rate. Dividing both the numerators and denominators of q_1 and q_3 by $\epsilon(f, i)$ shows the following: (a) If $\epsilon(s, i_e)$ and the sum of the interest elasticities of the time-deposit ratio approach zero while $\epsilon(f, i)$ is non-zero, q_1 and q_3 approach the critical values $1/\alpha$ and 1, respectively. (b) If $\epsilon(s, i_e)$ and the sum of the interest elasticities of the t ratio remain bounded while $\epsilon(f, i)$ approaches minus infinity, the same results are obtained. We have found no other assumptions about components approaching plus or minus infinity that imply asymptotic traps for M_1 if $\epsilon(s, i_e)$ remains bounded.

Some implications of one of the above sets of assumptions are discussed in n. 22.

3 Some Empirical Evidence for the Propositions

We have now shown that most of the absolute traps and several of the asymptotic traps are inconsistent with the theory of money and bank credit. The evidence presented in this section supports the theory and suggests that it is a reasonably good summary of the money–bank-credit process. The findings, therefore, support the conclusions that have been reached and increase our confidence in the analysis that led us to reject many of the liquidity traps. In addition, the data cast substantial doubt on the likely occurrence of those traps that require a particular elasticity to reach (or approach) a critical value. The results suggest that the estimated values and the critical values are far apart.

To obtain empirical estimates, the rates of interest on commercial-bank loans and on corporate bonds were used to measure i_e and i_o, respectively, and the elasticities of the monetary and asset multipliers with respect to the reserve-requirement and currency ratios were assumed to be constant.[32] A demand equation for money, similar to the equation used in several of our papers,[33] was estimated as a part of the money–bank-credit process. The results of reduced-form and/or two-stage least-squares regressions of the i_e, M_1 and D_m equations are shown in appendix 3.3, sections C.1 and C.2, along with the computed values of the parameters of the bank-credit and money-supply equations (tables C1 and C2).

The evidence generally supports our hypothesis about the signs of the elasticities of interest rates and money with respect to policy and other variables and thus supports the analysis that led to the rejection of a number of liquidity traps. The residuals from the computed supply and demand equations for money furnish additional support. Large, systematic overestimates of the quantity of money supplied in the late thirties, and large underestimates of the quantity demanded, would suggest that the banks and the public substantially increased the quantities of reserves and money demanded relative to the amounts they would be expected to hold at the prevailing levels of the policy variables, interest rates, wealth, etc. Table 3.5 presents the data

[32]The assumption of constant elasticities for m and a with respect to r^d, r^t, and k is one of the simplest that can be made. It appears to be quite reasonable for the postwar years but is a somewhat poorer approximation for some of the prewar years that have been included in the data. The difficulties are particularly apparent in the early thirties, 1930–4, when there were substantial changes in the currency ratio. For the postwar period, computation of the elasticities from monthly data for the period January, 1947–March, 1964, supports the assumption of constancy reasonably well. A formal statement of our procedure is given in appendix 3.3, sec C.1 and C.2.

[33]Brunner and Meltzer (1963, 1964c) and Meltzer (1963a). The sources of the data for the supply and demand equations are given in these papers.

Table 3.5   Values[a] of the residuals of the money equations in the late thirties

	Residual form	
Year	The demand equation percent	The supply equation percent
1937	−0.4	−1.6
1938	−1.3	−2.0
1939	−1.1	−0.5
Average absolute value (30 years)	0.8	0.9

[a] A negative value means that the actual quantity is less than the predicted quantity. The correlation of the residuals from the two equations for the entire period is zero. Both positive and negative residuals are found in the supply and demand equations during the thirties.

and shows that, although our equation overestimates the quantity of money supplied in the late thirties, the overestimate is not substantial.[34] Moreover, the overestimates of the nominal quantity demanded suggest that the public held a slightly *smaller* quantity of money than would be expected from their behavior in other periods. This finding provides no support for the notion of a trap in the demand for money.

In table 3.6 we have listed the conditions for some of the liquidity traps that cannot be rejected without estimates of particular parameters. The results in appendix 3.3, used to obtain the values shown in the table, suggest that the parameter values required for these traps differ from the values suggested by our estimates. Most of the conditions listed were discussed in detail above, so the findings require only brief comment. A value of $\epsilon(a, i_e)$ > $\epsilon(m_1, i_e)$ is inconsistent with the first condition listed. To obtain the estimate of $\epsilon(a, i_e)$, we assume that $\epsilon(s, i_e)$ approximately equals $-\epsilon(s, i_o)$ and use this value with the first sum shown in table C1 of appendix 3.3. The same assumption is used to obtain the value of $\epsilon(s, i_e)$ and to reject the second trap in the list. One of the conditions for the third trap requires that $\epsilon(s, i_e)$ approach minus infinity. If this occurs, q_1 and $\epsilon(i_e, B^a)$ approach zero. Our

[34]Note that the residuals in the supply equation for money do not suggest that the residuals in the banks' demand equation for total reserves is small in the late thirties. We have not estimated the demand equation for reserves separately. However, comparison of the residuals in the money-supply equation for 1937 and 1938 with the residual for 1939 and other years suggests that the larger residuals for 1937–8 may be due to the changes in the reserve-requirement ratios that were imposed at the time. Large changes in the reserve-requirement ratios change the values of some of the elasticities used to construct the data in the regression equations, contrary to our assumptions. See appendix 3.3.

Table 3.6   Empirical findings about the critical conditions for various traps

Type of trap	Critical conditions	Finding	Conclusion
1. Absolute base traps	$\epsilon(t, i^t)\epsilon(i^t, i) + \epsilon(t, i) < 0$ $\epsilon(m, i_e) = \epsilon(a, i_e) - \epsilon(s, i_e)$	$\epsilon(a, i_e) - \epsilon(m_1, i_e) \cong 0.2$ $\epsilon(a, i_e) - \epsilon(s, i_e) = 1.96$ $\epsilon(m, i_e) = 0.94$	Reject Reject
2. Complete, absolute bank-credit trap	$\epsilon(s, i_e) = 0$	$\epsilon(s, i_e) \cong -0.83$	Reject
3. Asymptotic trap for i_e, i^*, and D_m	$\epsilon(D, i^*) \rightarrow -\infty$ $\epsilon(s, i) \rightarrow \pm\infty$	$\epsilon(D, i^*) = -0.47$ q_1 is significantly different from zero	Reject Reject
4. Partial trap for M_1 with respect to reserve-requirement ratios and rediscount rate	$q_1 = 1/\alpha$ in the thirties	$q_1 = 0.48$ $1/\alpha \cong 0.7$ in the late thirities	Reject

Read $\cong$ as "approximately equal."

estimates show that $1 - q_1\alpha$ is significantly different from zero and thus assign a very small probability to $q_1 = 1$.

In short, the data support the conclusions reached earlier and lend strength to the analysis that rejected various types of liquidity traps. The connection between monetary policy and the money supply, interest rates, bank credit, and the demand for money does not appear to have been broken.

4 Conclusion

Our analysis has implications for monetary theory in the broader sense of macroeconomic general-equilibrium analysis and in the narrower sense of the supply and demand for money. Many of the conclusions for the latter branch of monetary theory have been stated already. Of these the most important is that monetary policy has not become "ineffective." This conclusion follows from the denial of various forms of the liquidity trap, denials that are implied by the hypothesis and/or supported by the evidence that has been introduced.

While our analysis is based upon the institutional arrangements prevalent in the United States, the implications for the various liquidity traps do not depend particularly on these arrangements. They apply to any economy in which the monetary base is not zero, in which banks issue types of deposits that are not perfect substitutes and respond to cost and yield changes when adjusting their reserve positions. These conditions are met in the monetary systems of most developed countries.

Differences in the response to policy operations of money and bank credit – variables that are frequently used as indicators of the direction of monetary policy – were discussed. Both money and bank credit are treated as endogenous variables, and their partial-equilibrium responses to monetary-policy changes include a response to the changes in interest rates induced by policy operations. Recognition of the endogeneity of the money supply and other monetary variables permits the factors determining the differences in the relative responses to be analyzed and leads to the conclusion that open-market operations induce a larger relative change in the money supply than in the money supply plus time deposits or in bank credit.

The observed cyclical pattern in the ratio of bank credit to money can be interpreted in terms of the differences in the relative responses of the two variables to policy and other changes. The movements of the bank-credit–money ratio, implied by our analysis and parameter estimates, are consistent with our finding that postwar changes in policy variables have been procyclical rather than countercyclical on the average (Brunner and Meltzer, 1964a, 1964b). It appears likely that failure to carefully distinguish between money and bank credit misleads the Federal Reserve in its interpretation of the direction of its policy actions. By watching the rate of change of bank credit, rather than changes in the money supply or the monetary base, policymakers often become convinced that a policy of relative ease is in effect when they are pursuing a policy of relative restraint.

Similar conclusions apply to the use of changes in interest rates on financial assets as indicators of the direction of recent monetary policy. The empirical findings suggest that, when the relative growth rates of the monetary base and the principal determinants of the public's supply of earning assets to banks are equal, changes in the determinants of the public's supply of earning assets dominate the movements of interest rates. Thus, the evidence suggests that rising or falling interest rates are not a useful indicator of the current direction of monetary policy.

The effects of monetary policy on real output and prices have not been investigated here. Hence the paper does not discuss these effects or attempt to compute the responses of real variables to changes in monetary policy. Nevertheless, the results have implications for macroeconomic theory.

Our denials of the various liquidity traps do not depend on particular assumptions about the structure of the real sector. Any of a number of widely used models, in which expenditure functions are not completely interest inelastic and in which money wages adjust more slowly than the monetary variables, yields the conclusion that monetary policy affects the pace of economic activity once the liquidity trap is denied. Of course, each hypothesis has different properties that may imply differences in the magnitude of the response to monetary policy. But our conclusion that monetary policy has an effect on the real variables does not appear to be sensitive to changes in the hypotheses about the real sector.

Part of this conclusion is not novel. Most economists agree that open-market operations change prevailing interest rates, alter the relative prices of assets and output, and hence affect real variables. Denial of the liquidity trap, however, adds important support to the generality of this conclusion and suggests that the ability of monetary authority to introduce or remove an excess demand for real balances does not depend on the real-balance effect. In the absence of a liquidity trap in both the supply and demand functions for money, there is little reason to believe that the effectiveness of monetary policy ever requires the assumption that the government sector is unconcerned by the change in the value of its outstanding debt or that the public is unconcerned about changes in future tax burdens.[35]

Appendix 3.1

Alphabetical List of Principal Symbols Used in the Paper

A	Discounts and advances of member banks
a	The earning-asset multiplier
B	The monetary base
B^a	The adjusted monetary base, $B - A$
b	The ratio of member-bank borrowing to total deposits
C	Treasury currency outstanding
C_p	Total currency held by the public
c	Treasury cash in the sources statement of the base
D (or D_m)	The quantity of money demanded
D_p	Demand deposits of the public
D_t	Demand deposits of the Treasury at commercial banks
d	The ratio of Treasury deposits at commercial banks to the public's demand deposits.
E	Earning assets of commercial banks net of Treasury deposits and the banks' net worth
E_b	The banks' demand for earning assets (net of Treasury deposits and capital accounts)
E_p	The public's supply of earning assets to banks
e	The ratio of desired excess reserves to total deposits
$f*$	Deposits of foreign banks at Federal Reserve Banks

[35]For a summary of the discussion on these points, see Johnson (1962, pp. 337–43).

f	The ratio of free reserves to total deposits $= e - b$
g	Deposits of the Treasury at the Federal Reserve Banks
i_e	An index of interest rates on bank earning assets
i_o	An index of interest rates on financial assets other than bank earning assets
i^t	The interest rate paid by banks on time deposits
$i*$	An index of rates on all financial assets, a weighted average of i_e and i_o
k	The ratio of currency held by the public to demand deposits of the public
K	A weighted sum of the logarithms of the policy variables and the currency ratio
M_1	The money supply, $C_p + D_p$
M_2	The money supply plus time deposits $M_1 + T$
m_1	The monetary multiplier
m_2	The multiplier for the money supply plus time deposits
n	The yield on private capital
o	The difference between other liabilities plus net worth and other assets on the consolidated balance sheet of the Federal Reserve Banks
P	The Federal Reserve's portfolio of earning assets net of discounts and advances
P_a	The deflator for wealth
p	The income deflator
q	A ratio of interest elasticities
$R*$	Total commercial-bank reserves – base money held by banks including vault cash counted as reserves
R_e	Desired excess reserves of commercial banks
R_r	Required reserves of commercial banks
r	The sum of weighted averages of demand- and time-deposit reserve-requirement ratios plus the vault-cash ratio
r^d	The weighted-average reserve-requirement ratio for demand deposits
r^t	The reserve-requirement ratio for time deposits
r_1	The interest rate on loans at commercial banks
r_{20}	The long-term interest rate, the Durand measure of the interest rate on twenty-year bonds
T	Total commercial-bank time deposits
t	The ratio of time deposits to the public's demand deposits
U	The gold stock
V	Vault-cash holdings of commercial banks not counted as required reserves
v	The ratio of vault-cash holdings to total deposits
W	The nominal stock of wealth held by the public

W/P_a — The deflated stock of wealth held by the public

Y/Y_p — The ratio of net national product to "permanent" net national product, an index of transitory income

Z — A combination of elasticities in the denominators of the elasticities of table 3.4

α — The ratio $m_2/a[=m_2/(m_2 - 1)]$

β — The ratio of a/m_1

γ — The ratio $(D_p + D_t)/(D_p + D_t + T)$

δ — The ratio of member-bank demand deposits of the Treasury and the public to total demand deposits

Δ — The denominator of the simple elasticities in appendix 3.2 and of the monetary and asset multipliers

ϵ — An elasticity

π — Used to represent unspecified variables in the equations of appendix 3.2

ρ — The rediscount rate

τ — The ratio of member-bank time deposits to total commercial-bank time deposits

Appendix 3.2

Equations of the Underlying Money-Supply Bank-Credit Hypothesis and the Derived Elasticities Required for the Text

Basic Definitions	*Description*
(D1) $B = P + U + C - g - o - f^* - c$	Sources of the base
(D2) $B = R^* + C_p$	Uses of the base, total reserves plus currency
(D3) $B^a = B - A$	The adjusted base, the base minus borrowed reserves
(D4) $M_1 = D_p + C_p$	The money supply
(D5) $M_2 = M_1 + T$	The money supply plus time deposits
(D6) $E = D_p + T - (R^* - A)$	Bank credit net of Treasury deposits and the banks' net worth

From eqns (D3), (D4), and (D6), we note that $M_1 = E$ if and only if $B^a = T$.

Other Equations of the Monetary Systems

The ratio of required reserves plus vault cash outside required reserves to total deposits of member and non-member banks is a weighted average:

$$V + R_r = r(D_p + D_t + T);$$
$$r = \gamma\delta r^d + (1 - \gamma)\tau r^t + v. \tag{A1}$$

The desired excess-reserve, borrowing, and free-reserve ratios are:

$$R_e = e(i, \rho, \pi_1)(D_p + D_t + T), \quad e_i < 0 < e_\rho;$$
$$A = b(i, \rho, \pi_2)(D_p + D_t + T), \quad b_i > 0 > b_\rho;$$
$$\frac{R_e - A}{D_p + D_t + T} = f(i, \rho), \qquad f_i < 0 < f_\rho; \tag{A2}$$

The ratio of Treasury deposits to the public's demand deposits is taken as a policy variable,

$$D_t = dD_p. \tag{A3}$$

The currency ratio k is dependent on a variety of costs and returns as well as on wealth and other factors. In this paper it is treated as given:

$$C_p = kD_p. \tag{A4}$$

The time-deposit ratio t is assumed to depend on interest rate, wealth, and other variables:

$$T = t\left(i^t, i, \frac{W}{P_a}, p, \frac{Y}{Y_p}, \pi_3\right)D_p; \quad t_i^t, t_w > 0; t_i < 0. \tag{A5}$$

Solutions for the Monetary and Asset Multipliers

(A1)–(A5) and (D2)–(D6) permit us to solve for the monetary and asset multipliers and obtain

$$m_1 = \frac{1+k}{(r+f)(1+t+d)+k}. \tag{A6}$$

$$m_2 = \frac{1+k+t}{(r+f)(1+t+d)+k}. \tag{A7}$$

and, since $E = M_2 - B^a = (m_2-1)B^a$,

$$a = m_2 - 1 = \frac{(1+t)-(r+f)(1+t+d)}{(r+f)(1+t+d)+k}. \tag{A8}$$

The Elasticities of the Monetary and Asset Multipliers

We denote by $\epsilon(m_1, x)$, $\epsilon(m_2, x)$, and $\epsilon(a, x)$ the simple elasticities of the monetary and asset multipliers with respect to the factors shaping the multipliers. The discussion in the text makes use of the following relations:

$$\epsilon(m_1, f) = \frac{-(1+t+d)f}{\Delta}, \tag{A9}$$

where Δ is the denominator of the monetary and asset multipliers in equations (A6)–(A8),

$$\epsilon(m_1, t) = \frac{-(\tau r^t + f + v)t}{\Delta}, \tag{A10}$$

$$\epsilon(a, f) = \epsilon(m_1, f)\alpha, \tag{A11}$$

$$\epsilon(a, t) = \frac{t}{\Delta}(\alpha - 1) + \epsilon(m_1, t)\alpha, \tag{A12}$$

$$\epsilon(m_2, f) = \epsilon(m_1, f), \tag{A13}$$

and

$$\epsilon(m_2, t) = \epsilon(m_1, t) + \frac{t}{1+k+t} \; ; \left(\frac{t}{1+k+t} = \frac{T}{M_2}\right),$$

where

$$\alpha = \frac{m_2}{a} = \frac{1+k+t}{(1+t)-(r+f)(1+t+d)}.$$

The ratio $\alpha > 1$, since $a = m_2 - 1 < m_2$.

Solutions similar to (A9) and (A11) are obtained for the parameters r^d, r^t, δ, and τ (but not k). For example,

$$\epsilon(m_1, r^d) = \frac{-\gamma\delta(1+t+d)r^d}{\Delta}, \tag{A14}$$

and

$$\epsilon(a, r^d) = \epsilon(m_1, r^d)\alpha. \tag{A15}$$

Appendix 3.3

Solution for Equilibrium Values; Derivation of the Elasticities in Tables 1 and 2 of the Text; Values of the Empirical Coefficients

Assume (1) that the elasticities of monetary and asset multipliers in appendix 3.2 may be approximated by constants and (2) that the public's supply of assets to banks, eqn (3.4) of the text, is linear in the logarithms of the variables.

A. Solution for i_e on the Bank-Credit Market

$$\text{Log } E_b = \log B^a + \epsilon(a, r^d) \log r^d + \epsilon(a, i_e) \log i_e,$$

plus similar terms for r^t, k, ρ, W/P_a, p and Y/Y_p, where the last three terms occur because of their influence on t.

$$\text{Log } E_p = \epsilon(s, i_e) \log i_e + \epsilon \left(s, \frac{W}{P_a}\right) \log \frac{W}{P_a} + \epsilon(s, i_o) \log i_o,$$

plus similar terms for p, Y/Y_p, and n. The equilibrium stock of bank credit, E, and i_e are simultaneously determined.

$$\text{Log } i_e = \frac{1}{\epsilon(a, i_e) - \epsilon(s, i_e)} \left\{ \left[\epsilon \left(s, \frac{W}{P_a}\right) - \epsilon \left(a, \frac{W}{P_a}\right) \right] \log \frac{W}{P_a} \right.$$
$$\left. + \epsilon(s, i_o) \log i_o - \log B^a - \epsilon(a, r^d) \log r^d \right\}, \qquad \text{(A16)}$$

plus similar terms for r^t, k, p, n, etc.

The elasticities of i_e with respect to B^a, r^d, W/P_a, and i_o shown in table 3.1 are obtained from eqn (A16). The values of the coefficients are shown in table C1.

B. Solution for the Money Supply and Bank Credit

Equation (3.1) of the text may be written as

$$\log M_1 = \log B^a + \epsilon(m_1, r^d) \log r^d + \epsilon(m_1, i_e) \log i_e, \qquad \text{(A17)}$$

plus similar terms for r^t, k, etc.

Substitution of the solution for $\log i_e$ from eqn (A16) gives the equilibrium solution for the money supply incorporating the elasticities and variables of the E_p and E_b equations.

It is shown in appendix 3.2 that $\epsilon(a, r^d) = \epsilon(m_1, r^d)\alpha$. Define

$$q_1 = \frac{\epsilon(m_1, i_e)}{\epsilon(a, i_e) - \epsilon(s, i_e)}.$$

Substituting eqn (A16) into (A17) gives:

$$\log M_1 = (1 - q_1) \log B^a + \epsilon(m_1, r^d)(1 - q_1\alpha) \log r^d \qquad \text{(A18)}$$
$$+ \{\epsilon(m_1, p) - q_1[\epsilon(a, p) - \epsilon(s, p)]\} \log p + \epsilon(s, i_o)q_1 \log i_o,$$

plus similar terms for other variables and parameters, W/P_a, Y/Y_p, r^t, n, k, and ρ. By the same procedure the equilibrium solutions for M_2 and R are obtained in terms of q_2 and q_3. These solutions are used to obtain the elasticities shown in table 2 of the text. Regression estimates for eqn (A18) are shown in section C.2 below.

C.1. Values of Coefficients and Parameters of the Bank-Credit-Market Equation

Using data for 1919–41 and 1952–8, the regression estimates (t statistics are in parentheses) of the reduced-form equation for i_e are:

$$\log r_1 = -6.306 \;\; -0.510 \, K_3 + 0.908 \log \frac{W}{P_a} + 0.423 \log r_{20}$$
$$(-4.49) \qquad (6.67) \qquad\qquad (2.32)$$

$$+ 0.017 \log \frac{Y}{Y_p} + 0.744 \log p + 0.254 \log \rho$$
$$(4.90) \qquad\qquad (4.44) \qquad\quad (3.98)$$
$$(R^2=0.983),$$

where r_1 is the interest rate on bank loans, r_{20} is the Durand yield on corporate bonds,

$$K_3 = \log B^a + \epsilon(a, r^d) \log r^d + \epsilon(a, r^t) \log r^t + \epsilon(a, k) \log k,$$

(with elasticities in K_3 computed according to the formulas given in appendix 3.2), and n was omitted from the regression owing to problems of measurement.

The regression coefficients suggest that the parameters have the values shown in table C1.

C.2. Values of the Coefficients and Parameters of the Supply and Demand Equations for Money

Using data for 1919–41 and 1952–8, the regression estimates (t statistics are in parentheses) of the supply equation for money are:

$$\log M_1 = -4.359 + 0.347\, K_1 - 0.145 \log \rho + 0.501 \log\frac{W}{P_a} - 0.459 \log r_{20}$$
$$(2.10) \qquad (-2.27) \qquad\qquad (2.90) \qquad\quad (-2.43)$$

$$+ 0.926 \log p - 0.008 \log \frac{Y}{Y_p} \quad (R^2=0.996; \text{ Durbin–Watson}=1.40),$$
$$(4.12) \qquad\quad (-1.64)$$

Table C1   Estimated credit market parameters

Variable	Interpretation of reduced-form parameter	Value of credit-market parameter
K_3	$\dfrac{-1}{\epsilon(a, i_e) - \epsilon(s, i_e)}$	$\epsilon(a, i_e) - \epsilon(s, i_e) = 1.96$
$\log \dfrac{W}{P_a}$	$\dfrac{\epsilon[s, (W/P_a)] - \epsilon[a, (W/P_a)]}{\epsilon(a, i_e) - \epsilon(s, i_e)}$	$\epsilon\left(s, \dfrac{W}{P_a}\right) - \epsilon\left(a, \dfrac{W}{P_a}\right) = 1.78$
$\log r_{20}$	$\dfrac{\epsilon(s, i_0)}{\epsilon(a, i_e) - \epsilon(s, i_e)}$	$\epsilon(s, i_0) = 0.83$
$\log \dfrac{Y}{Y_p}$	$\dfrac{\epsilon[s, (Y/Y_p)] - \epsilon[a, (Y/Y_p)]}{\epsilon(a, i_e) - \epsilon(s, i_e)}$	$\epsilon\left(s, \dfrac{Y}{Y_p}\right) - \epsilon\left(a, \dfrac{Y}{Y_p}\right) = 0.03$
$\log p$	$\dfrac{\epsilon(s, p) - \epsilon(a, p)}{\epsilon(a, i_e) - \epsilon(s, i_e)}$	$\epsilon(s, p) - \epsilon(a, p) = 1.46$
$\log \rho$	$\dfrac{-\epsilon(a, p)}{\epsilon(a, i_e) - \epsilon(s, i_e)}$	$\epsilon(a, p) = -0.50$

where

$$K_1 = \log B^a + \epsilon(m_1, r^d) \log r^d + \epsilon(m_1, r^t) \log r^t + \epsilon(m_1, k) \log k$$

(with elasticities in K_1 computed according to the formulas in appendix 3.2).
Two-stage least-squares estimates of the demand equation were obtained
using the interest rate (r_1^*) estimated from the bank-credit-market equation.
Again, t statistics are shown in parentheses; the Durbin–Watson statistic is
from the one-stage least-squares estimate. The estimates suggest that the
"combined" interest elasticity of the demand for money, $\epsilon(D, i^*)$, is approximately -0.5. The lack of significance of one rate in these regressions most
likely results from the very high correlation between r_1^* and r_{20}.

$$\text{Log } D_m = -0.995 + 0.831 \log\frac{W}{P_a} + 1.317 \log P_a - 0.004 \log \frac{Y}{Y_p}$$
$$\quad\quad\quad\quad\quad (8.71) \quad\quad\quad (21.20) \quad\quad\quad\quad (1.18)$$

$$- 0.073 \log r_{20} - 0.399 \log r_1^*$$
$$(-0.340) \quad\quad (-3.06) \quad\quad (R^2 = 0.997; \text{ Durbin–Watson} = 1.22).$$

Estimates of the M_1 and D_m equations obtained from three-stage least-
squares regressions do not differ in any important respect and are omitted.
The regression estimates for the M_1 supply equation can be combined with
the estimates from the r_1 (or i_e) equation to obtain the elasticities of the
monetary multiplier (see table C2).

Table C2   Elasticities of the monetary multiplier

Variable	Interpretation of parameter	Elasticities of the monetary multiplier[a]
K_1	$1 - q_1\alpha$[b]	$q_1 = 0.48$; $\epsilon(m_1, i_e) = 0.94$
ρ	$\epsilon(m_1, \rho)(1 - q_1\alpha)$[c]	$\epsilon(m_1, \rho) = -0.42$
$\dfrac{W}{P_a}$	$\epsilon\left(m_1, \dfrac{W}{P_a}\right) - q_1\left[\epsilon\left(a, \dfrac{W}{P_a}\right) - \epsilon\left(s, \dfrac{W}{P_a}\right)\right]$	$\epsilon\left(m_1, \dfrac{W}{P_a}\right) = -0.35$
ρ	$\epsilon(m_1, \rho) - q_1[\epsilon(a, \rho) - \epsilon(s, \rho)]$	$\epsilon(m_1, \rho) = 0.23$
$\dfrac{Y}{Y_p}$	$\epsilon\left(m_1, \dfrac{Y}{Y_p}\right) - q_1\left[\epsilon\left(a, \dfrac{Y}{Y_p}\right) - \epsilon\left(s, \dfrac{Y}{Y_p}\right)\right]$	$\epsilon\left(m_1, \dfrac{Y}{Y_p}\right) = -0.021$[a]
α		$\alpha = 1.35$, the average value for the period

[a] The coefficient of i_o has a sign opposite to the sign implied by our theory and has been omitted from the table.

[b] There is a small approximation error. The correct interpretation of the product of the coefficient and variable is

$$(1 - q_1) \log B^a + (1 - q_1\alpha)[\epsilon(m_1, r^d) \log r^d + \epsilon(m_1, r^t) \log r^t] + \left[\frac{k}{1 + k} - \frac{k}{\Delta}(1 - q_1)\right] \log k,$$

where Δ is the denominator of the monetary and asset multipliers in appendix 3.2.

[c] An alternative estimate of q_1 can be obtained using $\epsilon(a, \rho) = -0.50$ from table C1 and the equation $\epsilon(a, \rho) = \epsilon(m_1, \rho)\alpha$. This estimate gives $\epsilon(m_1, \rho) = -0.37$ and $q_1 = 0.45$.

References

Bronfenbrenner, M. and T. Mayer. 1960. Liquidity functions in the American economy. *Econometrica* 28, 819–34.
—— 1963. Rejoinder to Professor Eisner. *Econometrica* 31, 539–44.
Brunner, K. 1965. Institutions, policy, and monetary analysis. *Journal of Political Economy* 73, 197–218.
—— and A. H. Meltzer. 1963. Predicting velocity: Implications for theory and policy. *Journal of Finance* 18, 319–54.
—— 1964a. *An Alternative Approach to the Monetary Mechanism*. Washington: House Committee on Banking and Currency, August.
—— 1964b. *The Federal Reserve's Attachment to the Free Reserve Concept*. Washington: House Committee on Banking and Currency, April.
—— 1964c. Some further investigations of demand and supply functions for money. *Journal of Finance* 19, 240–83.
—— 1966. A credit market theory of the money supply. *Rivista internaz. sci. econ. e commerciali* 13, May.
—— 1967. The meaning of monetary indicators. In *Monetary Process and Policy: A Symposium*, ed. G. Horwich. Homewood, Ill.: Richard. D. Irwin.
Burstein, M. 1963. *Money*. Cambridge, Mass.: Schenkman Publishing Co.
Christ, C. F. 1963. Interest rates and portfolio selection among liquid assets in the United States. In *Measurement in Economics*, ed. C. F. Christ. Stanford, Calif.: Stanford University Press.
Feige, E. 1964. *The Demand for Liquid Assets: A Temporal Cross-Section Study*. Englewood Cliffs, NJ: Prentice-Hall.
Fellner, W. 1948. Employment theory and business cycles. In *A Survey of Contemporary Economics*, ed. H. S. Ellis. Philadelphia: Blakiston Co.
Friedman, M. and A. J. Schwartz. 1963. *A Monetary History of the United States, 1867–1957*. Princeton, NJ: Princeton University Press for the National Bureau of Economic Research.
Frost, P. A. 1966. The Banks' Demand for Reserves. Unpublished PhD dissertation, University of California, Los Angeles.
Hester, D. 1962. An empirical examination of a commercial bank loan offer function. *Yale Economic Essays*.
Horwich, G. 1963. Effective reserves, credit and causality in the banking system of the thirties. In *Banking and Monetary Studies*, ed. D. Carson. Homewood, Ill.: Richard D. Irwin.
Johnson, H. G. 1962. Monetary theory and policy. *American Economic Review* 52, 335–84.
Keynes, J. M. 1936. *The General Theory of Employment, Interest and Money*. New York: Harcourt, Brace & Co.
Klein, L. R. 1947. *The Keynesian Revolution*. New York: Macmillan Co.
Maisel, S. J. 1957. *Fluctuations, Growth, and Economic Forecasting*. New York: John Wiley & Sons.
Meiselman, D. 1962. *The Term Structure of Interest Rates*. Englewood Cliffs, NJ: Prentice-Hall.
Meltzer, A. H. 1963a. The demand for money: The evidence from the time series. *Journal of Political Economy* 71, 219–46.

—— 1963b. Yet another look at the low level liquidity trap. *Econometrica* 31, 545–9.

Modigliani, F. 1944. Liquidity preference and the theory of interest and money. *Econometrica* 12, 45–88.

Patinkin, D. 1965. *Money, Interest and Prices*, 2nd edn. New York: Harper & Row.

Shaw, E. S. 1950. *Money, Income, and Monetary Policy*. Homewood, Ill.: Richard D. Irwin.

Tobin, J. 1947. Liquidity preference and monetary policy. *Review of Economics and Statistics* 29.

US Congress. 1935. *Hearings on H. R. 5327* (Banking Act of 1935). 74th Congress, 1st session Washington: House Committee on Banking and Currency.

—— 1961. *Hearing on the Annual Report of the Federal Reserve for the Year 1960.* 87th Congress, 1st session. Washington: Joint Economic Committee.

Villard, H. 1948. Monetary theory. In *A Survey of Contemporary Economics*, ed. H. S. Ellis. Philadelphia: Blakiston Co.

Warburton, C. 1950. Monetary velocity and the rate of interest. *Review of Economics and Statistics* 32.

4

An Aggregative Theory for a Closed Economy

Karl Brunner and Allan H. Meltzer

1 Introduction

For more than a generation, aggregative analysis of a closed economy has remained within the confines of the Keynesian framework as interpreted by Hicks (1937). Metzler (1951), Patinkin (1965) and others provided an alternative interpretation of Keynes (1936). Later extensions introduced anticipations and growth without altering the main qualitative conclusions. In both interpretations, the short-run response to monetary and fiscal policy is transmitted mainly by interest rates and depends on properties of the demand function for money and the expenditure function. A large interest elasticity of the demand for money increases the short-run response of output to fiscal policy. A large interest elasticity of consumption or investment expenditure increases the short-run response of output to monetary policy.

The meaning of "interest rates" differs in the two interpretations, and the adjustment processes differ as a consequence. In the common textbook version, interest rates are borrowing costs and portfolio adjustment consists of substitution between money and a narrow range of finanical assets called bonds. Metzler's financial asset is a composite representing claims to real capital. Bonds are perfect substitutes for such claims, and interest rates are the yield per period of a unit of real capital.

In Metzler's analysis real resources are fixed, so long-run output is fixed. The long-run effects of monetary and fiscal policies are on prices and interest rates. Changes in money change the price level but leave interest rates and real balances unchanged. Open market operations and changes in tax rates

This paper appeared in J. Stein (ed.), *Monetarism.* Amsterdam: North-Holland, 1976, pp. 69–103. Reprinted with permission. Helpful comments have been received from many readers. We are grateful to all of them and particularly to Pieter Korteweg. We are indebted to the National Science Foundation for continued support of our work.

transfer ownership of claims to streams of real income between the government and the private sector. Interest rates rise in response to open market sales and reductions in tax rates and fall in response to open market purchases and tax increases. Open market operations induce larger changes in the price level than tax changes that transfer securities of equal value, but the effects on real balances are identical. Open market purchases raise the equilibrium price level; open market sales lower the equilibrium price level.

All of the above conclusions are derived from a static model of exchange in which government is, at most, an agency for redistributing income by changing the ownership of wealth. Similar conclusions have been obtained for a growing economy under similar assumptions. In the Hicksian version, the government purchases goods and services. The long-run implications for prices and interest rates of issuing and withdrawing bonds are rarely discussed.

The basic difference between Hicks' and Metzler's analysis of portfolio adjustment reflects a difference in the assumptions about transaction costs. The Hicksian approach makes the cost of adjusting real assets in portfolios infinite. The Metzler approach sets these costs approximately equal to the transaction costs for securities, at or near zero. An intermediate position permitting adjustment of real capital, or claims to real capital, bonds and money seems to us more appropriate for aggregate analysis.

Our version of the monetarist hypothesis analyzes an economy in which costs of adjusting real capital in portfolios are neither zero nor infinite. Finite transaction costs place a wedge between the price of current output and the price of existing real capital. Substitution is not limited to two assets but includes the entire spectrum of assets. Adjustment is not limited to "the interest rate" but includes the relative prices of real capital and financial assets.

In two previous papers (1972, 1974a), we developed a general framework involving interaction between three assets. Wealth owners may accumulate or decumulate each of the assets – money, financial assets, and real capital – and may purchase current output. The economy is closed and, as in most of our discussion here, there is no growth in the stock of real capital, population or effective labor force. Interest rates, the prices of output and real capital are variable, however, and there is a government that purchases goods and services, taxes, finances deficits and surpluses and engages in open market operations.

Several of the conclusions obtained from a model with only two assets do not hold in a three-asset model. We have shown (Brunner and Meltzer 1974a) that the slopes of the expenditure functions and the demand function for money do not determine the relative size of the responses to fiscal and monetary policies. Contrary to frequent assertions, the major issues in aggregative analysis cannot be reduced to propositions about the relative slopes of the *IS* and *LM* curves.

In this paper, we consider standard propositions about the effects of policy changes in a closed economy. The following two sections present the model, develop conditions for equilibrium on the markets for assets and output, and show that the interaction of policy variables and market variables determine interest rates, prices, output and the government's budget position. Next, we consider the effects of monetary and fiscal policies and the financing of deficits and surpluses. The conclusion examines the main empirical conjectures that separate monetarist and Keynesian views.

2 The Framework

In the economy that we analyze, private decisions to hold, acquire or dispose of assets and to consume are made in response to prices and anticipated prices including the prices of current output, existing real capital and the market rate of interest. Government decisions on tax rates, expenditure and the financing of the budget surplus or deficit are summarized in a budget equation. For given tastes, opportunities and anticipations, and given wage rates, the decisions of the government and private sectors determine the level of output, the market rate of interest, the size of the budget deficit or surplus and the prices of real capital and current production. The economy is closed, and the capital stock and money wages are given. At a few points we relax the last constraints and permit the capital stock or money wage to change.[1]

2.1 The Output Market

Three principal equations describe the output market. Equation (4.1), is an equilibrium condition. Real output produced by the private sector, y, is absorbed by the private and government sectors. Real government expenditure, g, is set by government. Private expenditure, d, depends on prices and wealth, as shown in eqn (4.1'). Equation (4.1'') describes the pricing behavior of producers. Output prices, p, are revised in response to current market conditions expressed by y, real capital stock, K, efficiency wage rate, w, and suppliers' anticipations of prices, ϕ.[2]

$$y = d + g, \tag{4.1}$$

---

[1]More attention is given to longer-run consideration in Brunner (1974b). The international aspects were integrated in some detail in Brunner and Meltzer (1974b).

[2]There is no labor market in our model. The influence of the labor market on output, prices and other variables come through w and W_h, the efficiency wage and the value of current and future income from labor services. In a more complete analysis, w would be replaced by a solution of the labor market equations. Wage rates and interest rates are net of income and other taxes.

$$d = d(i - \pi, p, p^*, P, e, W_n, W_h) \qquad d_1, d_2 < 0; d_3, \ldots, d_7 > 0, (4.1')$$

$$p = p(y, K, w, \phi), \qquad p_1, p_3, p_4 > 0; p_2 < 0. \qquad (4.1'')$$

The variables affecting private expenditure are: i, the market rate of interest; π, the rate of inflation anticipated on the credit market; p^*, the price level anticipated by purchasers; P, the current price of existing real capital; e, the anticipated return to real capital per unit of capital; W_n and W_h are, respectively, human and non-human wealth at market value.

Differences between anticipated and actual outcomes affect the output market in a number of ways. The anticipated return to real capital may differ from the real rate of interest received and paid by lenders and borrowers on the credit market. Prices anticipated by purchasers may differ from the prices anticipated by suppliers, and both may differ from prevailing prices. The market rate of interest is related to prices and to anticipated returns, and in long run, steady state equilibrium, satisfies the equation

$$i = (p/P)e + \pi.$$

Elsewhere, the equality need not hold.

Both W_h and e depend on the level of real income and on the tax rates applicable to income from labor and capital. We assume that, for given tax rates, there is sufficient regularity in the distribution of income to permit us to neglect explicit references to the effect of changes in the distribution on expenditure, borrowing, lending or money holding. Human wealth, W_h, depends on wages, prices, and the tax rates applicable to income of this kind. Tax rates on non-human wealth affect the expected return to capital, e, and the returns received by owners of real assets, pe/P.

Non-human wealth at market value is the sum of base money, B, government securities held by banks and the non-bank public, S, and the stock of capital,[3]

$$W_h = PK + v(i, \tau)S + (1 + \omega)B.$$

S is the face value of the stock of government debt, and v is the market value per unit of debt. The market value of the debt depends on the difference between market and coupon rates, on maturity, and on the tax rates applicable to income from this source. The market value, v, depends negatively on i with an elasticity, $\epsilon(v, i)$ dependent on maturity structure; $\epsilon(v, i)$ rises algebraically as the maturity declines. The parameters τ and ω represent a vector of tax rates and the net worth multiplier of the banking system, respectively. The latter reflects a Pesek–Saving (1967) effect resulting from a regulated, non-competitive banking system and the real resources invested in the banking system but not included in K. The monetary base, B, is the total

---

[3]This expression is equivalent to the public's net worth.

monetary liability of the monetary authorities and is equal to total bank reserves and currency outstanding.

The output market proximately determines real output and the price level for given values of the other variables. Interest rates and asset prices affect the output market but are proximately determined in the asset markets. Money wages, anticipated prices, tax rates and real government expenditure are treated as given. In a closed economy, base money and outstanding securities are cumulated sums remaining from the financing of fiscal and monetary policies. Current changes in the base and the outstanding stock of securities depend on policy decisions and the position of the economy. The remaining component of wealth, real capital, is taken as given until the restriction is relaxed below.

2.2 The Asset Markets

Two asset markets, a credit market and money market, proximately determine the interest rate, i, and the asset price level, P. Interaction of the credit and money markets redistributes the components of existing wealth – money, government securities (or non-money financial assets) and real capital – among wealth holders until all assets are willingly held. Money is a substitute for securities and real capital, not for securities alone.

The credit market distributes the stock of outstanding securities between banks and the non-bank public and proximately determines the market rate of interest, i. Credit is defined as the asset portfolio on the consolidated balance sheet of the banking system and consists of bank loans and the banks' holdings of government securities. The stock of credit is the product of the monetary base, B, and the bank credit multiplier, a. The latter depends on all of the arguments of the expenditure function,[4] with derivatives shown in eqn (4.2), and on policy variables such as the discount rate and the reserve requirement ratios represented by the dots in the a-function. The public's supply of earning assets to banks, σ, depends on all the variables introduced in our discussion of the output market, and on the outstanding stock of securities, S. Equation (4.2) is an equilibrium condition for the stock of bank credit,

$$a(i, p, P, W_n, W_h, e, \ldots)B = \sigma(i - \pi, P, p, p^*, \phi, e, S, W_n, W_h), \quad (4.2)$$
$$a_1, a_3, a_4 > 0 > a_2; \sigma_1, \sigma_2 < 0; \sigma_3, \ldots, \sigma_7 > 0.$$

For the public, buying securities is an alternative to repaying loans, and

---

[4]More complete discussion of the bank credit and money multipliers – and the credit and money markets – can be found in several of our earlier papers. See Brunner and Meltzer (1968, 1974a), Brunner (1974a), or Burger (1972). Equations (4.2) and (4.3) can be interpreted as partially reduced forms.

selling securities is an alternative to borrowing from banks. The derivatives of the first six terms of the σ function show that prices, anticipated prices and returns affect the two components of σ – the public's desired borrowing and the excess supply of securities offered to banks – in the same way. Changes in wealth affect the two components in opposite ways. Hence, the derivatives with respect to wealth are small and of uncertain sign.

The demand for money is not equivalent to the public's supply of earning assets to banks, and the stock of money is not identical to the stock of bank credit. The money market of our analysis proximately determines the asset price level, P, and for given values of p and e, determines the real rate of return on real capital.

The asset price level is distinct from the price level of new production. Costs of adjustment associated with the acquisition of real captial, and costs of acquiring information about market opportunities, assure that p and P are, generally, not equal. In full long run adjustment to a steady state, with all costs variable, all opportunities realized, and all anticipations equal to actual values, existing capital sells at reproduction cost, and the real return to real capital equals the expected return, e.

Equation (4.3) is the equilibrium condition for the money market. The stock of money is the product of a money multiplier, m, and the monetary base. Interest rates, asset prices and wealth affect the money multiplier and the stock of money by changing the distribution of money between currency and demand deposits and the distribution of deposits between time and demand accounts. Reserve requirement ratios and the discount rate affect the money multiplier by changing the distribution of reserves between required and surplus reserves or by increasing or decreasing borrowing from the central bank.

$$m(i, p, P, W_n, W_h, \ldots)B = L(i, p^*, \phi, e, p, P, W_n, W_h),$$
$$m_1, m_2 > 0; m_3, m_4 < 0; \tag{4.3}$$
$$L_1, \ldots, L_4 < 0; L_5, \ldots, L_8 > 0.$$

The demand for money depends on all of the arguments of the σ function except S. However, the properties of the two functions differ. Changes in anticipated prices, the anticipated rate of price change, the anticipated yield on real capital, and the asset price level shift L and σ in opposite directions. Moreover, the wealth elasticities of L are considerably larger than the wealth elasticities of σ.

Our analysis explicitly rejects the traditional Keynesian view that identifies the demand for money with the supply of earning assets of banks (Gramley and Chase, 1965). Failure to separate the markets for money and credit restricts such analysis – for example, *IS–LM* analysis – to a world in which there are at most two assets. We do not believe it is possible to correctly analyze the adjustment of prices and output to government fiscal and monetary policies without separating the credit and money markets, or alternatively, distinguishing money, bonds and real capital.

2.3 The Government Sector

An understanding of the effects of monetary and fiscal policy requires analysis linking the government budget deficit or surplus and the financing of the budget with the markets for assets and output (Christ, 1972; Silber, 1970). Changes in tax rates or government expenditure affect the output market directly. Changes in the volume of base money and securities issued to finance the budget deficit also change expenditure, and more importantly, change the position of the asset market. Even a constant, maintained deficit or surplus affects the markets for assets and output. The reason is that the financing of any deficit or surplus alters the nominal stocks of base money and securities and changes the prices of assets and output.

Equation (4.4) is the government's budget equation. The government's purchase of goods, pg, labor services, $\bar{w}lg$, and interest payments (net of taxes), $I(i)S$, are financed by tax revenues, $t(p, y, \bar{w}lg; \tau)$, and by issuing base money and securities. All bonds are issued at par,

$$pg + \bar{w}lg + I(i)S - t(p, y, \bar{w}lg; \tau) = \overset{\circ}{B} + \overset{\circ}{S}. \tag{4.4}$$

In a closed economy, most changes in the base and the stock of securities result from the financing of the current deficit or from open market operations.

The government hires labor at the market money wage $\bar{w}$, and pays interest on its outstanding debt. Interest payments depend on the maturity and volume of debt. Expenditure g (or pg) the number of workers hired, lg, or expenditure for labor services, $\bar{w}lg$, and the tax rate schedule, τ, are set by policy decisions. We are free to choose either $\overset{\circ}{B}$ or $\overset{\circ}{S}$ or some combination as an additional policy variable. The proper choice depends on the institutional arrangements prevailing in a given economy. Most central banks and governments do not choose explicitly but, instead, attempt to damp fluctuations in interest rates. Let μ be the portion of the current deficit or surplus financed by issuing or withdrawing base money, and let ν be the amount of base money issued or withdrawn by open market operations conducted independently of deficit finance. $\overset{\circ}{B} = \nu$ whenever the budget is balanced. If the budget is unbalanced, $\nu = 0$ whenever $0 < \mu < 1$. More generally,

$$\overset{\circ}{B} = \mu(pg + \bar{w}lg + IS - t) + \nu,$$

and

$$\overset{\circ}{S} = (1 - \mu)(pg + \bar{w}lg + IS - t) - \nu.$$

We treat μ as a policy parameter describing the financing of the government budget.

3 Interaction of the Budget and the Markets for Assets and Output

Every displacement of the equilibrium position of the credit, money or output market affects the other markets and the budget equation. Every change in the budget position affects the markets for assets and output. Every change in stocks, flows or the budget changes relative prices, tax collections and the amounts of base money and securities issued or withdrawn. In this section, we analyze the interaction of the system and show the conditions for stock-flow equilibrium. Diagrams illustrate the main points.

The position of flow equilibrium must satisfy the equilibrium condition, eqn (4.1), relating actual and desired output or expenditure. Desired expenditure depends on P and i. Changes in the stocks – B, S, or K – affect P and i and shift the position of flow equilibrium, so the flow equilibrium depends upon the position of the asset market.

To take account of the effect of the asset markets on the flow equilibrium, we first solve the asset market equations for P and i. The solutions for P and i depend on p and y because the multipliers m and a and the L and σ functions depend on prices and output. The dependence on y reflects the presence of W_h and e in the asset equations. Let $\epsilon(i, y|AM)$, $\epsilon(P, y|AM)$ and similar expressions with output price (p) in lieu of y, denote the elasticities of i and P with respect to prices and output derived from the equilibrium conditions for the asset markets given the position of the output market.[5] Next we substitute the solutions for i and P obtained from the asset market equations into the d function and obtain an implicit function, shown by the $d + g$ line, involving p and y. Then we differentiate the equilibrium condition for the output market with respect to y and solve for $\epsilon(p, y|d+g)$, the slope of the $d + g$ curve in figure 4.1. The slope is the elasticity of p with respect to y obtained from the expenditure and asset market equations. The bars on $\bar{\epsilon}(d, i)$ and $\bar{\epsilon}(d, P)$ indicate that these elasticities include the effect on expenditure of the change in wealth induced by changes in interest rates and asset prices.

$$\begin{aligned}
\epsilon(p, y|d+g) = &\{1 - (1-\gamma)[\bar{\epsilon}(d, i)\,\epsilon(i, y|AM) + \bar{\epsilon}(d, P)\,\epsilon(P, y|AM) \\
&+ \epsilon(d, W_h)\,\epsilon(W_h, y) + \epsilon(d, e)\,\epsilon(e, y)]\} \\
&\times \{(1 - \gamma)[\epsilon(d, p) + \bar{\epsilon}(d, i)\,\epsilon(i, p|AM) \\
&+ \bar{\epsilon}(d, P)\,\epsilon(P, p|AM) + \epsilon(d, W_h)\,\epsilon(W_h, p)]\}^{-1}
\end{aligned}$$

The numerator and denominator depend on the proportion of total output absorbed by government, $\gamma = g/(d + g)$, and on the relative responses of expenditure to asset prices, interest rates and output prices. The elasticity is likely to be negative.[6] The magnitude increases (numerically) as γ increases.

---

[5]The appendix describes the asset market responses discussed in the text.

[6]The homogeneity properties of the d function assure that $\epsilon(d, p)$ is large relative to the elasticities with respect to P, W_h, W_n and p^*. The denominator is unambiguously negative. A very

The rate of use of resources, y/K, also affects the size of the elasticity. At low rates of utilization the numerator is smaller than at high rates. The reason is that $\epsilon(i, y|AM)$ and $\epsilon(P, y|AM)$ change with the utilization of capacity and the distribution of income.[7] To simplify the notation, we rewrite the slope of $d + g$ as

$$\epsilon(p, y|d+g) = \{1 - (1-\gamma)\,\bar{\epsilon}(d, y)\}\{(1-\gamma)\,\bar{\epsilon}(d, p)\}^{-1}$$

The barred values of the elasticities are defined by the corresponding expressions in the brackets above. The position of the $d + g$ curve depends on anticipations and stocks. The curve is the locus of all p, y combinations satisfying the output and asset market equations simultaneously.

The supply curve (s) of output is obtained from the price setting function, eqn (4.1″). The price elasticity of the supply of output increases as capacity utilization increases. The position of the supply curve depends on K, w and ϕ. The slope of the supply curve is denoted $\epsilon(p, y|s)$.

Figure 4.1a shows a flow equilibrium at the intersection of $d + g$ and s. The equilibrium position depends on the stocks of financial assets and real capital, the efficiency wage and anticipations. The size of the financial stocks depends, in turn, on the history of the government's budget and the financing parameter, μ.

In a closed economy with no growth, there cannot be full stock–flow equilibrium with an unbalanced budget. The relation between the government's budget and the position of the economy is expressed by the balanced budget equation and shown by the *bbe* curve in figure 4.1. The *bbe* curve is the locus of all p, y combinations that satisfy the asset market equations and the balanced budget equation. To obtain the curve, we substitute the solution for i from the asset market equation into the balanced budget,

$$i = i(y, p, B, S),$$
$$pg + \bar{w}lg + I(i)S = t(p, y, \bar{w}lg, \tau).$$

The position of the curve depends on fiscal and monetary polices. Increases in g, lg, or S move the line to the right; increases in τ move the line to the left. The slope of the line, holding w constant, is

$$\epsilon(p, y|bbe; g) = \frac{\epsilon(t, y) - \epsilon(I, i)\,\epsilon(i, y|AM)\,IS/t}{pg/t - \epsilon(t, p) + \epsilon(I, i)\,\epsilon(i, p|AM)\,IS/t} < 0.$$

---

large positive value of $\bar{\epsilon}(d, P)\,\epsilon(P, y|AM)$, substantially greater than unity, is required to turn the numerator negative and determine an ascending "demand" curve. This is unlikely. The $d + g$ curve is an equilibrium position for expenditure, not an expenditure relation as we incorrectly described it in an earlier paper (1974a). J Marquez-Ruarte pointed out the error. The $d + g$ line is the locus of all combinations (p, y) simultaneously satisfying asset markets and output markets.

[7] The distribution of income changes with fluctuations in income. At low rates of utilization, changes in y have larger effects on e than on W_h, while at high rates of utilization, the opposite is true. The elasticities $\epsilon(e, y)$ and $\epsilon(W_h, y)$ are components of $\epsilon(i, y|AM)$ and $\epsilon(P, y|AM)$. On the supply side, $\epsilon(p, y|s)$ rises monotonically with the degree of utilization.

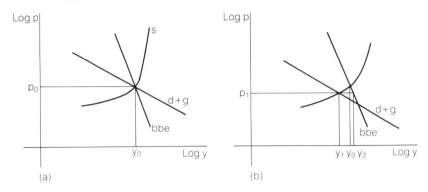

Figure 4.1   Conditions for stock–flow equilibrium.

The elasticity $\epsilon(I, i)$ rises from zero to unity as the average maturity of the debt declines. With a positive wage bill and a positive volume of outstanding government debt, the ratio $pg/t < 1$. The *bbe* line is negatively sloped for all tax revenue functions at least proportional in the price level, i.e., for $\epsilon(t, p) \geq 1$.[8] If, as we have assumed, government sets the level of real expenditure, g, the *bbe* line is relatively steep. If the government directs its fiscal policy at nominal expenditure, pg, the elasticity becomes

$$\epsilon(p, y \,|\, bbe; pg) = \frac{-\epsilon(t, y) + \epsilon(I, i)\,\epsilon(i, y\,|\,AM)\,IS/t}{\epsilon(t, p) - \epsilon(I, i)\,\epsilon(i, p\,|\,AM)\,IS/t},$$

and the value of the elasticity is approximately -1.

All points on the *bbe* line are, by definition, positions of budget balance. Any price output combination to the right of the line generates a budget surplus, and any point to the left of the line generates a budget deficit. Every budget deficit or surplus requires the banks and the public to increase or decrease holdings of base money and debt, so any departure from the *bbe* line affects the position of the $d + g$ line. Changes in financial stocks change P and i and modify the $d + g$ line. If follows that all points of stock–flow equilibrium must lie at the common intersection of the *bbe* line, the $d + g$ line and the *s* line. An equilibrium of this kind is shown at $p_0 y_0$ in figure 1a.

3.1 Short-Run Equilibrium

Suppose the output market comes into short-run flow equilibrium with output less than y_0, for example at p_1, y_1 in figure 4.1b. With current fiscal

---

[8]A positive slope of the *bbe* line does not alter the main conclusions of the analysis unless the slope of the *bbe* line exceeds the slope of the *s* curve. For the problem to arise, the share of taxes allocated to interest payments must be so large that increases in output increase interest rates and raise the budget deficit and reductions in expenditure induce ever-increasing budget surpluses.

policies shown by the position of the *bbe* line, the government budget has a deficit. The size of the deficit increases with the horizontal distance, $y_1 - y_2$, between the position of flow equilibrium at the intersection of $d + g$ and s and the position of budget balance of the *bbe* line at the prevailing price level, p_1. A budget surplus forces a reduction in the stocks of base money and securities, and a budget deficit requires an increase in the stocks of these financial assets. The relative size of the changes in each stock depends on the financing parameter, μ, and the speed of adjustment to a balanced budget equilibrium depends on μ also. As the value of μ increases, the change in the base and the speed of adjustment to a new equilibrium increase. However, for given w, K and unchanged position of s, the total size of the adjustment from $p_1 y_1$ to a position of stock–flow equilibrium declines as μ increases.

3.2 Intermediate-Run Equilibrium

We refer to the resulting stock–flow equilibrium, at an intersection of the $d + g$, s, and *bbe* curves, as an intermediate-run equilibrium to emphasize that money wages are constant and s remains fixed. The adjustment to intermediate-run equilibrium involves changes in the $d + g$ line and the *bbe* line. These changes are the responses to the changes in B and S issued to finance the deficit – or retired if a surplus replaces the deficit – in figure 4.1b.

Financing the deficit increases B and S in the proportion defined by μ. Increases in B and S shift the $d + g$ line to the right. The size of each shift is obtained by differentiating the output market equation with respect to B or S after replacing i and P with their respective solutions from the asset market equations, holding the value of y constant. The two vertical shift elasticities are

$$\epsilon(p, B|d + g) = \left[- \bar{\epsilon}(d, i) \, \epsilon(i, B|AM) + \bar{\epsilon}(d, P) \, \epsilon(P, B|AM) + \right.$$

$$\left. + \epsilon(d, W_n) \frac{(1+\omega)B}{W_n} \right] [\bar{\epsilon}(d, p)]^{-1} > 0,$$

$$\epsilon(p, S|d + g) = \epsilon(p, B|d + g) \left\{ \left[\bar{\epsilon}(d, i) \, \epsilon(i, S|AM) + \bar{\epsilon}(d, P) \, \epsilon(P, S|AM) \right. \right.$$

$$+ \epsilon(d, W_n) \frac{\nu S}{W_n} \right] \left[\bar{\epsilon}(d, i) \, \epsilon(i, B|AM) \right.$$

$$\left. \left. + \bar{\epsilon}(d, P) \, \epsilon(P, B|AM) + \epsilon(d, W_n) \frac{(1+\omega)B}{W_n} \right]^{-1} \right\} > 0.$$

Both elasticities are positive, so the direction in which the $d + g$ line shifts is independent of the method of financing the deficit or surplus.[9] The $d + g$

---

[9] A low interest elasticity of expenditure $\epsilon(d, i)$ is clearly not sufficient to eliminate the effect of

line always shifts in the direction of the *bbe* line, toward a position of budget balance. The size of the shift depends on the relative amounts of base money and debt issued (or withdrawn in the case of a surplus). The larger the value of μ, the larger is the instantaneous shift in the $d + g$ curve. This is shown by the elasticity formulas. The response of the $d + g$ line to a unit change in debt, $\epsilon(p, S|d+g)$, is proportional to $\epsilon(p, B|d+g)$, the response to a unit change in the base. The denominator of the proportionality factor, or ratio, is positive, but the first two terms of the numerator are of opposite sign. The ratio is less than one, so the response of the $d + g$ line to a unit change in the base exceeds the response to a unit change in debt.

The vertical shift in $d + g$ and the slopes of the $d + g$ and s curves determine the position of flow equilibrium to which the system moves in response to changes in B and S. We use $\epsilon(p, B|0, AM)$, $\epsilon(y, B|0, AM)$ and similar expressions with S replacing B to denote the responses of prices and output to financial stocks. As before, the responses combine the adjustment of the asset markets and the output market to changes in the financial variables, holding the position of s constant. The $0, AM$ elasticities define the movement of the flow equilibrium point determined by $d + g$ and s in figure 4.1.

$$\epsilon(p, B|0, AM) \quad = \frac{-\ \epsilon(p, B|d + g)\ \epsilon(p, y|s)}{\epsilon(p, y|d + g) - \epsilon(p, y|s)} > 0, \qquad (4.5')$$

$$\epsilon(y, B|0, AM) \quad = \frac{-\ \epsilon(p, B|d + g)}{\epsilon(p, y|d + g) - \epsilon(p, y|s)} > 0. \qquad (4.5'')$$

The responses of p and y to S (or g) are similar to eqns (4.5') and (4.5''); S (or g) replaces B in the first term of the numerator.

The response of the flow equilibrium position to a given deficit is a weighted combination of the separate responses of B and S with weights fixed by financial policies. Let D be the cumulated deficit. In a closed economy, the current stocks of B and S record past financial policy,

$$B = B_0 + \bar{\mu}D, \qquad (4.6')$$

$$S = S_0 + (1 - \bar{\mu})D, \qquad (4.6'')$$

---

monetary policy. The sign of the denominator of $\epsilon(p, B|d + g)$ is discussed in the appendix. The sign of the numerator depends on $\epsilon(i, B|AM) < 0$ and $\epsilon(P, B|AM) > 0$. The former is unambiguous; the latter occurs if the interest elasticity of the excess supply of credit exceeds the interest elasticity of the excess supply of money. The signs of the elasticities of i and P with respect to B and S are shown in the appendix. The positive sign of $\epsilon(p, S|d + g)$ requires that in the numerator

$$|\bar{e}(d, i)\ \epsilon(i, S|AM) < \bar{e}(d, P)\ \epsilon(P, S|AM) + \epsilon(d, W_n)\nu S/W_n.$$

The restriction assures that issues of debt to finance expansive fiscal policies increase expenditure and prices. A very large $\bar{e}(d, i)$ reverses the response of output and prices to debt-financed fiscal policy. The stability of the system requires that the inequality above holds.

where $\bar{\mu}$ is the mean value of the financing parameter, and B_0 and S_0 describe stocks of base money and government securities acquired independently of the budget process. B_0 and S_0 are the values of any prehistoric stocks of base money or securities modified by the cumulated effect of pure open market operations, ν.

The weighted shift of the $d + g$ curve induced by a deficit (or surplus), per unit, is

$$\epsilon(p, D|d+g) = \epsilon(p, B|d+g)\bar{\mu}\, \frac{D}{B} + \epsilon(p, S|d+g)(1-\bar{\mu})\, \frac{D}{S} > 0.$$

All terms are positive, so the direction of response is independent of current and past financial policies. The magnitude of the response depends on both current and past policies. A large value of $\bar{\mu}$ raises $\epsilon(p, D|d + g)$ and the adjustment speed of the flow equilibrium.

The movement to a new flow equilibrium position reduces the initial deficit (or surplus). However, the size of the deficit depends on the distance between the flow equilibrium position and the *bbe* line. The position of the *bbe* line is also changed by the financing of the deficit or surplus and the direction of change depends on the way in which the deficit is financed. The vertical shifts of the *bbe* line, per unit change, are expressed as elasticities. The elasticities are obtained by differentiating the government budget equation with respect to B and S taking into account the effect of price changes on interest rates, holding money wages constant. The numerators of the two elasticities are of opposite sign. The denominators are negative wherever tax revenues are not sufficiently regressive.

$$\epsilon(p, B|bbe; g) = \frac{-\,\epsilon(I, i)\,\epsilon(i, B|AM)\,IS/t}{pg/t + \epsilon(i, p|AM)\,\epsilon(I, i)\,IS/t - \epsilon(t, p)} < 0,$$

$$\epsilon(p, S|bbe; g) = \frac{-\,[\epsilon(I, i)\,\epsilon(i, S|AM) + \epsilon(I, S)]IS/t}{pg/t + \epsilon(i, p|AM)\,\epsilon(I, i)\,IS/t - \epsilon(t, p)} > 0.$$

An increase in B lowers the *bbe* line, whereas an increase in S raises the line. The size of the change in the *bbe* line depends on the relative sizes of the numerators of the two shift elasticities. With $\epsilon(I, S)$ equal to unity, $\epsilon(p, S|bbe)$ probably exceeds $|\epsilon(p, B|bbe)|$. At high values of μ, deficits shift the *bbe* line to the left and surpluses shift the *bbe* line to the right. At low values, of μ, deficits move the *bbe* line to the right and surpluses move the line to the left.

The speed of convergence to intermediate-run equilibrium and the equilibrium position depend on the value of μ. With $\mu = 1$, the $d + g$ line shifts up when there is a deficit and down when there is a surplus. The *bbe* line shifts the opposite way, down when there is a deficit and up when there is a surplus. The process converges to equilibrium at an intersection of $d + g$, s and *bbe*. In figure 4.1b, with $\mu = 1$ the *bbe* curve slides down the s curve until it meets the rising $d + g$ curve. For values of μ near unity, similar movements take place, but as μ declines, the change in the position of the *bbe* curve becomes smaller relative to the change in the position of $d + g$.

We reach a critical value of μ at which the position of the *bbe* line is fixed. The adjustment to intermediate-run equilibrium is now described by the movement of the $d + g$ curve along s. If the intersection of *bbe* and s is a position of long-run equilibrium, the economy returns to long-run equilibrium at unchanged prices and output.

The diagram cannot show a determinate result for low values of μ. The reason is that the *bbe* and $d + g$ lines moves in the same direction. Convergence requires that the *bbe* line moves less than the $d + g$ line. Otherwise, the deficit continues and the stocks of financial assets increase forever. Prices rise continuously as $d + g$ chases *bbe* along s. The system never reaches intermediate-run equilibrium. At the polar position, $\mu = 0$, if the system does not converge to equilibrium, prices rise with a constant monetary base.

Can there be inflation with a constant monetary base? To show that the system converges to an intermediate-run equilibrium for all values of μ, we substitute in the government budget equation until the equation contains only variables taken as givens in the determination of flow equilibrium. The price level p is replaced by the price setting function. The values of i and y are replaced by their flow equilibrium solutions. The 0, AM elasticities, as in eqn (4.5), describe the properties of these solutions. Further, we use eqn (4.6) to replace B and S with the cumulated deficit and the stocks B_0 and S_0. We obtain a differential equation relating the current deficit (or surplus) to the cumulated deficit.

$$\overset{\circ}{D} = f(D; B_0, S_0, \mu; g, \tau).$$

The stability of the stock–flow system and convergence to intermediate-run equilibrium require that the derivative $f_D < 0$.

The derivative is

$$\frac{\partial f}{\partial D} = \frac{\partial f}{\partial B} \bar{\mu} + \frac{\partial f}{\partial S} (1 - \bar{\mu});$$

$$\frac{\partial f}{\partial B} = \frac{t}{B} \left\{ \epsilon(y, B | 0, AM) \left[\epsilon(p, y | s) \left(\frac{pg}{t} - \epsilon(t, p) \right) - \epsilon(t, y) \right] \right.$$

$$\left. + \epsilon(I, i) \, \epsilon(i, B | 0, AM) \, \frac{IS}{t} \right\} < 0,$$

$$\frac{\partial f}{\partial S} = \frac{t}{S} \left\{ \epsilon(y, S | 0, AM) \left[\epsilon(p, y | s) \left(\frac{pg}{t} - \epsilon(t, p) \right) - \epsilon(t, y) \right] \right.$$

$$\left. + \left[1 + \epsilon(I, i) \, \epsilon(i, S | 0, AM) \right] \frac{IS}{t} \right\}$$

The necessary conditions for stability and convergence, with any value of

μ are $\epsilon(y, S|0, AM) > 0$ and a non-regressive tax function. The first condition is discussed in note 9 and the accompanying text. The second condition is required to assure $\partial f/\partial S < 0$. The second term of $\partial f/\partial S$ is positive. The derivative remains negative, however, if net interest payments are sufficiently small relative to tax revenues and tax revenues are not overly regressive.

Analysis of stock–flow adjustment to an intermediate-run equilibrium yields four principal conclusions. First, the relative sizes of the shift elasticities $\epsilon(p, B|d + g)$ and $\epsilon(p, S|d + g)$ imply that the *instantaneous* rate of adjustment of output to a budget deficit or surplus increases with the value of μ. Second, the *total* adjustment of output and prices, measured from the initial displacement to the intermediate-run equilibrium, *decreases* as μ increases. The change along a given s curve reaches a maximum with debt finance, $\mu = 0$, and a minimum with base money finance, $\mu = 1$. Third, any change in μ changes the equilibrium position of the *bbe* line and therefore affects prices and output. Fourth, maintenance of stock flow equilbrium at constant prices requires a balanced budget and no open market operations. The first of these restrictions assures that $\overset{\circ}{D} = 0$; the second maintains a constant ratio of B_0 to S_0. Both are required for equilibrium in a non-growing economy.

3.3 Long-Run Equilibrium

Money wages cannot be held fixed if prices and output change. The dynamics of the labor market push the system toward a longer-run position determined by long-run output and the long-run *bbe* line. In figure 4.2 long-run output is shown as a vertical line drawn at y_0. The position of y_0 depends on productive opportunities, resources, and tastes. The long-run position of flow equilibrium and the long-run position of the *bbe* line depend on the adjustment of money wages. Even in a closed economy with no growth, the long-run position of stock–flow equilibrium differs from the intermediate-run position if prices and money wages change. To reveal the general nature of long-run adjustment, we permit efficiency wages to adjust to market conditions.

The wage adjustment process can be divided into two parts. One links wage movements to prices and completes our analysis of the response to changes in B, S, and government expenditure; the other develops the general relation between changes in prices, in efficiency wages and in the deviations of output from its long-equilibrium value. Only the first process is discussed here. The second is developed in Brunner (1974b).

The elasticity $\epsilon(w, p)$ describes the (eventual) adjustment of efficiency wages to prices. Adjustment of wages shifts the supply of output and changes the position of flow equilibrium. The response of the s curve is

$$\epsilon(p, w|s)\,\epsilon(w, p)\,\epsilon(p, x|0, AM, s).$$

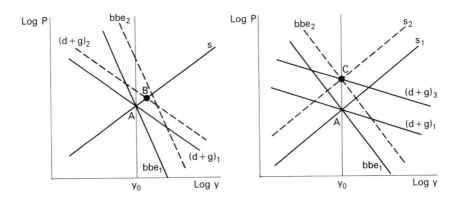

Figure 4.2 Factors determining the long-run position of stock–flow equilibrium.
4.2a short-run response of system from A to B to an increase in government expenditures.
4.2b final adjustment of system from A to C after full adjustment of wages and prices.

The responses of the price level and output are

$$\epsilon(p, x|0, AM, s) = \{-\epsilon(p, x|d + g)\,\epsilon(p, y|s)$$
$$+ \epsilon(p, y|d + g)\,\epsilon(p, w|s)\,\epsilon(w, p)\,\epsilon(p, x|0, AM, s)\}$$
$$\times \{\epsilon(p, y|d + g) - \epsilon(p, y|s)\}^{-1},$$

$$\epsilon(y, x|0, AM, s) = \{-\epsilon(p, x|d + g) + \epsilon(p, w|s)\,\epsilon(w, p)\,\epsilon(p, x|0, AM, s)\}$$
$$\times \{\epsilon(p, y|d + g) - \epsilon(p, y|s)\}^{-1},$$

for $x = B, S, g$.

Rearrangement yields

$$\epsilon(p, x|0, AM, s) = \{\epsilon(p, x|d + g)\,\epsilon(p, y|s)\}\,\{\epsilon(p, y|d + g)$$
$$\times [1 - \epsilon(p, w|s)\,\epsilon(w, p)] - \epsilon(p, y|s)\}^{-1} > 0,$$

$$\epsilon(y, x|0, AM, s) = \{-\epsilon(p, x|d + g)\}/\{\epsilon(p, y|d + g) - \epsilon(p, y|s)\}$$
$$\times 1 + [\epsilon(p, w|s)\,\epsilon(w, p)\,\epsilon(p, y|s)]/[den]\},$$

where *den* is the denominator of $\epsilon(p, x|0, AM, s)$.

With $\epsilon(p, w|s)\,\epsilon(w, p)$ approximately 1,

$$\epsilon(p, x|0, AM, s) \sim \epsilon(p, x|d + g),$$

and

$$\epsilon(y, x|0, AM, s) \sim 0.$$

In the limiting case of flexible money wages, real output is unaffected by monetary and fiscal policies. The instantaneous shift effect of policy variables on output prices is identical to the long-run effect.

The value of the product $\epsilon(p, w|s) \cdot \epsilon(w, p)$ describing the wage adjustment process probably lies between 0 and 1. The results obtained holding the s line fixed correspond to $\epsilon(p, w|s) \cdot \epsilon(w, p) = 0$. This state describes short-run processes and is dominated by the response of output. At the opposite pole the price level absorbs all the effects of wage adjustment, and output is not affected. We conjecture that in the intermediate run, the value for $\epsilon(p, w|s) \cdot \epsilon(w, p)$ produces a noticeable output response. Subsequent wage adjustments strengthen the price response and dampen the output response.

Wage adjustments change little in the dynamics of the intermediate financial stock–flow process. To show this result, we again substitute the solutions from the flow equilibrium system into the deficit function and obtain a differential equation determining the motion of D. The main differences from results without wage adjustment are in the properties of the p and y function. With $\epsilon(p, w|s) \cdot \epsilon(w, p) = 0$ the p function was simply the price setting function, whereas it is now a solution function with arguments B, S and g and properties established in previous paragraphs. The derivative of the deficit function with respect to D is again a linear combination of derivatives with respect to B and S with weights μ and $(1 - \mu)$.

$$f_B = \frac{t}{B}\left[\epsilon(p, B|0, AM, s) \left\{\frac{pg}{t} - \epsilon(t, p) + \epsilon(w, p) \left(\frac{wlg}{t} - \epsilon(t, \bar{w}lg)\right)\right\}\right.$$

$$\left. - \epsilon(t, y) \cdot \epsilon(y, B|0, AM, s) + \epsilon(I, i) \cdot \epsilon(i, B|0, AM, s) \frac{IS}{t}\right],$$

$$f_S = \frac{t}{S}\left[\epsilon(p, S|0, AM, s) \left\{\frac{pg}{t} - \epsilon(t, p) + \epsilon(w, p) \left(\frac{wlg}{t} - \epsilon(t, \bar{w}lg)\right)\right\}\right.$$

$$\left. - \epsilon(t, y) \cdot \epsilon(y, S|0, AM, s) + [1 + \epsilon(I, i) \cdot \epsilon(i, S|0, AM, s)] \frac{IS}{t}\right]$$

The interaction of wages and prices raises the third component of both derivatives algebraically and lowers the second component algebraically. Both changes narrow the constraints required to assure stability in the case of debt finance. For stability the system may require a minimal value of μ to prevent the destabilizing influence arising from a numerically small but positive derivative f_s. Instability reflects an inadequate financing procedure of the government and becomes most relevant when interest payments are large relative to taxes.

The operation of the wage adjustment process moves the intermediate-run system expressed by the $d + g$, s and bbe lines towards an intersection on the vertical long-run output line. Convergence of the system allows us to discuss general directions of longer-run movements by concentrating attention on the intersection between the (long-run) *bbe* line and the vertical long-run output line. Changes in this intersection determine the system's underlying trend movement in prices and output. An examination of longer-run aspects requires a clear description of the long-run *bbe* line.

The line is obtained by replacing i with the solution for i from the asset market (AM) equations and replacing B and S by $B_0 + \mu D$ and $S_0 + (1 - \mu)D$. With these changes, the balanced budget equation becomes

$$pg + \bar{w}lg + I\{i[B_0 + \mu D, S_0 + (1 - \mu)D; p, y]\} [S_0 + (1 - \mu)D]$$
$$= t(p, y, \bar{w}lg; \tau).$$

The position of the line depends on the value of D. The slope of the line, with g as a policy variable, is

$$\epsilon(p, y|bbe; g) = \{\epsilon(t, y) - \epsilon(I, i)\epsilon(i, y|AM) IS/t\}\{pg/t + \epsilon(\bar{w}, p) \bar{w}lg/t$$
$$+ \epsilon(I, i)\epsilon(i, p|AM) IS/t - \epsilon(t, p) - \epsilon(\bar{w}, p)\epsilon(t, \bar{w}lg)\}^{-1} > 0.$$

We previously noted that allowing for the adjustment of money wages lowers the denominator numerically; the slope of the *bbe* line becomes slightly steeper. A non-regressive tax revenue function assures that the slope is negative.

The position of the long-run *bbe* line depends on D, the cumulated deficit. Once the fiscal policy variables, g and τ, and the parameter μ have been fixed, the balanced budget determines D. This is necessary to assure that in the long-run *bbe* and long-run output, y_0, intersect at a price level consistent with the long-run solutions of the output market equations and the government budget equation. The solution for D acts as a scale value that places the *bbe* line at its long-run position.

The value of long-run output depends on opportunities, resources, and tastes. With a stationary population and a constant value of K, long-run output y_0 and the expected return to capital are fixed. The output and asset market equations determine two ratios and the rate of interest, given long-run output,

$$p/D = \bar{p}(\mu, g, lg, \tau, B_0/D, S_0/D, y_0),$$
$$P/D = \bar{P}(\mu, g, lg, \tau, B_0/D, S_0/D, y_0),$$
$$i = \bar{\imath}(\mu, g, lg, \tau, B_0/D, S_0/D, y_0).$$

The price-setting function can be used to determine the money wage consistent with long-run equilibrium. This permits the replacement of w in the budget equation by an expression that is linear, homogeneous in p. If we now replace p with $\bar{p}D$, y with y_0, and i with $\bar{\imath}$ in the government budget equation, the equation determines a value of $D = D^*$ associated with given fiscal and monetary policy. With proportional taxes, $\epsilon(t, p) + \epsilon(t, \bar{w}lg) = 1$, and $S_0 = B_0 = 0$ the value of D^* is arbitrary. Otherwise, the budget equation determines a unique D^*. D^* determines the position of the long-run *bbe* line, and the intersection of the line with y_0 determines the price level at which the economy reaches stock equilibrium.

Changes in the intersection between the long-run *bbe* line and long-run equilibrium output, y_0, determine the general direction in which the price level changes. Fiscal policy (g, lg, τ) and monetary policy, (μ, B_0, S_0) affect the relative changes in the position of *both* lines. Increases in the government's absorption of output, g or absorption of labor, lg, or lower tax rates, raise the *bbe* line and the price level to which the economy adjusts. Open market operations determine the size of B_0 relative to S_0, and the choice of $\bar{\mu}$ determines the proportion in which B and S are issued or withdrawn to finance budget deficits and surpluses. Increases in $\bar{\mu}$ lower the *bbe* line and reduce the price level to which the economy adjusts.

In the long run, all costs are variable, capital sells at replacement cost, $p = P$, and the market rate of interest equals the expected return to capital per unit of capital. The system cannot determine values for $\bar{p}D$, $\bar{P}D$ and $\bar{\iota}$ that ignore these constraints. If the capital stock is fixed and monetary policy sets μ, fiscal policy cannot be predetermined but must adjust to the system. Or, if lg, g and τ are set and K remains fixed, the system determines μ and B_0 or S_0.

There is a third alternative. We may choose both fiscal variables, B_0 and S_0. The long-run conditions $p = P$ and $i = e + \pi$ determine K and μ. All real stocks are then determined endogenously and adjusted to policy variables. The long-run level of economic activity is conditioned by the stock of real capital, the labor force, the absorption of labor by the government sector, the amount invested in human capital such as skills and knowledge. These determinants of the level at which y_0 settles depend on fiscal and monetary policies. If expenditure, transfer and tax policies and the means of financing deficits and surpluses are set by political or policy decisions, the capital stock, the productivity of capital, and long-run output, y_0, must adjust.[10]

4 Monetary Policy

The interaction of stocks and flows with the budget deficit or surplus provides a framework within which we can trace the effects of monetary and fiscal policy on prices and output. Population and the capital stock are fixed. There is an efficient long-run output, y_0, corresponding to the optimal rate of use of fixed capital and manpower for unchanging tastes, opportunities and realized anticipations. Every departure from equilibrium produces a budget deficit or surplus and requires a decision about the financing of the budget, a choice of μ. The speed of adjustment to a new equilibrium and the characteristics of the new equilibrium depend on the choice. In this section, we

---

[10]Brunner (1974b) examines these longer-run aspects in greater detail. Discussion of a growing economy requires some minor changes discussed there.

analyze the response to changes in monetary policy – changes in the monetary base. Tax rates and real government expenditure remain fixed. In the following section we analyze the response to fiscal changes – changes in government expenditure and tax rates.

We start from a position of stock–flow equilibrium such as p_0, y_0 in figure 4.2. The intersection of the *bbe* line and the vertical line at y_0 determines the position of long-run stock equilibrium. The budget is balanced; all stocks are fixed, unchanging and willingly held at prevailing prices and anticipations. The intersection of $d + g$ and s at y_0 determines the position of full employment flow equilibrium. Equilibrium positions to the right and left of y_0 are admissible positions of flow equilibrium but not positions of full stock equilibrium. In a growing economy, capital and the effective labor force grow; y_0 is the rate of output per man with the optimal stock of capital per man. Very little in our discussion depends on the difference between a growing and a non-growing economy, so the capital stock is fixed unless we note the contary.

Suppose the central bank undertakes an open market operation. A purchase or sale of securities changes B_0 and S_0, disturbs the asset market equilibrium and thereby changes P and i. The initial responses to any change in B and S are weighted sums of the elasticities of i and P with respect to B and S. The elasticities and their signs are shown in the appendix. The signs of the elasticities indicate that, initially, asset prices fall and interest rates rise with open market sales. Asset prices rise and interest rates fall with open market purchases. The responses of i and P to open market operations are weighted combinations of the responses to B and S. Inspection of the elasticities shows that the responses to changes in the base and to open market operations are approximately equal in modern economies with large outstanding public debt.

$$\epsilon(i, 0M0|AM) = \epsilon(i, B|AM) B_0/B - \epsilon(i, S|AM) B_0/S < 0,$$
$$\epsilon(P, 0M0|AM) = \epsilon(P, B|AM) B_0/B - \epsilon(P, S|AM) B_0/S > 0.$$

In an open market operation, B_0 and S_0 change in opposite directions. Open market operations amplify the response of i and moderate the response of P relative to fiat changes in the base.

An open market operation disturbs the flow equilibrium. The position of flow equilibrium shifts in proportion to a weighted sum of $\epsilon(p, B|0, AM)$ and $\epsilon(p, S|0, AM)$ with weights shown in the previous section. We noted there that the sum is dominated by the response to the base. If we start from full employment, the new position of flow equilibrium is above full employment equilibrium output following an open market purchase and below full employment equilibrium output following a sale. In figure 4.2, we have shown the response to an open market purchase. Flow equilibrium is at output y_1, and there is a budget surplus.

Open market operations also change the position of the *bbe* line. Purchases lower the line by reducing the outstanding stock of securities and interest payments. The response of the *bbe* line reinforces the output effect; the surplus increases as shown in figure 4.2.

The budget imbalance induced by monetary policy starts a process that restores stock equilibrium. The budget surplus reduces B and S. The reductions of B and S shift $d + g$ to the left, reducing expenditure. With s constant, the position of flow equilibrium moves toward the *bbe* line. Output and prices decline. The speed of adjustment depends on the financing of the budget, i.e., on the choice of μ. A large value of μ raises the rate at which the intersection of $d + g$ and s converges to an intersection with *bbe*. The common intersection is a position of intermediate-run equilibrium.

The position of the *bbe* line depends on the financing of the surplus. If pure open market operations cease, B_0 and S_0 remain at their new values. Further changes in B and S arise from the financing of the budget and depend on the choice of μ. There is a critical value of μ that holds the *bbe* line constant. A value of μ less than the critical value reinforces the effect of the open market purchase on the position of the *bbe* line. The *bbe* line shifts away from the initial position shown by the solid *bbe* line in figure 4.2. A large value of μ offsets the downward shift induced by the initial open market purchase. In this case, the broken *bbe* line in figure 4.2 moves in the direction of the solid *bbe* line.

Fiscal policy (g, τ) and monetary policy (μ, B_0, S_0) determine the position of the long-run *bbe* line. The intersection of the long-run *bbe* line and the long-run output line, y_0, determines the long-run equilibrium price level. With fiscal policy constant, the long-run equilibrium price level is *lowered* by an open marked purchase. And the larger μ is relative to the critical value following the open market purchase, the larger is the decline in the price level.

Figure 4.2 shows the adjustment. The solid lines are the initial position of equilibrium. An open market purchase raises P and lowers i, shifting the $d + g$ curve to the position shown as $(d + g)_1$. The *bbe* line moves down, as shown by the broken line. There is a budget surplus, proportional to $y_1 - y_2$. With money wages and anticipations unchanged, the position of the s curve is fixed. The surplus moves $d + g$ back along the s curve until s, *bbe*, and $d + g$ intersect. The intersection is a position of intermediate-run equilibrium. The intermediate-run equilibrium is at an output below y_0; the precise location depends on the choice of μ. Money wages gradually adjust to prices, so the efficiency wage declines, and the s curve shifts to the right. Output increases, and prices fall.

Stock–flow equilibrium at output y_0 can occur only if the equilibrium price level is fully anticipated by purchasers and producers and embedded in wage contracts. Unless money wages eventually fall during the adjustment to an open market purchase and rise during the adjustment to an open market sale, real output cannot return to y_0. With money wages fixed, open market purchases first raise employment, output and prices but adjustment of asset and output markets lowers employment, output and prices. Open market sales have the opposite effects on prices, output and employment.

If there were no adjustment in money wages, real output, or per capita real output, and the price level would be correlated positively. The adjustment of money wages removes the correlation between prices and output, but the price level does not return to its previous value. Output prices and market interest rates are lower at full employment following an open market purchase and higher following an open market sale. The response of interest rates is similar to the conclusion about the effects of open market operations reached by Metzler (1951). The response of prices differs.

Not all conditions for long-run full equilibrium have been satisfied at this point. We note that $\epsilon(P, B|AM) - \epsilon(P, S|AM)$ is positive. Asset prices remain higher relative to output prices after adjustment to an open market purchase and relatively lower after adjustment to an open market sale. Since there cannot be full stock–flow equilibrium with $P \neq p$, further adjustment is required to reach full equilibrium.

To restore full stock–flow equilibrium with unchanged fiscal policy, the composition of expenditure and the size of the capital stock must change. With output prices and market interest rates lower, and asset prices higher, after adjustment to an open market purchase, investment increases relative to consumption, so the capital stock increases. Open market purchases increase the equilibrium stock of capital, or capital per man, and open market sales reduce the equilibrium stock of capital. Long-run output, y_0, depends on the capital stock and changes as the capital stock changes.

Changes in the *bbe* line and the level of long-run output imply that the adjustments following an open market operation do not return the economy to the previous equilibrium. In the equilibrium reached after full adjustment of *bbe* and y_0 to an open market purchase, output, or output per man, is higher and prices are lower. Open market sales reduce equilibrium output and raise prices. In the long run prices and output are negatively related. After full adjustment, real balances and the stock of real capital are complements; bonds and real capital are substitutes.

The qualitative conclusions from our analysis of the long-run adjustment to an open market operation do not depend on whether equilibrium is disturbed by the purchase or sale of securities, as in Metzler (1951) and Patinkin (1965). Suppose, as is customary, that money is distributed by airplane, destroyed in a furnace, delivered like milk, or withdrawn by vacuum cleaner. Each of these operations changes B_0 and, therefore, the relation of B_0 to S_0. The position of full employment stock–flow equilibrium depends on B_0 and S_0 and changes as either magnitude changes. The signs of $\epsilon(i, B|AM)$, $\epsilon(P, B|AM)$ and $\epsilon(p, B|O, AM)$ are the same as the corresponding elasticities with respect to open market operations. Money wages must *fall* to restore full employment following an increase in the base and must *rise* in the full adjustment to a decrease in the base. The equilibrium capital stock is higher following an increase in base money and lower following a decrease. Prices and real output are negatively related in the long-run response to a change in money just as in the case of an open market operation.[11]

To this point, we have assumed that the government maintains real expenditure and keeps tax rates unchanged. The size of the budget deficit or surplus, at each price–output combination, depends on these assumptions. For a given tax rate schedule a policy of maintaining constant nominal expenditure, pg, produces a larger deficit when the base is reduced and a larger surplus when the base is increased relative to the deficit or surplus when fiscal policy holds g constant.

Maintaining constant nominal government expenditure, pg, increases the contribution of policy to the stability of aggregate real expenditure. The counter cyclical increases in debt and money induced by shifts in expenditure are larger than under the policy of keeping g constant. Moreover, the shift in the position of the bbe line is larger algebraically per unit change in B but smaller numerically. The size of the shift in the bbe line induced by a change in the base is

$$\epsilon(p, B \mid bbe; pg) \; = \; \frac{- \; \epsilon(i, B \mid AM) \; \epsilon(I, i) \; IS/t}{\epsilon(i, p \mid AM) \; IS/t - \epsilon(t, p)} \; < \; 0,$$

The elasticity $\epsilon(p, S \mid bbe; pg)$ is algebraically and numerically smaller than the elasticity for fixed g. A policy of maintaining constant pg lowers the absolute value of the response of the equilibrium price level to changes in money. It remains true, however, that changes in money change the equilibrium stock of real capital, output, prices and real returns.

5 Fiscal Policy

Monetary policy consists of setting reserve requirement ratios, discount rates and choosing values of μ, B_0 and S_0. Fiscal policy consists of setting government expenditures and tax rates. Fiscal policy determines the relative size of the private and public sectors and the distribution of income.

Policies interact. The speed of adjustment to changes in monetary policy depends on a fiscal decision, the decision to maintain constant real or nominal govenment expenditure. The size of the "automatic" or "built-in" stabilizers increases, at any deviation from full employment output, if the maintained fiscal policy holds nominal expenditure constant. The response

---

[11]A qualification to these propositions is that an initial increase in B, and S unchanged, followed by a financial policy of maintaining $\mu = 1$ restores the previous equilibrium. This is the analogue of a fiat change in money when the government budget equation is acknowledged.

to a change in tax rates or real government expenditure varies with the method of financing the resulting deficit or surplus, the choice of μ.

In this section, we analyze the response to changes in g on short- and long-run equilibrium. To separate the effects of fiscal and monetary policy, we assume throughout this section that μ remains constant at the prevailing value of B/S. Base money and securities are issued or withdrawn in proportion to the ratio of B to S prevailing before the fiscal change. B_0 and S_0 are constant also.

Every change in g (or τ) disturbs both the flow equilibrium and the stock equilibrium. Per unit percent change in g the $d + g$ curve shifts by an amount

$$\epsilon(p, g|d + g) = -\gamma/[(1 - \gamma)\,\bar{\epsilon}(d, p)] > 0.$$

The denominator is negative, as discussed previously, so an increase in government expenditure raises prices and output, and a reduction in g lowers prices and output. The size of the response depends on the distribution of expenditure between the government and the private sector. The larger is γ, the larger is the relative size of the government. The size of the response of prices of fiscal policy on the output market increases as γ increases.

The change in the stock equilibrium position depends on the method of financing the resulting deficit or surplus, the value of μ, on the tax revenue function, and on the choice of g or pg as a budget or expenditure policy. Holding g constant at the level reached after the change induces a much larger shift in the stock equilibrium position than holding nominal government expenditure constant. The reason is that with real expenditure constant the price level must rise or fall until the private sector releases or absorbs an amount of real output equal to the change in g. Holding pg constant, following a change in real expenditure, distributes the effect of the induced price change between the real expenditure of the government and private sectors. The effects of the alternative policies on the stock equilibrium position are shown by comparing the changes in the position of the bbe line,

$$\epsilon(p, g|bbe; g) = \frac{-[pg/t]}{pg/t - \epsilon(t, p) + \epsilon(I, i)\,\epsilon(i, p|AM)\,IS/t} > 0,$$

$$\epsilon(p, g|bbe; pg) = \frac{-[pg/t]}{-\epsilon(t, p) + \epsilon(I, i)\,\epsilon(i, p|AM)\,IS/t} > 0.$$

The relative responses to the two types of expenditure policy depend only on the denominators. The denominator of $\epsilon(p, g|bbe; pg)$ is approximately unity, so the ratio of the two elasticities is approximately equal to

$$(pg - t)/- t = IS/t,$$

the ratio of interest payments to tax collections. At current values, the policy of holding g constant raises the response of the price level to fiscal changes by a factor of 9 or 10.

An increase in g raises both the $d + g$ line and the bbe line. The relative magnitudes of the two vertical shifts determine the system's subsequent adjustment. If the shift of the $d + g$ line exceeds the shift of the bbe line, the flow equilibrium at an intersection of $d + g$ and s lies to the right of the bbe line. The financial stock-flow equilibrium on bbe associated with the new level of g is below the new flow equilibrium position. The increase in g produces a *surplus*, lowering B and S and driving the $d + g$ line back to the bbe line. If the response of the bbe line is larger than the response of $d + g$, the new flow equilibrium occurs below the new bbe line. There is a budget deficit. The resulting deficit accelerates B and S, expands output and raises prices. The additional increases in p and y are responses to the financial consequences of the deficit.

The position of intermediate-run stock-flow equilibrium reached after adjustment to the change in g and the resulting deficit or surpls depends on the slopes of the $d + g$, s, and bbe curves and on the size of the shifts, $\epsilon(p, g | d + g)$ and $\epsilon(p, g | bbe)$. Both the slope and the position of the balanced budget equation depend on the choice of budget policy – constant real or nominal expenditure. Moreover, the slope of the price setting function depends on capacity utilization. All that can be said without considering relative orders of magnitude is that, for given anticipations, money wages and stock of capital, stock–flow equilibrium lies at higher output and prices following the adjustment to an increase in g and at lower output and price level following a reduction in g.

With constant anticipations and money wages, expansive fiscal policy lowers real wages; and fiscal contraction increases real wages (per efficiency unit). The change in real wages is a main reason that stock–flow equilibrium can be achieved temporarily at a position above or below full employment. Restoring real wages to the level of the previous full employment equilibrium by changing money wages does not restore the price level that prevailed at the previous full stock–flow equilibrium. The bbe line and therefore the position of stock equilibrium has changed. If, as we have assumed, real or nominal expenditure and μ are maintained, the price level remains higher than in the previous equilibrium following an increase in g, and prices remain lower after a reduction in g. The magnitude of the price change depends, of course, on the choice of expenditure policy.

The economy cannot return to full stock–flow equilibrium if asset prices and output prices are unequal. Increases in g raise p and, generally, lower P and increase i. The changes in P and i are a consequence of the redistribution of income and the effects of the redistribution on the credit and money markets. The changes in P, i and p assure that the intermediate-run stock-flow equilibrium reached following adjustment to a change in g is not maintained. Even if money wages remain unchanged, the stock equilibrium and the flow equilibrium cannot persist. The increase in p and reduction in P, following an increase in g, leave the price of existing assets lower than the price of current output. Any increase in money wages further increases prices and interest rates and lowers asset prices. To restore full equilibrium, the distribution of expenditure between consumption and investment must change. An increase in consumption and a reduction in investment move the economy toward equilibrium, the capital stock (or capital per man) is smaller following an increase in g and larger following a reduction in g. For the longer-run adjustment of the price level to a change in g, the effects on bbe and long-run output are reinforcing. The level of prices is positively related to g.

Fiscal policy has short-run, intermediate-run and long-run effects. Figure 4.3 brings out aspects of these adjustments. We start from a full stock–flow equilibrium, at the intersection of the solid lines in figure 4.3a. The budget is balanced; and the flow markets are in equilibrium at long-run output to y_0. An increase in g, with μ, B_0 and S_0 given, raises the bbe line to bbe_1 and the $d + g$ line to $(d + g)_1$. Comparison of the two responses to g shows that $\epsilon(p, g|d + g)$ is a small fraction of $\epsilon(p, g|bbe; g)$. The sizes of the relative shifts assure that the flow equilibrium at the intersection of $(d + g)$ and s is to the left of bbe_1. The government budget is in deficit. Point A shows the short-run flow equilibrium.

The financing of the deficit gradually moves the $d + g$ line to the right. With fixed B_0 and S_0, and μ below the critical level, the cumulated deficit, D, moves the bbe line to the right along the s curve. The economy reaches point B, a position of intermediate-run equilibrium at the intersection of bbe_2, s and a $d + g$ curve. Output and prices are higher. The movement from the initial position to A is the pure fiscal effect of fiscal policy and the movement from A to B shows the financial effect of the same policy.

The system does not remain at the intermediate-run position, B. Output at B is above the long-run level; wages and prices rise, and the s line moves to the left. A further round of financial stock–flow adjustments moves the flow

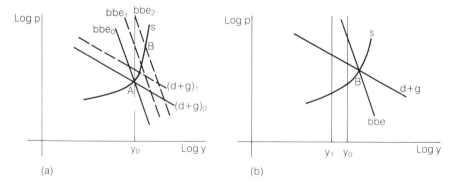

Figure 4.3   Aspects of adjustment to fiscal policy in the short, medium, and long run.

equilibrium system along a northwesterly path toward the intersection of the long-run *bbe* line and the new level of long-run output, y_1, in figure 4.3b. Fiscal policy has real and nominal effects in the short and in the long run. Our discussion of figure 4.3 shows that the expansive effect of an increase in *g* is eroded in the longer run by the operation of the wage adjustment process. Eventually, the adjustment of the stock of real capital converts the initial expansion of output into a decline of long-run output. Prices are higher in both the short and long run relative to the price level in the initial equilibrium. A reduction in *g*, depresses real output in the shorter run but increases long-run output of the private sector. Prices are lower following the reduction in *g*.

Similar conclusions are obtained from the analysis of changes in tax rates. Increases in tax rates reduce output prices, interest rates and asset prices and raise real wages in the short run. The size of the price and interest rate changes depends on expenditure policy. A policy of maintaining constant nominal expenditure induces smaller changes in the position of stock equilibrium than a policy of maintaining constant real expenditure. Full adjustment to an increase in tax rates is not completed until money wages fall and asset prices are again equal to output prices. The composition of real expenditure changes to adjust the capital stock.

6 Monetarist Implications and Conjectures

What makes our theory a monetarist theory instead of a Keynesian, neo-Keynesian or quantity theory? We trust that the careful reader finds many points at which we do not differ from other economists, including economists who would not christen their theories "monetarist." Often, labels remain, sustained by the intellectual laziness that postpones careful examination of implications and propositions long after hypotheses have changed and distinctions have blurred. There is, therefore, reason to end this paper by pointing to the characteristics that we regard as "monetarist," if a label is to be assigned, and to point out also the relation of the implications and conjectures to the hypothesis.

A theory is not a monetarist theory unless three conditions are met. One, the long-run position to which the system moves is determined by stocks, particularly the stock of money, and not by flows. Stocks and flows interact, but in the longer run, flows adjust to stocks. Two, the adjustment to a change in money involves substitution between money, other assets and new production. Adjustment is not confined to a narrow range of assets, called bonds, or a single price, "the" interest rate. Changes in money modify relative prices and initiate a process of substitution that spreads to the markets for existing capital, securities, loans and current output. Three, the economic system is stable. Cumulative movements of prices or output result mainly from the decisions or actions of governments not individuals or private institutions. The private sector has a stabilizing influence, so that the economy adjusts to any maintained policy.

Together, or separately, we and other "monetarists" have made these statements, or similar statements, for many years. Contrasts and conflicts between "monetarists" and non-monetarists are most apparent in policy recommendations or criticisms and discussions of past and future courses of action. These discussions reveal differences in analysis and interpretation of events that cannot be reduced to differences about the slopes of standard *IS* and *LM* curves of Hicks' or the similar curves of Metzler's analysis, as is often suggested (Okun 1971; Samuelson 1969).

The transmission of monetary changes, in our analysis, does not depend on the interest elasticities of the demand for money and expenditure. The relative interest elasticities that matter are the interest elasticities of the money and credit markets. As long as the credit market response to interest rates exceeds the money market response, increases in the base raise the prices of real assets and reductions in the base lower asset prices. Moreover, a small response of expenditure to interest rates, "elasticity pessimism," has no implication for the effectiveness of monetary policy. Monetary policy affects expenditure by changing interest rates and asset prices, so the combined effects of the changes, not the separate effects, determine the response of expenditure.

The difference in implications reflects differences in the transmission or adjustment process. In Hicksian analysis, real capital is locked in portfolios and is not affected by the substitution and adjustment processes. There are markets for money and bonds, but Walras' law is used to eliminate analysis of the bond market. The money market remains as the only relevant asset market. In Metzler's interpretation, real output is fixed and all non-monetary assets are perfect substitutes, so a single asset price or interest rate is all that is required for the analysis of substitution between money and other assets.

Metzler's analysis clarified a number of outstanding issues. However, he did not analyze positions other than long-run full equilibrium or permit prices of existing assets to differ from replacement costs. To move beyond his analysis, we assume that bonds and claim to real capital are not perfect substitutes. The money market is supplemented by another asset market, the credit market.[12] Asset prices join interest rates in the transmission of monetary (and fiscal) changes. Once these changes are made, the response of assets and output to policy variables becomes more pervasive than in Keynesian models.

---

[12]The real capital market is related by Walras' law to the credit and money market. The choice of the two markets involves no logical issue. It reflects a judgment about a useful strategy for empirical research.

Long-run positions of stock–flow equilibrium are adjustments to the position determined by past policies, real resources, tastes, opportunities and realized anticipations. The accumulated effects of past policies determine the outstanding stocks of money and debt. Fiscal policy determines the size of budget deficits or surpluses and monetary policy determines the distribution of stocks of financial assets between money and debt. If fiscal and monetary policies remain fixed, long-run equilibrium requires adjustment of the prices of assets and output and the stock of real capital. In the long-run, government securities and real capital are substitutes; base money and capital are complements.

The price level and real output settle at a position determined by the stocks of money, debt and capital, for given resources, tastes and opportunities. In stationary, long-run equilibrium the budget must be balanced and the stocks of money and debt unchanging. We show that, if the system is stable and there are reasonable restrictions on the tax revenue function, the economy converges to an equilibrium for any combination of debt and base money issued or withdrawn to finance budget deficits or surpluses.[13] The principal long-run effects of maintained government policies are on the level of prices, the distribution of output between consumption and investment expenditure and the level of output at which the economy reaches equilibrium, not on the existence of equilibrium. The private sector adjusts to any set of maintained government fiscal and monetary policies.

Of particular interest is the response to a maintained change in real or nominal government expenditure financed entirely by issuing debt. Our analysis implies that the interaction of stocks and flows brings the budget into balance at a constant price level, under the conditions reiterated in note 13. Fiscal changes induce once and for all adjustments of the equilibrium price level, long-run equilibrium output and the stock of capital.

A maintained fiscal position does not induce steady inflation or deflation whether financed entirely by debt or by base money. The main differences between money and debt finance are on the level of long-run output and prices and on the speed of adjustment to equilibrium. The speed of adjustment to a deficit rises with the ratio of base money to debt issued (or withdrawn in the event of a surplus). The long-run price level is *lower* and output is higher the larger the ratio of base money to debt accumulated in the financing of deficits and surpluses and resulting from open market operations.

The stability of the private sector, one of the principal monetarist

---

[13]The qualifications apply to fiscal policy financed by debt issues. The response of real output to a change in debt depends on a combination of negative and positive responses $\bar{\epsilon}(d, i)$ $\epsilon(i, S|AM) + \bar{\epsilon}(d, P) \epsilon(P, S|AM)$ that must be non-negative if the system is stable. Also a slightly progressive tax revenue function may be required to balance the budget at the higher or lower interest payments resulting from the financing of fiscal policy solely by issuing or withdrawing debt.

conjectures, is an implication of our stock flow analysis. Keynesians typically assume that the private sector is unstable. Waves of optimism or pessimism, stable Phillips curves and the "autonomy of the wage unit"[14] determine the rate of inflation. Any proposition asserting that prices or wages move independently of current and past market conditions and the values of financial variables is inconsistent with the monetarist proposition and with our analysis. The evidence is not conclusive but we believe that the weight of the evidence, including the evidence from large econometric models, supports us.

The stability of the private sector supports another of the principal monetarist propositions. Inflation (or deflation) can occur, in our analysis, only if some impulse is maintained. A one-time change in base money, government expenditure, tax rates, debt, or anticipated real returns produces at most a one-time adjustment of prices. Inflation or deflation cannot occur unless some impluse is maintained. We observe secular increases in the share of output absorbed by the government sector in many countries, but we have not observed sporadic increases capable of explaining observed inflation or deflation. Nor do we know of any evidence of steady changes in the expected return to capital or the monopoly positions of unions and corporations that is capable of explaining current or past rates of price change. The absence of such evidence is inconsistent with the eclectic–agnostic view and the "special factors" explanations of inflation and deflation. Evidence showing the effect of monetary growth on inflation and deflation is consistent with our analysis, supports our hypothesis and the monetarist proposition that the monetary impulse is the dominant impulse in inflations or deflations.

The three conjectures constitute the core of monetarism, but they are not the only monetarist propositions. Differences between monetarists and some Keynesian and eclectic economists are not limited to conjectures about the impulses initiating major changes in prices and output, or the processes transmitting such changes from one market to another, or the stability of the private sector. There are differences in methods also. Monetarists have not developed large-scale econometric models – models with twenty or more behavior equations – to analyze or predict aggregate behavior. The reason is that many Keynesians treat allocative detail as central to an explanation of aggregative behavior, and monetarists do not. Nowhere in our discussion of short- and intermediate-run adjustment did we find reason to mention the distribution of output between consumption and investment or the many

---

[14]An explicit statement of the "autonomy" of prices and wage movements is in a recent paper by Lerner (1974). He argues that excess demand creates inflation and deficient demand creates depression (at unchanged prices or wages). Therefore, if one observes "stagflation" one necessarily has a demand deficiency. But, we also require recognition of a supplementary force driving prices independently of market conditions.

kinds of consumption and investment spending. For us, the distribution of private expenditure is determined by relative prices and wealth in response to monetary and fiscal policies. The distribution is not invariant. In the long run, fiscal policy determines the absolute size of the government sector and the relative size of the private and the government sector. Both the stock of private capital and the level of long-run output change inversely to the size of the government sector and the stock of securities. Changes of this kind have important long-run but not short-run effects on output and the price level.

On the asset market of our analysis, the excess supply of government securities and the excess supply of money simultaneously determine the asset price level and the market rate of interest. The allocation of credit by type of loan securities plays no role and has no effect on aggregates. In large, econometric models, and in policy discussions, many Keynesians assign importance to the allocation of credit. Selective credit controls, changes in the stock of mortgages, and other changes in the distribution of financial assets have effects on the composition of spending and on aggregate output. "Credit rationing" and institutional practice are used to justify these hypotheses and policy recommendations.

Once again, the difference in analysis reflects a difference in the roles assigned to relative prices. To us, "credit rationing" means that the empirical counterpart of the term "price" often includes the terms and conditions of a contract or agreement. The adjustment of relative prices includes such changes in terms. Changes in terms and conditions under which borrowing and lending occur change the allocation of financial assets but have very little effect on the allocation of real resources and no effect on total spending.

A century of assertions has not produced any reliable or persuasive evidence that the phenomenon called "credit rationing" affects the composition of spending or its total. The absence of such evidence is support for the monetarist proposition and our hypothesis that assign no role to allocative detail.

Discussion of the conjectures and implication dividing economists, and their relation to the formal analysis of the paper, can be extended. Perhaps enough has been said to justify our contention that monetarism is *not* a set of empirical conjectures about the slopes of *IS* and *LM* curves or a proposition denying any effect of fiscal policy.

Appendix 4.1   Some Asset Market Responses

(1) Response to the base,

$$\epsilon(i, B|AM) = -\frac{\epsilon(MM, P) - \epsilon(CM, P)}{\epsilon(CM, i)\cdot\epsilon(MM, P) - \epsilon(MM, i)\cdot\epsilon(CM, P)} < 0,$$

$$\epsilon(P, B|AM) = -\frac{\epsilon(CM, i) - \epsilon(MM, i)}{\Delta},$$

where Δ is the same denominator as in $\epsilon(i, B|AM)$. The components of the expression defining the two elasticities are

$$\epsilon(CM, i) = \epsilon(a, i) - \epsilon(\sigma, i) > 0, \qquad \epsilon(MM, i) = \epsilon(m, i) - \epsilon(L, i) > 0,$$

$$\epsilon(CM, P) = \epsilon(a, P) - \epsilon(\sigma, P) > 0, \qquad \epsilon(MM, P) = \epsilon(m, P) - \epsilon(L, P) < 0.$$

Inspection of these expressions yields the following interpretation:

$\epsilon(CM, i)$ the interest elasticity of the excess supply of "bank credit" or earning assets,

$\epsilon(MM, i)$ the interest elasticity of the excess supply of money.

A similar interpretation applies to the two elasticities with respect to P.
The following inequality is the basic order constraint of our analysis,

$$\epsilon(CM, i) > \epsilon(MM, i) > 0.$$

The reader should note that with $\epsilon(CM, i) = \epsilon(MM, i)$ the extended range of substitution relations induced by changes in B becomes irrelevant. Debt and real capital remain less than prefect substitutes, and our analysis of fiscal policy is unaffected.

(2) Response to government securities,

$$\epsilon(i, S|AM) \sim \{\epsilon(MM, P)/\Delta\} (S/aB) > 0,$$

$$\epsilon(P, S|AM) \sim -\{\epsilon(MM, i)/\Delta\} (S/aB) > 0.$$

The approximations ($\sim$) denote that minor effects of wealth are omitted.

(3) Response to p,

$$\epsilon(i, p|AM) = -\{\overset{-}{\epsilon(CM, p)}\cdot\overset{-}{\epsilon(MM, P)} - \overset{-}{\epsilon(MM, p)}\cdot\overset{+}{\epsilon(CM, P)}\}/\Delta > 0,$$

$$\epsilon(P, p|AM) = -\{\overset{+}{\epsilon(CM, i)}\cdot\overset{-}{\epsilon(MM, p)} - \overset{+}{\epsilon(MM, i)}\cdot\overset{-}{\epsilon(CM, p)}\}/\Delta < 0,$$

where

$$\epsilon(CM, p) = \epsilon(a, p) - \epsilon(\sigma, p) < 0, \quad \epsilon(MM, p) = \epsilon(m, p) - \epsilon(L, p) < 0.$$

The sign for $\epsilon(P, p|AM)$ is based on the order condition $0 > \epsilon(CM, p) > \epsilon(MM, p)$. Note that $|\epsilon(P, p|AM)| < 1$.

(4) Response to y,

$$\epsilon(i, y|AM) = -\{\overset{-}{\epsilon(CM, y)}\cdot\overset{-}{\epsilon(MM, P)} - \overset{+}{\epsilon(MM, y)}\cdot\epsilon(CM, P)\}/\Delta > 0,$$

$$\epsilon(P, y) = \{\epsilon(CM, i)\cdot\epsilon(MM, y) - \epsilon(MM, i)\cdot\epsilon(CM, y)\}/\Delta,$$

where

$$\epsilon(CM, y) = [\epsilon(a, W_h) - \overset{+}{\epsilon(\sigma, W_h)}] \epsilon(W_h, y)$$
$$\overset{-}{} \quad \overset{+}{}$$
$$+ [\epsilon(a, e) - \epsilon(\sigma, e)]\epsilon(e, y) < 0,$$
$$\overset{-}{} \quad \overset{+}{}$$
$$\epsilon(MM, y) = [\epsilon(m, W_h) - \epsilon(L, W_h)] \epsilon(W_h, y)$$
$$+ \quad +$$
$$+ [\epsilon(m, e) - \epsilon(L, e)] \epsilon(e, y) \geqq 0.$$

References

Brunner, K. 1971. A survey of selected issues in monetary theory. *Schweizerische Zeitschrift für Volkswirtschaft und Statistik* 107, 1–46.

—— 1974a. A diagrammatic exposition of the money supply process. *Schweizerische Zeitschrift für Volkswirtschaft und Statistik* 109, 481–533.

—— 1974b. Inflation, money and the role of fiscal arrangements: An analytic framework for the inflation problem. Conference on the New Inflation (Milan, June 24–26, 1974).

—— and A.H. Meltzer. 1968. Liquidity traps for money, bank credit and interest rates. *Journal of Political Economy* 76, 1–37.

—— 1972. A monetarist framework for aggregative analysis. *Proceedings of the First Konstanz Seminar on Monetary Theory and Monetary Policy, Kredit und Kapital*. Duncker & Humblot, Berlin 31–88.

—— 1974a. Money, debt and economic activity, *Journal of Political Economy* 80, 951–77.

—— 1974b. Monetary and fiscal policy in open, interdependent economies. In *Paris-Dauphine Conference on Monetary Theory* ed. E. Claassen and P. Salin forthcoming in this series.

Burger, A. 1972. *The Money Supply Process*. Belmont, Calif.: Wadsworth.

Christ, C. 1972. A simple macroeconomic model with a government budget restraint. *Journal of Political Economy* 76, 53–67.

Gramley, L. and S. Chase. 1965. Time deposits in monetary analysis. *Federal Reserve Bulletin* 51, 1380–406.

Hicks, J.R. 1937. Mr. Keynes and the "classics": A suggested interpretation. *Econometrica* 5, 147–59.

Keynes, J.M. 1936. *The General Theory of Employment Interest and Money*. New York: Macmillan.

Lerner, A.P. 1974. From the treatise on money to the general theory. *Journal of Economic Literature* 12, 38–42.

Metzler, L. 1951. Wealth, saving and the rate of interest. *Journal of Political Economy* 59, 93–116.

Okun, A. 1971. Rules and roles for fiscal and monetary policy. *In Issues in Fiscal and*

Monetary Policy: The Eclectic Economist Views the Controversy ed. J. Diamond. Chicago, De Paul University Press, III. 51–74.

Patinkin, D. 1965. *Money, Interest and Prices*, 2nd edn. New York: Harper & Row.

Pesek, B. and T. Saving. 1967. *Money, Wealth and Economic Theory*. New York: Macmillan.

Samuelson, P. 1969. The Role of Money in National Economic Policy, Controlling Monetary Aggregates. Boston, Mass.: Federal Reserve Bank of Boston.

Silber, W.L. 1970. Fiscal policy in IS–LM analysis: A correction. *Journal of Money, Credit, and Banking* 2, 461–72.

5

Money and Economic Activity, Inventories and Business Cycles

Karl Brunner, Alex Cukierman, and Allan H. Meltzer

1 Introduction

The observation that unanticipated changes in money cause fluctuations in real wages, inventories and economic activity is almost as old as systematic discussion of economics.[1] Currently, two hypotheses are offered. One uses nominal wage contracts to explain the real effects of money. Gordon (1976), Fischer (1977), and Phelps and Taylor (1977) are examples. Increases in money can induce increases in real output by raising prices and thereby reducing real wages earned under prevailing contracts. Studies of cyclical changes in real wages by Cargill (1969) and others do not find evidence that this pattern is dominant. A second hypothesis emphasizes that wages (or prices) are set in local markets. Expectations are formed rationally, using all available information, but the information available in local markets does not permit people to separate absolute and relative price changes promptly. The confusion between relative and absolute price changes is responsible for the short-term responses of real output to money.[2] This class of models

This paper appeared in *Journal of Monetary Economics* 11 (May). Amsterdam: Elsevier, 1983, pp. 281–319. Reprinted with permission. We are indebted to Alan Blinder, Benjamin Eden, Lars Hansen, Dorit Hochbaum, Edi Karni, Finn Kydland, Leo Leiderman, Michael Parkin, Walter Wasserfallen, and to the participants of the NBER summer institute group on inventories for helpful comments. An earlier version of this paper was presented at the 1980 Konstanz conference.

[1]Henry Thornton (1802, pp. 118–20) refers to a "very great and sudden reduction" of money instead of an "unanticipated reduction in money" and develops the consequences for inventories, employment and production. The core of his argument is that if the fall in prices is believed to be temporary money wages change less than prices, and manufacturers accumulate (unintended) inventories.

[2]This line of argument was developed in Lucas (1972, 1973) and extended in Sargent (1973), Barro (1976), Cukierman (1979) and elsewhere.

implies that unemployment and deviations of output from capacity or 'normal' output are serially uncorrelated, contrary to common observations.[3] More recently Blinder and Fischer (1981) resurrect the idea that inventories can lead to persistence when people confuse absolute and relative price changes; increasing marginal costs of production, at the level of the industrial firm, make it profitable to smooth production by partially accommodating demand out of inventories.

This paper reopens the analysis of business cycles in a monetary economy with inventories. All markets are expected to clear each period, and expectations are formed rationally using available information and knowledge of the deterministic and stochastic structure. Product and labor markets differ from financial markets, however, in the speed with which they adjust to new information. Prices, wages and employment are set at the start of the period using all information available at the time. Once set, these variables remain unchanged until the beginning of the next period. They are then reset in light of new, available information. Financial markets clear within the period. Nominal stocks of money and bonds are willingly held at a market rate of interest that reflects both beliefs about all shocks that occur during the period and the actual values of the shocks.

The deterministic segment of the economy is dichotomized. All real variables, including the real rate of interest, depend only on real values and are independent of the money stock. The price level is fixed each period, however, so real and monetary shocks that occur within the period change interest rates and cause unintended changes in inventories. Firms hold inventories to increase expected profits by decreasing the probability of stockouts.[4] Within the period they accommodate demand passively, within some range.[5] Production technology is linear in labor so there is no production smoothing at the level of the individual firm.

Gradual adjustment of inventories and production smoothing develops for macroeconomic reasons that are related to the intertemporal substitution of labor supply. The model reconciles the intertemporal substitution theory of labor supply with the observed effects of lagged money on output and employment after allowing for the effect of intertemporal substitution.[6] A depletion of inventories at the aggregate level increases aggregate labor demand. The labor market clears at a higher real wage rate and higher

---

[3]Lucas (1975) demonstrates that an accelerator effect on the demand for capital transforms serially uncorrelated errors into serially correlated deviations of real variables from "normal" values. Sargent and Wallace (1975) also obtain serially correlated errors through the capital stock. Other models with persistence include Sargent (1979) and Kydland and Prescott (1982).

[4]The contribution of inventories to expected profits is modeled directly rather than through a downward sloping inventory carrying cost function as is customary in some of the inventory literature. (See, for example, Maccini, 1976.)

[5]The range is set by the optimal choices of the individual firm.

[6]Evidence is presented in Hall (1980).

employment; workers substitute current for future leisure as in Lucas and Rapping (1969). The higher real wage rate also makes it profitable to rebuild inventory over several periods. As a result, a given unanticipated monetary shock induces a cycle in inventories, employment and output. The duration and amplitude of the cycle is systematically related to the magnitude of the effects of the real wage on labor demand and supply and other parameters of the macroeconomy.

The adjustment of inventories gives rise to several characteristic features of modern business cycles. Monetary and real shocks have persistent effects on output and employment. Unemployment rates and deviations of output from "normal" or "capacity" output are serially correlated. Real wages move procyclically and adjust more slowly than unemployment.[7] Prices move in direct proportion to money only when inventories have settled at their permanent, steady-state level. In other states, prices depend on both money and on the cyclical position of the economy.

The plan of the paper is as follows. Section 2 sets out the deterministic and stochastic features of the macroeconomic environment and develops the implications for aggregates of individual firm's behavior. Aggregate labor demand and product supply are derived from an underlying model of firms' optimizing choices in section 3. This section also establishes the internal consistency or "rationality" of the model. Section 4 shows that aggregate inventories follow a partial adjustment process and characterizes the behavior of planned and unintended changes in inventories. A general framework of analyzing the cyclical fluctuations set off by real and nominal shocks is presented. This framework is then specialized to focus on the channels through which money affects economic activity. A conclusion completes the paper.

2   The Macroeconomy: Fast Clearing versus Fixed Price Markets and the Dynamic Behavior of Expectations

In the economy, we consider the macrostructure and the microstructure are interrelated, but they are presented separately. The demand facing each firm depends on aggregate demand and on factors specific to the firm. Each firm solves a dynamic optimization problem to determine its expected sales and its demand for labor. Firms hold inventories to reduce the (negative) effect of stockouts on expected profits. The individual firm's decisions are derived in section 3. This section uses the aggregate of the expected sales and labor demand functions derived in section 3 as aggregate expected sales and labor demand functions. The macro model determines the level of aggregate demand and the prices and interest rates on which the individual firm's

---

[7]For evidence on the relative sluggishness of wages and unemployment see Hall (1977).

decisions depend. These macro results become inputs for the micro decisions analyzed in the next section.

The underlying framework of the macroeconomy is conventional. There are four markets: The goods market, the labor market, the money market and the bond market.[8] The first two markets clear in an ex ante or "contract" sense while the last two markets clear continuously and reflect the realization of shocks that occur during the current period. There is a fixed number of firms, N, in the economy; each is endowed with the simple production function

$$y_i = l_i,$$

where y_i is the ith firm's homogeneous output and l_i its labor input.[9]

2.1 The Commodity Market

Aggregate demand in period t, D_t is

$$D_t^a = \alpha Y^p + \beta(r_t^a - \pi_{\tau+1}) + \epsilon_t, \qquad \alpha > 0, \beta < 0, \tag{5.1}$$

where Y^p is (constant) permanent income, r_t^a is the nominal rate of interest, ϵ_t is a stochastic shock to current demand, with expected value of zero, and $\pi_{t+1} = P_{t+1}/P_t^a - 1$ is the rate of inflation expected to occur between t and $t+1$ as of the beginning of period t. The superscript 'a' on a variable designates the *actual* value of that variable. A variable without the superscript 'a' designates the value of that variable rationally expected by individuals at the beginning of the period for that period.[10] P_t^a is period t's price level and P_{t+1} is the price level expected for period $t+1$.[11]

Firms hold inventories, so the commodity market clears when aggregate demand is equal to expected sales rather than to current output. Expected aggregate sales, $\bar{S}_t$, reflects the combined, optimal supply decisions of firms,

---

[8]Since these markets are related through the budget constraint, one market can be eliminated from the analysis. We chose to drop the bond market.

[9]In general, we will denote by the corresponding upper case letters the aggregate values of these variables.

[10]Since much of the discussion involves these expectations, this notational choice economizes on the use of symbols. Whenever the time at which an expectation is formed is not mentioned explicitly, it should be understood as referring to the beginning of the period.

[11]Several of the structural variables of the economy, e.g., income, appear in three forms: (1) as an actual value with the superscript 'a', Y^a; (2) as an expected value without any superscript, Y; (3) as a permanent or steady-state value, Y^p. For *some* variables – output, employment, the real wage rate and the price level – the actual and the expected values of the variable for the current period are equal. For sales, demand and the interest rate actual and expected values are not necessarily equal, as explained below. Precise definitions of expectations and permanent values appear in the subsections on ex ante equilibrium and permanent values later in this section. The notational rule does not apply to random shocks. Realizations of shocks do not carry any superscripts.

$$\bar{S}_t = K_0 + K_1(H_t^a + Y_t^a) + K_2 D_t, \qquad 0 < K_1, K_2 < 1, \tag{5.2}$$

where H_t^a is economy wide finished good inventories at the beginning of period t, Y_t^a is period t's income and D_t is the forcast of aggregate demand for the period using all the information available to firms at the beginning of the period.

Equation (5.2), including the restrictions on K_1 and K_2, results from optimization and an aggregation over all firms in the economy. Each firm chooses its optimal level of employment and production for the period by maximizing the present value of expected future profits. Demand facing the individual firm depends on aggregate demand as well as on factors specific to the firm. All firms have the same average size. Given D_t the demand facing an individual firm is stochastically distributed around the firm's average shares of aggregate demand. The more the individual firm decides to produce at the beginning of the period, and the larger its inventories, the smaller the probability that it will stockout during this period and the larger its expected sales. As a result, expected sales of the individual firm depend on opening inventories and, its optimally chosen, current production level. Expected average demand per firm is given by

$$\mu_t = D_t/N. \tag{5.3}$$

2.2 The Labor Market

The aggregate demand for labor at the beginning of period t is

$$L_{dt} = \bar{L}_d + (\gamma_1\beta + \gamma_2)v_t + \gamma_3 w_t - H_t^a, \qquad 1 > \gamma_1 > 0, \gamma_2, \gamma_3 < 0, \tag{5.4}$$

where L_{dt} is aggregate demand for labor in period t, $\bar{L}_d$ is constant, γ_1 is the sensitivity of labor demand with respect to average expected demand per firm, γ_2 is the direct sensitivity of labor demand with respect to the expected real rate of interest, γ_3 is the sensitivity of labor demand with respect to the real wage rate, w_t, and

$$v_t \equiv r_t - \pi_{t+1} \tag{5.5}$$

is the expected value of the real interest rate.[12] Each firm chooses its optimal labor input. Aggregation of the individual demands leads to eqn (5.4) including the restrictions on the coefficients. Note that the demand for labor is inversely related to the opening level of inventories and to the relative prices, v and w.

Aggregate supply of labor is given by

$$L_{st} = \bar{L}_s + \omega(w_t - w^p), \qquad \bar{L}_s > 0, \omega > 0, \tag{5.6}$$

where L_{st} aggregate is labor supply in period t and w^p is the (time-independent) permanent value of the real wage rate. The supply function embodies

---

[12]r_t is the expected value of the nominal rate.

the main idea of the Lucas and Rapping (1969) intertemporal substitution theory of labor supply. Workers substitute leisure in low wage periods for leisure in high wage periods.[13] If we interpret the real wage rate as an index or proxy for all dimensions of the employment agreement, eqn (5.6) states that the supply of labor increases when a suitably weighted average of all the benefits a worker anticipates from a current offer of employment increases relative to the permanent value of the benefits he expects to command.

The dependence of labor supply on current and permanent real wage rates leads to the same definition of unemployment as in Brunner, Cukierman and Meltzer (1980). When the current wage rate is below the rate believed to be permanent, part of the labor force finds it profitable to abstain from accepting employment. These workers appear in the statistics as unemployed until actual and permanent real wage rates are equal. Within the context of the model, unemployment is defined as the difference between labor supply when $w_t = w^p$ and labor supply when actual and permanent wages differ. The number of unemployed workers is given by[14]

$$n_t^q = \omega(w^p - w_t). \tag{5.7}$$

The steady-state rate of unemployment is zero by definition, but the actual rate of unemployment may be positive or negative.

In the models of Friedman (1968), Phelps (1967) and Lucas (1973), unemployment is a consequence of faulty perceptions about the price level. Here workers are unemployed when they expect their labor to command more benefits than the market currently offers.[15]

2.3 The Money Market

The demand for nominal money is

$$P_t^a[Y^p + g(Y_t^a - Y^p) + br_t^a - \theta\epsilon_t], \qquad g, \theta > 0, b < 0. \tag{5.8}$$

Equation (5.8) makes the demand for real money balances an increasing function of both permanent and transitory income and a decreasing function of the nominal rate of interest. We assume that g is relatively small. The term $\theta\epsilon_t$ shows that any shock to aggregate demand is partly a shock to the demand for money in the opposite direction. The parameter θ measures how

---

[13]We assume for simplicity that equal changes in actual and permanent wage rates do not change the supply of labor. Qualitative results do not depend on this assumption.

[14]Recall that in eqn (5.4) the demand for labor is set at the beginning of the period and does not respond to changes in v_t that occur within the period. We do not mean to imply that this is the only kind of unemployment reflected in the statistics. However, it is probably an important element in the cyclical component of the measured rate of unemployment.

[15]A more complete analysis of unemployment requires discussion of the pecuniary and non-pecuniary components of w^p and of changes in w^p.

much of the shock to aggregate demand individuals desire to finance by changes in their money holdings.[16]

Money supply at the beginning of period $t+1$ is given by

$$M^a_{t+1} = M^a_t(1+m_t),$$ (5.9)

where m_t is the stochastic rate of growth of money supply between the beginning of period t and the beginning of period $t+1$. m_t has a time-independent expected value denoted $\bar{m}$.[17]

2.4 Financial Versus Real Markets and Ex Post Versus Ex Ante Equilibrium

A basic feature of the economy is that employment, output, the real wage rate and the price level are set at the beginning of each period at levels which clear all markets in an ex ante sense before the realization of the aggregate shocks (ϵ and m) and the individual demand shocks. By contrast, the nominal rate of interest, r^a_t, is determined after the realization of these shocks by the clearing of the money market. The actual values of both aggregate and individual demands reflect the shocks that occur during the period. This asymmetry is designed to capture the more rapid clearing of markets for nominal stocks relative to markets for real product and labor. Recontracting in real markets within the period is prohibitively costly because of the complex nature of production and distribution activities. By contrast, the relative ease with which financial obligations are exchanged makes it possible for financial markets to clear more frequently. We assume, along the lines of Alchian (1969), that because of the informational efficiency to buyers of a fixed price for the period, firms that do not post price in advance lose customers to firms that do. Furthermore, alteration of the price, within the period after it has been posted, is prohibitively costly to the firm. As a consequence, all firms post a price for the product at the beginning of each period and adhere to it for at least one period.[18, 19]

[16]The rest is financed in the bond market.

[17]More generally, imperfectly perceived permanent changes could occur in $\bar{m}$ over time. The implications of this case for the cycle are briefly investigated at the end of section 4.

[18]This temporary price fixity can be viewed as an implicit contract between firms and buyers. Several models with a temporary fixity of the *nominal* wage have appeared in the recent literature. See Fischer (1977) and Phelps and Taylor (1977). In these models, monetary policy affects real variables by temporarily decreasing the real wage rate. This channel of monetary policy is absent here since the *real* wage rate is determined along with the level of employment and the price level at the beginning of the period. Unlike the above-mentioned models, our "contract" is immune to the criticism raised by Barro (1977), since both the real wage rate and employment are determined concurrently at ex ante market clearing values. Costs of adjustment prevent employment from adjusting to shocks within the period.

[19]Since the price level is fixed for the period, it does not matter whether the contract is made in terms of the nominal wage rate or not. In either case, the real wage rate and employment are predetermined and independent of the current monetary shock.

The demand for labor and expected sales depend on opening inventories, so the ex ante equilibrium of the economy also depends on these inventories. Shocks occur after the decisions about employment, output, the real wage and the price level have been made. Generally, firms respond to the shocks passively, selling from opening inventories and current production until they stockout.[20] Since the realization of demand and the ex post equilibrium usually differ from the forecast at the beginning of the period, end of period inventories differ in general from the ex ante plan made at the beginning of the period. The new, and partly unanticipated, level of inventories affects firms' decisions in the next period. Unanticipated inventories are the channel through which current unanticipated shocks affect the future equilibrium of the economy.

We now show the nature of these adjustments and the way in which they occur. Firms set plans. Aggregations of the planned values yields the market ex ante equilibrium values. The ex ante values, the expected permanent values and the unforeseen shocks that occur during the period determine the ex post realizations. Firms adjust plans using the new information.

2.5 The Ex Ante Equilibrium

All firms and individuals know the deterministic and stochastic structure of the economy. At the beginning of period 0 each obtains information on the aggregate level of inventories, H_0^a, and on the money supply, M_0^a, inherited from the previous period. Information about the aggregate level of inventories and the money supply at the end of period 0 (or beginning of period 1) does not become available until the beginning of period 1. The ex ante market clearing values of the various variables are obtained by equating demand and supply in all markets after setting the shocks' values equal to their respective expected values. This yields the system[21]

$$D_0 = \alpha Y^p + \beta \nu_0 = a(H_0^a + L_0) + \frac{K_0}{1-K_2}, \qquad 1 > a \equiv \frac{K_1}{1-K_2} > 0, \qquad (5.10\text{a})$$

$$\bar{L}_d + (\gamma_1\beta + \gamma_2)\nu_0 + \gamma_3 w_0 - H_0^a = \bar{L}_s + \omega(w_0 - w^p) = L_0, \qquad (5.10\text{b})$$

$$M_0^a(1 + \bar{m}) = P_0[(1-g)Y^p + gY_0 + br_0], \qquad (5.10\text{c})$$

$$r_0 = \nu_0 + P_1/P_0 - 1, \qquad (5.10\text{d})$$

where use has been made of the fact that $Y_0 = L_0$. Equations (5.10a and b)

---

[20]The condition under which such behavior is optimal is shown at the end of section 3.
[21]Eqn (5.10a) is obtained by equating (5.1) and (5.2), putting $D_0 = D_0^a$, $\epsilon_0 = 0$ and rearranging. Eqn (5.10b) is obtained by equating (5.4) and (5.6). Eqn (10c) is obtained by equating (5.8) and (5.9) after restriction $a < 1$ follows from micro considerations established in section 3.

constitute a system of three equations from which the ex ante market clearing values v_0, w_0 and $L_0 = Y_0$ can be solved in terms of H_0^a and the known, constant values of Y^p and w^p. Given these values, (5.10c) and (5.10d) determine P_0 and r_0 in terms of P_1 and $\bar{m}$.[22] The ex ante equilibrium of the economy is dichotomized, so real variables like employment, production, the real wage and the real rate of interest are determined by the subsystem (5.10a)–(5.10b). The price level and the nominal rate of interest are determined by (5.10c) and (5.10d) as functions of expected inflation and the quantity of money.

The ex ante market clearing values are the values that individuals expect the respective variables to take in period 0 given the (identical) information they have at the beginning of the period. For Y, L, w and P, as we saw earlier, expectations are equal to actual values. ($Y_0^a = Y_0$, etc.) The common expected value of sales, $\bar{S}_0$, and of aggregate demand, D_0, can also be solved in terms of H_0^a by substituting the solution for v_o into eqn (5.1) with $\epsilon_0 = 0$. The solutions for some of the expectations for period 0 are

$$Y_0 = L_0 = \bar{Y} - C_y H_0^a, \tag{5.11a}$$

$$w_0 = \bar{w} - (C_y/\omega)H_0^a, \tag{5.11b}$$

$$v_0 = \bar{v} + (a/\beta)(1 - C_y)H_0^a, \tag{5.11c}$$

$$D_0 = \bar{S}_0 = \bar{\bar{S}} + a(1 - C_y)H_0^a, \tag{5.11d}$$

where $\bar{Y}$, $\bar{v}$, $\bar{w}$ and $\bar{\bar{S}}$ are some constants which depend on Y^p, w^p and the parameters of the model and

$$0 < C_y \equiv \frac{\omega[\beta(1 - a\gamma_1) - a\gamma_2]}{-\beta\gamma_3 + \omega[\beta(1 - a\gamma_1) - a\gamma_2]} < 1. \tag{5.12}$$

The inequalities in (5.12) hold, provided the commodity market is dynamically stable in the sense that an increase in the real rate of interest decreases excess demand on this market.[23] The intuitive meaning of this condition can be understood as follows: Ceteris paribus, an increase in the real rate of interest decreases both aggregate demand and expected sales. The latter reflects the supply behavior of firms. Dynamic stability requires that the decrease in demand be larger than the decrease in supply. Equations (5.11a) through (5.11d) imply that employment, output, the real wage rate and the expected real rate are all lower the higher the initial level of inventories. By contrast, expected sales are higher the higher the initial level of inventories.

---

[22]The solution appears below.
[23]For a proof, see part A.1 of appendix 5.1.

2.6 Determination of Permanent Values

The permanent values are the values generated by the general equilibrium of the economy when the exogenous shocks are at their expected values – $\bar{m}$ and 0 – and inventories are at their permanent level H^p. Operationally, the permanent values of all real variables can be obtained from eqns (5.11) by replacing H_0^a with H^p and using eqns (5.10).

$$Y^p = K_0 + K_1(H^p + Y^p) + K_2(\alpha Y^p + \beta \nu^p) = D^p = \bar{S}^p, \tag{5.13a}$$

$$\alpha Y^p + \beta \nu^p = a(H^p + Y^p) + K_0/(1-K_2), \tag{5.13b}$$

$$\bar{L}_d + (\gamma_1 \beta + \gamma_2)\nu^p + \gamma_3 w^p - H^p = \bar{L}_s = L^p = Y^p. \tag{5.13c}$$

Equation (5.13a) is the steady-state condition which states that no inventory change is planned, so output and expected sales are equal. The solutions to the five eqns (5.13a – c) are the permanent values H^p, Y^p, L^p, w^p and ν^p. The solutions are omitted for brevity.

2.7 The Ex Post Equilibrium

The market interest rate, aggregate demand and sales are affected by shocks that occur within the period, so the actual values of these variables differ from the values expected at the beginning of the period. The interest rate, determined by clearing of the money market with the period, depends on the price level. The path of interest rates depends on the path of prices, analyzed below. After rearrangement of the demand for money,

$$r_0^a = \frac{1}{b}\left[\frac{M_0(1+m_0)}{P_0^a} + \theta\epsilon_0 - (1-g)Y^p - gY_0^a\right]. \tag{5.14}$$

The actual value of aggregate demand is given by eqn (5.1). Actual sales are

$$S_0 = \min[D_0^a, H_0^a + Y_0^a] = \min[\alpha Y^p + \beta(r_0^a - \pi_1) + \epsilon_0, H_0^a + Y_0^a]. \tag{5.15}$$

As long as aggregate demand is less than current production plus carryover stocks of inventories, $H_0^a + Y_0^a$, actual sales equal aggregate demand.[24] If

---

[24]Writing actual sales in this way involves three assumptions. First, whenever a particular firm stockouts and other firms have merchandise for sale, customers find the other firms within the period. Customers fail to complete purchases only if there are stockouts at the aggregate level. Second, the real rate is non-negative. Third, observation of the within-period value of the interest rate r_0^a, does not alter expected inflation for the period. This assumption is made for simplicity and without much loss of generality since, as demonstrated in part A.2 of the appendix, its removal does not change the qualitative results to be discussed in the text. Explicit incorporation of the informational value of r_0^a in the model increases the effect of unanticipated money on aggregate demand. This fact also constitutes an answer to Siegel's (1981) criticism of a similar mechanism presented in Cukierman (1981). Those who believe that stockouts are unimportant can disregard the minimum throughout.

aggregate demand exceeds $H_0^a + Y_0^a$, sales are constrained to equal $H_0^a + Y_0^a$. The actual level of inventories at the beginning of period 1 is then

$$H_1^a = H_0^a + Y_0^a - \min[D_0^a, H_0^a + Y_0^a]. \tag{5.16}$$

2.8 The Dynamic Behavior of Expected Inventories

The expected change in inventories during period 0 is the difference between the sum of output planned by individial firms and the expected level of sales or demand. H_1 is the level of inventories that firms in the aggregate currently expect to hold at the start of period 1,[25]

$$H_1 = H_0^a + Y_0^a - D_0. \tag{5.17}$$

Substituting (5.11a) and (5.11d) into (5.17) and rearranging terms gives

$$H_1 = \bar{H} + (1-a)(1-C_y)H_0^a, \tag{5.18}$$

where $\bar{H}$ depends on the constant values of Y^p and w^p and on the model's parameters. Given H_1, (5.18) can be used to calculate H_2, since the level of inventories expected at the beginning of period 2 bears the same relationship to H_1 as H_1 bears to H_0^a. In general,

$$H_t = \bar{H} + AH_{t-1}, \text{ and} \tag{5.19a}$$

the permanent level of inventories is

$$H^p = \bar{H}/(1-A), \text{ where} \tag{5.19b}$$

$$0 < A \equiv (1-a)(1-C_y) < 1. \tag{5.20}$$

The solution for H^p is the same as the solution obtained from eqns (5.13). Equation (5.19a) is a monotonically convergent first order difference equation. The steady state level of expected inventories (which is also their permanent level) is obtained by setting $H_t = H_{t-1} = H^p$ for all t in (5.19a). The solution for the dynamic, expected behavior of future inventories is

$$H_t = H^p + A^t(H_0^a - H^p). \tag{5.21}$$

Equation (5.21) shows that the expected level of inventories converges to its permanent value. If the current level of inventories is larger than H^p, the economy is expected to decumulate inventories. Similarly, if $H_0 < H^p$, (5.21) implies that inventories are expected to increase until they reach H^p.[26]

---

[25]Again, to avoid repeating information on timing, current expectations refer to expectations formed at the start of period 0. Note 38 below shows that firms never *plan* to stockout. Stockouts occur only because of unanticipated shocks. This assures that in eqn (5.17) H_1 is always strictly positive.

[26]The current level of inventories of any individual firm may deviate from the economy-wide average. A firm with inventories below their expected permanent level may at times expect its own inventories to go up while simultaneously expecting the aggregate level of inventories to go down.

2.9 The Dynamic Behavior of Other Expectations

By adding and substracting the term $C_y H^p$ on the right-hand side of (5.11a) and leading by t periods, the level of output and employment expected for period t at the beginning of period 0 becomes

$$Y_t = L_t = Y^p - C_y(H_t - H^p). \qquad (5.22a)$$

Proceeding similarly with eqns (5.11b to d),

$$w_t = w^p - \frac{C_y}{\omega}(H_t - H^p), \qquad (5.22b)$$

$$v_t = v^p + \frac{a}{\beta}(1 - C_y)(H_t - H^p), \qquad (5.22c)$$

$$\overline{S}_t = D_t = N\mu_t = \overline{S}_p + a(1 - C_y)(H_t - H^p). \qquad (5.22d)$$

The time paths in eqns (5.22a) through (5.22d) describe, in addition to expectations, the actual path that the economy follows if, after period 0, there are no further unanticipated shocks to demand or to money. Any shock that raises H_t above its steady-state value, H^p, reduces Y, w and v and raises $\overline{S}$. Adjustment to the shock continues until H_t converges to H^p. The deviation of each of the expected values from its permanent value is uniquely determined by the deviation of (expected) inventories from the permanent value of inventories.

2.10 The Path of Prices and Inflation

When inventories are at their permanent position, the demand for real money balances is constant. In this special circumstance, the price level is proportional to the permanent money stock. If the permanent money stock changes at the rate $\bar{m}$, prices are expected to change and for the permanent rate of inflation. The path can be computed from[27]

$$M_0(1 + \bar{m})^t = P_t^p[Y^p + b(v^p + \bar{m})]. \qquad (5.23)$$

Generally, inventories are not at their permanent value, so the path of expected prices differs from the path of expected permanent prices. We showed above that because A is a proper fraction, planned inventories adjust gradually. The gradual adjustment of inventories causes gradual adjustment of expected output and other expected real variables, as shown by (5.22).

---

[27]Eqn (5.23) is obtained by substituting permanent instead of expected variables in (5.10c), using (5.10d) and noting that along the permanent path $P_t/P_{t-1} - 1 = \bar{m}$. The path of expected permanent prices is the path followed by the price level in the absence of unforseen shocks once inventories have reached their permanent level.

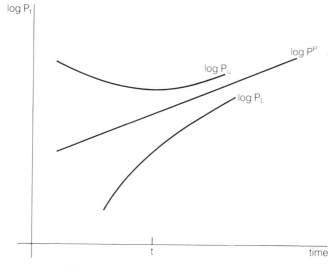

Figure 5.1   Price adjustment path.

The expected demand for money depends on expected output and interest rates, so the gradual adjustment of planned inventories causes gradual adjustment of expected real money balances (and prices) to the permanent or steady-state level.

Figure 5.1 illustrates the adjustment of prices. The line labelled log P^p is the path of the permanent price level obtained from (5.23). The slope of log P^p is approximately $\bar{m}$; the permanent rate of inflation equals the maintained rate of money growth. The lines labelled log P_i, $i=U, L$ are the paths of prices before the economy settles at its permanent position.[28]

Two cases are illustrated in figure 5.1. Along log P_L the expected rate of inflation exceeds the rate of monetary growth: $\pi_t > \bar{m}$; P_t approaches P^p from below. The reason is that the response of income and interest rates to inventory adjustment lowers the real demand for money. The converse happens along log P_U. Note that the slopes of the lines log P_U and log P_L, which are approximately equal to the expected rate of inflation, approach the long-run rate of inflation $\bar{m}$ gradually.[29] In general, if P_t is a converging path, a necessary and sufficient condition for $P_t > P^p_t$ is $\pi_t < \bar{m}$.[30]

---

[28]Although the word "expected" does not always appear here it should be understood that these are expected price paths or alternatively the actual paths on which P_t adjusts in the absence of any further unanticipated shocks.

[29]This is a direct consequence of the discussion on pp. 110–11 in Cukierman (1981). The statement presupposes convergence; see note 30.

[30]This statement can be proved by assuming the converse – that when $\pi_t < \bar{m}$, $P_t < P^p_t$ – and establishing a contradiction. Let $\pi_t < \bar{m}$. As shown in corollary to proposition 1, of Cukierman (1981) convergence is monotonic, so $\pi_{t+k} < \bar{m}$ for $k \geqq 0$. If $P_t < P^p_t$, P never converges to P^p.

Substituting (5.11a), (5.11c) and (5.10d) into (5.10c) and rearranging

$$P_0^a = P_0 = \frac{M_0(1+\bar{m}) + |b|P_1}{B_0 + B_1 H_0^a} \equiv x_0[M_0\rho + |b|P_1], \qquad (5.24)$$

where B_0 is a positive constant of no particular interest, $\rho \equiv 1 + \bar{m}$, x_0 is implicitly defined by the last equality of (5.24), and x_0 depends on H_0^a.

$$B_1 \equiv a \frac{b}{\beta} (1 - C_y) - gC_y. \qquad (5.25)$$

We assume that g, the sensitivity of money demand with respect to transitory income, is relatively small, so $B_1 > 0$. Equation (5.24) suggests that period 0's expected price depends on P_1, the price expected for period 1, which in turn through the same relation depends on P_2 and so on. Leading (5.24) by one period to express P_1 in terms of P_2, substituting the resulting expression into eqn (5.24) and continuing, eventually we get[31]

$$P_0^a = P_0 = M_0[x_0\rho + x_0x_1|b|\rho^2 + \ldots + x_0x_1 \ldots x_{t-1}|b|^{t-1}\rho^t]$$
$$+ |b|^t x_0 x_1 \ldots x_{t-1} P_t^p. \qquad (5.26)$$

Here use has been made of the assumption that prices eventually converge to their permanent path.

Equation (5.26) is a unique well-determined expression for the current period's price level in terms of the expected path of inventories and P_t^p. The uniqueness of the path contrasts with the multiple solutions for the price level found in some recent rational expectations models. (See Taylor, 1977 and Blanchard, 1979.) The two reasons that rational expectations do not give rise to non-unique solutions in our model are (1) the real economy is expected to converge eventually to fixed permanent values, and (2) stock equilibrium determines a unique permanent price level. If real balances always have a positive, finite value, the price level converges to its permanent value and is strictly proportional to the stock of money. Thus the current price level is pinned down by the permanent value of the demand for real money balances.

Equation (5.21) shows that, ceteris paribus, an increase in H_0^a increases H_t for all $t \geq 0$. Since $B_1 > 0$, x_t falls. This leads to the following proposition:

(Similarly for $\pi_t > \bar{m}$ and $P_t > P_t^p$.) Economic reasoning exludes non-convergence of P to a unique equilibrium at P^p. The reason is, as we see from (5.23), that both P^p and the permanent value of real balances have unique finite values when Y and ν are at their permanent values, Y^p and ν^p. We know also that, Y, ν, H and other real variables converge to permanent values. If P_{t+k} does not converge to P_{t+k}^p (in fact diverges) real balances approach zero or infinity as k increases. Non-convergence implies, therefore, that with all remaining real variables constant, real balances approach zero or infinity. An algebraic proof of convergence cannot be provided because the system is dichotomized. Using (5.26) below, it is easy to see that P approaches P^p, if there is convergence.

[31]Here, $x_t \equiv 1/(B_0 + B_1 H_t)$ for $t > 0$.

Proposition 1. An increase in beginning of period inventories reduces the price level for small g.

This result is reminiscent of a similar result at the micro level according to which upward deviations of actual from 'desired' inventories cause downward deviations of the current price set by a firm from its long-run price. (See, for example, Maccini, 1980.) The reason is completely different, however. The micro result arises because the firm attempts to decrease its relative price. Our result concerns the general price level; ceteris paribus, a higher current level of inventories decreases expected real and nominal rates of interest, increases the expected demand for money and, thus reduces the current price level.

3 Microfoundations of the Firms Sector: Derivation of Labor Demand and Expected Sales

At the beginning of a period, each firm chooses employment, output, inventories and prices by maximizing the present value of expected real profits given its perceptions about the state of the economy in the current and future periods. Demand facing the representative firm depends on aggregate demand and on factors specific to the firm. Both components of demand are stochastic, but the uncertainty in the individual component of demand is large relative to macroeconomic uncertainty.

Expected average demand per firm at the beginning of period 0 is equal to μ of eqn (5.3). Firms use this expectation when setting price. At this level of demand and at the price $P_0^a = P_0$, from eqn (5.26), the representative firm faces a kinked demand curve. The kink is sufficiently strong that no firm sets its price higher or lower than P_0. As a consequence of this assumption, all firms in the economy post the same price, P_0. At the posted price, the stochastic demand facing the individual firm, given μ, is

$$d = z + \delta\mu, 0 < \delta < 1, \tag{5.27}$$

where z is the stochastic demand factor specific to the firm. The distribution of z is the same for all firms but its realizations differ across firms. Further, z is i.i.d. and is statistically independent of the macroeconomic shocks, m and ϵ. The expected value, Ez, is positive for all μ. This last assumption means that in the relevant range, part of the systematic demand facing the individual firm is not related to movements in the systematic part of aggregate demand.[32]

---

[32]The restriction $\delta < 1$ in (5.27) is implied by the assumption that $Ez > 0$ for all μ together with equilibrium in the commodity market. This is shown at the end of this section.

3.1 The Single Firm's Optimization

The representative firm maximizes the present value of its stream of real expected profits, given the forecasts of the relevant macroeconomic variables from eqn (5.22). Formally, at the beginning of period 0, the firm's problem is

$$J_0(h_0) \equiv \max_{\{l_0, l_1, \ldots\}} E_{-1} \sum_{i=0}^{\infty} \left(\Pi_i(l_i) \Big/ \prod_{s=0}^{i-1} (1 + \nu_s) \right), \qquad (5.28)$$

subject to

$$h_i = h_{i-1} + l_{i-1} - \delta\mu_{i-1} - z_{i-1}, \quad i = 1, 2, \ldots,$$
$$h_i \geq 0, \qquad l_i \geq 0, \qquad\qquad i = 0, 1, 2,$$
$$h_0 \quad \text{given}$$

where l_i is the amount of labor employed by the firm in period i, h_i the level of its inventories at the beginning of period i. It is understood that $\Pi_{s=\tau}^{i-1}(1+\nu_s) = 1$, for $i - 1 < \tau$.

$$\Pi_i(l_i) = \bar{s}_i(h_i + l_i) - w_i l_i \qquad (5.29)$$

are the expected real profits of the firm in period i, measured in units of the product, $\bar{s}_i(h_i + l_i)$ the expected sales of the firm, and $h_i + l_i$, the total that firm has available for sale.[33] The dependence of $\bar{s}_i$ on $h_i + l_i$ arises because the firm stocks out at realizations of demand above $h_i + l_i$. Stockouts truncate the positive effect of high realizations of demand on expected sales, $\bar{s}_i(\cdot)$ and, thus, create a positive dependence of $\bar{s}_i(\cdot)$ on $h_i + l_i$. Each firm takes the macro forecasts of the real wage and the real rate of interest, w_i and v_i as determined from (5.22b) and (5.22c), given H_0^a.

Let $g(z)$ and $G(z)$ be respectively the probability density and the cumulative probability density of the specific demand shock z. We assume that the probability of zero sales at the firm's level is zero, so that $g(-\delta\mu) = G(-\delta\mu) = 0$, and that in the upper tail of z, $g(z)$, although small, is positive for large $z - s$. Backlogs are not permitted. The firm either sells in the period in which a given demand materializes or loses the sale. Let

$$x \equiv h + l \qquad (5.30)$$

---

[33]The expected value operator E_{-1} in (5.28) is over the distribution of the firm specific demand shocks $z_0, z_1, z_2, \ldots$ given the information available to the firm at the beginning of period, 0. Since this expectation is formed on the basis of information up to and including period -1, before the realizations of period 0's shocks are known, it carries the index -1. The latest information included in this information set is H_0^a, M_0 and h_0. Note that h_0 is an actual value whereas the h_i, $i > 0$, are random variables. The index "a" for "actual" is not attached to h_0 for simplicity.

be the total amount of the product the firm has available for sale in a given period. Using eqn (5.27) and the distribution function of z, $\bar{s}$, the expected value of sales conditional on the forecast μ, can be computed as[34]

$$\bar{s}(x) = \delta\mu + \int_{-\delta\mu}^{x-\delta\mu} z\,\mathrm{d}G(z) + [1 - G(x - \delta\mu)][x - \delta\mu]$$

$$= G(x - \delta\mu)\delta\mu + [1 - G(x - \delta\mu)]x + \int_{-\delta\mu}^{x-\delta\mu} z\,\mathrm{d}G(z). \qquad (5.31)$$

Partial differentiations of $\bar{s}$ with respect to x yields

$$\partial\bar{s}/\partial x = 1 - G(x - \delta\mu) > 0. \qquad (5.32)$$

Any increase in the total available for sale, x, increases expected sales by decreasing the probability of stockouts. Inventories are held, therefore, to increase expected sales and profits.

By the principle of optimality, eqn (5.28) can be rewritten

$$J_0(h_0) = \max_{l_0} \left[E_{-1}(\bar{s}_0(h_0 + l_0) - w_0 l_0) + \frac{T_1(h_0 + l_0 - \delta\mu_0)}{1 + \nu_0} \right], \qquad (5.33)$$

where

$$J_1(h_1) = \max_{\{l_1, l_2, \ldots\}} E_0 \sum_{i=1}^{\infty} \left(\Pi_i(l_i) \bigg/ \prod_{s=1}^{i-1} (1 + \nu_s) \right), \qquad (5.34)$$

and

$$T_1(h_0 + l_0 - \delta\mu_0) \equiv E_{-1}J_1(h_0 + l_0 - \delta\mu_0 - z_0). \qquad (5.35)$$

In the expected value, $E_{-1}J_1$, if $z_0 \geqq h_0 + l_0 - \delta\mu_0$, $h_1 = 0$. Note that eqn (5.33) can be written as a decision problem in $x_0 \equiv h_0 + l_0$, provided $h_0 \leqq x_0$.[35]

Each unit of labor produces one unit of the product. A necessary condition for positive production at the permanent position of the economy is that the permanent wage, per unit of labor supplied, is less than unity, so we assume $w^p < 1$. With this assumption, an interior maximum for x_0 in eqn (5.33) exists. (See part A.3 of the appendix.) The optimum that the firm chooses is the same whether x_0 or l_0 is the decision variable. The first order (necessary) condition (using (5.31) specialized to period 0) is

---

[34]This expected value is always smaller than or equal to the expected value of demand, $Ed = Ez + \delta\mu$, which does not permit stockouts.

[35]If $h_0 > x_0$, x_0 is not a decision variable (negative production is not possible) so the firm's demand for labor is zero. We assume $h_0 \leqq x_0$ to be the typical case. Tracing out the effects of $h_0 > x_0$ through the macroeconomy complicates the analysis without changing the qualitative nature of the results.

$$1 - G(h_0 + l_0 - \delta\mu_0) - w_0 + \frac{T_1'(h_0 + l_0 - \delta\mu_0)}{1+\nu_0} = 0, \qquad (5.36\text{a})$$

and the second order (sufficient) condition is

$$R'' = -g(h_0 + l_0 - \delta\mu_0) + \frac{T_1''(h_0 + l_0 - \delta\mu_0)}{1+\nu_0} < 0, \qquad (5.36\text{b})$$

where T'_1 and T_1'' are respectively the first and the second order partial derivatives of the function T_1. Equation (5.36a) determines optimal l_0 for given initial inventories, h_0, or determines optimal x_0. All firms choose the same level of x_0 independently of their initial inventories.[36]

3.2 From Individual to Aggregate Expected Sales

This section derives eqn (5.2) in the macro problem. Differentiating $\bar{s}$ from eqn (5.31) partially with respect to μ, we have

$$\partial\bar{s}/\partial\mu = \delta G(x - \delta\mu). \qquad (5.37)$$

Equations (5.32) and (5.37) imply that

$$0 < \partial\bar{s}/\partial x < 1 \text{ and } 0 < \partial\bar{s}/\partial\mu < 1. \qquad (5.38)$$

Furthermore,

$$\partial\bar{s}/\partial x + \partial\bar{s}/\partial\mu = 1 - (1-\delta)G(x - \delta\mu) < 1, \qquad (5.39)$$

and

$$0 < \frac{\partial\bar{s}}{\partial x} \Big/ \left(1 - \frac{\partial\bar{s}}{\partial\mu}\right) = \frac{1 - G(x - \delta\mu)}{1 - \delta G(x - \delta\mu)} < 1. \qquad (5.40)$$

Approximating $\bar{s}(x)$ linearly around the point $x = Ez + \delta\mu^p$ for $\mu = \mu^p$, we obtain

$$\bar{s} = k_0 + K_1 x + K_2\mu, \text{ where} \qquad (5.41)$$

$$k_0 \equiv \int_{-\delta\mu}^{Ez} z \, dG(z), \quad K_1 \equiv 1 - G(Ez), \quad K_2 \equiv \delta G(Ez). \qquad (5.42)$$

From eqns (5.38), (5.39), (5.40) and the definitions in (5.42), we see that

$$0 < K_1, K_2 < 1, \ 0 < K_1 + K_2 < 1, \ 0 < a \equiv \frac{K_1}{1-K_2} < 1. \qquad (5.43)$$

Since all firms choose the same x, the aggregate level of expected sales for the whole economy is obtained by summing (5.41) over all (N) firms and using (5.3) to get

---

[36]The last two statements are strictly true only when $h_0 \leqq x_0$, and x_0 is the decision variable.

$$\bar{S} = N\bar{s} = K_0 + K_1 X^a + K_2 D, \tag{5.44}$$

where $K_0 \equiv Nk_0$ and $X^a \equiv Nx = H^a + Y^a$. Equation (5.44) is the expected aggregate sales function that appears as eqn (5.2) of the macro model. Equation (5.43) shows that the restrictions imposed on eqns (5.2) and (5.10a) of the macro model are implications of the micro model.

3.3 Comparative Statics and the Demand for Labor

By differentiating the first order condition (5.36a) with respect to period 0's variables, we derive the restrictions on the coefficients of the aggregate labor demand function, eqn (5.4),

$$\partial l_0 / \partial h_0 = -1, \tag{5.45a}$$

$$1 > \gamma_1 \equiv \partial l_0 / \partial \mu_0 = \delta > 0, \tag{5.45b}$$

$$\gamma_2 \equiv \partial l_0 / \partial \nu_0 = \frac{1}{R''} \left[\frac{T_1'(\cdot)}{(1+\nu_0)^2} \right] < 0, \tag{5.45c}$$

$$\gamma_3 \equiv \partial l_0 / \partial w_0 = \frac{1}{R''} < 0. \tag{5.45d}$$

The sign of γ_2 requires discussion. $T_1'(\cdot) = E_{-1} J_1'(h_1)$, where J_1' is the derivative of the optimized function in eqn (5.34) with respect to beginning inventory. An increase in beginning inventory increases expected sales and therefore expected profits, in some states of nature, but may not affect these variables in others; so for all h_1, $J_1'(h_1) \geq 0$, and for some h_1 it is strictly positive. It follows that $T_1'(\cdot)$ (being a linear combination over states of nature of $J_1'(\cdot)$) is also positive.

The firm in our model has no reason to smooth inventories at the micro level.[37] Equation (5.45a) shows that a unit increase in inventories decreases production (and the demand for labor) equiproportionally. This result differs from much of the micro literature on inventories. See Amihud and Mendelson (1982), Reagan (1982), Blinder and Fischer (1981) and Blinder (1981). There, a unit increase in inventories decreases production by less than one unit: diminishing marginal productivity and fluctuating demand induce firms to smooth production and hold inventories. In contrast, we have assumed constant returns to scale for labor. Our firm plans to hold a positive amount of inventory, on average, to increase expected profits.[38] Since the effects of an additional unit of current production and an additional unit of

---

[37]The macroeconomic model implies that $dY^a/dH^a = dL^a/dH^a > -1$, however, so there is "smoothing" for macro reasons, as shown in section 4.

[38]That the firm plans to hold a positive amount of inventories, on average, can be seen from eqn (5.31). $\bar{s}(x)$ is a weighted average of x and of demand which is lower than x, so it must be lower than x. Therefore, $h_1 = h_0 + l_0 - \mu_0 = x_0 - \bar{s}(x_0) > 0$.

inventories on expected profits are the same, the firm treats current production and inventories as perfect substitutes.

Approximating labor demand of the jth firm linearly, we have[39]

$$l_{0j} = \tilde{\gamma}_0 + \gamma_1\mu_0 + \tilde{\gamma}_2\nu_0 + \tilde{\gamma}_3 w_0 - h_{0j}, \tag{5.46}$$

where in view of eqn (5.45), $0 < \gamma_1 = \delta < 1$, $\tilde{\gamma}_2 < 0$, $\tilde{\gamma}_3 < 0$. Summing eqn (5.46) over all firms, the aggregate demand for labor is

$$L_0^d \equiv \sum_{j=1}^{N} l_{0j} = N\tilde{\gamma}_0 + \gamma_1(N\mu_0) + N\tilde{\gamma}_2\nu_0 + N\tilde{\gamma}_3 w_0 - \sum_{j=1}^{N} h_{0j}$$

$$= \gamma_0 + \gamma_1 D_0 + \gamma_2\nu_0 + \gamma_3 w_0 - H_0^a, \tag{5.47}$$

where $\gamma_0 \equiv N\tilde{\gamma}_0$, $\gamma_2 \equiv N\tilde{\gamma}_2 < 0$, $\tilde{\gamma}_3 \equiv N\tilde{\gamma}_3 < 0$. Substituting expected aggregate demand from (5.10a) into (5.47) and rearranging, we obtain the aggregate demand for labor function postulated in eqn (5.4) of the macro section,

$$L_0^d = \bar{L}_d + (\gamma_1\beta + \gamma_2)\nu_0 + \gamma_3 w_0 - H_0^a, \quad 0 < \gamma_1 < 1, \quad \gamma_2, \gamma_3 < 0, \tag{5.47'}$$

where $\bar{L}_d \equiv \gamma_0 + a\gamma_1 Y^p$.

3.4 Recapitulation of the Linkages Between the Macro and the Micro Structures

In section 2 we postulated the forms of the aggregate expected supply function and the aggregate labor demand by firms, eqns (5.2) and (5.4), and derived the expectations of firms concerning the future time paths of relevant economic variables. In this section, the individual firm chose its optimal employment and production, for given expectations. Then, we showed that aggregation of the individual firm's expected sales and labor demand functions, derived from their optimizing choices, yielded the aggregate functions postulated in the macro section. (Compare (5.44) with (5.2) and (5.47') with (5.4).) This establishes the consistency between the macro and the micro structures as well as the rationality of the various epxectations derived in the macro section.

Before closing this section, two remarks are in order. First, we note that whatever view the firm holds about future prices during period 0, it always chooses to carry out the plan made at the beginning of this period provided that the realized real rate is non-negative.[40] The firm does not alter its current

---

[39] l_{0j} also depends on the expected time paths of μ, ν and w for future periods from period 1 on. We know that these time paths eventually converge to some constant permanent values, so we approximate the dependence of l_{0j} on those paths by making it a function of μ^p, ν^p and w^p. The permanent values are constant over time, and the dependence is subsumed in the constant, γ_0 in (5.46).

[40] This also establishes that even if the firm changes its view about future prices within the period (along the lines of part A.2 of the appendix), it does not change behavior within the period.

price by assumption, but it can refrain from selling some of the product on hand in order to sell it in future periods. For small shocks the firm never finds it profitable to refuse sales. The reason is that one unit of product not sold today decreases the present value of expected real profits by exactly one unit and increases the present value of future expected real profits by less than one unit. This can be seen by noting that, whatever the price level expected for period 1, the transfer of one unit of inventories to period 1 increases the present value of expected *real* profits by

$$\frac{1-G(x_1-\delta\mu_1)}{1+r_0^a-\pi_1}, \tag{5.48}$$

which is always smaller than 1 for a positive real rate of interest. Transfer of this unit to more distant future periods increases the present value of expected profits by even less. Hence, as long as they do not stockout, firms satisfy demand passively out of current production and opening inventories as assumed in the macro section.[41] Second, our claim that $Ez > 0$ for all μ, implies that $\delta < 1$ is demonstrated. Taking the expected value of (5.27) over the distribution of z,

$$Ed = Ez + \delta\mu. \tag{5.49}$$

For the case $\mu = Ed$, the ex ante equilibrium condition in the commodity market together with (5.49) imply

$$\mu = Ed = Ez + \delta\mu, \tag{5.50}$$

which implies that $\delta < 1$ since both Ez and μ are positive.

4 Money, Business Cycles and Macroeconomic Aspects of Inventory Behavior

If real markets and financial markets clear simultaneously, money is neutral in our model. Non-neutrality of money results from a one-period difference in the speed of response to unanticipated shocks. The nominal stock of money is always willingly held at the market clearing rate of interest, so the markets for money and securities reflect all shocks instantly. Efficient production and sales require advance planning of real output and expected sales. To plan production and sales, firms set prices and agree with workers on employment and real wages one period at a time. These "contracts" are

---

[41]Note that speculation on future changes in relative prices is excluded since all firms charge the same price. A large shock to the money stock can make $r_0^a - \pi_1$ negative for a period by driving the nominal rate of interest below the expected rate of inflation. In this case, the value of eqn (5.48) can exceed unity. If this happens, optimizing behavior leads firms to withhold sales and carry inventory to the next period.

revised each period using all available information, but they remain fixed during the period for which they are set. Consequently unanticipated shocks to the growth rate of money change interest rates immediately but do not affect prices, employment and real wages until "contracts" are revised. Unanticipated increases in the growth of money reduce interest rates, increase sales and reduce end of period inventories; unanticipated reductions in money growth raise interest rates, reduce sales and increase end of period inventories. At the start of each period, everyone knows the changes in money growth, sales and aggregate inventories that has occurred; prices, real wages, employment, output, planned inventories and expected rates of interest reflect the new information. Nevertheless, persistent deviations from permanent values occur, and the deviations are serially correlated.

Producers do not restore inventories to their (known) permanent value in the period following an unintended change but, instead, spread the response over several periods. A main reason is that the aggregate labor supply curve is positively sloped. Each firm knows that the larger the increase in the aggregate demand for labor, the larger is the rise in the real wage and the larger the cost of rebuilding inventories. The speed of response, and the length of time for which deviations from permanent values persist, depends not only on the slope of the labor supply function but also on the slope of the labor demand function and on the sensitivity of aggregate demand to the interest rate.

In this section we show that, despite the absence of production smoothing at the micro level, rational expectations provides a macro reason for aggregate inventories to follow a partial adjustment process. Then, we present a general analysis of the response of inventories to unanticipated changes. The analysis is specialized to the case in which there are only monetary shocks. This permits a more compact analysis of the the cyclical responses of output, unemployment and other real variables to unanticipated money growth. We show that errors in judging the persistence of shocks to money growth contribute to the serial correlation. The section closes with a comparison of our results to some previous studies.

4.1 Production Smoothing – Macro Versus Micro Considerations

Individual firms do not smooth inventories as shown by eqn (5.45a);

$$\partial y/\partial h = \partial l/\partial h = -1, \tag{5.51}$$

but, for the aggregate, we know from eqn (5.11a) of section 2 that

$$\partial Y/\partial H^a = \partial L/\partial H^a = -C_y > -1. \tag{5.52}$$

A given decrease in economy-wide inventories increases aggregate production by less than the decrease in inventories

The origin of the difference in response lies in the familiar distinction between a "market" and an "individual" experiment and depends on the rational expectations of producers who know the structure of the model and anticipate the aggregate response. An unexpected exogenous decrease in aggregate inventories increases the aggregate demand for labor as firms try to rebuild stocks. The increased demand for labor increases the real wage rate along the aggregate labor supply schedule in (5.6). At the higher real wage rate, firms spread the rebuilding of inventories over time, reducing the planned increase in current period output and employment. Because firms know that the increase in the aggregrate demand for labor increases the real wage, they spread inventory rebuilding activity over time. Although there is no production smoothing at the level of the individual firm, there is production smoothing because of macroeconomic reasons under rational expectations. The intensity of the smoothing is inversely related to C_y and thus, depends on structural parameters. The effects of these parameters on C_y are summarized in the following proposition:

Proposition 2. C_y is smaller and macroeconomic smoothing stronger, the lower ω, the higher $|\gamma_2|$ and $|\gamma_3|$ and the lower $|\beta|$.[42]

The less sensitive labor supply is to the real wage rate (low ω), the more the real wage rate increases and the less employment and production increase following a decrease in inventories. The more sensitive labor demand (high $|\gamma_3|$) to the real wage, the more the increase in the real wage discourages production. As can be seen from (5.11d), lower initial inventories also partially reduce expected sale (since $0 < a(1-C_y) < 1$). To maintain commodity market equilibrium, aggregate demand falls. This is brought about by an increase in the real rate of interest. The rise in the real rate, ceteris paribus, decreases labor demand, employment and production. The less sensitive is aggregate demand to the real rate (low $|\beta|$), the larger is the necessary increase in the real rate, the more sensitive labor demand is to the real rate (large $|\gamma_2|$), the stronger, ceteris paribus, is the negative effect of the higher real rate on current employment and production. Therefore, a low $|\beta|$ and a high $|\gamma_2|$ lead to a rather lengthy period of inventory rebuilding activity. Similar reasoning, later in this section, shows that the same parameters that determine the degree of macroeconomic smoothing play an important role in determining the amplitude and the length of the cycle.

4.2 The Partial Adjustment Feature of Aggregate Inventories

By adding and subtracting AH^p to the right-hand side of (5.19a), we get, after rearrangement

$$H_t - H_{t-1} = (1-A)(H^p - H_{t-1}), \tag{5.53}$$

---

[42]These results follow directly from (5.12) and by noting that $\partial C_y/\partial\beta$ has the same (negative) sign as $-\omega a\gamma_2\gamma_3$.

where from (5.20), (5.42), (5.43) and (5.45b)

$$A \equiv (1-a)(1-C_y)=(1-a) \; \frac{-\beta\gamma_3}{-\beta\gamma_3+\omega[\beta(1-\delta a)-a\gamma_2]} \; ,$$

$$a \equiv \frac{1-G(Ez)}{1-\delta G(Ez)} \; . \tag{5.54}$$

Equation (5.53) describes the anticipated path of aggregate inventories. In the absence of further unanticipated shocks, actual and anticipated inventories adjust to the permanent level by following a simple stock adjustment equation of the Koyck variety. The speed of adjustment is a decreasing function of A, which in turn is a decreasing function of C_y. Thus, the same factors that increase macro smoothing in Proposition 2 also increase the lag in the adjustment of inventories to their permanent or "desired" value.

4.3 Unintended and Planned Inventory Changes

Since decisions about production, employment and inventories are made at the beginning of each period, before the realizations of the shocks in that period, end of period inventories can differ from planned. As a result, total inventory investment has two components. The planned or anticipated component follows a path described by eqn (5.21). Unintended changes occur only if there are unanticipated shocks to aggregate demand or to money growth.[43] The unanticipated change in inventories is determined by the unanticipated component of demand which, (using eqn (5.1)), is

$$D_0^a - D_0 = \beta(r_0^a - r_0) + \varepsilon_0. \tag{5.55}$$

Unanticipated demand depends on ε, the unanticipated component of aggregate demand, and on the unanticipated change in the normal rate of interest.[44] The latter is obtained by rearranging (5.10c) and subtracting from (5.14),

$$r_0^a - r_0 = \frac{1}{b} \; [(M_0^a/P_0^a)(m_0 - \bar{m}) + \theta\varepsilon_0] \tag{5.56}$$

so both shocks affect aggregate demand and unanticipated inventory change through their effect on interest rates. Substituting (5.56) into (5.55), and

---

[43]By contrast, in the *macro* inventory model of Blinder and Fischer (1981), decisions are made after the resolution of uncertainty, so there is no room for unanticipated changes in inventories. In recent *micro* inventory models, that is not always the case. See, for example, Amihud and Mendelson (1980) and Blinder (1981).

[44]Firms accommodate demand within the period. Except for the case discussed in note 41, such behavior is optimal for the individual firm. We limit our analysis to the case in which there are no stockouts in the aggregate.

recalling that unanticipated inventory change is the mirror image of unanticipated shocks to demand, we can write the former as[45]

$$H_1^a - H_1 = -(D_0^a - D_0) = -\left[\frac{\beta}{b}\left(\frac{M_0^a}{P_0^a}(m_0 - \bar{m}) + \theta\varepsilon_0\right) + \varepsilon_0\right].$$ (5.57)

Positive random shocks to either the rate of monetary growth or to aggregate demand cause unanticipated decumulations of inventories. The shock to money growth has this effect through the rate of interest. The shock to aggregate demand has this effect directly and, by changing the within-period demand for money, through the interest rate as well.

Actual changes in inventory include planned and unintended changes,

$$H_1^a - H_0^a = H_1^a - H_1 + H_1 - H_0^a$$ (5.58)

The planned change is, using eqn (5.53),

$$H_1 - H_0^a = (1 - A)(H^p - H_0^a).$$ (5.59)

Planned changes in inventory are independent of current monetary shocks and depend only on actual and permanent values of real variables. Past monetary shocks continue to affect planned changes in inventory, however. The reason is that, as shown in (5.59), planned changes are a decreasing function of the inherited level of inventories, H_0^a. Since inventories adjust gradually, as shown in (5.53), the inherited level of inventories reflects the influence of past monetary (and real) shocks.

4.4 A General Characterization of the Cycle

The permanent values of the variables in our model are the values that rational individuals perceive as steady state, trend values. To characterize cyclical fluctuations, we use the deviations of actual values from (constant) permanent values as a measure of the cycle. These differences can be positive or negative.

Equations (5.21) and (5.57) specify the adjustment of inventories in any period, t, as the sum of two components – the planned adjustment toward the permanent value and the unanticipated shock that occurs in period t. Combining these terms, we have

$$H_t^a - H^p = -\left[\frac{\beta M_t^a}{b P_t^a}(m_t - \bar{m}) + \left(1 + \theta \frac{1}{b}\right)\varepsilon_t\right] + A[H_{t-1}^a - H^p].$$

(5.60)

---

[45]If the effects of the information contained in r_0^a on aggregate demand are incorporated explicitly, the response of $H_0^a - H_0$ to unanticipated shocks increases. See part A2 of the appendix and note 24.

By lagging eqn (5.60) one period, and substituting the result into (5.60), we can write the cyclical deviation on the left in terms of the gradual adjustment that occurred in $t-2$ and the shocks in $t-1$. Continuing this procedure, we eventually obtain the cyclical amplitude of inventories expressed as a function of past unanticipated shocks,[46]

$$H_t^a - H^p = - \sum_{i=1}^{t} A^{i-1} \left[\frac{\beta}{b} \frac{M_{t-i}^a}{P_{t-i}^a} (m_{t-i} - \bar{m}) + \left(1 + \theta \frac{\beta}{b} \right) \varepsilon_{t-i} \right].$$

$$(5.61)$$

Equation (5.61) suggests that the impact of past unanticipated shocks on the current cyclical deviation of inventories increases with the damping factor A. From (5.54), we know that A is larger the lower is C_y. A large A (low C_y) slows the adjustment of inventories to their permanent position. We find, therefore, that the same factors that increase the lag in the adjustment of inventories also prolong the effect of past unanticipated shocks on the cyclical deviation of inventories. In view of proposition 2 and eqn (5.61), we have:

Proposition 3. The effect of past unanticipated shocks on the current cyclical deviation of inventories is larger and more durable the lower ω and the higher $| \gamma_2$ and $| \gamma_3 |$.

4.5 A Monetary Cycle

To focus on the effects of unanticipated money growth, we eliminate all uncertainty with respect to ε_t by setting it equal to its expected value (zero) for all t.[47] In this case, eqn (5.61) specializes to

$$H_t^a - H^p = - \frac{\beta}{b} \sum_{i=1}^{t} A^{i-1} \frac{d_{t-i}}{1+\bar{m}} (m_{t-1} - \bar{m}), \qquad (5.62)$$

where $d_{t-i} \equiv M_{t-i}(1+\bar{m})/P_{t-i}^a$ is the expected value of real money balances in period $t-1$ as of the beginning of period $t-1$. By substituting (5.62) into eqns (5.22) and using the definition of unemployment from (5.7), we get the effect of unanticipated money on the cyclical deviations of other variables. These are summarized in eqns (5.63),[48]

---

[46]The term $A^t[H_0^a - H^p]$ is deleted since for large t, $A^t \to 0$.

[47]The analysis in this section is easily generalizable to the case in which ε_t is stochastic.

[48]Note that the cyclical deviations of output, employment and unemployment are measured by deviations of actual values from permanent values while the real rate and sales are in terms of expectations of those variables as conceived at the beginning of each period. The cyclical deviation of actual sales is discussed below. Cyclical behavior of real rates is discussed at length in Cukierman (1981).

$$Y_t^a - Y^p = L_t^a - L^p = \frac{\beta}{b} C_y \left[\sum_{i=1}^{t} A^{i-1} \frac{d_{t-i}}{1+\bar{m}} (m_{t-i} - \bar{m}) \right], \qquad (5.63a)$$

$$w_t^a - w^p = \frac{\beta}{\omega b} C_y \left[\sum_{i=1}^{t} A^{i-1} \frac{d_{t-i}}{1+\bar{m}} (m_{t-i} - \bar{m}) \right], \qquad (5.63b)$$

$$n_t^a = -\frac{\beta}{b} C_y \left[\sum_{i=1}^{t} A^{i-1} \frac{d_{t-i}}{1+\bar{m}} (m_{t-i} - \bar{m}) \right], \qquad (5.63c)$$

$$\nu_t - \nu^p = -\frac{a}{b\beta} (1-C_y) \times \left[\sum_{i=1}^{t} A^{i-1} \frac{d_{t-i}}{1+\bar{m}} (m_{t-i} - \bar{m}) \right], \qquad (5.63d)$$

$$\bar{S}_t - D^p = -\frac{a}{b} (1-C_y) \times \left[\sum_{i=1}^{t} A^{i-1} \frac{d_{t-i}}{1+\bar{m}} (m_{t-i} - \bar{m}) \right]. \qquad (5.63e)$$

Equations (5.63) have four main implications for business cycles. First, cyclical deviations of all real variables are serially correlated. The reason is that the deviations depend on past, unanticipated shocks to the rate of money growth, and the responses to these shocks damp only gradually. Second, as sensitivity of money demand to the interest rate falls – as $|b|$ declines – the response of each of the real variables to an unanticipated monetary shock becomes larger in magnitude and persists longer. A small value of $|b|$ implies that the interest rate changes more, on impact, in response to a given monetary shock. A relatively large change in interest rates causes larger and more persistent cyclical deviations of real variables from their permanent values. Third, proposition 3 applies to the cyclical deviations of all real variables in (5.63) since these deviations depend on the cyclical deviation of inventories. Fourth, the lower is the maintained rate of inflation, $\bar{m}$, the higher, ceteris paribus, real money balances, d_{t-i}, in every period, and the higher the impact of past unanticipated shocks to the rate of monetary growth on current cyclical deviations. Our analysis implies, therefore, that the dynamic Phillips curve is steeper in periods of high inflation and flatter in periods of low inflation. This effect depends on the properties of the money market, through d_{t-i}. Proposition 4 summarizes some principal determinants of the magnitude and duration of cycles in real variables:

Proposition 4. Ceteris paribus, the effects of monetary shocks on real variables is larger in magnitude and more persistent in time the smaller the maintained rate of inflation, $\bar{m}$, the smaller ω and $|b|$ and the larger $|\gamma_2|$ and $|\gamma_3|$.

The effect of past unanticipated monetary growth on the cyclical deviations of output, employment, the real wage rate and the expected real rate of interest is positive.[49] The effect on the cyclical deviations of unemployment and expected sales is negative. The directions of response accord with intuition. Past, unanticipated, positive shocks to money growth, reduce actual inventories and, therefore, start a process of inventory rebuilding. Current production and employment increase, so the real wage rate rises and unemployment falls. To bring actual and expected demand down to the level of the reduced supply (planned sales), the expected real rate of interest rises; the rise in the real rate reduces planned sales.

4.6 A Monetary Cycle with Persistent Errors about Money Growth

The model can be extended easily to incorporate uncertainty about the systematic rate of monetary expansion by respecifying the distribution of m_t as

$$m_t = m_t^p + m_t^q, \quad \Delta m_t^p \sim N(0, \sigma_p^2), \quad m_t^q \sim N(0, \sigma_q^2). \tag{5.64}$$

The observed rate of monetary expansion is now the sum of a permanent (random walk) component and a transitory (white noise) component. The optimal predictor of future rates of monetary growth, given the information available at the end of period $t - 1$, becomes

$$E_{t-1} m_{t+j} = \lambda \sum_{i=0}^{\infty} (1-\lambda)^i m_{t-1-i}, \quad j \geqq 0, \tag{5.65}$$

where $0 < \lambda < 1$. λ is an increasing function of σ_p^2/σ_q^2, the ratio of the variance of the permanent component to the variance of the transitory component.[50] All the analysis above, including, in particular, eqns (5.61), (5.62) and (5.63) continues to hold with $m_{t-i} - \bar{m}$ replaced by the forecast errors,

$$m_{t-i}^a - E_{t-1-i} m_{t-i} \equiv m_{t-i}^a - m_{t-i}, \tag{5.66}$$

where the expected value in (5.66) is computed using (5.65). When a large permanent change in m^p occurs, forecast errors display ex post serial correlation for a number of periods after the change.[51] This phenomenon arises because individuals confuse permanent and temporary changes.

Figure 5.2 shows the adjustment paths. Up to period t, the economy is at an equilibrium; $H_t = H_t^p$. During period t, there is an unanticipated increase

---

[49][49]Inventory stocks are negatively related to the real rate of interest over the cycle. Further implications for interest rates appear in Cukierman (1981). For recent evidence on a negative relationship between target inventories and the cost of capital, see Irvine (1981a, b).

[50]For further details, see Muth (1960), and Brunner, Cukierman and Meltzer (1980).

[51]In Brunner, Cukierman and Meltzer (1980) we discuss these errors more fully. Forecast errors are serially correlated in the sense that, looking back on the past, economists or historians can find evidence of serial correlation. At the time, no one is aware of serial correlation.

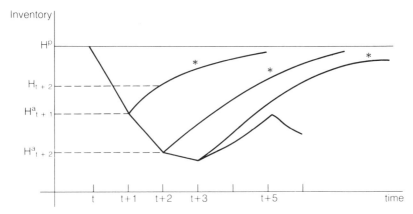

Figure 5.2   Expected and actual inventory adjustment. Asterisks indicate the expected paths; the outer envelope shows the actual path.

in money growth. Interest rates fall; with prices fixed for the period, aggregate demand increases, and inventories are reduced. Inability to identify permanent shocks means that the perceived value of m changes as information about the rate of monetary expansion becomes available. Forecast errors remain on one side of zero for several periods. Forecast errors reinforce the cyclical deviation of inventories. A large permanent increase in money growth, that is not immediately recognized as permanent, increases m_t and adds to the cyclical deviation of inventories.

The reduction in inventories sets off a process of adjustment of output and inventories. The path along which inventories are expected to adjust at the onset of period $t - 1$ is shown by the positively sloped line from H^a_{t+1} to the permanent level of inventories, H^p. Along this path, a typical firm plans to produce output in excess of expected sales and build inventories.[52] The expected value of inventories by the end of period $t + 1$ is shown as H_{t+2}. If the monetary shock is correctly perceived as transitory and there are no further shocks, firms adjust along the planned path and achieve the values of inventories, H_{t+2}, H_{t+3} in successive periods until the permanent value, H^p, is restored.

Suppose, however, that the increase in money growth persists. In period $t + 2$, interest rates are again pushed below the value expected for the period, and actual inventories, H^a_{t+2}, are, again, below the value expected, H_{t+2}, as shown in figure 5.2. At the beginning of period $t + 2$ firms and households expect the economy to adjust along the new path, from H^a_{t+2} to H^p. The new path reflects all the available information about the shocks, including beliefs about the permanence of the change in money growth and

[52]Recall that all firms do not have the same inventories.

knowledge of the structural parameters. The process shown in eqn (5.64) governs the speed with which people change their views about permanence or persistence of shocks. If the variance of the transitory component of money growth is large relative to the variance of the permanent component, adjustment to permanent changes is relatively slow. Inventories can fall below their expected value for several periods and, thus, move away from H^p.

Additional information about the permanence of the shock that first occurred in period t is revealed each period, so the path of adjustment toward H^p is not smooth. As time passes, however, the addition to information is small. After $t + 3$ in figure 5.2, inventories adjust toward H^p unless another shock – another unanticipated increase in money growth – lowers inventories and starts a new process of learning and adjusting.

Actual inventories follow the outer envelope in figure 5.2; expected inventories, H, follow the adjustment paths that start at the actual values for each period. The figure shows principal features of our model of inventory behavior, augmented by the effect of permanent–transitory confusion. Deviations from H^p are on one side of H^p for several periods because of the slow adjustment of inventories. This feature occurs even if all shocks are white noise. In addition, information about the permanence of shocks becomes available gradually. People use all information and their beliefs about permanent values to determine the adjustment path, but they make unavoidable errors because they learn about the permanence of shocks gradually.

Obviously a similar analysis can be carried out for each of the real variables which appears in eqns (5.63). This is not done for brevity. Instead, we conclude this discussion with the general observation that the model predicts that the effects of unanticipated money growth on the economy take the form of distributed lags of past money growth. Unanticipated changes in money causes procyclical movements in the levels of output, employment and real wages and countercyclical movements in unemployment. The path of each variable is qualitatively similar to the inventory adjustment shown in figure 5.2. Even if money growth is underestimated in only one period – and is predicted without error in all subsequent periods – employment, output, real wages and real rates of interest are above their permanent values for a number of periods. Expected sales and unemployment are below their permanent values. In addition, persistent errors in the prediction of the money supply provide additional reason for serially correlated cyclical deviations.

The more slowly people learn about the permanent rate of money growth, the longer is the period during which permanent money growth is underestimated. The speed with which people learn about the rate of money growth depends on the variance of the permanent component, σ_p^2, relative to the transitory component, σ_q^2. Increases in σ_p^2/σ_q^2 reduce the length of time required to learn about the permanence of the change. When the ratio of variances is low, unanticipated permanent monetary acceleration induces a larger increase in output and employment. For the same reason, efforts to slow inflation cause more persistent unemployment as well as longer periods with high interest rates.

4.7 Unemployment and Real Wages during Cycles

The permanent level of employment is a constant and, by definition, permanent unemployment is set at zero. Actual unemployment rises above the 'natural' or permanent rate when inventories are above their permanent value. Unemployment is lower than the natural rate when inventories are below their permanent value. As inventories are reduced or replaced, unemployment moves toward the natural rate.

In eqn (5.63c), the unemployment rate in any period, n_t^a, depends on the past history of monetary growth. An unanticipated increase in money growth pushes the actual rate of unemployment below the natural rate for several periods.[53] As the effect of the monetary shock on inventories decays, employment returns to L^p as shown in (5.63a), and unemployment returns to zero. During the adjustment, unemployment rates are serially correlated.

Hall (1977) found that the real wage rate adjusts more slowly than the unemployment rate. Based on this finding, he concluded that real wage rates are not the only factor explaining unemployment. Hall interpreted his result as evidence of disequilibrium in the labor market.

In our model, employers and workers are always on their respective labor demand and labor supply curves. Changes in employment and unemployment are the result of changes in the real wage rate caused by past monetary acceleration and deceleration. Although workers respond only to market incentives, the model implies that the wage rate typically adjusts more slowly than the rate of unemployment. This can be seen by noting from eqn (5.7) that

$$n_t^a/n_{t-1}^a = (w^p - w_t)/(w^p - w_{t-1}).$$

Dividing numerator and denominator on the right-hand side of this equation by the product $w^p w_{t-1}$ and rearranging, we obtain

$$\left| \frac{w_t - w_{t-1}}{w_{t-1}} \right| = \left| 1 - \frac{w^p}{w_{t-1}} \right| \cdot \left| \frac{n_t - n_{t-1}}{n_{t-1}} \right|.$$

No separate, or additional explanation is required to reconcile our hypothesis with the observed sluggish response of real wages to unemployment. The percentage change in the real wage rate associated with a given change in the rate of unemployment is very likely to be considerably smaller than the

---

[53]Unanticipated real changes in demand have similar effects on real wages and unemployment.

percentage change in unemployment. For example, if over the cycle w_t does not deviate from w^p by more than 20 percent, percentage changes in the real wage rate are, at most, one-fifth of the associated percentage changes in unemployment. As w_t approaches w^p the relative response of real wages decreases monotonically towards zero.

4.8 Intertemporal Substitution in the Labor Market

In a recent empirical study, Hall (1980) tested the intertemporal substitution model of labor supply. He (p. 1) found that, "This model stands up reasonably well on its own ground. The elasticity of labor supply is around one-half." However, Hall also found that when a distributed lag on money is added to the pure intertemporal substitution model, the predictive power of the model of employment and real output increased substantially. Hall concluded that the pure substitution model is untenable in the light of this evidence.

The framework presented here suggests that the intertemporal substitution model is entirely consistent with the observation that current and lagged money affects output and employment. The resolution of the apparent puzzle raised by Hall's work comes from the response of labor *demand* to unanticipated money. Intertemporal substitution is the mechanism by which the effect of monetary shocks on the real rate increases the demand for labor, raises the real wage and increases employment. Rather than constituting a contradiction to the observed real effects of money, the substitution model is one of the links in the transmission mechanism through which current unanticipated monetary growth affects future employment and output.

5 Concluding Comments

One of the challenges raised by the existence of a short-run trade-off between inflation and economic activity is to explain the trade-off within a consistent macroeconomic framework. Several alternative explanations have been offered. The oldest, used by Thornton (1802), Keynes (1936) and many others, relies on nominal wage rigidity but offers no explanation for wage rigidity. Modern formulations of this approach base the effects of money on output on the existence of nominally denominated labor contracts.[54]

The most articulate explanation of the short-run effects of money on output postulates that suppliers of labor services in localized markets react to nominal impulses because they confuse changes in the aggregate price level

---

[54]See Gray (1976), Fischer (1977), Phelps and Taylor (1977) and Cukierman (1980).

and changes in relative prices.[55] Blinder and Fischer (1981) present a macro model with inventories in which production smoothing by individual firms and confusion between aggregate and relative price changes lead to serially correlated deviations of output from trend. These authors also investigate the effects of perfectly anticipated money through the (Mundell) effect of inflation on real rates of interest.

Our explanation does not rely on the aggregate relative confusion; all individuals have identical information. Nor do we rely on prearranged *nominal* wage contracts; wage contracts are made in real terms.[56] Instead, we rely on two assumptions that are consistent with, and based upon, many economists' observations. First, the activities performed in real flow markets, like employment, production and distribution, require advance planning and commitment over some (possibly small) future discrete time period. Second, firms advertise prices in advance of the market period.[57] As a result of these assumptions, the real wage rate, employment and the price level are predetermined at the start of each period for one period; these variables do not reflect shocks that occur during the market period. The clearing of financial markets, on the other hand, occurs continuously.

Monetary shocks change the real rate of interest and cause unanticipated inventory changes. These changes arise because prices are fixed for a period and financial markets clear continuously. Since all firms have the same constant returns to scale technology, there is no reason for production smoothing at the micro level. There is, however, production smoothing in the aggregate. The reason is that each firm recognizes that the cost of rebuilding inventories rises with the real wage. The real wage depends on the demand for labor and, therefore, on the speed with which firms in the aggregate choose to rebuild (or run down) inventories. More generally, the speed of adjustment to permanent values of real variables, the amplitude of business cycles, and the advantages of inventory smoothing at the macro level depend on structural parameters of the model.

All real variables reflect the influence of the inventory cycle and show sustained responses to monetary and real shocks. The longer or more persistent the deviations of the aggregate inventory from its permanent value, the longer or more persistent are the deviations of other real variables from their permanent values. And the larger the amplitude of inventory fluctuations, the larger are the cyclical deviations of other real variables from their permanent values.

---

[55]See Lucas (1973, 1975), Barro (1976). Hall (1980) claims that in view of the speed with which information about aggregate variables becomes available, it is hard to believe that misperception of aggregate variables is an important source of non-neutrality in a modern economy.

[56]We also do not rely on the Mundell effect. The model does not have a real balance effect.

[57]For an argument for infrequent changes in prices as a means of preserving the informational efficiency of the price system, see Alchian (1969).

Our model has a Keynesian, non-neutral, element in the very short run since aggregate demand is satisfied, at a fixed price, out of buffer stock inventories. The price level fully reflects all information available at the beginning of each period, so prices change as new information becomes available. Everyone has the same information about the determinants of relative and absolute prices. Nevertheless, prices deviate persistently from their expected permanent value. The reason is that the demand for real balances responds to the induced changes in interest rates and income that result from shocks. Since the shocks have persistent real effects on all real variables, the demand for real balances changes cyclically.

The rate of price change fully reflects current monetary growth only in the long run. Elsewhere, price changes reflect all of the information the public has about current money growth and, in addition, reflect the lagged effects of past monetary growth on the demand for real balances. When all real variables are at their permanent values, the price level is at its permanent value.[58]

To keep the paper within manageable proportions, we have assumed, for the most part, that random shocks are completely transitory. We show that the model can be easily extended to the case in which there are persistent changes in the shocks that affect the economy. Within the extended framework, individuals cannot distinguish permanent and transitory shocks. Errors of forecast become serially correlated, in an ex post sense, whenever large permanent changes occur. When there is uncertainty about the permanence of monetary shocks, a permanent monetary change may produce, for a while, a bunching of overestimates or underestimates of money growth. The inability to separate permanent and transitory changes adds an additional cyclical disturbance to the disturbance produced by the slow adjustment of inventories.

Appendix 5.1

A.1 Proof that $0 < C_y < 1$

Using (5.1), (5.2) and (5.4), the systematic part of the excess demand for goods can be written

$$D - \bar{S} = \overline{ED} + (1 - K_2)[\beta(1 - a\gamma_1) - a\gamma_2]\nu - K_1\gamma_3 w,$$

where $\overline{ED}$ is a combination of constant parameters of no particular interest. We know from (5.43) that $1 - K_2 > 0$, so the excess demand for

---

[58]Economic reasoning suggests that prices converge to their permanent level, but an algebraic proof cannot be supplied because the system is dichotomized.

goods is a decreasing function of the real rate of interest, ν, provided $\beta(1-a\gamma_1) - a\gamma_2 < 0$. Since $\omega > 0$ and $-\beta\gamma_3 < 0$, this implies in conjunction with eqn (5.12) in the text that $0 < C_y < 1$.

A.2 Incorporation of the information contained in the within-period observation on the interest rate

Equation (5.56) of the text implies that $r_0^a - r_0$, the error in forecasting the nominal rate, conveys some information about m_0 and therefore about money growth at the beginning of period 1 and, thus about the level of inventories at the beginning of period 1. In particular if $r_0^a < r_0$, rational individuals attribute at least part of this discrepancy to the excess of the actual over the anticipated rate of growth of money. They therefore revise their forecast of P_1^a upward. Defining $P_1^* \equiv E[P_1/(r_0^a-r_0)]$ this implies that $P_1^* > P_1$, where P_1 is the forecast of the price in period 1 as conceived at the beginning of period 0. The fact that $r_0^a < r_0$ allows individuals to infer that aggregate demand is higher than expected and therefore that the level of inventories at the beginning of period 1 is lower than had been expected. If g is relatively small, ceteris paribus, the relation between the price level and inventories is negative. (See proposition 1 at the end of section 2.) This implies a further increase in $P_1^* - P_1$. It follows that $P_1^*/P_0 - P_1/P_0 = -\rho(r_0^a-r_0)$, where ρ is a positive coefficient. This implies that the expected rate of inflation goes up when the nominal rate is lower than expected so the effect of a decrease in the nominal rate on aggregate demand increases. More formally, when consumers are allowed to draw inferences from r_0^a, aggregate demand becomes

$$D_0^a = \alpha Y^p + \beta\nu_0 + \beta(1+\rho)(r_0^a-r_0) + \varepsilon_0.$$

The discussion in the text assumes $\rho = 0$ which weakens (but does not change the sign of) the effects of unanticipated shocks, through the interest rate channel, on aggregate demand.

A.3 Proof that for $w^p < 1$ there exists an interior maximum for x_0

$w^p < 1$ implies, using (5.6), that at zero unemployment the real wage demanded by a marginal unit of labor is always less than 1 since $w_t = w^p - \bar{L}_s/\omega < 1$ for $\bar{L}_s > 0$. Substituting the constraints in (5.28) and (5.29) and using the definition of x_i

$$\Pi_i(x_i, x_{i-1}) = \bar{s}_i(x_i) - w_i x_i + w_i \max[0, x_{i-1}-\delta\mu_{i-1}-z_{i-1}], \quad i = 1, 2, \ldots,$$
$$(5.A.1)$$

and

$$\Pi_0(x_0) = \bar{s}_0(x_0) - w_0(x_0-h_0). \qquad (5.A.2)$$

Let $x_0^*, x_1^*, x_2^*, \ldots$ be an optimal solution. We assume that $x_0^* = 0$ and prove by establishing a contradiction. From (5.A.2) and (5.32)

$\partial \Pi_0(0)/\partial x_0 = 1 - w_0 > 0,$

so a small increase in x_0^* at zero increases $\Pi_0(\cdot)$ and does not decrease $\Pi_i(\cdot)$ for $i \geq 1$ whatever the realization of z_{i-1}. It follows that x_0^* must be positive. On the other hand $\bar{s}_0(x_0)$ is bounded by Ed. It follows from (5.A.2) that the optimal value of x_0 is finite. Hence $0 < x_0^* < \infty$.

References

Alchian, A.A. 1969. Information costs, pricing and resource unemployment. *Economic Inquiry*, June, 109–28.

Amihud, Y. and H. Mendelson. 1980. Monopoly under uncertainty: The enigma of price rigidity. Research working paper no. 305A, Graduate School of Business, Columbia University, March.

—— 1982. The output inflation relationship: An inventory adjustment approach. *Journal of Monetary Economics* 9, 163–84.

Barro, R.J. 1976. Rational expectations and the role of monetary policy. *Journal of Political Economy* 84, 1–32.

—— 1977. Long term contracting, sticky prices and monetary policy. *Journal of Monetary Economics* 3, 305–16.

Blanchard, O.J. 1979. Backward and forward solutions for economies with rational expectations. *American Economic Review, Papers and Proceedings* 69, 114–18.

Blinder, A.S. 1981. Inventories and sticky prices: More on the microfoundations of macroeconomics. Manuscript, July.

—— and S. Fischer. 1981. Inventories rational expectations, and the business cycle. *Journal of Monetary Economics* 8, 277–304.

Brunner, K., A. Cukierman and A.H. Meltzer. 1980. Stagflation, persistent unemployment and the permanence of economic shocks. *Journal of Monetary Economics* 6, 467–92.

Cargill, T. 1969. An empirical investigation of the wage-lag hypothesis. *American Economic Review* 59, 806–16.

Cukierman, A. 1979. Rational expectations and the role of monetary policy: A generalization. *Journal of Monetary Economics* 5, 213–29.

—— 1980. The effects of wage indexation on macroeconomic fluctuations; A generalization. *Journal of Monetary Economics* 6, 147–70.

—— 1981. Interest rates during the cycle, inventories and monetary policy – A theoretical analysis. In: The costs and consequences of inflation, ed. K. Brunner and A. Meltzer. *Carnegie–Rochester Conference Series on Public Policy* 15.

Fischer, S. 1977. Long term contracts, rational expectations and the optimal money supply rule. *Journal of Political Economy* 85, 191–205.

Friedman, M. 1968. The role of monetary policy. *American Economic Review* 58, 1–17.

Gordon, R. 1976. Recent developments in the theory of inflation and unemployment. *Journal of Monetary Economics* 2, 185–219.

Gray J.A. 1976. Wage indexation: A macroeconomic approach. *Journal of Monetary Economics* 2, 221–36.

Hall, R.E. 1977. Expectation errors, unemployment and wage inflation. Center for Advanced Study in the Behavioral Science, Sept. manuscript.

—— 1980. Labor supply and aggregate fluctuations. In: On the state of macroeconomics, ed. K. Brunner and A. Meltzer. *Carnegie-Rochester Conference Series on Public Policy* 12.

Irvine, F.O. Jr. 1981a. A study of automobile inventory investment. *Economic Inquiry* 19: July.

—— 1981b. Retail inventory investment and the cost of capital. *American Economic Review* 71, Sept.

Keynes, J.M. 1936. *The General Theory of Employment, Interest and Money*. London: Macmillan.

Kydland, F. and E. Prescott. 1982. Time to build and aggregate fluctuations. *Econometrica*. 50, 1345–70.

Lucas, R.E. Jr. 1972. Expectations and the neutrality of money. *Journal of Economic Theory* 4, 103–24.

—— 1973. Some international evidence on output inflation tradeoffs. *American Economic Review* 63, 326–35.

—— 1975. An equilibrium model of the business cycle. *Journal of Political Economy* 83, 1113–44.

—— and L. Rapping. 1969. Real wages, employment and inflation. *Journal of Political Economy* 77, 721–54.

Maccini, L.J. 1976. An aggregate dynamic model of short-run price and output behavior. *Quarterly Journal of Economics* 90, 177–96.

—— 1980. On the theory of the firm underlying empirical models of aggregate price behavior. *International Economic Review*.

Muth, J.F. 1960. Optimal properties of exponentially weighted forecasts. *Journal of the American Statistical Association* 55, 299–306.

Phelps, E.S. 1967. Phillips curves, expectations of inflation and optimal unemployment over time. *Economica* (NS) 34, 254–81.

—— and J.B. Taylor. 1977. Stabilizing powers of monetary policy under rational expectations. *Journal of Political Economy* 85, 163–90.

Reagan, P. 1982. Inventory and price behavior. *Review of Economics and Statistics* 49, 137–42.

Sargent, T.J. 1973. Rational expectations, the real rate of interest and the natural rate of unemployment. *Brookings Papers on Economic Activity* 2, 429–80.

—— 1979. *Macroeconomic Theory* New York: Academic Press.

—— and N. Wallace. 1975. Rational expectations, the optimal monetary instrument, and the optimal money supply rule. *Journal of Political Economy* 83, 24–54.

Siegel, J.J. 1981. Interest rates during the cycle, inventories and monetary policy – A theoretical analysis – A comment. In: The costs and consequences of inflation, ed. K. Brunner and A. Meltzer. *Carnegie-Rochester Conference Series on Public Policy* 15.

Taylor, J. 1977. Conditions for unique solutions in stochastic macro-economic models with rational expectations. *Econometrica* 45, 1377–85.

Thornton, H. 1802. *An Enquiry into the Nature and Effects of the Paper Credit of Great Britain*, repr. 1965. New York: Kelley.

6

The Uses of Money: Money in the Theory of an Exchange Economy

Karl Brunner and Allan H. Meltzer

One of the oldest unresolved problems of monetary theory is to explain the use and holding of money. Resolution of the problem is central to an understanding of the difference between a monetary and a nonmonetary or barter economy, and there have been numerous attempts at resolution. The use of money or the existence of a positive demand has been made to depend on such diverse factors as the anticipation of price or interest rate changes, uncertainty, the embarrassment of default, legal restrictions, or some undefined set of "services" – such as "liquidity" – that money provides. Probably the dominant, current explanation posits the existence of a number of ostensibly separate "motives for holding money." This explanation coexists with vestiges of an earlier preferred explanation that made the use and/or holding of money depend on the "functions" performed by money, such as medium of exchange, store of value and unit of account.

Four recent developments have increased economists' interest in the problem. First, money has remained in use in a number of countries even in periods of accelerating inflation, most recently in Brazil. The continued acceptance of existing monies under conditions of ever-increasing holding cost calls into question the relevance of treating money as an asset that provides little or no return. Second, proponents of a new international monetary unit have claimed benefits to the world economy that exceed the saving of resources arising from the substitution of paper money for commodity money. Third, recent work (Pesek and Saving, 1967; Friedman and Schwartz, 1970) has revived interest in the properties of a medium of exhange, in the appropriate definition of money, and in the relation between

This paper appeared in *American Economic Review* 61 (Dec.) Nashville: American Economic Association, 1971, pp. 784–805. Reprinted with permission. We have benefited from the helpful suggestions of Jack Hirshliefer, Thomas Saving, Jerome Stein, Terry Turner, and especially Axel Leijonhufvud. Their many comments and suggestions improved the paper.

the assets that serve as medium of exchange and the assets that serve as money. Fourth, growth theorists have introduced an asset called "money" into models of economic growth. Some of their studies (Sidrauski, 1967; Tobin, 1965) conclude that the introduction of money either reduces the community's nonmonetary real wealth and lowers the capital-labor ratio or has no effect at all on society's real wealth.[1] The economy of these growth models becomes monetized only because of a difference between private and social returns from the use or holding of money.

A large literature has developed to explain why individuals and/or societies forego consumption so as to hold an asset that adds nothing to individual wealth or utility,[2] or in some versions, has negative marginal social product.[3] Aspects of this literature have been surveyed several times (John Gilbert, Arthur Marget, Will Mason, Don Patinkin) and summarized by Keynes (1936, ch. 15) who based three of his four motives for holding money on the principal arguments advanced by his predecessors. The main arguments, used alone or in combination, invoke (1) time, (2) uncertainty, (3) lack of synchronization of receipts and expenditures, (4) costs of transacting, and (5) the existence of non-pecuniary returns. Of these, the most common is one or another of the many versions of the synchronization argument. This argument is valid only in the simple barter economy of the textbooks.[4]

---

[1] Quoting Tobin, ". . . as viewed by the inhabitants of the nation individually, wealth exceeds the tangible capital stock by the size of what we might call the fiduciary issue. This is an illusion, but only one of the many fallacies of composition which are basic to any economy of any society" (1965, p. 656).

[2] This position is very old and was stated clearly by Henry Thornton, one of the best of the early monetary theorists (1965, p. 234) when discussing the holding of Bank of England notes.

> It presents to the holder no hope of future profit from the detention of it. Not only does it bear no interest, but it offers no substitute for interest; . . . the quantity held by each person is only that which the amount of payments to be effected by it renders, in his opinion, necessary.

However, in Chapter III, Thornton recognizes that resource costs are reduced when paper money replaces gold and silver and (pp. 91ff.) he criticizes Smith, whom he credits with this argument, for failing to see that resources are also saved when bills of exchange replace notes.

[3] Recent exceptions are David Cass and Menahem Yaari (1966) and Jürg Niehans (1969) who show that social efficiency rises if the community agrees to use money. Cass and Yaari discuss the use of money as a medium of exchange (or in their terminology intermediation) and show that money is productive under the circumstances of their model. However, they restrict barter exchange to a single "double coincidence" transaction and assume that each trader knows, or can obtain at zero cost, information about the exchange ratio or prices at which all other transactors are willing to trade. Our earliest attempt to relate the productive contribution of money to the saving of costs of information was published in 1964 (pp. 258–62).

[4] It is easy to see why "lack of synchronization" does not imply that money is used and held. Consider an economy that has neither a medium of exchange nor money. If there are no costs of acquiring information, differences in the timing of receipts and payments are adjusted by

Friedman (1956) and Patinkin recognized that previous analyses yielded scarcely any information about the productivity of money. Building partly on work by Paul Samuelson (1947, pp. 118–20) they identified the productive services of money with a nonobservable, nonpecuniary return to money. But the nature of the services yielded by money and the conditions governing the marginal productivity of money have not been much explored in their work. The most extensive discussion of the coexistence of money, bonds and real capital in portfolios explains the use of money by asserting that, "Intuitively, money seems to be a more efficient carrier of nonpecuniary services . . . than bonds . . ." (Friedman, 1969, p. 25).[5]

The most casual observation suggests that a limited number of assets is used to make or receive payments in all but a few primitive societies. Very similar assets are used in very different places. The standard theory of exchange, or price, however, provides no hint as to why dominant mediums of exchange emerge.[6] Any asset or combination of assets is equally likely to be selected as a medium of exchange, and the allocation of resources is not affected by the choice. In the next two sections we reconsider the services rendered by money, extend the theory of choice to include the choice of the assets individuals use as mediums of exchange and then use diagrams to illustrate the main points of our analysis.

Our argument requires the use of two postulates that are not part of conventional exchange theory. They are:

1. For each transactor in an exchange economy, the marginal cost of acquiring information, measured in units of consumption sacrificed, depends on the goods or services selected.
2. The marginal cost of acquiring information about the properties of any

---

issuing verbal promises in exchange for goods and, later, delivering goods. More generally, in a barter credit economy, commitments or promises to pay "bridge the gap between receipts and payments." Gilbert discusses several versions of the "synchronization" argument and provides references to the more prominent writers and to those who stated their arguments most clearly. We have found no one who discusses barter-credit. A simple statement of the synchronization argument is due to Joseph Schumpeter (1939, p. 547) who argued that if people are paid on Saturday and stores are closed until Monday, firms hold money from Monday to Saturday and households from Saturday to Monday because "the institutional arrangement so wills it." For a comparison with current notions of the Hicksian week, see Patinkin (1965, pp. 13–14).

[5]Friedman does not explain why money is superior to bonds as a carrier of nonpecuniary services. In his analysis, the only uncertainty is about the timing of receipts. We find nothing to prevent individuals in his model from holding interest-yielding bonds and using verbal promises to pay when expenditures temporarily exceed receipts.

[6]Although specialization has long been invoked to explain exchange, economic theory explains specialization in exchange as the result of a corner solution. For much the same reason that theory offers no explanation of the concentration of the medium of exchange function in a narrow range of assets, theory provides no explanation of the specialization of traders in other inventories and types of exchange.

asset does not vary randomly within a social group and declines as the frequency with which the group uses a particular asset increases.

The two postulates are necessary and sufficient conditions for the use of a medium of exchange. They emphasize the point that will concern us throughout – that it is the uneven distribution of information, and not the existence of an undifferentiated uncertainty, that induces individuals to search for, and social groups to accept, alternatives to barter.

Social choice of an asset used as money is separate from, though not entirely independent of, individual decisions to hold money. We believe it is useful to separate the analysis of the choice of the asset used as money from the analysis of the optimal amount of money to produce and from the individual's choice of a desired money balance. Our interest here is in the individual and social choice of the assets used as money, the services money provides to individuals and societies, the relation of these services to the choice of a monetary unit, and some implications of these decision.

1 The Services of Money to Individual Transactors

One of the main productive activities of a household in a developed market economy is the acquisition of the goods and services consumed by the household. The provision of these goods and services requires not only the sale of income-yielding productive services but the use of resources to acquire information, arrange payments, and schedule purchases. Shopping, budgeting, and planning expenditures are productive tasks that both absorb resources and yield benefits to the skilled or knowledgeable purchasers or sellers who make advantageous exchanges. The use of a medium of exchange permits the household to economize on the amount of resources absorbed by these activities and to enjoy a larger and more diversified basket of goods and more leisure.

Potential transactors possess very incomplete information about the location and identity of other transactors, about the quality of the goods offered or demanded, or about the range of prices at which exchanges can be made. Uncertainty about quality characteristics is a main reason for the dispersion of prices of any commodity, and uneven distribution of information about the qualities of commodities increases the dispersion of prices both within the community and between bid and ask quotations.[7] Transactors can

[7]Relatively low cost of acquiring information and a smaller dispersion of prices is one of the many meanings of the term liquidity, a property often attributed to money. Reducing the cost of acquiring information raises liquidity. We conjecture from this line of reasoning that the announcement that shares are to be moved from the over-the-counter market to an organized exchange such as the New York Stock Exchange raises the average price of the shares. The price increase is a measure of the value to the stockholders of the reduced dispersion of bid and ask prices.

acquire information most readily and at lowest cost about commodities that are most widely used and best known, so the prices of these commodities have the least dispersion. When the qualities of a commodity are less certain, acquisition of information requires greater use of valuable resources, and dispersion increases. If risk aversion is prevalent, uncertainty about the properties or quality of an asset further lowers the average demand price of the asset.

The use of money reduces uncertainty and expands trade in a number of ways. One way is by providing a unit of account, or standard, in which prices are expressed. If there are N commodities in a barter economy and the unit of account is randomly selected, anyone wishing to organize or participate regularly in a market must know (or be able to obtain) each of the $N(N-1)/2$ independent, exchange ratios in the barter exchange matrix. Social choice of a unit of account reduces the matrix to an $N \times 1$ vector of exchange ratios expressed in the unit of account. The cost of acquiring, processing and storing information falls. The gain from the use of a unit of account is analogous to the gain that comes from introducing a common unit of measure such as height, weight or temperature.

The gain from using a unit of account is limited by the size of the market, but the size of the market expands after agreement on a unit of account because resources devoted to trade receive higher net returns. As information about the unit spreads and the market expands, additional private and social benefits result from the development of the market system. Additional exchange ratios are expressed in the unit; it becomes efficient to use the unit where other units were used previously.[8]

A second and considerably more important way in which the use of money reduces uncertainty and contributes to the expansion of trade and the market system is through service as the medium of exchange. The frequency with which the same unit serves both as medium of exchange and as unit of account suggests that it is efficient to perform both functions with a single unit, but the functions are distinct and require separate analysis.

To analyze the medium of exchange function, we consider a transactor who has an initial endowment of resources including his own labor time and some information about exchange ratios and qualities of commodites. He has several alternative ways of transforming his initial endowment into a preferred bundle. As in standard price theory, he can use his endowment for

---

[8]An example is the spread of the decimal and dollar system or the metric system to countries where the pound or foot has long served as the standard. The Euro-dollar market suggests the way in which a unit of account begins to acquire the properties of a medium of exchange and other attributes of money through the efforts of private traders. Conversely, where trade between countries is small and infrequent, it is not profitable to devote resources to establishing a unit of account or medium of exchange and barter-credit predominates.

production, consumption, or exchange. In addition, he has two options that are neglected in traditional price theory. (1) He can use resources to increase his information about the qualities of goods and opportunities for exchange. If the transactor uses resources in this way, we say that he invests in information. (2) He can engage in indirect or roundabout methods of exchange, accepting goods with low marginal cost of acquiring information, transferring and storing, then exchanging these goods for others until he obtains an optimal bundle. We describe the resources allocated in this way as the (real) costs of transacting or exchanging. The resources used in this way are, of course, distinct from the resources exchanged.

Under conditions of uncertainty[9] about the quality of goods offered in exchange and about prevailing market opportunities, the costs of acquiring information and exchanging are neither zero nor identical for every good or service. Our first postulate, introduced above, recognizes that the marginal cost of the resources the transactor uses to acquire information or to carry out transactions is the amount of consumption or endowment sacrificed. This marginal cost depends on the goods or services he selects (or about which he chooses to acquire information) and is subject to substantial variance.

By choosing a sequence of transactions – a transaction chain – involving assets with low marginal cost of information, the transactor can lower the marginal cost of exchanging. He incurs transfer and carrying costs and uses existing information about the qualities of particular goods instead of investing resources to acquire information about other goods or other trading arrangements. However, transfer costs increase with the length of the transaction chain, forcing the rational transactor to compare the marginal cost of acquiring information to the marginal cost of rearranging the transaction chain and to the benefits obtained from these and alternative uses of resources.

The formal statement of our analysis involves the maximization of utility subject to a budget constraint under conditions of uncertainty about market opportunities and the qualities of goods. An individual seeks to obtain the optimum combination of goods and services by investing in information and engaging in exchange. Numerous sequences of transactions are open to him. His problem is to find the optimal sequence of transactions and the optimal investment in information while choosing an optimal bundle of goods or consumption plan. Production of the standard type is disregarded.

Let the individual's utility function be

$$U = U(\epsilon, v; Q); U_1 > 0; U_2 < 0; U_3 > 0 \tag{6.1}$$

[9]Note that uncertainty in our account differs from the types of uncertainty emphasized in past discussions of money. The latter include uncertainty about (1) the price level, (2) the timing of receipts, and (3) interest rates (see Gilbert, 1953). For other recent attempts to relate search and costs of acquiring information to resource allocation, see Simon (1959) and Stigler (1961).

where ϵ is the expected bundle of goods the transactor obtains by allocating resources to the various options, v is the variability of the bundle associated with the uncertainty about market conditions, and Q is the information available to the transactor about the qualities or properties of goods. We regard Q as a partition of the state space summarizing the full range of qualities. A skilled trader or market professional has valuable information about the qualities of goods, the location of other traders and their tastes and preferences. His market opportunities differ from those of an unskilled trader or infrequent participant in the market. The more certain a transactor is about the qualities (or properties) of goods, and the more he is able to discern differences in performance or other quality characteristics, the higher his utility. The more information the transactor has about market conditions and the characteristics of goods, the lower the variability of the bundle he obtains and the higher his utility.

The budget constraint is

$$R_0 = C_0 + X_0 + I_0 + S_0. \tag{6.2}$$

The transactor can allocate his resources, R,[10] to reservation demand, C, to exchange, X, to acquire information about market opportunities, I, or to execute transactions, S. The conditions for advantageous exchange depend on the information available to the transactor. By using resources to acquire information, he lowers the amount of resources remaining available for reservation demand and trade. However, the new information reduces uncertainty about market conditions and exchange opportunities and lowers the variability of the return from trading. Optimal information is achieved when the marginal utility of resources withdrawn from consumption (reser-

---

[10]The variables R_0, C_0, X_0, I_0, and S_0 denote diagonal non-negative matrices. Each of the symbols is defined in the text, but some discussion of the difference between allocations to S_0 and I_0 may clarify the analysis that follows. No "generally accepted" medium of exchange is imposed on the economy discussed in the text. A transactor can forgo consumption and use resources to sample the exchange ratios at which other transactors (including potential transactors) are willing to offer goods of the quality he desires for the goods he presently holds. We use the symbol I_0 to describe the resources allocated to sampling or search of this kind. The goods the transactor holds may include "intermediate" goods, goods acquired in previous transactions for use in later transactions. Alternatively, a transactor can seek to improve his knowledge of transaction arrangements by (1) learning about the properties of goods that other transactors desire to acquire either for consumption or as intermediate goods, or (2) by learning about the relative costs of storing or transporting goods, or (3) by learning about the costs of completing exchanges using different sets of intermediate goods. We use the symbol S_0 to summarize the resources used to acquire information about transaction arrangements and to carry out exchanges. Resources must be used for similar purposes even if a few assets are generally accepted as means of payment. "Shopping" is a common means of acquiring information about price–quality combinations. Resources must also be used to learn about the advantages of immediate payment over deferred payment, the costs and benefits of using coin or currency rather than checks in general and in specific exchanges, etc.

vation demand) equals the marginal utility of an improved trading position and reduced uncertainty.

Transactors' uncertainty with respect to market opportunities is conditioned by a distribution of exchange ratios governing the social exchange process.

$$\pi = \pi(E|P) \tag{6.3}$$

The term E is a matrix of exchange ratios whose generic elements e_{ij} denote the jth unit obtained per unit of i, and P summarizes the information about market opportunities and exchange ratios available to transactors.[11] Since bid and ask prices are generally not the same in the presence of costs of acquiring and maintaining information and transferring goods, the matrix is not anti-sysmmetric, and $e_{ij}e_{ji} \neq 1$.

At any time the transactor knows a maximal E, denoted E^*, that describes the best market opportunities available to him if he relies on the information carried over from the past. We treat E^* as a random variable conditional on the transactor's information about market opportunities, P. There is a unique expected value of E^* corresponding to each state of knowledge about market opportunities. A transactor can improve his information about market opportunities by using a portion of his endowment to acquire additional information, i.e., by investment in information. Although a larger sample does not necessarily increase the maximal sample value, under weak constaints on π, a larger sample raises the expected value of the sample maximum and reduces the variance of the exchange ratios at which the transactor trades. We postulate that the mean and variance of the distribution, π, depend on the amount invested in information and the transaction arrangements, T, and are denoted

$\epsilon(E^*|I, T)$ and $v(E^*|I, T)$ with

$$\frac{\partial \epsilon}{\partial I} > 0; \quad \frac{\partial v}{\partial I} < 0; \quad \frac{\partial^2 \epsilon}{\partial I^2} < 0; \quad \frac{\partial^2 v}{\partial I^2} > 0.$$

Once a transactor allocates I_0 to improve his information, only $R_0 - I_0$ of the initial endowment remains available for consumption and exchange.

---

[11]P is a vector whose coordinates summarize market information. The coordinates depend on the individual's and the community's information. Increased investment in information refines the available information, and reduces the generalized variance. Technological change reduces information and increases the variance of π by reducing information about the qualities of goods. The coordinates of P are the partitions, Q, of the state spaces – characterizing each individual's information. An example helps to describe Q and P. An individual's utility increases if, with unchanged market opportunities, he acquires information that permits him to develop his tastes. An ability to distinguish between Botticellis and "paintings" increases Q but does not change other elements of P. If everyone acquires the same discriminating tastes, all Qs change and therefore P changes.

Exchange operations involve allocation to two distinct components, X and S, with X the bundle offered in exchange and S the resources used to produce the exchange. An exchange matrix T^{12} characterizes the transformation via exchange transactions of a bundle X_0 into a new bundle, Y_1. The off-diagonal elements of the T matrix are the proportions of the ith good exchanged for the jth good. The resource cost (S) of executing a set of transactions T depends on T; $S = S(T)$. A market exchange is a transformation of the inputs X, $S(T)$ to an output $\epsilon(Y_1)$. The selection of the amounts offered in exchange, X, and the division of resources between C, X, and T depends, of course, on the information summarized by $\epsilon(E^*)$ and $v(E^*)$ and therefore on I and T.

The total volume of physical resources available to the transactor after the market transformation is expressed by the diagonal matrix $\epsilon(R_1)^{13}$

$$\epsilon(R_1) = \epsilon(Y_1) + C_0 \tag{6.4}$$

and consists of the reservation demand C_0 plus the bundle $\epsilon(Y_1)$ the transactor expects to obtain via market exchange. Replacing X_0 in the description of $\epsilon(Y_1)$ (from note 13) we can express $\epsilon(Y_1)$ as a function

$$\epsilon(Y_1) = Y_1[R_0 - C_0 - I_0 - S(T_0), I_0, T_0; \pi]$$
$$= \sum_j X^j[R_0 - C_0 - I_0 - S(T_0), T_0] \tag{6.5}$$
$$\epsilon(E_j^*/I_0, T).$$

The function $\epsilon(Y_1)$ depends on the initial endowment R_0, the reservation demand C_0, the transaction arrangement T_0, the investment in information I_0, the distribution of exchange ratios and, therefore, on E^* via π. The mean,

---

[12] T is a non-negative hollow matrix whose element t_{ij} describes the portion of the ith good allotted in exchange for the jth good and whose diagonal elements, $t_{ij} = 0$. Also, $1 \geq t_{ij} \geq 0$ for $i \neq j$, and $\Sigma_j t_{ij} = 1$.

[13] The trade matrix $T'X$ can be described as a sum of matrices X^j, i.e., $T'X = \Sigma_j X^j$. This decomposition is uniquely determined by the form of the matrix $T'X$. The generic matrix X^j consists of zero row vectors with the exception of the jth row vector which is identical to the jth row vector of $T'X$. The index j ranges over all the rows of $T'X$. Under the circumstances specified, the constituent matrices X^j are functions of the exchange X and the transaction T, i.e., $X^j = X^j(T, X)$. Once the decomposition of $T'X$ has been defined a matrix $\epsilon(E_j^*)$ is associated with X^j. The matrix $\epsilon(E_j^*)$ consists of zero column vectors with the exception of the jth column which is identical to the jth column of matrix $\epsilon(E^*)$. The product $X^j \cdot \epsilon(E_j^*)$ denotes a diagonal matrix with zero diagonal elements except in the jth row. This diagonal matrix describes the acquisition of the jth good by means of an exchange X and a transaction arrangement T. The sum $\Sigma X^j \epsilon(E_j^*)$ is a diagonal matrix describing the result of the market transformation defined by the pair (X, T) and, since E^* is a random variable, the expected value of this sum is $\Sigma X^j \epsilon(E_j^*)$. The result is denoted by $\epsilon(Y_1)$, i.e.,

$$\epsilon(Y_1) = \sum_j X_0^j(T_0, X_0) \cdot \epsilon[E_{j0}^*(I_0)]$$

ϵ, and variance, v, of the transactor's utility function can now be expressed as the functions

$$\epsilon = \epsilon[Y_1|R_0 - C_0 - I_0 - S(T_0),\ T_0,\ I_0] + C_0 \tag{6.6}$$

$$v = v[Y_1|R_0 - C_0 - I_0 - S(T_0),\ T_0,\ I_0] \tag{6.7}$$

A transactor can change his utility by three distinct types of allocation, represented in our analysis by C_0, I_0, and T_0. The transactor trades whenever the utility associated with $\epsilon = C_0 = R_0$ and $v = 0$ is less than the utility associated with some $C_0 < R_0$.

Taking derivatives of ϵ and v with respect to I_0 and solving the resulting equations shows that the optimal investment in information depends on the effects on mean, ϵ, and variance, v. Increased investment (I_0) either lowers reservation demand (C_0) or the resources devoted to exchange (S_0, X_0). With S_0 and X_0 held constant, an increase in I_0 lowers the variance $v(Y_1)$ and has two, opposing effects on the mean $\epsilon(R_1)$. Increased I_0 raises, and the associated reduction in reservation demand lowers $\epsilon(R_1)$. The investment in information raises the expected maximal ratio, expressed by $\epsilon(E^*)$. The rise in $\epsilon(E^*)$ changes the optimal amount offered in exchange, X_0, and this in turn changes, C_0 and T_0 and the transactor's utility.

The transactor acquires information until the gain in utility from an increment ΔI_0 equals the loss resulting from the decrease in resources available for reservation demand and exchange imposed by the constraint

$$\Delta I_0 = -(\Delta C_0 + \Delta S_0 + \Delta X_0). \tag{6.8}$$

The second derivatives of ϵ and v with respect to I_0 assure that the marginal utility of investment in information decreases as investment increases. Moreover, the continued decrease of C_0 and X_0 generates an increasing loss of welfare, and the continued decrease of S_0 imposes increasingly severe constraints on the choice of transaction arrangements and (given $\partial^2 U/\partial \epsilon^2$ to form a negative definite Hessian matrix) a nondecreasing loss of utility. The allocation of resources to acquire information necessarily reaches an optimum.

A similar argument applies to the choice of transaction arrangement or reservation demand. Utility increases as more resources are allocated to market transformations, T, and the wider search for transaction arrangements, S_0. The larger S_0 and $S(T_0)$, the larger the admissible set of transaction arrangements and the greater is a transactor's opportunity to exploit differences in the marginal cost of information, associated with various goods. For example, by using indirect or roundabout exchange arrangements that reduce uncertainty, the transactor can lower v by allocating resources to S_0 while keeping I_0 constant. The increase in S_0 (holding I_0 constant) reduces C_0 and X_0, and therefore lowers ϵ. But the allocation to S_0 permits the transactor to choose from a wider range of transaction arrangements, raising ϵ. The optimal allocation to S is reached when the gain in utility from the smaller variance and more advantageous transaction arrangements just equals the loss in utility due to a smaller C_0 and X_0.

By neglecting costs of search and exchange, the traditional analysis of barter exchange sets S and I to zero and thus omits important aspects of resource allocation and choice under uncertainty. In the usual analysis, a transactor either engages in a single, double-coincidence transaction, $C_1 = R_1$, or does not trade, $C_0 = R_0$. In our analysis, a transactor is not forced to choose between autarchy and a single, double-coincidence transaction. He can engage in a sequence of transactions, expressed by a sequence of matrices or transaction chain $[T_0, T_1, \ldots, T_n]$ chosen so as to exploit differences in the marginal cost of acquiring information and exchanging. The length of the transaction chain – the optimal number of exchanges – is determined jointly with the choice of commodity bundle $C_n = R_n$ that maximizes utility. The bundle, R_n, is defined recursively in equation (6.9):

$$
\begin{aligned}
R_n &= Y_n + C_{n-1} \\
&= Y_n + R_{n-1} - [X_{n-1}+I_{n-1}+S_{n-1}(T_{n-1})] \\
&= Y_n + Y_{n-1} + C_{n-2} - [X_{n-1}+I_{n-1}+S_{n-1}(T_{n-1})] \\
&= Y_n + Y_{n-1} + R_{n-2} - [X_{n-1}+I_{n-1}+S_{n-1}(T_{n-1})] - \\
&\quad [X_{n-2}+I_{n-2}+S_{n-2}(T_{n-2})]
\end{aligned}
$$

$$
R_n = \sum_{i=1}^{n} Y_i + R_0 - \sum_{i=1}^{n-1} [X_i+I_i+S_i(T_i)] \tag{6.9}
$$

for convenience the expected value operator is omitted in the statement of the definition. Moreover, every Y_i is a function of T_{i-1}, X_{i-1} and the sequence of investments in information $(I_0 \ldots I_{i-1})$ given by

$$
\epsilon(Y_i) = \Sigma X_{i-1}^j(T_{i-1}, X_{i-1}) \cdot [E_{j,i-1}^*(I_0, I_1 \ldots, I_{i-1})] \tag{6.10}
$$

as shown in note 13. Both ϵ_n and v_n are, therefore, functions of the transaction chain $(T_0, \ldots, T_{n-1})$, the sequence of exchanges $(X_0, \ldots, X_{n-1})$ and the sequence of inventments in information $(I_0, \ldots, I_{n-1})$ according to the definition

$$
\epsilon_n = \epsilon(R_n); \quad v_n = v(R_n). \tag{6.11}
$$

Where information about the qualities and exchange ratios varies with the commodities, there are corresponding differences in the marginal cost of acquiring information, so transactors are not indifferent about the commodities they accept for use in subsequent exchanges. By choosing transaction arrangements T_i that induce the transactor to include in his transaction chain commodities or assets whose qualities are better known and less uncertain, the transactor can reduce the variance $v(Y_i)$ and the resources I_i that he uses to acquire information about exchange opportunities. At each step in the sequence, more resources become available for exchange and for reservation demand, so utility increases. By careful choice of the elements in the triplet C, T, I, a transactor is able to obtain the commodity bundle with mean and variance ϵ_n and v_n that maximize utility.

Our first postulate, introduced earlier, makes the marginal cost of acquiring information depend on the good or service selected. Unless transactors ignore the information they acquire, the postulate implies that intermediate transaction matrices in the chains they select (i.e., matrices up to the last) do not exhibit a random distribution of nonzero elements. In the first matrix of the chain, clusters of nonzero elements appear most frequently in the columns identified with assets that reduce uncertainty, provide more reliable information and lower marginal information costs. In the last matrix of the chains, the nonzero elements tend to be in the rows associated with commodities that have these same properties.

The distribution of costs of acquiring and maintaining information gives the transactor an opportunity to reduce the resource cost of acquiring his preferred commodity bundle by substituting knowledge about transaction arrangements for investment in information about market conditions and the qualities of goods offered in exchange. Cost reduction occurs in two ways. First, detailed information about market conditions such as location and identification of transactors, the quality and type of commodity bundles they hold and the exchange ratios at which they trade probably decays more rapidly than knowledge about optimal transaction chains. Second, as the use of an asset in exchange increases, the transactor learns more about the asset's properties. With growing use of particular transaction chains and improved knowledge of the properties of the assets exchanged, uncertainty and the variances and covariances in the general covariance matrix describing the overall density $\pi(E)$ decline.

The marginal productivity of transaction arrangements can be expressed in terms of the smaller investment in information required to keep the variance $v(R_n)$ unchanged. By choosing transaction arrangements that reduce the cost of acquiring information and exchanging, a transactor can allocate additional resources to exchange or reservation demand without raising the variance of the bundle he obtains. Indeed, if this were not so, direct exchange would predominate.

The usual discussion of a barter economy neglects the marginal productivity of transaction arrangements by limiting exchange to a single, double coincidence transaction. Once the transactor is given a choice of I and S, both the length of this optimal chain and the assets that enter depend on differences in the productivity and cost associated with alternative chains. Thus, our first postulate assures that the choice transaction chain and of the assets used in exchange is neither random nor determined solely by the exchange – i.e., by the initial and terminal bundles.

To show that individuals' optimizing behavior leads to the social choice of a small number of medium of exchange assets, we use our second postulate. This postulate states (1) that the marginal cost of acquiring information does not vary randomly within a social group and (2) that the marginal cost declines as the frequency with which an asset is used increases. Transactors can acquire information about a particular subset of the available assets at comparatively low marginal cost once these assets are used frequently.[14]

Our second postulate implies that the transaction chains of the numerous participants in the market process exhibit some common properties. These properties can be expressed as a clustering of the nonzero elements in the columns of the first matrix and in the rows of the last matrix of the chain. The repetitive use of a relatively small number of transaction chains by the members of the social group further reduces the marginal cost to each transactor of acquiring information about the assets most frequently used. The lower costs of acquiring information and transacting induce further clustering and the convergence of individuals' chains toward a common pattern.

There are many stages of development between double-coincidence barter and a fully monetary economy. At some stage, a few assets are used with dominant frequency in transactions. Once this stage is reached, a majority of the transaction chains consists of two matrices, the first containing a few (nonzero) columns and the second a few (nonzero) rows. Thus, money as a medium of exchange, as a transaction-dominating asset, results from the opportunities offered by the distribution of incomplete information and the search by potential transactors to develop transaction chains that save resources.

The analysis also explains the emergence of specialized trading functions such as brokerage and other market arrangements. They develop from the conditions that shape the (social) convergence to a dominant medium of exchange. Where information is complete and both information and readjustment are costless, specialization of trading functions yields no economic advantages and has no utility. Where information and readjustment are not free, the situation changes. Specialized services lower the costs of acquiring information and trading by providing more complete information about the range of qualities and market conditions. With a smaller investment of resources a transactor acquires the same information, and more resources can be used for reservation demand or trade.

2 A Diagrammatic Exposition

By simplifying the argument and omitting several aspects, we can use diagrams to demonstrate some main points of our analysis. We start with a nonmonetary economy in which there are two goods. One is the initial

---

[14]Differences in technological properties of commodities contribute to differences in the costs of acquiring information and transferring. Monetary literature has long recognized that portability, divisibility, durability, etc. are useful properties for assets used as mediums of exchange.

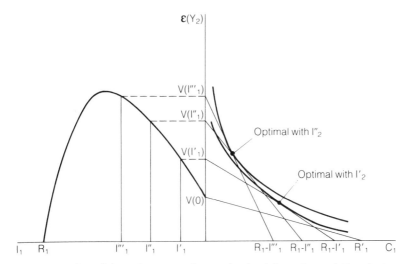

Figure 6.1   Conditions for an optimum budget line: the relation between information (left panel) and budget line (right panel).

endowment of a transactor, R_1; the other is the good, Y_2, acquired by trading in the market. We disregard the resources used in the trading process and allocate the initial endowment to reservation demand, C, to exchange in the market, X, and to the acquisition of information about market opportunities and exchange ratios, I.

$$R_1 = C_1 + X_1 + I_1. \tag{6.12}$$

The exchange ratio between R_1 (or C_1) and Y_2, denoted e_{12}, states the units of Y_2 obtainable per unit of R_1. Market opportunities are not known with certainty. By investing resources I_1 to acquire information, a transactor obtains a sample of potential exchange ratios. The sample has a maximal value e_{12}^*, the latter a random variable dependent on the underlying distribution. As above, we make the expectation and variance of e_{12}^* a function of investment, I.[15] Market exchange is a productive process that transforms the inputs (X_1, I_1) into an output $Y_2 = X_1 e_{12}^* (I_1)$. The value of the bundle after an exchange is $R_2 = Y_2 + C_1 e_{12}^*$.

The transactor seeks to maximize the utility of the bundle available for consumption. The arguments of the utility function are C_1 and the expected value and variance of Y_2. The indifference curves of figure 6.1 are drawn for a given value of the variance $v(Y_2)$. A change in variance moves the entire surface or, what is the same thing, requires a relabelling of the indifference

---

[15]To simplify notation we write e_{12}^* for the expectation of the maximal sample value, and where there is no chance of confusion, we use Y_2 instead of $\epsilon(Y_2)$.

curves to associate a higher level of utility with an unchanged combination of Y_2 and C_1, if the variance of Y_2 decreases and a lower level of utility if the variance increases.

Unlike the standard analysis, neither the slope nor the position of the budget line is independent of the transactor's allocation of resources. Increased investment in information raises the expectation of the maximal sample value e_{12}^* and the slope of the budget line, $-e_{12}^*$. With increased investment, the budget line becomes steeper, and the transactor obtains more Y per unit of C.

The relation between investment in information, the value of information and the position of the budget line is developed in the left panel of figure 6.1. On the horizontal axis, we measure the resources used to acquire information on a scale running from zero at the origin to R_1, the transactor's endowment. By sacrificing a unit of real consumption and investing in information, a transactor enlarges his sample of exchange ratios and, in general, raises the value of e^*. The marginal cost of information is the consumption sacrificed. The value of the information is the gain or loss in $\epsilon(Y_2)$ obtained from the exchange of a smaller (R_1-I_1) endowment of real resources at a higher exchange ratio. The curve in this panel shows the value of information $V(I_1)$ as a function of the amount invested. The intercept of the curve on the Y_2 axis is the value of the information, in $\epsilon(Y_2)$ units, that the transactor carries over from previous trades. If he relies entirely on past experience, the best he can do is trade at the ratio $e_{12}^*(0)$; the maximum Y_2 he can obtain by exchanging all his endowment at this ratio is shown as $V(0)$. By investing in information, at a cost equal to I_1, he increases his information about market conditions. The change in the value of information is shown by the projections of the curve in the left panel on the Y_2 axis. If he invests an amount I_1', he has available for exchange only $R_1 - I_1'$, but he can exchange at the higher ratio $e_{12}^*(I_1')$ and obtain a maximum value of $Y_2 = V(I_1')$. The distance $V(I_1') - V(0)$ on the Y_2 axis is the value of the information obtained with an investment I_1'.[16]

For any investment I_1, the value of information is given by

$$V(I_1) = (R_1-I_1)e_{12}^*(I_1). \tag{6.13}$$

Inspection makes clear that if the entire endowment is used to acquire infor-

---

[16]The cost of acquiring information, I_1, is clearly visible in two places on figure 6.1. One is the horizontal axis on the left panel. The other is the difference between R_1 and the intercept of any budget constraint on the C_1 axis, $R_1 - I_1$. The difference defines the maximum C_1 associated with any given I_1. As the figure is drawn, each increment to investment $(I_1''-I_1', I_1'-0)$ and each distance between intercepts of the budget line on the C_1 axis is the same size. The decreasing incremental value of information is shown by the decrease in the distance between the successive intercepts of the budget line on the Y_2 axis. The relations of I to $V(I)$ depends on the vector, P, discussed in note 11.

mation, nothing is left for trade or consumption, so $V(R_1) = 0$. To find the value of I_1 that maximizes $V(I_1)$, we take the derivative

$$\frac{\partial V}{\partial I_1} = e^*_{12}(I_1) \left[\frac{R_1 - I_1}{I_1} \, \eta(e^*_{12}, I_1) - 1 \right] \qquad (6.14)$$

where $\eta(e^*_{12}, I_1)$ is the elasticity of e^*_{12} with respect to I_1. It follows from diminishing marginal productivity of investment that the increase in the expected sample value falls as investment increases, and the elasticity falls as I_1 increases. Moreover, as I_1 approaches R_1, $(R_1 - I_1)/I_1$ approaches zero. The value of information V reaches a maximum when the share of the endowment invested in information is

$$\frac{I_1}{R_1} = \frac{\eta}{1 + \eta} < 1. \qquad (6.15)$$

If the elasticity is low, investment in information raises the expected sample value and improves market opportunities very little. The maximum V then occurs at a very low value of I_1.

The optimal amount of resources invested in information is determined jointly with the optimal reservation demand and allocation to trade by maximizing utility. Differentiating

$$U = U[\epsilon(Y_2), C_1, v(Y_2)]$$
$$U_1, U_2 > 0; \quad U_3 < 0 \qquad (6.16)$$

with respect to C_1 and I_1, we obtain the necessary conditions for a maximum,

$$U_1 e^*(I_1) = U_2 \qquad (6.17)$$

$$\frac{\partial V}{\partial I} = C_1 \frac{\partial e^*_{12}}{\partial I} + \frac{-U_3}{U_1} \frac{\partial v}{\partial I}. \qquad (6.18)$$

Solving these two equations for C_1 and I_1 and substituting the solutions in the budget constraint $R_1 = C_1 + I_1 + X_1$ gives the optimal allocation to reservation demand, investment in information and trade.

The first of the two necessary conditions is the familiar condition for tangency between the indifference curve and the budget line obtained in the standard analysis of consumer choice. The second equation goes beyond the standard analysis and states the condition for the optimal *position* of the budget line. The equation has two components. The first is the increment to the value of reservation demand, measured in units of Y_2, obtained from investment in information, the second is the marginal gain or loss from reducing the variance. The position of the budget line is optimal when the sum of these components equals the marginal value of information, $\partial V/\partial I_1$, measured in units of Y_2.[17]

---

[17]Interpretation of the second component of the second necessary condition is made clearer

The conditions for an optimum are shown in figure 6.1. The slopes of the budget lines show the exchange ratio e_{12} for different values of I. The position of the budget lines is determined by the amount invested and the value of the information obtained. The relation between the two is given by the curve in the left panel. We disregard, for the moment, the gain or loss in utility resulting from changes in the variance. As the figure is drawn, it is suboptimal to restrict investment in information to I'_1. The transactor can reach a higher indifference curve by increasing investment to I''_1. A further increase to I'''_1 lowers utility. In the absence of any effect of variance, the transactor would choose an investment I''_1 and trade at the corresponding exchange ratio. The investment I''_1 and the associated allocations to C_1 and Y_2 represent an optimum for any transactor unconcerned by the variance, i.e., for any risk neutral transactor.

For a risk neutral transactor $U_3 \equiv 0$. For such transactors, the optimal position of the budget line is always below the projection of the maximum value of information on the $\epsilon(Y_2)$ axis. The same is true for transactors who are not risk neutral whenever $\partial v / \partial I = 0$. In these cases, the optimal value of information is always reached before the maximum value of information. This can be verified by noting that in these cases $\partial V / \partial I$, therefore $\partial e^*_{12} / \partial I$, must be positive since $\partial V / \partial I = C \cdot \partial e^*_{12} / \partial I$.

Transactors who are willing to sacrifice resources to reduce uncertainty and obtain more reliable information are important in our analysis. For them, investments in information not only shift the budget line but also change the utility surface. A reduction in variance means that there is less uncertainty about the outcome of an exchange. With uncertainty reduced, the transactor receives more utility from a smaller bundle of commodities. The effect of reducing uncertainty can be shown in figure 6.1 by relabelling each of the indifference curves so as to attach more utility to every commodity bundle or by shifting each indifference curve in figure 6.1 vertically downward thereby raising the utility assigned to any Y_2, C_1 combination.

The size of the shift in the indifference curves resulting from the effect of investment in information on the variance provides another interpretation of the second component of the optimality condition. The vertical shift, measured in units of Y_2, $(-U_3/U_1)\,(\partial v/\partial I_1)$, is the amount of $\epsilon(Y_2)$ that provides just as much utility as the reduced variance $v(Y_2)$.

The effect of a reduction in variance on utility implies that the optimal position involves more investment in information than I''_1. The bundle available for exchange and consumption declines. In terms of figure 6.1, the downward shift in the indifference curves – the gain in utility from reduced

---

by noting that $-U_3/U_1 = dY_2/dv$ so the component can be written $[dY_2/dv]\,[dv/dI] = dY_2/dI$. The left side of this last expression shows the change in Y_2 associated with an increment to investment as the product of the change in variance resulting from an increment of information weighted by the appropriate marginal rate of substitution.

variance – at first offsets the loss of utility from the decline in the bundle. Where the product of the marginal reduction in variance $\partial v/\partial I$ and of the marginal rate of substitution between variance and Y_2, $-U_3/U_1$, is large, the optimal value of information may not be reached until we are on the negatively sloped segment of the $V(I)$ curve. Pronounced risk aversion, a relatively large $-U_3$ raises the portion of the resources a transactor allocates to investment in information and reduction of uncertainty.

We now introduce a third good into the nonmonetary economy we have considered. This good has zero direct marginal utility for each transactor.[18] It contributes to utility indirectly, however, by improving a transactor's information and by reducing the variance of exchange ratios and thus the uncertainty about the bundles obtained in market exchange. We assume that the third good has the following properties:

$$\frac{\partial e_{13}^*}{\partial I} > \frac{\partial e_{12}^*}{\partial I} < \frac{\partial e_{32}^*}{\partial I}$$

$$\frac{\partial v(e_{13}^*|I)}{\partial I} < \frac{\partial v(e_{12}^*|I)}{\partial I} > \frac{\partial v(e_{32}^*|I)}{\partial I} .$$

(6.19)

These conditions state that the third good reduces the transactor's cost of acquiring reliable information. With the same investment in information, he increases the expected value of the sample maxima (e_{13}^*, e_{32}^*) and reduces uncertainty.

The introduction of a roundabout method of exchange using a good that gives transactors increased value of information at relatively low cost offers an opportunity not previously available. Transactors are no longer restricted to choosing between allocations to reservation demand, trade, and investment in information. They may now choose transaction arrangements, i.e., they can obtain Y_2 either by exchanging part of R_1 directly at the exchange ratio e_{12}^* or by first acquiring the new good at exchange ratio e_{13}^* and using good 3 to obtain Y_2 at the exchange ratio e_{32}^*.

As before the initial constraint in terms of R is

$$R_1 = C_1 + X_1 + I_1.$$

(6.12)

The transactor wishes to acquire Y_2 by trading X_1 and investing I_1. The market transformation is expressed by $Y_2 = X_1 t^i(I_1)$ where

[18]We do not make this assumption in the formal analysis of the previous section. The assumption is introduced here only to simplify the graphical presentation, specifically to avoid superimposing a second indifference map on the map in the figure. In the more general analysis of the previous section there are a large number of commodities and potential transaction chains. The number of chains depends on the number of commodities. Under our maximizing procedure, at least one of these chains is optimal. In the graphical analysis of figure 6.2, V_2 represents this chain.

$$t^1(I_1) = e^*_{12}(I_1)$$
$$t^2(I_1) = e^*_{13}(I_1) \cdot e^*_{32}(I_1)$$

(6.20)

The transactor desires to maximize the utility function

$$U[\epsilon(Y_2), C_1, v(Y_2)]$$

(6.16)

by suitable choices of C_1, I_1 and market transformation t^i, subject to the endowment constraint. The optimizing problem can be rewritten as the maximization of the function

$$U[(R_1 - C_1 - I_1)t^i, C_1, v[(R_1 - C_1 - I_1)t^i]]$$

with respect to C_1, I_1 and t^i ($i=1, 2$). The first-order conditions for C_1 and I_1 are

$$U_1 t^i = U_2$$

(6.21)

$$\frac{\partial V(t^i)}{\partial I_1} = C_1 \frac{\partial t^i}{\partial I_1} + \frac{-U_3}{U_1} \frac{\partial v(t^i)}{\partial I_1}$$

(6.22)

where $V(t^i) = (R_1 - I_1)t^i$, and $v(t^i) = v[X_1 \cdot t^i]$. The two equations determine C_1 and I_1 as a function of t^i. Replacement in the utility function gives

$$U[X_1(t^i)t^i, C_1(t^i), v[X_1(t^i)t^i]]$$

and the stage is set for the choice of the optimal transaction arrangement.

Figure 6.2 shows the choice of transaction arrangement. With this choice, the transactor determines the value of information obtained from a given investment, I_1. The curves V_1 or V_2 represent two alternative transaction arrangements. The difference in the value of the information obtained from a given investment depends on the properties of the joint conditional distribution $\pi(e^*_{12}, e^*_{13}, e^*_{32}/I_1)$ of the three exchange ratios. Since information about types of transaction chains decays slowly, the intercept of the curve V_2, describing chain t^2, is above the intercept of V_1. The diagram also shows an earlier and higher maximum for transaction chain t^2. Since V_2 lies above V_1 throughout the ascending branch of V_1, a trader gains from using transaction arrangement t^2 throughout this range. This effect is reenforced by the shift of the indifference map resulting from the greater reduction in variance per unit of I. The selection of t^2 and the use of an asset with well-known properties permits the transactor to trade at a more favorable exchange ratio and reduces uncertainty. Thus, the choice of t^2 instead of t^1 raises the transactor's welfare.

Figure 6.2 shows the productivity gain resulting from the choice of transaction arrangements in two distinct ways. One measure of the gain in the smaller investment in information required to obtain information of given value. For example, the transactor can obtain information with value OM either by investing I'_1 and using transaction arrangement V_1 or by making no investment in information and using transaction arrangement V_2. The pro-

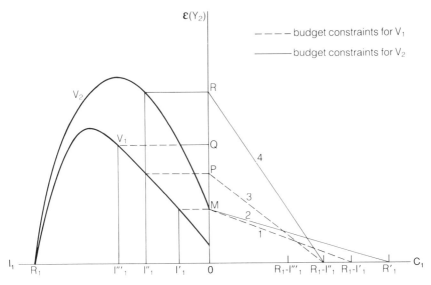

Figure 6.2   Choice of transaction arrangement.

ductivity gain is equal to the saving of resources (I_1'). This saving permits the transactor to trade at the maximal exchange ratio represented by (the solid) budget line 2 instead of the maximal ratio represented by (the dashed) line 1. Similarly, point OQ shows that the combination of V_1 and I_1''' produces the same value of information as the combination V_2 and I_1'. By choosing transaction arrangement V_2, the transactor reduces the cost of acquiring information of value OQ by $I_1''' - I_1'$. The saving in cost becomes available for consumption and exchange. The production of unchanged value of information with a smaller input of resources is a measure of the marginal productivity of transaction arrangement V_2.

An alternative measure of the productivity gain is the increase in the value of information obtainable with unchanged investment. The distance PR on the $\epsilon(Y_2)$ axis is the increased value of information (in units of Y_2) obtained with investment I_1'' and the choice of transaction chain V_2 instead of V_1. By using V_2 the transactor is able to trade at the ratio given by budget line 4 rather than the lower exchange ratio given by constraint 3. Thus, careful choice of transaction arrangements increases the productivity of a transactor's resources and his utility.

The results obtained in our world of three commodities apply to an n-commodity world in which there are numerous alternative transaction arrangements and many transactors. Each transaction arrangement can be represented by a curve on the left panel of figure 6.2 showing the value of information obtained with a given investment of resources in information.

Our first postulate implies not only that the curves differ substantially but that the optimal transaction arrangement for an individual transactor – the highest curve – involves indirect exchange, i.e., the use of an intermediate asset that reduces his cost of acquiring information about market opportunities. Our second postulate implies that what is true for the individual is true for most members of the social group. The transaction arrangements that are most productive for the individual are also most productive for a dominant portion of the group.

The assets used to reduce the cost of acquiring information and transacting are money for the group or society. The social and private productivity of a medium of exchange results from the use of transaction chains involving assets with these properties. Where knowledge of market opportunities and the qualities of goods is neither costless to obtain nor uniformly distributed, the use of money as a medium of exchange reduces the resource cost of exchanging. In the following section we consider the social productivity of money and some implications of the analysis for the type of assets chosen as mediums of exchange and used as money.

3 The Social Services of Money

For individuals, money is a substitute for investment in information and labor allocated to search. By using money, individuals reduce the amount of information they must acquire, process, and store, and they reduce the number of transactions in which they engage to exchange their initial endowments for optimal baskets of goods. The use of money increases the welfare of each money user by reducing uncertainty, the length of transaction chains, and the variance of price ratios and by increasing expected wealth and time available for leisure. Whatever other services create a demand for the assets that serve as mediums of exchange, their use as mediums of exchange increases demand. Individuals find it advantageous to allocate part of their wealth to money.

What is true for individuals is in this case true for society. The convergence of optimal transaction arrangements generates an aggregate demand for the assets used as mediums of exchange. The increased demand to hold inventories of these assets (money) is independent of the previous uses of the assets and, of course, increases the (relative) prices of the assets. The average amount held in inventories depends on the prices of the assets held, the prices of alternative assets and, thus, on the relation between net marginal productivity and marginal cost.

Once inventories of money are held, payments and receipts are no longer synchronized. Lack of sychronization, however, does not explain the use of holding of money any more than the holding of money explains the lack of synchronization. Both are a result of the superior productivity of indirect methods of exchange, the smaller resource cost of acquiring information and transacting in a monetary economy.[19]

The use of money encourages the development of the market system by lowering the costs of acquiring information and transacting. With the expansion of the market, opportunities increase for professional middlemen and specialized traders to exploit the partial and incomplete distribution of information about particular commodities. Specialized traders substitute for a wider and more general distribution of information. The use of money also affects the intertemporal allocation of resources. Deferred payments, borrowing, credit and the payment system expand when a standardized asset with well-known properties becomes available. The reason is that transactors become more willing to enter into contracts calling for deferred payment.

The magnitude of the net social productivity of money is not constant but varies with the degree of uncertainty about market conditions, including exchange ratios and the quality of goods. Accelerated technological changes or innovations that change the qualities of goods and increase the number or types of goods raise the productivity of money. Large fluctuations in economic activity also raise costs of acquiring information and the productivity of money. Our analysis implies that the demand for mediums of exchange is higher in periods of rapid change than in periods of gradual or relatively steady change. The longer the period of steady, gradual change continues, the lower the productivity of money and the smaller the demand for assets that reduce costs of acquiring information by serving as mediums of exchange.

A stationary state or a world of steady growth are the limiting cases of economic theory. Tastes, technology, anticipations, population, and types of product are either invariant or change in a known, fully anticipated way at a steady rate. The marginal cost of acquiring information falls and in the limit approaches zero. Transaction chains no longer differ by the saving of costs of acquiring information and differ only by the costs of transfer. The main condition leading to the selection of a small group of assets as money, and therefore the main source of the distinction between money and

---

[19]In a well-developed market economy, most of the net *marginal* productivity of money probably results from the saving of costs of transacting, while the *total* productivity of money depends on the reduction in cost of acquiring information and costs of exchanging. The difference between our analysis and the usual analysis of "transaction costs" (see Baumol, 1952; Tobin, 1956) is that the *total* productivity of money in the familiar Baumol and Tobin analyses is almost the same as the *marginal* productivity in our analysis. The reason is that Baumol–Tobin transactors face fixed payment schedules, whereas our transactors optimize over all transaction arrangements. The Baumol–Tobin analysis has been used recently by Samuelson (1969), Clower (1970) and Johnson (1970) to equate the productivity of money with the "shoe leather" saved by avoiding trips to the bank or the market place. Their analyses understate the total contribution of money to wealth by neglecting the improvement in the opportunity set shown in figure 6.2 and discussed in the text.

nonmonetary assets, disappears in the stationary state or world of steady growth.[20]

Hyper-inflation and hyper-deflation provide examples of changes in the marginal cost and marginal productivity of holding and using money. In both, the increased frequency of change in market conditions increases uncertainty and the variance of exchange ratios and thus raises the marginal productivity of money. But the marginal cost of holding money increases in hyper-inflation as the rate of inflation increases. Transactors are induced to choose transaction chains that avoid the inflation tax, even if such chains use more resources for transactions.

The search for new transaction chains and the abandonment of old is commonly mistaken for a return to barter. The process does not restore either double-coincidence exchange or the random selection of mediums of exchange. Transactors concentrate their search on these transaction chains that offer at least the same expected gain in wealth as existing mediums of exchange. The assets that replace existing money may have higher marginal costs of acquiring information and transacting. If so, they must have lower marginal holding costs than the existing money.

Our analysis implies that continued and accelerated hyper-inflation eventually comes to an end. The economy gradually adopts a new money and a new set of transaction arrangements. The process of search and social convergence is not costless for the individual transactors or the society. Governments or private producers can reduce the social cost of introducing new mediums of exchange and the transition to the new transaction arrangements by introducing new assets with properties similar to the old and effectively controlling the quantity produced.

A large deflation also increases uncertainty and induces transactors to reconsider transaction chains. Unlike hyper-inflation, the search for new transaction chains in a deflation does not replace existing mediums of exchange but adds new ones. The relatively high yield on money puts a premium on the search for assets that are close substitutes for the existing mediums of exchange – have similar information and transfer costs – and lower yield. New types of money evolve to supplement the existing money and increase the available stock of real balances. Adjustment to severe deflation, therefore, is not concentrated solely on the price level and rate of price change as in growth theory. New supplies of real balances are produced by the search for alternative transaction chains.

Our analysis of the use of money implies that both inflation and deflation

---

[20]In the terms of our formal analysis, the effect is conveyed by the distribution $\pi(E|P)$. The coordinates of the vector P summarize the representative individual's information about market opportunities. The greater the frequency of change in market conditions, the poorer his information. In the stationary state his information increases without offset and approaches full information. The variances and covariances of the π function decline. See note 11.

are stable in a certain technical sense. In inflation new monies are substituted for old; in deflation supplementary monies are introduced. But the evidence, from periods of hyper-inflation and severe deflation alike, reveals the sizeable resource costs associated with the stabilizing mechanism. Hyper-inflation or deflation reach relatively high levels before transactors begin to replace existing money or add new money. The high costs that individuals are willing to pay before beginning to search for new or supplementary arrangements suggests the size of the benefits received from the use of dominant medium of exchange.

The size of the net social productivity of money also depends on the assets selected as mediums of exchange. Once the community uses some assets as money, the private and social benefit can be increased by substituting claims against commodities for commodity money. Individuals gain from the use of substitutes for commodity money if the reduction of costs of acquiring information and transacting more than compensates for the increased variability of exchange ratios. Society gains because the use of claims and fiat paper money reduces the resources used to make exchanges in three main ways. First, paper money permits society to develop a fractional reserve money system and to produce the same nominal stock of money at lower resource cost. Second, the use of claims encourages the development of privately produced money and with it the development of the payments system. The cost of acquiring information about the qualities of paper money, whether produced by government or by private producers, is lowest if the paper money starts as a claim against commodity money. When information about the paper money becomes widespread, paper money retains the property of general acceptability even if the claim against commodites is removed. Third, paper money frequently lowers the resource cost of transfer and exchange. This somewhat less than general proposition recognizes that both costs and benefits are affected and that the size of the net benefit from the use of paper money depends on the prevailing monetary arrangements. We also note that a paper money system moves without an anchor constraining the behavior of the price level. Its social costs include the cost of variable and possibly permanent inflation.

Monetary history offers numerous examples of changes in monetary arrangements that reduced marginal costs of information or transfer for the assets used in optimal transaction chains. Coinage is one of the earliest, and bank credit cards one of the most recent steps extending the range and use of mediums of exchange by reducing these costs.[21] Suppose, however, paper

---

[21]Credit cards centralize information about deposit users, reduce a seller's cost of acquiring information, encourage the separation of payments and purchases and thereby increase (relatively) the use of deposits as a medium of exchange, lowering the ratio of currency to deposits. Lowering the costs of acquiring information and transferring via deposits lowers the net

money is not introduced by a central bank or government but emerges in response to the public's search for optimal transaction chains. Many different producers are induced to issue paper money as a claim against commodity money. The social benefit resulting from the use of lower cost money is partly offset by the higher cost individuals pay to acquire information. The legislation of 1844 in England and Wales and of the 1860s in the United States that reduced the number and types of notes in circulation by restricting the right to issue notes are examples of institutional changes that raised economic welfare by reducing costs of acquiring information. The requirement of par collection of checks under the Federal Reserve Act is another example.

Nothing in our analysis implies either that society converges to a single medium of exchange or that the productivity of money and the contribution of money to wealth is limited to a single monetary asset. Different types of assets – some privately, some publicly produced – appear in the transaction chains adopted by members of the group and in the transaction chains of a single transactor at different times. These differences in the choice of transaction chain reflect differences in marginal cost that depend on the type of transaction and the transactor's information. Even in highly developed economies with extensive monetary institutions, transactors can use specialized information to develop transaction arrangements that lower transfer costs by avoiding the use of money. Moreover, sectors of an economy that develop specialized information about the properties of particular assets often find it useful to develop specialized mediums of exchange.[22]

Our analysis suggests an extension of Gresham's law – cheap money drives out dear at fixed exchange rates – to the case of multiple mediums of exchange with variable or floating exchange rates. With floating exchange rates, stable monies drive out variable monies. Consequently, government or private producers desirous of maintaining the circulation of government and privately produced monies have found it desirable to provide arrangements for exchange of one money for the other on demand.[23] More importantly, issuers of privately produced money expand the market for their product by maintaining a fixed exchange rate. By doing so, they lower the users' cost of information and increase the demand for their product. Businessmen, bankers, and government officials have used similar reasoning to press for

---

marginal productivity of deposit inventories. Average inventories of deposits are reduced; velocity increases.

[22]The development of the Federal funds market is an example. Corporate mergers offer examples of the way in which the allocation of human wealth (skilled specialists) reduces cost by avoiding money as a medium of exchange. By offering the owners of the merged firm deferred equity claims of various kinds, the purchasers reduce or defer the tax liabilites of equity owners, raising the owners' wealth and reducing the cost of acquisition.

[23]This is the rationale for the instant repurchase clause discussed by Pesek and Saving.

fixed exchange rates between national monies. The advantages of a fixed rate system are however not obtained without a cost.

Throughout our analysis we have indentified money with the medium of exchange. This usage has been criticized on two grounds. Tobin (1963) is one of the last in a long line emphasizing the existence of close substitutes for money. Tobin's criticism is part of a position discussed above, that ignores costs of acquiring information and attributes the total productivity of money to its role in synchronizing receipts and payments and reducing brokerage costs. Friedman and Schwartz (1970) also criticize the notion that money is a medium of exchange. They describe money as a "temporary abode of purchasing power" and argue that the term medium of exchange is an a priori notion devoid of empirical content. As an example of the deficiency of the medium of exchange concept, they cite the difficulty of using units of currency with large denominations or using checkable deposits in unfamiliar environments. Their argument is insufficient for the conclusion they have drawn. The use of checks and bills of large denomination often involves substantial costs of acquiring information and exchanging. On our analysis, it is not surprising that neither circulates in unfamiliar environments.[24]

Defining money as a temporary abode of purchasing power does not distinguish between properties of assets or between a monetary and a barter economy in a manner independent of the medium of exchange function. As our earlier discussion shows, transactors hold intermediate goods temporarily in a barter economy – as one of the items in a transaction chain – if their best information suggests that by doing so they can make more advantageous exchanges.

The recognition of the central role of a medium of exchange does not imply that the collection of assets that serve as medium of exchange is most appropriate for explaining movements of the general price level. A definition embracing a larger collection of assets is appropriate if there are close substitutes for the medium of exchange on the supply side. In this case, slight changes in relative prices reallocate output between the medium of exchange and other assets, so the collection of assets most useful for explaining changes in the general price level differs from the assets that serve as medium of exchange. However, even if evidence suggests that a broader collection is justified empirically and the term money is used to refer to the broader collection, the significance of the medium of exchange function and its importance for explaining the productivity of monetary assets remains.

---

[24]Five and ten thousand dollar notes never circulated widely but were used primarily for transactions between banks where the marginal cost of acquiring information about the notes was low. With the development and extension of the Federal funds market and other lower cost means of making interbank transfers, the use of bills of large denomination declined markedly.

4 Conclusion

The use of money remained puzzling as long as the theory of exchange was restricted to the case of perfect certainty, a world in which information about market prices and the qualities of goods and services is obtained at zero cost. Standard price theory eliminated the main reasons for the existence and use of money by confining choice to three options – production, consumption and exchange – and setting costs of acquiring information about exchange opportunities and qualities of goods to zero. With costs of executing transactions zero and information a free good, there are no costs of shopping to assure that exchanges take place at the most favorable prices and no benefits from reducing the resource cost of executing transactions and eliminating cross-hauling of commodities. Any asset is just as usable as any other for executing transactions and discharging obligations. As a result, attempts to explain the use of money generally accept some consequences of the use of money – such as lack of synchronization – as an explanation of the existence of money.

Our analysis extends the theory of exchange to include the cost of acquiring information about market arrangements, relative prices, or exchange ratios. Individuals search for those sequences of transactions, called transaction chains, that minimize the cost of acquiring information and transacting. The use of assets with peculiar technical properties and low marginal cost of acquiring information reduces these costs. Money is such an asset, and the private and social productivity of money is a direct consequence of the saving in resources that the use of money permits and of the extension of the market system that occurs because of the reduction in the cost of making exchanges.

Money is a substitute for the specialized market skills that are part of a transactor's stock of knowledge or "human wealth." Resources allocated to search and to maintaining market information can be reallocated once money is used as a medium of exchange. Trade and the market system expand, and the economy becomes increasingly monetized. More and better quality information becomes available with the expansion of the market and the opportunities for division of labor that lead to the development of professional transactors such as brokers and specialists. The use of a unit of account further reduces the cost of making exchanges.

We do not attempt to explain the holding of money except in the trivial sense that the use of an asset implies that the asset is held. Nevertheless the analysis helps to explain why money continues to be used even in periods of accelerating inflation when the cost of holding money reaches very high levels.

By analyzing the productivity of money and relating the productivity of money to the analysis of trade in an exchange economy, we clarify the meaning of the phrase "the services of money" and suggest by implication the benefits that would accrue to the world economy from the use of a medium of exchange. Since the saving in brokerage costs or "trips to the bank," that is generally presented as the total product of money, is only the marginal product of money in our analysis, the gains from using money in international as in domestic exchange are considerably larger than is generally claimed. (See Baumol (1952), Clower (1970), Johnson (1970), Samuelson (1969), Tobin (1965).) Once we leave the world of certainty and costless information, both the private and social productivity of money rise; the use of money ceases to be puzzling and becomes, instead, an implication of optimizing behavior.

References

Baumol, W.J. 1952. The transactions demand for cash: An inventory theoretic approach. *Quarterly Journal of Economics* 66, 545–56.

Brunner, K. and A.H. Meltzer. 1964. Further investigations of demand and supply functions for money. *Journal of Finance* 19, 240–83.

Cass, D. and M. Yaari. 1966. A reexamination of the pure consumption loans model. *Journal of Political Economy* 74, 353–67.

Clower, R. 1970. Is there an optimal money supply? *Journal of Finance* 25, 425–33.

Friedman, M. 1956. The quantity theory of money, A restatement. In *Studies in the Quantity Theory of Money*, ed. M. Friedman. Chicago.

—— 1969. The optimum quantity of money. In *The Optimum Quantity of Money and Other Essays*, ed. M. Friedman. Chicago.

—— and A.J. Schwartz. 1970. *The Monetary Statistics of the United States*. National Bureau of Economic Research, *Studies in Business Cycles* 20.

Gilbert, J.C. 1953. The demand for money: The development of an economic concept. *Journal of Political Economy* 61, 144–59.

Johnson, H. G. 1970. Is there an optimal money supply? *Journal of Finance* 25, 435–42.

Keynes, J. M. 1936. *The General Theory of Employment, Interest and Money*. London: Macmillan.

Marget, A. W. 1938; 1942. *The Theory of Prices*. New York, vols I and II.

Mason, W.E. 1963. *Clarification of the Monetary Standard*. University Park, Pa.

Niehans, J. 1969. Money in a static theory of optimal payment arrangements. *Journal of Money, Credit, and Banking* 1, 706–26.

Patinkin, D. 1965. *Money, Interest and Prices*, 2nd edn. New York: Harper & Row.

Pesek, B.P. and T.R. Saving. 1967. *Money, Wealth and Economic Theory*. New York.

Samuelson, P.A. 1947. *The Foundations of Economic Analysis*. Cambridge, Mass.

—— 1969. Non-optimality of money holding under laissez-faire. *Canadian Journal of Economics* 2, 303–8.

Schumpeter, J. 1939. *Business Cycles*. New York.

Sidrauski, M. 1967. Rational choice and patterns of growth in a monetary economy. *American Economic Review* 57, 531–44.

Simon, H.A. 1959. Theories of decision making in economics and behavioral science. *American Economic Review* 49, 253–83.

Stigler, G. 1961. The economics of information. *Journal of Political Economy* 69, 213–25.

Thornton, H. 1802. An enquiry into the nature of the paper credit of Great Britain. London, repr. New York, 1965.

Tobin, J. 1956. The interest elasticity of transactions demand for cash. *Review of Economics and Statistics* 38, 241–7.

—— 1963. Commercial banks as creators of money. In *Banking and Monetary Studies*, ed. D. Carson, Homewood. Ill.

—— 1965. Money and economic growth. *Econometrica* 33, 671–84.

7

Fiscal Policy in Macro Theory: A Survey and Evaluation

Karl Brunner

1 Background

Almost twenty years ago the "fiscalist issue" emerged as a major focus on macroeconomic debates. Milton Friedman and David Meiselman initiated the discussion with an article eventually published in the volumes of the Commission on Money and Credit. The debate was subsequently joined in the middle 1960s by Albert Ando, Michael De Prano, Donald Hester, Thomas Mayer, and Franco Modigliani. Jerry Jordan and Leonall Andersen, with other members of the research staff at the Federal Reserve Bank of St. Louis and their critics, continued the discussion toward the end of the 1960s into the early years of the 1970s.

Another round of discussions followed in the first half of the 1970s. The focus had somewhat changed, however. The Keynesian side acknowledged real effects of monetary influences, and the monetarists participating in the discussion recognized temporary real effects and permanent nominal effects of fiscal policy. Starting from this position, the contribution by Carl Christ (1968), Blinder and Solow (1974), Brunner (1976), and Brunner and Meltzer (1972a, 1972b, 1976) addressed mainly the feedback via the asset markets resulting from prevailing budgetary policies. This work reemphasized the idea of a "crowding out" of private capital formation associated with the financing of a budget deficit.

The appearance of "rational expectations" with the seminal work of Robert Barro, Robert Lucas, and Thomas Sargent modified our approach to monetary processes. It affected also the analysis of fiscal policy. The basic thrust provided by the prevailing formation of "rational expectations" encouraged the revival of an idea originally pondered by Ricardo. Rational expectations of agents expressing concern for future generations destroys the

This paper appeared in R.W. Hafer (ed.) *The Monetary versus Fiscal Policy Debate*. Totowa, NJ: Roman and Allanheld, 1986, pp. 33–116. Reprinted with permission.

significance of financial decisions in the budget process. The financing of current expenditures with tax revenues or the sale of bonds yields the same results under the circumstances. Deficit finance determines future tax liabilities with a present value just matching the tax revenues currently suspended. Wealth position and opportunities of agents remain unchanged. Deficit finance affects, therefore, neither interest rates nor aggregate demand for output. This aspect of fiscal policy thus offers no wedge for influencing the aggregate evolution of the economy. This result contrasts both with Keynesian and inherited monetarist analysis. The ensuing discussions, however, uncovered processes linking tax policies (even lump sum policies) with real effects operating independently of direct portfolio and asset market effects. These processes are centered on intergenerational wealth transfers associated with debt and tax policies. The macroeconomic role of tax policies depends ultimately, so it appears, on the assumption of "intergenerational self-interest" or on specific risks and uncertainties.

An important role of tax policies apparently survives the emergence of rational expectations and so does a role for expenditure policies. Total expenditures and their structure still affect, in the context of this neoclassic analysis, consumption, investment, aggregate real demand for output, the supply of output, and real rates of interest. But the detailed nature of the mechanism differs radically from the Keynesian story. The government sector operates essentially as a production process absorbing products from the private sector as an input to produce an output. This output either competes with private consumption or contributes to the private sector's production process. This approach was originally suggested by Martin Bailey (1971) but disregarded by aggregate analysis. Both Keynesian and monetarist arguments treated "government" as a sinkhole swallowing a portion of private sector output. The emphasis on "government" as a production process operating with distortionary taxes changes the macroeconomic focus of fiscal policy in important ways.

The momentum of academic discussions substantially changed in retrospect the range of issues surrounding fiscal policy. The analytic evolutions and the resulting discussions modified many questions and emphasized new dimensions. Academic discussions were also influenced in recent years by political events and discussions in the public arena. The emergence of a comparatively large and possibly "permanent" deficit in the Federal budget motivated another round of discussions. There appeared voices claiming that such deficits produce, in contrast to Keynesian arguments, *negative* short-run effects on output. Others emphasized the long-run effects on normal growth. Many concentrated on linking high interest rates with the prevailing large deficit. The inflationary significance of the deficit was also considered. Some arguments seem to recognize a direct link between deficits and inflation. More carefully developed arguments emphasize the longer-run effect of persistent deficits on monetary policy. It would appear that an anti-inflationary policy pursued in the context of a permanent deficit cannot persist. Fiscal policy appears under the circumstances as the longer-run determinant of monetary policy and a crucial characteristic of the ultimately prevailing monetary regime. It follows that no reliable change in monetary regime is really feasible without an associated change in the long-run fiscal regime. This argument introduced a new focus and attention to fiscal policy.

The evolution of questions, issues, and analysis over the past nineteen years since the "war between the radio stations" (FM, AM, DM) in the *American Economic Review* (1965) justified in the judgment of the Conference organizers, and also in my judgment, an appraisal of our intellectual positions. My paper is addressed to this task. It offers essentially a survey over major strands of the discussion evolving over the past twenty years. This survey remains somewhat selective even within its confined range of macroeconomic issues. Neither does it cultivate a "neutral" account. It involves interpretations and evaluations referring to aspects of arguments advanced or to dimensions of the analysis that require more attention.

The first section covers the fiscalist–monetarist debate of the late sixties and early seventies. It evaluates the empirical work bearing on the central questions addressed at the time. The following section attends to the range of issues raised by the neoclassical-cum-rational-expectations approach. Section 4 examines a number of problems recently associated with transitory and permanent deficits. The last section assesses the consequences of our intellectual position with respect to fiscal policymaking and the choice of fiscal regime.

2 The Fiscalist Issue

2.1 The Fiscalist – Monetarist Debate

2.1.1. The Evolving Theme

The debate emerged gradually in the late 1950s and was fully focused at the time of the conference on monetary theory organized by the National Bureau of Economic Research in Pittsburgh (1963). The intellectual state was conditioned at the time by the critical response of an increasing number of economists to the prevailing Keynesian analysis of fiscal and monetary policy. The core of Keynes's *General Theory* presents a real theory of a low-level output trap. It is supplemented by a real theory of business cycles. The central theme emphasizes the operation of two fundamental failures embedded in economic organizations relying on markets for the social coordination of activities. These market failures center on the stock market, as a guide for investment activities, and the labor market. They severely damage the ability of a market system to function as an instrument of social coordination. The peculiar characteristics of the stock market shape, so the story goes, a price behavior randomly related to the social function of rational resource allocation. These characteristics also suspend a reliable feedback from the saving–consumption nexus to an investment decision. Persistent mass unemployment suggested, moreover, to Keynes that potentially beneficial transactions remained suspended. Such potentialities are expressed by an excess of the labor suppliers' marginal utility of the wage product over the marginal disutility of labor. The market process apparently fails to provide a sufficient range of coordinating mechanisms.

These basic failures embedded in the structure of the economic process could not be offset by increased wage flexibility or monetary manipulations. Such endeavors would produce, at most, temporary deviations from the low-level output trap (Meltzer, 1981). A more powerful instrument was required to move the economy out of such doldrums and push it nearer to full employment. Fiscal policy seemed to offer the instrumental opportunities needed for Keynes's purpose. The underlying analysis suggested that fiscal policy could be shaped to influence directly aggregate expenditures and to affect indirectly, via the multiplier, the level of consumption expenditures and total output and employment.

The message infiltrated the profession with some variations on the theme. Alvin Hansen's secular stagnation centered on the basic real phenomenon subsequently formalized by the "Keynesian cross." This formulation reenforced the "fiscalist thesis" emerging from the Keynesian analysis, a thesis that attributed dominant positive and normative significance to fiscal policy as an instrument conditioning the level of output and employment. Sir John Hicks's reinterpretation in terms of the IS/LM ("islamic") paradigm complicated the pattern somewhat with its inclusion of a feedback via asset markets and portfolio adjustments. But the assumption of accommodating monetary policy or the prevailing view attributing low-interest elasticity to aggregate demand and high-interest elasticity to money demand yielded a close approximation to the implications of the "Keynesian cross." The professional literature of the late forties and fifties reveals this state very clearly. The article on monetary policy by Seltzer (1945) in the late 1940s effectively reflects the dominant intellectual mood. The book *Policies to Combat Depressions* (1956) based on a conference organized by the National Bureau of Economic Research expresses the basic theme. It concentrated fully and only on fiscal policy. The slowly evolving flood of textbooks conveyed the same message and so did, to mention another example, Tinbergen's book *On the Theory of Economic Policy* (1952).

The existing professional state must be clearly perceived in order to understand the subsequent intellectual developments. Doubts and reservations bearing on the central underlying theme of market failure never vanished entirely. The victorious sweep of the fiscalist thesis did not silence some expressions of doubt. Clark Warburton pursued the classic program of monetary analysis, offering a substantive alternative to the Keynesian vision.

Milton Friedman (1952) reenforced the questioning with an examination of the comparative role of government expenditures and monetary movements in three wartime experiences. The classic research program rejected the market-failure approach introduced by Keynes as a serious misinterpretation of market economics and of specific events observed in the 1930s. Substantial doubts about the role assigned to fiscal policy by the Keynesian position was unavoidable under the circumstances. The evolution of monetarist ideas thus continues essentially a classical program. These ideas reject the dominance of fiscal policy as a determinant of both short- and long-run, aggregate, nominal or real demands. At least some strands of the analysis acknowledge an effect of fiscal policy on short- and long-term *nominal* demands, and a short-term effect on real demand for output, but they deny any effect on long-term aggregate real demand. However, all strands attribute to monetary shocks substantial short- and long-term nominal effects and a definite short-term real effect. This basic position was, however, sharpened with a specific "impulse hypothesis" incorporated into monetarist analysis. This position reversed the Keynesian thesis and assigned a comparatively dominant role to monetary impulses within the general pattern described above. This thesis of a comparative dominance was not advanced as an "ontological proposition." It was interpreted to reflect simultaneously the response characteristics of the economic mechanism and the historical circumstances expressed by the relative magnitude and variability of fiscal and monetary impulses. The dominant impulse hypothesis maintained by the monetarists was thus quite sensitively dependent on the choice of financial regime.

2.1.2. The Empirical Work
The professional state characterizing the earlier postwar period outlined in the previous paragraph needs to be fully appreciated in order to assess the empirical work initiated in the late 1950s by Milton Friedman and David Meiselman. This article motivated critical responses by Donald Hester (1964), Ando and Modigliani (1965), and De Prano and Mayer (1965). Another round of empirical discussion was unleashed by Leonall Andersen and Jerry Jordan (1968) with an article in the *Review* published by the Federal Reserve Bank of St. Louis. Other members (Michael Keran and Keith Carlson) of the St. Louis Fed's staff extended the discussion and so did Keynesian critics from the Board's staff in Washington (de Leeuw and Kalchbrenner 1969) and the Brookings Institution (Goldfeld and Blinder 1972).

Harry Johnson (1971) asserted in the early 1970s that the empirical discussion of the 1960s was fundamentally flawed and methodologically inadequate. Tobin (1981) recently repeated Johnson's assessment. The two authors thus convey an impression that little, if anything at all, can be learned from the first round of discussion about the role and significance of fiscal policy. Neither one of the authors, however, provides any references or offers any arguments or clues supporting their contention. The methodological objections raised at the time by Keynesians were apparently accepted at face value without further examination. It is noteworthy, therefore, that Keynesian critics justified their rather categorically formulated conclusions in terms of the same methodological procedure. An array of objections advanced with a categorical import frequently involved, moreover, nothing beyond invocations of possibly alternative, but unassessed, hypotheses. A retrospective appraisal from the vantage point of our current state of discussion may be useful for our purposes.

Consider first the basic purpose of the empirical work. It was addressed to a preliminary assessment of a wide and influential class of macroeconomic hypotheses. An array of formulations filling textbooks and conveyed to the academic world with a sense of empirical relevance implied the dominant significance of fiscal policy and the irrelevance of monetary policy in shaping the evolution of output and nominal magnitudes. These implications were also mirrored by many policy statements supplied to the public arena. These broad statements about the nature of the economic process were the subject of a first round of searching investigation.

The examination, guided by the dominant underlying theme, essentially addressed a basic *class* of Keynesian theories. The class was determined by the specification of the income variable Y, the autonomous expenditure variable A, and the linearity constraint. These specifications yielded the induced magnitude defined by $I = Y - A$ and the reduced forms $Y = \alpha + \beta A + \epsilon$ or $I = \gamma + \delta A + v$. A wide range of specific theories formulated with any given definition of Y and A yields the specific reduced forms. Changes in the definition of Y and A modify the relevant class under consideration. The dependence of the definition of I on the definitions of Y and A is crucial in this context. This requirement was occasionally violated by some authors. This basic class was contrasted with a "quantity-theory" of the form $Y = \alpha + bM + \mu$ or $I = c + dM + w$. The "simple" K-class implies that β and δ are significantly positive, whereas b and d are zero. The "simple" version of the quantity-theory asserts the opposite.

The investigation extended beyond the basic class of income–expenditure theories. They included classes defined by the reduced forms $Y = \alpha + \beta A + \gamma M + \epsilon$ or $I = a + bA + cM + \mu$. These formulations subsume all standard versions constructed in accordance with the "islamic" paradigm. The underlying theme to be assessed implies that β dominates γ (or b dominates c) in significance.

The empirical assessment exploited both versions of the reduced form. The I-form offered a useful check on the Y-form. The latter produces a biased estimate of the A-coefficient due to the implicit correlations between Y and A, which would yield an apparently significant coefficient estimate for A even in the absence of any relevant systematic connection between I and A.

A remarkable fact emerged once the investigation was under way. We seemed to have been conditioned to assume that we understood what Keynesian theory meant. But such understanding required that the profession agree on the specification of autonomous expenditures. The investigations, however, revealed a remarkable disarray and confusion. The critical comments advanced by Friedman and Meiselman (1965, p. 73) in this respect are still worth noting today:

> We and our critics all used the same measures (for the money stock) without much ado. The contrast with "autonomous expenditures" could hardly be sharper. Among us, we have produced more measures than there are critics. We settled on one; AM on a different one, which is the sum of two separable components; DM, after running "basic test . . . on 20 different, but not unreasonable, definitions of autonomous expenditures" settle on two, but also carry two others along for the ride; Hester came up with four measures that only partly overlap the others. And all of us harbor serious doubts about the measures we settled on. However useful "autonomous expenditures" may be as a theoretical construct, it is still far from having any generally accepted empirical counterpart.

Another passage in Friedman and Meiselman's comments also deserves our current attention. It cautions against the potential evaluation of Keynesian theory by choosing larger portions of Y as A:

> By our model, we in effect treated the income–expenditure theory as saying: if you know from other sources what is going to happen to roughly one-tenth of Y or N, then the multiplier analysis will tell you (or give you an estimate of) what will happen to the other nine-tenths. AM converts the model into one that says: if you know from other sources what is going to happen to nearly half of Y or over one-third of N, then the multiplier analysis will tell you what will happen to the other half of Y or two-thirds of N. DM's two models treat only slightly less of total income as autonomous. If AM and DM were to continue along this line of "improving" the model by having it predict a smaller and smaller percentage of income more and more accurately they would soon arrive at the point where it is predicting nothing – perfectly! In the old saw, with such friends, the income–expenditure theory hardly needs any enemies.

These issues found little attention at the time. They did reveal, however, that the sweep of Keynesian ideas, in spite of a vast literature and influential textbooks, had not been translated into a useful empirical theory. The strong assertions conveyed by the basic core of the income–expenditure approach, which frequently spilled over into categorical policy statements, were thus shown to have little substantive foundation.

2.1.3. The Nature of Objections and Critique

An evaluation of the first-round discussion especially needs to consider the major objections advanced that possibly influenced Johnson's judgment, which was repeated by Tobin. Ando and Modigliani (1965), for instance, objected vehemently against the "single equation–single variable approach." They also criticized the use of "simple models" in lieu of "sophisticated models." Ando and Modigliani emphasized, in particular, at a later round of discussions that the regressions applied in the investigations under consideration were demonstrably inadequate to assess fiscalist propositions on the basis of observations controlled by a world conforming to a specific, large, econometric model (1976). Closely associated with these points was the accusation (or condemnation) that the procedure chosen reflected a "reduced form methodological commitment." This "simplistic" commitment was juxtaposed to the "sophistication" of a "structural" model. Authors were also inclined to criticize on grounds of "grievous misspecification." Ando and Modigliani, moreover, declared categorically that the examinations executed by Friedman and Meiselman are "basically irrelevant for the purpose of assessing the *empirical* uselessness of the income–expenditure framework." Disputes arose over the choice of exogenous variables. The other party's choices were naturally wrong, most particularly if one's own selection yielded approximately the desired estimate. Lastly, one author (Hester) asserted that "theory or intuition" was necessary to specify (correctly?) "the components of autonomous expenditures." This argument could, of course, be extended to the choice of exogenous variables.

These objections involve two important issues and reflect the confusions frequently emerging in the interpretation of the profession's empirical work. The first issue addressed by the critique emphasizes the "reduced form methodology," the "single-equation–single-variable" fallacy, or the propensity for simple, in lieu of, (more realistic?) "sophisticated" models. These objections essentially fail to recognize the rather specific and limited purpose of the investigations. This failure is especially visible in the quote drawn from the comments made by Ando and Modigliani. The "battery of tests" undertaken by Friedman and Meiselman and also the subsequent work contributed by the staff of the Federal Reserve Bank of St. Louis were not immediately directed to an assessment of the income–expenditure *framework*. A direct assessment of such a framework is logically impossible. Such assessments pertain to specific hypotheses or classes of hypotheses formulated in accordance with general criteria characterizing the framework. An assessment of the framework emerges ultimately from the cognitive fate of the hypotheses it generates. It would thus be clearly understood that none of the critical investigations was addressed to the framework. Previous passages emphasized that the assessment was directed at *particular classes* of hypotheses yielding strong propositions about the comparative significance of autonomous expenditures and at least potentially about fiscal policy. And once more, the prevalent intellectual state with its underlying theme fully justified this limited purpose – that is, limited relative to the general framework and its possible translation into classes of hypotheses.

The other three objections associated with the first issue involve different aspects or verbalizations of the same problem. The attribution of a methodological legislation insisting, as a matter of principle, on a reduced-form procedure reflects a pervasive misunderstanding about the logic of the procedure characterized above. The statements under examination pertaining to relative dominance of A do not bear *specifically* on any *particular* structure; that is, they do not characterize or single out in a detailed fashion a particular hypothesis. They consistently describe a whole class of hypotheses and actually pertain to *properties of the class*. The most efficient procedure, under the circumstances, for systematic assessment of such statements uses the reduced form as a test statement. The properties of the reduced form reflect the properties of the class of hypotheses under examination. Structural estimation of a single member of the class is inefficient and essentially uninformative for the purpose. No methodological legislation is thus involved.

The use of a single equation with a single independent variable should now be clear. It was the appropriate choice for an assessment of the core class. It did not represent a single equation *model* or a disposition to favor simple, as against sophisticated, models. The "single equation with single variable" was the appropriate choice for an evaluation of a class of hypotheses seriously presented in textbooks and class teachings. The objection thus either misses the point or really tells us that all the chapters and classes elaborating the Keynesian cross or widely used versions of the "islamic" framework should be clearly labeled as irrelevant pastimes without any use for the justification of any policy statements. This would also involve a major separation from Keynes, Hansen, and an influential literature controlling undergraduate teaching during the 1950s and in our hinterlands still today.

A second issue embedded in the discussion bears on a pervasive confusion between logical issues and psychological effects. Our discussions frequently suffer under a disposition to *reject* an argument or hypothesis simply on the grounds that one is capable of formulating an alternative. Such ability offers, of course, no information about the cognitive status of the hypothesis under consideration. Objections adducing "misspecifications" are thus, by themselves, an empty gesture. They may be interpreted, however, as defining implicitly a program of further research. But the formulation of such a program possesses, by itself, no evidential value with respect to the initial hypothesis.

Some authors found that Friedman and Meiselman or Andersen and Jordan had committed some serious misspecifications. Ando and

Modigliani developed, in particular, a "more sophisticated model" within the general "income–expenditure framework." They concluded from this construction that the evaluations made by Friedman and Meiselman were useless and irrelevant. We note first that the "laborious battery of tests" executed by Friedman and Meiselman and others is indeed irrelevant with respect to a wide class of hypotheses subsumable under the general income–expenditure paradigm. This critique would be properly addressed to *general* conclusions about the role of fiscal policy drawn from the empirical work actually executed. Friedman and Meiselman and Andersen and Jordan carefully avoided such sweeping conclusions. Their evaluations were made relative to a specific class of "Keynesian-type" models and their significance is conditioned by this context. The evaluations would still be correct but irrelevant and useless if the class of hypotheses under consideration was demonstrably neglected, disregarded, and without any influence on the profession's policy thinking. But the latter condition hardly describes the professional situation of the earlier postwar period.

Hester's argument pertaining to the choice of autonomous magnitudes deserved special attention in this context; he suggested that theory or intuition determine this choice. But this choice determines the precise nature of the empirical theory. There exists no such theory involving a definite empirical context before this choice is made. The notion of a "theory" guiding the choice alluded to by Hester refers at best to a formal structure linking variables with generic names. The admissible range of semantic rules connecting variables via measurement procedures with observations still includes many diverse possibilities. Whatever a priori notions of "pre-empirical theory" or intuition we exploit for the specification of crucial magnitudes yield, however, no evidence of the empirical validity of the choice made. Neither Hester's notion of a "theory" nor any intuition can judge the empirically relevant choices. The suggestion fundamentally misconceives the nature of scientific procedures and confuses the context of search for an hypothesis with the context of evaluation on the basis of critical observation.

2.1.4. The Exogeneity Issue

Hester's issue naturally generalizes to the specification of exogenous variables. Objections addressed to the selection or construction of exogenous magnitudes form a standard procedure of mutual criticism. But once again the execution of a set of regressions with more "desirable" coefficient patterns based on alternative choices of exogenous variables expresses a rival hypothesis but offers per se no relevant evidence discriminating between the alternative hypotheses. Reliance on the correlation coefficient must be carefully examined in these matters. Such reliance is quite appropriate for the evaluation of the core class addressed by Friedman and Meiselman. The hypothesis of comparative dominance implies systematic differences among correlation coefficients. We note in contrast that the eventual observation of higher correlation under *alternative* choices of monetary and fiscal variables possesses no evidential value discriminating between the selections. Such value can ony exist relative to a specified class of hypotheses that *implies* statements about correlation patterns. This would require restriction on all the parameters, including a full description of stochastic properties under the alternative definitions. The observation of a comparatively high sample correlation and more "desirable" coefficient patterns under alternative exogeneity specifications in the absence of an initially formulated hypothesis therefore contains no discriminating cognitive significance. It forms at best the initial step in the formulation of an hypothesis still to be subsequently assessed against new data.

The exogeneity issue was further elaborated by Stephen M. Goldfeld and Alan S. Blinder (1972). The two authors explored in great and careful detail the implications of endogenous stabilization actions bearing on coefficient estimations in reduced forms. Their investigation is anchored by the reduced-form regressions used by Andersen and Jordan and expressed by eqn (7.1). The symbols F and M refer to fiscal and monetary

$$y = k + \alpha F + \beta M + \epsilon \qquad (7.1)$$

variables, and ϵ is a random term. It is, of course, well known that any correlation between F and M and ϵ as a result of an endogenous policy regime produces biased and inconsistent estimators of α and β. Goldfeld and Blinder pursue the matter well beyond this general statement and impose some structure on the nature of the correlations. This structure reflects a variety of assumptions about the nature of endogenous stabilization policies. The endogenous policy variables can be represented by a sum of a nonstochastic magnitude, which can be neglected for our purposes, and a stochastic term

$$F = \frac{\epsilon_F}{\alpha}, \quad M = \frac{\epsilon_M}{\beta},$$

where $\epsilon_F = \epsilon + u_F$, $\epsilon_M = \epsilon + u_m$, the variance of ϵ is σ^2, the variance of u_F is $\gamma^2 \sigma^2$ and the variance of u_M is $\delta^2 \sigma^2$. The u-terms reflect the forecasting ability of fiscal and monetary authorities exercised in the context of their stabilizing endeavors. The parameters γ and δ represent the authorities' forecasting ability. Lower values of γ and δ mean higher forecasting quality. Similar or coordinated forecasting may produce a correlation ρ between u_F and u_M. These assumptions imply the following probability limit for the ratios $\hat{\alpha}/\alpha$ and $\hat{\beta}/\beta$ of OLS estimates of the reduced form (7.1) to the true parameters

$$\frac{\hat{\alpha}}{\alpha} = 1 + \frac{\delta(\rho\alpha - \delta)}{\Delta}, \quad \frac{\hat{\beta}}{\beta} = 1 + \frac{\gamma(\rho\delta - \gamma)}{\Delta},$$

$$\Delta = \gamma^2 + \delta^2 - \alpha\rho\gamma\delta + \gamma^2\delta^2(1-\rho^2) > 0.$$

The three forecasting parameters associated with endogenous policy reactions clearly determine the outcome. Almost any combination of biases can be produced by shifting patterns of ρ, γ, and δ. With $\rho = 0$, δ large, and γ small, fiscal policy may appear to be insignificant in reduced-form regressions of eqn (7.1). An excellent stabilization record of the fiscal authorities supplemented with a poor record of monetary authorities could explain the Andersen–Jordan results even against the background of a substantial α-coefficient.

The authors' general result is confirmed by elaborations of the argument. These elaborations include erroneous assumptions about the multipliers made by the authorities and lagged policy responses to serially correlated ϵ-disturbances. They extend to the case of "policy interaction" where one authority's response takes into account the other agency's behavior. The argument also covers a more general model with exogenous variables added to eqn (7.1). All thes cases enlarge the range for potential bias beyond the initial parameters ρ, γ, δ.

Goldfeld and Blinder supplement their analytic investigation of statistic implications associated with endogenous policy responses with a Monte Carlo study. They use an econometric model originally published by Moroney and Mason to generate data sets on the variables incorporated. These data sets were applied to structural and reduced-form estimations. Structural estimations proceeded with and without inclusion of reaction functions describing the policymakers' endogenous responses. It would appear that structural estimates are comparatively little affected by non-recognition of endogenous policy responses. Direct estimation of the system's (exclusive of reaction functions) reduced form produces, in contrast, seriously biased multiplier estimates.

We should hardly quibble with the correctness of the argument advanced by Goldfeld and Blinder. Endogenous policy responses can yield seriously biased estimates of reduced forms exemplified by eqn (7.1). The meaning of this result must be carefully assessed, however. The authors usefully sharpen our awareness for some important qualifications applicable to the empirical work which emerged in the context of the "fiscalist debate." The results hold for classes of hypotheses recognizing an actual state of comparative exogeneity with respect to policy variables. Goldfeld and Blinder offer no argument or evidence bearing on the crucial issues of *whether, when* and *how* "policy was endogenous." The correctness of their analysis does not, unfortunately, establish its relevance. We still need to judge the occurrence and nature of endogenous policy responses. It is important to understand, however, that judgments based purely on standard regression analysis can seriously mislead us. We also need to examine carefully the institutional arrangements and explore special events in the manner of Friedman and Schwartz (1963). Institutional information may often tell us what regressions, if any, are advisable. A "mechanical" linking of policy variables with a

GNP gap hardly conforms to institutional situations prevailing over most periods or in most countries. The data used in regression estimates of eqn (7.1) by various researchers covered a variety of historical episodes and also different countries. One would conjecture that the existing institutional differences generate widely different endogenous responses. A consistent pattern of statistical results over periods and countries deserves more serious considerations under the circumstances, even with full acknowledgment of the argument advanced by Goldfeld and Blinder. It is very doubtful for instance that past episodes of US fiscal and monetary history exhibit a pronounced and approximately uniform stabilization policy. The available information about the Fed's strategy and tactical procedure suggests, moreover, the operation of a major random process affecting monetary growth over quarterly periods. This situation may, for all practical purposes, amount to an approximate exogeneity actually emphasized by Goldfeld and Blinder. The political economy of fiscal policy also suggests substantial doubts about the relevant occurrence of an endogenous fixed stabilization policy. "Stabilization" may be a useful rhetorical device addressed to academics and the public arena. But fiscal policy is dominated by other considerations associated with the incentive structure characterizing the existing policy institutions. This incentive structure implies that "fiscal policy" is dominated by redistributional interests with little substantive attention to "stabilization" per se. We should expect under the circumstances that regressions expressing fiscal reaction functions remain poorly defined and unstable over time. We may, of course, encounter situations justifying a substantial suspicion that endogenous policy responses do occur. But the implications with respect to estimates of eqn (7.1) are obscured until we know more about the nature of endogenous policy patterns. Information about occurrence only establishes that we need to be cautious in interpreting the results. But Goldfeld and Blinder still enriched our discussion. This contribution warns us essentially to extend the empirical work to as many different periods and situations involving different institutional arrangements as possible. This research strategy seems more promising than an approach relying on explicit statistical reaction functions of the usual kind embedded in a large structural model.

2.1.5. Some Problems of Statistical Theory

A retrospective evaluation guided by an interest to learn from the previous discussions for our present purposes cannot avoid an application of standards – criteria for procedures developed subsequent to the discussion under examination. Two aspects bearing on statistical procedures and matters of statistical theory require our attention. Most of the discussants used level data; Ando and Modigliani and De Prano and Mayer used data only in this form. Friedman and Meiselman also explored first differences, whereas Andersen and Jordan used only first differences. The proper choice between these alternative procedures poses a subtle but very important and widely neglected issue even today. The choice depends sensitively on the error structure in the formulated regression (Plosser and Schwert 1978) or the nonstationarity of the variables (Meese and Singleton 1982). Plosser and Schwert compare the problems posed by over- and under-differencing of data in regression analysis. They explore, in particular, the asymmetric effect of over- and under-differencing on statistical inferences. They show that over-differencing produces a regression with an error term controlled by an $MA(1)$ process with a unit coefficient, whereas under-differencing yields a regression with a nonstationary random term. Over-differencing still allows, under the circumstances, reliable estimation and inferences. Under-differencing, in contrast, poses a serious problem. The sample distribution of the estimator does not possess finite moments. No inferences are possible in this case.

The authors elaborate the general problem with the aid of several examples bearing quite directly on our issue. The first example explores a regression $\log y = \alpha + \beta \log m + \epsilon$, with y representing nominal income and m the money stock. The regression is estimated in level form, in levels modified with a time trend, with Cochrane–Orcutt adjustment, and also in first and second differences. The last four procedures yield essentially the same estimate for β. The first estimate derived from level data is separated by more than two standard errors from the estimate obtained on the basis of first differences. Most interesting is a comparison of the variances computed for the error term in the regressions. Over-differencing would imply that the variance associated with the first difference is twice the variance of the residual in the level regression. Under-differencing implies, in contrast, that the residual variance in the level regression exceeds the corresponding variance in the first difference. This implication is confirmed by the estimates.

The authors contrast this case with the "quantity theory of sunspots" expressed by the regression $\log y = \alpha + \beta \log s + \epsilon$, where s measures the accumulated sum of sunspots. The same five estimation procedures, previously mentioned, were carried out. The results based on level data convey the impression of a significant relation with a substantial correlation and a unit multiplier. The first difference yields a radically different result. The "multiplier" β-coefficient collapses to nonsignificance with a standard error almost equal to the coefficient estimate. The estimate derived from the second difference collapses even further and is hardly distinguishable from zero. The residual variance in the level regression is, moreover, almost 13 times the residual variance in first differences.

Lastly, the authors examine the data (A and M – in logs, however) used by Friedman and Meiselman. They compare the regressions $\log C = \alpha + \beta \log M + \epsilon$ with $\log C = \gamma + \delta \log A + \partial$. The results are remarkably different. The five estimation procedures yield the same results for β. The differences are not statistically significant when evaluated in terms of the standard error of β computed from first differences. Once again the residual variance of the level regression substantially exceeds this variance of the first differences. This pattern of residual variances occurs even more emphatically in the case of autonomous expenditures. The contrast offered by this regression appears, however, most particularly in the pattern of δ-estimates associated with the five estimation procedures. The coefficient collapses from 1.08 in level data to 0.14 in first differences and 0.09 in second differences. The differences in estimates are statistically highly significant. *All* estimates remain, however, significantly different from zero.

This analysis with the examples immediately related to our problem clearly reveals the danger associated with under-differencing and the misleading inferences obtainable under these circumstances. The results developed by Plosser and Schwert suggest a definite strategy for empirical investigations, at least in our range of problems. In the usual absence of sufficient information about the error structure we need to estimate both in terms of level data (unadjusted and adjusted for possible serial correlation in residuals), first differences, and, possibly, even second differences. The resulting pattern of residual variances and coefficient estimates determines our evaluation. A residual variance of level regressions substantially higher than the corresponding variance associated with first differences suggests the relevant application of first differences. The regression obtained from level data should, moreover, be considered seriously suspect whenever the estimated regression coefficients substantially collapse for first and second differences. It follows thus that the results presented by Ando and Modigliani or De Prano and Mayer yield little information until further reevaluation.

A possibly more basic problem was raised by Meese and Singleton (1982) and Wasserfallen (1985). The standard assumptions for regression analysis are satisfied for stationary stochastic variables and nonstochastic independent variables. The latter case hardly applies to a relevant analysis of data cast up by social processes. But nonstationary stochastic data pose a serious problem for estimation and inferences. It would appear that consistent estimates of a regression require that the diagonal terms of the covariance matrix of independent *exogenous* variables converge to infinity with the sample size. Alternatively, it seems sufficient that the independent (and exogenous) vector variable be controlled by a *finite* autoregressive process. These conditions offer, however, no basis for inferences. More structure must be imposed in order to derive an asymptotic sampling distribution. The weakest condition on the moment matrix of independent variables seems to have been formulated, according to Meese and Singleton, by Grenander (1954): "These conditions preclude exponential growth of any variable. . . Borderline non-stationarity (i.e., unit root) is allowed if regressors are fixed or strictly exogenous." Meese and Singleton emphasize that an independent error with finite variance is not a sufficient condition for asymptotic inferences. Quite generally, conditions on the regressors required for deriving inferences pose a troublesome issue. In the absence of good grounds supporting the relevant application of asymptotic distribution theory to inferences derived from nonstationary data, we may possibly obtain estimates but no judgment or evaluation. This argument reenforces the conclusion obtained from Plosser and Schwert's investigation: It seems advisable in the case of nonstationary data to derive the inferences from suitable transformation into stationary series. The neglect of this problem lowers the relevance of some empirical work presented in the "fiscalist" debate.

2.1.6. Some General Conditions
We should emphasize first that Johnson's indictment, recently repeated by Tobin after more than ten years, simply has no foundation. It reflects a somewhat casual misunderstanding of the nature of the argument. Friedman and Meiselman explicitly cautioned the reader that this assessment was quite provisional. It was also a definitely limited examination, and so was the work undertaken at the Federal Reserve Bank of St. Louis. The limitation is defined by the class of hypotheses implicitly addressed by the tests used. There do exist classes of hypotheses that cannot be subsumed under the assessments carried out. Friedman and Meiselman properly stressed therefore that their results are "not decisive." They are certainly not decisive with respect to the general paradigm and the general idea of fiscal effects on aggregate demand. But the tests were properly formulated and executed *relative* to the class of hypotheses considered. A reservation should be entered, however, with respect to the use of under-differenced and nonstationary variables. We should also note the reservation advanced by Goldfeld and Blinder. This reservation simply suggests some further examination in order to take account of potential effects of endogenous policy reactions.

The discussion also brought forth a perennial problem confronting our empirical work. The choice of exogenous variables forms an important component in the construction of an hypothesis (or class of hypotheses). The development of statistical analysis has sharpened somewhat our understanding and offered approaches to this issue. One lesson we should emphatically learn in this context emphasizes that we need to address more careful attention to the admissible interpretation of our work. Our imaginative invention of alternative specifications or constructions of exogenous magnitudes offers per se no rational grounds for the rejection of other specifications and choices. We need either (more or less) direct evidence bearing on the exogeneity of the variables concerned or to depend on the evaluation of the hypothesis as a whole. Correlation statements may appear as relevant test statements in this context, provided, however, as in the case of the core class examined by Friedman and Meiselman, the hypothesis under consideration *implies* comparative correlation statements. Comparison of correlations in the absence of such definite implications is meaningless and without any evidential value.

The substantive content of the discussion contributed in retrospect to some clarification. The hard Keynesian position dismissing monetary conditions was unanimously discarded. The relevance of monetary conditions became generally recognized. Substantial issues remained, however, in this range. Some Keynesians argued that the money stock or monetary growth exerts "permanent" (long-lasting) real effects. Monetarists confine, in contrast, (temporary) real effects to monetary accelerations (or decelerations). More important for our immediate purpose was the general recognition that fiscal policy did probably modify to some extent nominal aggregate demand for output. Substantial differences concerning orders of magnitude and persistence of real effects remained.

There occurred also a subtle but interesting shift with the Keynesian paradigm. This shift modified the meaning of "fiscal dominance." We observe well into the 1950s an argument assigning a steep slope to the IS curve and a flat slope to the LM curve. This assignment was justified in terms of a borrowing-cost interpretation for the interest elasticity of aggregate demand (Brunner, 1971). There clearly emerged a revision of this position during the 1960s. The relative slopes shifted sufficiently to offer monetary conditions a significant leverage. The inherited sense of "fiscal dominance" unavoidably disappeared. The appearance of the assignment problem and the policy mix analysis reveals this change. But the modified Keynesian analysis produced a new sense of "fiscal dominance" visible in the "Economic Reports" of the Kennedy–Johnson administration. Both monetary and fiscal policies were recognized to influence real magnitudes. Both policies were thus in principle applicable to stabilization purposes. Monetary policy was, however, judged to concentrate the social cost of stabilization policies on a small segment of the economy (housing). Fiscal policy, in contrast, spread these costs more "equitably." Fiscal policy was also judged to operate "directly," in contrast to the "indirect" effects of monetary policy, and, consequently, with shorter lags. These considerations determined that fiscal policy was proposed as the active component of a stabilization program with monetary policy assigned an essentially accommodating role defined in terms of an interest-rate strategy. This position was sensitively conditioned by the underlying paradigm summarized by the IS/LM approach and its economic interpretation. This paradigm with its confining view about the nature of the "transmission mechanism" remained, of course, on center stage in the dispute between "Keynesians" and "monetarists."

2.2 The Asset Market Effects of Fiscal Policy and the Stability of the System

The discussion covered in the previous paragraphs addressed the comparatively immediate output-market effects of fiscal policy. Neither Keynesians nor monetarists had at this stage integrated the ramifications of deficit financing via asset-market responses explicitly into their analysis. Attention focused by the early 1970s on the government's budget constraint. The relation between fiscal policy and asset-market responses generated by the mode of deficit financing and the resulting interaction between asset markets and output markets became the subject of further examination (Christ, 1979; Silber, 1970; Blinder and Solow, 1974, 1976; Infante and Stein, 1976; Brunner and Meltzer, 1972b, 1976; McCallum 1981). The participants in this discussion agreed that fiscal policy (including especially the effects of distortionary taxes and the *structure* of expenditures) affects actual output, normal output, price level, and real rates of interest. There remained, however, substantial variations in the details of the analysis and probably the order of magnitudes involved. The question pursued was addressed to the real and nominal consequences implicit in fiscal decisions beyond the effects attributable to (global) expenditures and taxes per se.

My summary of the issue exploits a scheme used in various papers by Brunner and Meltzer. The scheme involves an interaction between four lines represented in figure 7.1. The vertical line describes normal output. Some strands of analysis recognized the dependence of the line's position on taxes and most particularly on longer-run portfolio adjustments between government securities and real capital. The *bbe* line represents the balanced budget equation. It describes thus the locus of price level and output combinations (p,y) that satisfy a balanced budget. The position of the line depends on real government expenditures, the stock of outstanding debt held by the public, and a tax parameter. The slope of the line expresses the nonhomogeneity of the deficit function due to progressive taxation, yielding a "bracket creep." Under proportional taxation the *bbe* line would be vertical. The *d*-line presents a pseudodemand curve to be understood in a semireduced sense. The line summarizes the locus of all pairs (p,y) that satisfy simultaneously, for any given set of other variables, output- and asset-market equations. Lastly, the *s*-line describes the "structural" supply function. The position of this line moves with the expected price level, the stock of real capital, and technological progress.

The initial position in the diagram shows a state of full stock and normal output equilibrium. The short-run flow equilibrium determined by the interaction between pseudodemand and supply yields a state on the normal output line that simultaneously produces a balanced budget. Now consider an increase in real government expenditures (or a lower tax parameter). This

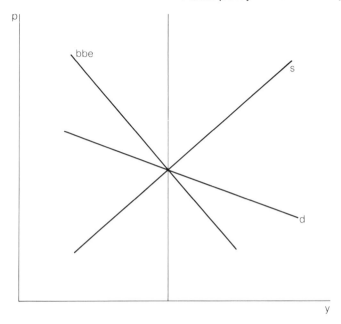

Figure 7.1   Budget, price level, demand, and output interactions.

raises the balanced budget line to the position bbe_1, and the pseudodemand line to d_1 (see figure 7.2). The fiscal stimulus thus immediately raises output, price level, and interest rates. It also produces a deficit expressed by the dis÷ tance of the *bbe* line from point A, which describes the new flow equilibrium. Suppose for the moment that the deficit is financed with a new issue of government bonds. The resulting increase in the stock of securities and interest rates pushes the *bbe* line further upward along the (vertical) normal output line. The net effect of a bond-financed deficit thus depends crucially on the interaction between asset markets and output markets. This interaction determines the movement of the pseudodemand curve relative to the balanced budget line induced by the fiscal action. The result depends, within the context of the IS/LM framework, on the relative magnitude of the vertical shifts imposed on the two curves. A comparatively larger upward shift of the IS curve due to wealth effects induced by the bond issue raises the d-line, whereas a comparatively larger wealth effect operating on the LM curve lowers the line. The Brunner–Meltzer asset-market analysis yields a somewhat more complex pattern modifying the wealth effect with substitution effects between financial and real assets. The absorption of a larger stock of government securities by the asset markets unleashes offsetting influences via interest rates on financial assets and via the asset price of real assets. The net effect thus remains quite ambiguous without constraining

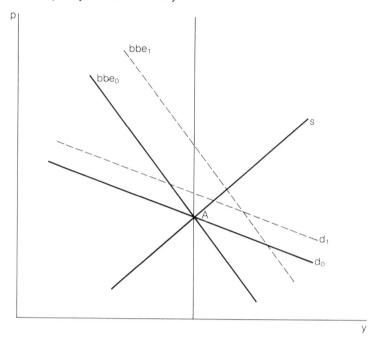

Figure 7.2   Effect of increased government expenditures.

order conditions. Neither argument thus yields, without specific order constraints, a definite answer. Even a positive response of the *d*-line is not
sufficient, however, for the stability of the stock equilibrium. This stability
requires that the upward shift in the *d*-line caused by deficit finance exceed
the corresponding upward shift of the *bbe*-line. This condition assures that
the *d*-line eventually catches up with the *bbe* line, and the flow equilibrium
produces a balanced budget.

Some variations in the analysis occur at this point. Some authors emphasize the transitory nature of movements along the *s*-curve. The latter will
shift upward in response to adjustments in the expected price level. The final
state of equilibrium will thus tend to the normal output line. But the conditions for stability appear under either the IS/LM or the Brunner–Meltzer
analysis quite unlikely. Instability associated with insufficient non-negative
or even negative responses of the *d*-line appear more likely in the context of
both analytic arguments.

In contrast, consider the case of a deficit financed with new base money.
The *d*-line is definitely raised, whereas the *bbe*-line is not further raised by
the increase in the money stock associated with deficit finance. The stability
of the stock equilibrium is thus ensured under the circumstances. The *d*-line
eventually intersects the *bbe*-line on the vertical. Several aspects should be

noted here. The total effect on the price level (and on output in case the natural rate hypothesis is rejected) is a multiple of the "immediate" effect associated with the flow equilibrium response to a fiscal impulse. The latter is described by the shift of the state point to point A, whereas the final state of stock equilibrium is controlled by the intersection of the budget line and the normal output line. The total effect of a bond-financed deficit is even large in the case where the stability conditions is imposed. This follows from the fact that the *bbe*-line moves during the adjustment processes beyond the position determined by the initial rise in real government expenditures. The total effect thus reflects in both cases the *financial* repercussions of fiscal policy decision.

The implications of the more likely *unstable* bond-financed deficit process deserve some more attention. Carl Christ (1979) emphasized that this result poses a problem for the imposition of a monetary rule. Such a rule confines the proportion of the deficit financed with base money below the critical level, assuring stability of the stock adjustment process, whenever the deficit is sufficiently large. Brunner (1976) and, recently, McCallum (1981) emphasized the (partial) alleviation of the problem produced by economic growth. Such growth moves the flow equilibrium with the normal output line to the right and closes the gap between the state point fixed by the flow equilibrium and a given budget line. For any given normal growth rate there exists an upper limit on the growth of real debt (and thus of the deficit) beyond which economic growth cannot produce stability; that is, the movement of the *bbe*-line to the right exceeds the growth-determined shift of the flow equilibrium. We should also consider that the analysis implies a negative effect of bond-financed deficits on the rate of normal growth via the longer-run adjustments in the stock of real capital.

But deficits beyond the critical level appear substantially more likely today than ten years ago. A low-level monetary growth would thus induce with substantial probability the unstable process above. This process would raise real and nominal interest rates over time and lower the normal rate of real growth. None of these consequences induces within the economic system, according to either type of analysis, any feedbacks eventually terminating the process. However, we need to broaden our vision at this stage and admit the interaction with the political process. The persistent increase in the real debt raises real interest rates and the relative burden of interest payments expressed by the ratio of interest payments to national income. This trend eventually induces rejection of low-level monetary growth in order to moderate the growth in real debt or even lower this stock with the aid of a higher price level. A change in fiscal regime offers an alternative avenue. The crucial conclusion from this stability analysis suggests that a stable noninflationary monetary regime is unlikely to persist in the absence of a *fiscal* regime effectively containing the average deficit. Both monetarist and Keynesian analysis developed at the time implied that the fiscal regime determines the longer-run opportunities of monetary policy. Alternatively, proposals for a *monetary* rule require a supplementary proposal of a *fiscal* rule.

3 The "Neoclassical" Contribution

The last phases of the discussion summarized in the previous section over-lapped with a new thrust in fiscal policy analysis. The "rational expectations revolution" also influenced, beyond the approach to monetary analysis, the analysis of the government's fiscal policy. A series of articles by Robert Barro, beginning in 1978, introduced a "neoclassical vision" into our discussion. The emerging analysis radically changed the economic significance of deficits. Deficits were interpreted similarly to the deviations between *current* income and *current* consumption of private households in the context of an intertemporal allocation. The public debt and its behavior thus reflect the public sector's intertemporal optimization conditioned by the pattern of permanent and transitory government expenditures. But decisions to issue bonds in order to finance expenditures affect, in contrast to both Keynesian and monetarist analyses, neither real interest rates nor the price level nor, even temporarily, output and employment. The stability issue discussed above does not exist under the circumstances. Traditional notions of stabilization thus offer no relevant motivation for public debt policy. This position bearing on deficits and debts does not extend to government expenditures on goods and services and "non-lump-sum" taxation. Budgetary policies expressed by expenditure and tax decisions do exert temporary and permanent real effects. This analysis, most especially developed by Barro (1981a), actually involved aspects of government budgetary operations, which, even if known in a general sense, were long neglected by macro-analysis. Standard macrotheory typically presented the public sector as a sinkhole for goods and services produced by the private sector. Martin Bailey moved beyond this "sinkhole theory" of the government sector and considered the government's supply of goods and services to the private sector. The substitutive or complementary nature of this supply with respect to private consumption and investment may substantially modify the traditional results. Barro (1981b, 1984a) revived Bailey's neglected initiative and also elaborated more carefully the impact of non-lump-sum taxation. He also revived in this context some earlier work by Miller and Upton (1974). The analysis addressed, beyond these aspects, different mechanisms yielding the real effects of budgetary decisions. It shares with monetary analysis an emphasis on wealth and substitution effects, in contrast to the Keynesian reliance on the income multiplier. Its emphasis on perpetual market clearing relative to *all* ongoing shocks differentiates it from both Keynesian and monetarist arguments.

3.1 The "Ricardian Theme"

Barro must be credited for having revived a theme originally considered by Ricardo. The stability analysis examined above assumed that the financial decision between bonds and taxes exerts a permanent real effect. Barro's argument persuasively challenges this position. He emphasizes that the traditional argument neglects to incorporate the future tax liability associated with current borrowing. A careful separation of issues requires, in this context, the assumption of lump-sum taxes. This assumption permits us to isolate the possible effects attributable to financial decision as such without contamination with the real effects of distortionary taxes. The forward-looking behavior emphasized by rational expectations interprets deficit finance essentially as an intertemporal reallocation of taxes. This implies that current deficits, expressed by a new sale of bonds, correspond to a shift of taxes from the present to the future. The present value of the forfeited (current) tax thus equals the present value of the future tax liability. This equality holds under an important assumption introduced by Barro and discussed subsequently. It holds, in particular, whether the bonds issues are maturing at a specified recognized date, according to a contingent state pattern (Chan, 1983), according to a probability pattern over time, or, lastly, whether the bonds are perpetuities.

The "Ricardian argument" requires the formal apparatus of intertemporal budget constraints for both a representative household and government. A first simple argument confines the repayment period of debt to the representative taxpayer's economic horizon. This constraint can be used to demonstrate that the present value of the future (expected) government expenditures plus the inherited government debt are equal to the present value of expected future taxes. Similarly, the household's budget constraint shows that the sum of the present values of expected future consumption and the present value of expected future taxes is equal to the present value of expected future income plus inherited assets. Any temporal reallocation of taxes combined with an unchanged stream of government expenditures produces an equality between current non-tax-financed government expenditures and the present value of future changes in tax liabilities. This result follows from the government's budget constraint. It implies in conjunction with the budget constraint of the representative household that the household's real opportunities are invariant with respect to the deficit. The household's wealth position defined by its present value of consumption remains unaffected and so does the present value of taxes and income. Households find the optimal choice of consumption pattern unchanged under the circumstances. The creation of a deficit thus cannot modify household consumption decisions. Substitution effects induced by distorting incentives are, moreover, excluded by the lump-sum character of taxes. The household's prior optimal consumption plan extends to the new situation, whatever the representative household's utility function may be. The deficit thus induces neither an intertemporal substitution nor a scale effect of consumption. The current deficit is perfectly matched under the circumstances by an increase in household saving. The government sector's dissaving is thus fully offset by additional private saving. The economy's total saving is therefore independent of the government's financial decision. This saving provides the necessary funds to absorb the new bonds into the household's portfolio. Optimal portfolio management determines this link between deficits, household saving, and bond acquisitions as a consequence of rational hedging. With portfolios optimally adjusted in terms of risk–return combinations before the new deficit emerges, households will find it advisable to hedge the expected tax liability by acquiring a corresponding amount of bonds. The optimal portfolio position will thus be maintained. In terms of the Brunner–Meltzer asset-market model, this result implies that the public's net (stock) supply of government securities disappears in the credit-market equation. It follows that variations in the stock of government securities exert no effects on asset markets. Asset prices and interest rates will not be affected. It follows, moreover, with respect to the stability analysis of section 2 that the d-line remains unaffected by the government's debt finance.

The argument establishing the Ricardian thesis is crucially conditioned by the two budget constraints. These constraints involve several important assumptions that decisively determine the conclusions. Barro explored these assumptions in careful detail and argued persuasively their a priori reasonableness as a good approximation to reality. Buiter and Tobin (1978) and Tobin (1980) examined the underlying assumptions with a matching vigor and argued persuasively their a priori unreasonableness as an approach to reality. There is no need to reproduce these excellent discussions here in depth. My comments concentrate on three aspects associated with the intertemporal budget constraints. These aspects bear on the horizon of the representative household, the nature of capital markets, and risks or uncertainties associated with deficit finance.

The simple fact of mortality combined with our knowledge of demographic structure and debt policies destroys the assumption that the representative household's horizon is at least as long as the repayment period of debt associated with a given tax cut. An "infinitely" living household would circumvent this problem for the Ricardian theme. Barro provided a subtle and extensive analysis interpreting this assumption in empirical terms. He introduced the notion of "operative intergenerational bequests and transfers" to link finitely living generations within an infinitely operating household. This is achieved analytically with an ingenious device. The utility of each generation depends on the utility level of the next generation. The implicit nesting of utility functions yields the appearance of an infinitely living decision unit. This does not imply that the consumption of future generations is weighted equally to the present generation's own consumption. Its implication denies, however, the dependence of consumption patterns on age characteristics of life cycle theories. Optimal consumption choices of infinitely living households produce a preferred pattern of intergenerational transfers (in either direction). Any intrusion by the government to modify this pattern via its budgetary operations necessarily fails under the circumstances. Impositions of tax burdens on future generations via a bond-financed deficit induces offsetting transfer of wealth from the present to the future generation financed with the additional current saving produced by the tax cut. The voluntarily determined optimal pattern of intergenerational transfers dominates the outcome and overrides or offsets the government's budgetary operations. The extension to an infinite budget constraint still assures that any cut in current taxes is exactly balanced by the present value of future tax liabilities. A shifting of the tax incidence beyond a mortal man's life span does not change his optimal intertemporal choice. The initial choice prevailing before the intertemporal tax shift remains optimal. This result implies that current tax cuts yield no wealth effects on current consumption or other real variables.

3.2 The Ricardian Theme: Its Qualification

3.2.1. Intergenerational Altruism and Intergenerational Selfishness
The invariance of intergenerational transfers with respect to budgetary operations is crucially conditioned by the assumption of "intergenerational altruism." This assumption justifies the infinite horizon. Consider, in contrast, the opposite assumption, "intergenerational selfishness," combined with the life cycle hypothesis of consumption (Kotlikoff, 1984). The latter hypothesis implies that the marginal propensity to consume increases with age. The assumption of "intergenerational selfishness" reenforces this pattern as older generations plan no bequests under the circumstances. Any transfer between generations modifies in this case aggregate real consumption. In particular, a transfer from the younger to the older generation raises aggregate consumption. A shift in taxes from the old to the young would produce this result. Replacing some current taxes with bonds maturing during the young generation's lifetime after the older generation's death would accomplish the necessary shift. The result emerges with even larger weight whenever the future tax liabilities fall on unborn generations. "Intergenerational selfishness" thus assures that any temporal reallocation associated with a deficit induces intergenerational transfers not "washed out" within an infinite intertemporal budget constraint. The intergenerational transfers are not offset and produce real consequences. They actually modify the relevant budget constraint for each generation.

The difference between the two cases may be conveyed in the following terms. Let the expression

$$A_{i+1} + C_i + T_i = Y_i + A_i$$

denote the ith generation's budget constraint, where A_{i+1} indicates the bequests transmitted to generation $i+1$ by generation i. C_i, T_i, and Y_i describe the present value of consumption, taxes, and income for generations i over its lifetime. With intergenerational altruism A_1 reflects the optimal transfer decisions in response to changes in T_0 and the matching changes in T_1. Thus follows the relevance of the infinite budget constraint. Intergenerational selfishness breaks up this pattern. Its strict and narrow application means that $A_{i+1} = 0$. A change in T_0 thus invariably induces a change in C_0 that exceeds, with the differential in marginal propensities, the change in C_1 in the initial period.

This analysis suffers, however, in comparison with the "intergenerational altruism" model from some immediate confrontation with reality. We do observe that wealth is actually transmitted from one generation to another. These transfers are excluded by the narrowly formulated "selfishness model." The occurrence of transfers is, however, not necessarily an expression of *voluntary* and *planned* transfers associated with intergenerational altruism once we move beyond the context of perfect information. Blanchard (1984) argued that an insurance scheme under risk yields the same result of no bequests. But such insurance does either not exist (specifically the one used by Blanchard) or is at most only used or offered partially by agents. But bequests apparently do occur. The context of risk could explain, however, the *appearance* of bequest without the bequest *motive* as formalized by Barro. Agents face some probability that the remaining life span exceeds the expected time. Risk averse agents will therefore adjust the use of their wealth in view of this uncertainty. Their problem is similar to the asymmetric risks associated occasionally with an inventory decision. The asymmetry is probably even more acute in this case. Using up all resources before death exposes a person to serious hazards. This is balanced by unused resources at death, reflecting lowered consumption before death. The comparatively lower level of consumption can be understood as a premium paid for self-insurance against the hazards of early exhaustion of one's resources. Wealth will be held under the circumstances beyond the requirements of the statistical expectations bearing on the remaining life span. It follows that, on average, unused wealth will be transmitted at death to the next generation without an "operative bequest motive." Intergenerational transfers operated by budget deficits would in this case still raise current consumption. The observation of substantial intergenerational transmission of wealth is thus consistent with the denial of "Ricardian equivalence."

It should be noted that this argument disregards the potential role of annuities to be purchased by the older generation. But even an actuarially fair supply of annuities would probably not completely replace the holding of tradeable wealth as insurance for old age hazards expressed by only partially insurable large expenses on health problems. The annuity business, moreover, operates at a cost. A comparison of this cost with the cost of self-insurance could be expected to leave a margin of tradeable wealth. But an entirely different argument, developed by Bernheim, Schleifer, and Summers (1985), explictly recognizes the occurrence of voluntary planned bequests and offers probably a more relevant critique of the Ricardian thesis of debt neutrality. This analysis will be examined in subsequent sections covering the empirical work.

3.2.2. Corner Solutions

The alternative hypotheses yield very different interpretations of social security. The Ricardian theme implies that such arrangements are offset by correspondingly larger transfers from the older to the next generation with no effect on current consumption. The alternative, articulated by Feldstein (1982), implies that this intergenerational transfer raises current consumption. An interesting explanation of the emergence of social security (Meltzer and Richard, 1985) reenforces the "non-Ricardian" hypothesis. Social security is interpreted as a substitute for the voluntary social arrangements made within the larger family. Social evolution gradually eroded such arrangements and raised the older generation's control problem associated with the extraction of the support. Social security emerged as a political solution to this problem. This explanation cannot be reconciled with a Ricardian equivalence. Its basic structure asserts, on the contrary, that the intergenerational link described by Barro has been suspended. This interpretation suggests, moreover, the occurrence of several important facts bearing on intergenerational transfers. Such transfers do not occur solely in the form of a tradeable wealth accumulated by the older generation and eventually inherited by the younger generation. Voluntary intergenerational transfers may frequently involve an intertemporal exchange between older and younger generations. The older generation invests initially in health, education, and other dimensions of the younger generation with the expectation of support (i.e., negative bequests) during old age. The extraction of support does not proceed without control and transactions costs, however. The hypothesis indicated above states basically that specifiable social changes raised these costs and increased the likelihood of corner solutions when unrestricted optimality yields negative bequests. Under the circumstances the government's intervention increases current real consumption. Lastly, we note that this argument also suggests that a single representative household does not adequately represent the actual diversity encountered in matters of intergenerational transfers.

The representative household's infinite intertemporal budget constraint requires, in addition to the special intergenerational link, an assumption about capital markets. This assumption removes the occurrence of another solution. The representative household's lending and borrowing rates coincide with the rates available to the government's operation. A violation of this condition produces wealth effects that suspend the Ricardian equivalence. Chan (1983) explored this theme in the context of an assumption approximating the problem in terms of liquidity constraints imposed on a subset of households. A debt-financed deficit operates under the circumstances to substitute government borrowing for constrained household borrowing. Households with no liquidity constraint or a nonbinding one respond to the deficit and its finance in the "Ricardian manner" with the offsetting behavior discussed above. Households suffering binding liquidity constraints before the event experience, through the intermediation of the government, a relaxation of the constraint. They will react by shifting future consumption into current consumption. The distribution of significant liquidity constraints or the distribution of differential borrowing rates of interest between government and households determines the net effect of a debt-financed tax cut on households' current consumption.

Some fundamental theoretical exploration about the conditions for Barro's "operative intergenerational bequests" qualifies the debt neutrality result. Barro's analysis is conditioned by the assumption that intergenerational transfers from old to young occur independently of debt. The emergence of debt changes neither opportunities nor preferences in the world described. No real consequences thus ensue. An interior solution is simply maintained. Philippe Weil (1984) examined the problem with great analytic care. His basic theme emphasizes the existence of a "deep connection between the efficiency properties of overlapping generation economies without bequest motive and the possible direction of intergenerational transfers." There exist, in particular, overlapping generation economies that "justify," in terms of efficiency, intergenerational transfers from young to old. Weil demonstrates that the existence of "operative bequests" in a suitably defined steady state depends on the discount applied by the old to the future utility of the young. This discount should not exceed a benchmark determined by the gap between the interest rate and economic growth rate in the Diamond-type model. Weil concludes that a "wide class of economies with a bequest motive" do not satisfy Barro's proposition about Ricardian debt neutrality. The limited significance of this analysis should be clearly understood. It essentially establishes that Barro's result is nonvacuous and places necessary and sufficient conditions on its occurrence. This purely analytic result cannot settle the crucial empirical issue at stake.

3.2.3. Risk and Uncertainty
Risk and uncertainty are essentially exorcised from the argument supporting the Ricardian theme. A firm link connects the household's benefits from the current tax cut with the future tax burden. The government's infinite intertemporal budget constraint also removes all risk and uncertainty with regard to the government's budgetary operation. Agents can rest assured that future tax liabilities guarantee the crucial equality of present values.

The pattern is substantially modified once we admit risk and uncertainty on two levels into the analysis. Barro (1981a) and Feldstein (1982) already noted in passing some consequences associated with uncertainty about the household's future tax liability. Barro suggested that uncertainty raises the perception of the present value attached to future tax liabilities by risk-averse households. Thus a debt-financed deficit *lowers* under uncertain future tax liabilities the representative household's perception of its wealth position. Current private consumption thus *declines* as a result of the deficit. The suggestive remark was developed by Chan (1983) in some explicit analytic detail. The argument still adheres to a state of lump-sum taxes with certainty concerning the future *aggregate* tax liability. Households suffer, however, incomplete information and consequently experience some risk about the distribution of the global burden among the taxpayers. The *individual* household's future tax burden is determined by a stochastic process. It follows that the individual's share of the current tax cut does not match his share of the future tax liability. This suspension of the crucial link produced by a stochastic tax incidence implies, under conventional restrictions on preferences, that a debt-financed deficit *lowers* current consumption. The larger the uncertainty about the incidence of the future tax liabilities, moreover, the *larger* is the negative effect of a deficit on current consumption. The result reveals that households hedge against the risk imposed on them by saving even more than determined under certainty. The hedging response induces a substitution of saving at the *expense* of consumption.

A similar theme, but different in its conclusion, was recently developed by Barsky, Mankiw, and Zeldes (1984). Risk-averse households encounter in this case not an uncertain tax incidence but an uncertain future income. An intertemporal reallocation of tax liabilities (with less now and more in the future) lowers the degree of uncertainty bearing on future income. The precautionary demand for savings declines and real consumption *increases* under the circumstances. This result is, moreover produced under strict "Ricardian conditions."

The analysis proceeds in the context of a two-period model characterized by three budget constraints. The two constraints describing the household's position appear as

$$W_1 = \mu_1 - C_1, \tag{7.2}$$

$$C_2 = (1 + R) W_1 + \mu_2 + \epsilon_2, \tag{7.3}$$

where C_1 and C_2 refer to consumption in periods 1 and 2, μ_1, and $\mu_2 + \epsilon_2$ designate income in the two periods, W_1 defines savings in period 1, and R is the interest rate. The magnitudes μ_1 and μ_2 are nonstochastic, whereas ϵ is the stochastic component of future income. A temporal tax shift is introduced by inserting T *positively* in eqn (7.2) and $(1 + R)T$ *negatively* in eqn (7.3). The signs are determined by the fact that any initial tax burden is impounded into μ_1 and μ_2. We thus rewrite the household's budget constraints as

$$W_1 = \mu_1 + T - C_1, \tag{7.4}$$

$$C_2 = (1 + R)W_1 - (1 + R)T + \mu_2 + \epsilon_2. \tag{7.5}$$

The government needs to levy taxes in the second period in order to finance the repayment of $(1 + R)T$. The required tax rate is thus determined by the relation

$$(1 + R)T = t\mu_2. \tag{7.6}$$

The revenues from extra taxation imposed on expected income should cover the repayment. The actual tax revenue is

$$t(\mu_2 + \epsilon_2) = (1 + R)T + \frac{(1 + R)T}{\mu_2}\epsilon_2.$$

The second period's household constraint can thus be rewritten once more as

$$C_2 = (1+R)W_1 - (1+R)T + \mu_2 + \left[1 - \frac{(1+R)T}{\mu_2} \right]\epsilon_2. \tag{7.7}$$

Lastly, the authors postulate a three-times differentiable utility function in C_1 and C_2 satisfying the conditions

$$(1 + R)U_{222} - U_{122} > 0.$$

The first-order optimality conditions are immediately derived:

$$EU_1(C_1, C_2) = (1 + R)EU_2(C_1, C_2).$$

A straightforward manipulation of this condition yields the marginal propensity to consume:

$$\frac{\partial C_1}{\partial T} = \frac{(1 + R)\text{Cov}[(1 + R)U_{22} - U_{12}, \epsilon_2]}{-\mu_2[EU_{11} - 2(1 + R)EU_{12} + (1 + R)^2 EU_{22}]} > 0. \tag{7.8}$$

A reduction in current taxes, appearing as a positive magnitude in the constraint, thus *raises* current consumption. Tax policies induce, under the circumstances, specified real effects in the economy. These effects emerge even with the household's definite perception that the present value of its expected future tax liabilities equals the taxes foregone in the present. The result is crucially conditioned by the positive covariance term in eqn (7.8). This result vanishes in the absence of the third-order derivative condition imposed on the utility function. Once we accept this condition the crucial aspect centers on the reduction in the variance of second period income produced by a nonvanishing tax rate $t = (1 + R)T/\mu_2$. The variance is actually reduced in the proportion $(1 - t)^2$.

The authors offer two distinct interpretations for the two-period model. One confines the model to the lifetime of a single individual. Income uncertainty bears in this case on an individual's uncertainty within the life cycle. The other interpretations introduce intergenerational relations. The second period refers to the economic uncertainty attached to a household's descendants. The uncertainty of both cases is incisively demonstrated by the authors. Extensive simulations proceeding under a variety of assumptions offer some insights beyond the qualitative result in eqn (7.8) about the order of magnitude of tax effects on real consumption.

The issue addressed by Barsky, Mankiw, and Zeldes was already analyzed by Chan (1983). The detailed formulation differs slightly, but the conclusion is the same once the preference structure is properly restricted. Chan emphasizes, however, that the insurance scheme introduced with the special tax policy arrangement is essentially independent of the debt–tax mix problem.

The infinite intertemporal budget constraint of government also reflects a crucial link suspending relevant risks and uncertainty. The equality of present values of expenditures and taxes expresses agents' certain knowledge that current expenditures will eventually be covered by taxation. Suppose, however, that large debt-financed deficits persist for 10, 100, or 1000 years. Is it reasonable to assume an invariant certainty that after $x + 1$ years all will be unwound with appropriately increasing tax liabilities? The basic thrust of rational expectations would suggest that agents learn. An experience of accumulating debt-financed deficits would induce doubts and reservations about the relevance of infinite intertemporal budget constraints. The time-inconsistency problem diligently discussed with examples from tax and monetary policies should actually be highly significant in this context (Baltensperger, 1984). Suppose that agents were exposed to a long series of deficits financed by issues of interest-bearing debt. This experience induces some revisions in agents' expectations. The probability assigned to possible defaults, particularly to default by inflation, will rise under the circumstances. The increasing risk associated with large and persistent deficits generates over time an anticipated purchasing-power risk attached to the government debt. This purchasing-power risk modifies the Fisher equation with the appearance of a specific covariance expression representing the purchasing-power risk. The emergence of this risk term implies an increase both of the nominal and the real rates of interest (Baghat and Wakeman, 1983). This problem will be reconsidered in a subsequent section attending to the long-run interdependence of monetary and fiscal policies, an issue raised by Sargent and Wallace (1982).

3.2.4. The Changing Nature of the Issue

The risk problem introduced in the previous paragraph bears essentially on long-run aspects associated with the cumulative effects of a long series of large deficits that erode the relevance of the infinite intertemporal budget constraint expressed in terms of ordinary taxes. This seems not to be the only aspect of risk and uncertainty associated with the macroeconomic consequences of the government's budgetary process. Such risk and uncertainty have so far not been integrated into macroeconomic analysis. Our most recent fiscal experiences suggest that a potentially useful research program would examine the impact of the uncertain amount and nature of tax liabilities on the public's balance-sheet risks and consequently on asset markets, with further effects on consumption and investment. This investigation moves us substantially away from the "Ricardian theme." This theme, restrained by the assumption of lump-sum taxes in order to isolate a possibly pure public-debt effect, can only admit uncertainty about the temporal distribution, the personal incidence of tax liabilities and future income. The first type of uncertainty does not modify the Ricardian theme, but the second and third violated the neutrality pattern of debt-financed deficits. Risk and uncertainty surrounding tax liabilities have a much wider field of operation once we introduce "non-lump-sum" taxes. The uncertain incidence of future tax liabilities on nonhuman wealth, human wealth, and consumption probably affects portfolio risks and thus the required average return. The consequent adjustment in asset values modifies consumption, saving and investment patterns. The importance of debt-financed deficits may, in this context, not so much emerge because of a *direct* effect of public debt on real interest rates in defiance of any "Ricardian equivalence." The deficits and the resulting increase in public debt yield possibly their most important effects via a different channel. These phenomena may be a signal of mounting uncertainty about future magnitude and incidence of tax liabilites. Agents' perceptions bearing on the interpretation of observed deficits would operate as a crucial link in the process. Balance-sheet risks and asset-market responses will vary with the perceived duration of the deficit.

This theme also offers an avenue for an analysis of fiscal *regimes* in contrast to the usual analysis of fiscal policy *actions* and their effects on the evolution of economic activity. Fiscal regimes could be differentiated according to their respective risk patterns parameterized in a specific mode. The procedure would follow the imaginative attempt made by Stulz and Wasserfallen (1985) for the case of monetary regimes. The investigation was motivated by the recognition of the comparative importance of the stochastic trend and the relatively modest significance of the stationary component in economic fluctuations (Nelson and Plosser, 1982). The array of *specific* policy *actions* addressed to the *cyclic* component remains, under the circumstances, confined to a smallish range of influence. Stulz and Wasserfallen show that, in contrast to influences exerted by specific actions, the influence of the *regime's* characteristics expressed by some risk parameters substantially contributes to global economic evolution by conditioning the properties of the stochastic trend. The uncertainty imposed by the regime affects the stochastic properties of assets, their risks, and the portfolio risk with consequences on returns and output behavior. These issues seem worthy of further exploration in a program designed to integrate finance and macro-economic analysis (Lucas, 1984; Plosser, 1984; Fischer and Merton, 1984).

3.2.5. Some Final Remarks on the Ricardian theme

It is interesting to reflect at this stage on the consequences of the discussion initiated with Barro's revival of the Ricardian theme. The neoclassic analysis rejects the "conventional" position that the government's financial decisions expressed by the debt–tax mix induce real consequences over both the short and long runs. The IS/LM framework concentrated on the wealth effects of debt policies as the crucial condition of real effects. The Brunner–Meltzer asset-market analysis, on the other hand, emphasized the comparatively small order of wealth effects associated with a pure-debt policy even when future tax liabilities were disregarded. The wealth effect measured as the vertical shift elasticity of the pseudodemand line in figure 7.1 occurs as a product of two terms. One term consists of components with opposite signs reflecting offsetting influences produced by interacting asset-markets. The other term is the ratio of government debt at market value to total nonhuman wealth. The real consequences of debt policies in the Brunner–Meltzer asset-market analysis were dominantly produced by substitution and relative price effects produced by the shifting composition of assets. The discussion of the stability analysis revealed furthermore that this short-run, pure-debt effect, again evaluated by shifts of the pseudodemand line, is at best very modest with respect to aggregate output and the price level. This portion of "conventional" analysis assigned more significance to the long-run effects of a pure-debt policy centered on the adjustment of the optimal stock of real capital and consequently the position of the normal output line in figure 7.1. Both mechanisms stressed by conventional analysis became suspended in the neoclassic analysis. Intergenerational altruism and optimal hedging removed both wealth and substitution effects.

The discussion seems hardly to restore the "conventional" position. Its most significant elements modifying the Ricardian theme do not suggest very potent effects of debt–tax mix policies per se. Kotlikoff's analysis directs our attention neither to any wealth nor substitution effects. This analysis implies, based on the assumption of "intergenerational selfishness," that debt policies induce intergenerational wealth transfers that modify current real consumption. Debt policy is, however, not a necessary condition for such transfers. Such transfers may occur without debt policy as a result of current tax shifts. But debt policies do induce, on the other hand, the transfers described by Kotlikoff. This analysis thus emphasizes the effect of debt policies on the composition of aggregate real demand. Debt policies raise real consumption and lower real investment in the short run and lower (comparatively) the capital stock and normal output in the long run. But the mechanism involved differs from those described by conventional analysis. We note, however, that Kotlikoff's analysis is consistent with the operation of a wealth and substitution effect (via asset markets) induced by debt policy.

The consequences of risk and uncertainty induced by debt-financed deficits, so clearly visible in the past five years, may also trace potentially important transmission channels for debt policies. The papers by Baltensperger and Chan are somewhat suggestive in this respect. The issue raised by Baltensperger suggests that an increasing risk of default by inflation associated with a permanent, large, debt-financed deficit raises the purchasing-power risk of government debt and consequently raises the (gross) real rate of interest. An alternative mode of approaching the same issue proceeds along lines suggested by Bomhoff (1983), Mascaro and Meltzer (1983), and Evans (1984). Permanent and large debt-financed deficits contribute to uncertainty about the course of monetary policy. This uncertainty produces a risk premium embedded in interest rates and raises real rates. And once we move beyond the realm of pure-debt policies and consider deficit policies in a world of distortionary taxes, the risk problem appears, on a first impression, to magnify. But we still lack at this stage an adequate analysis of portfolio risks induced by persistent deficits and the associated uncertain course of tax policies. This analysis would also extend to the effects of such portfolio risks on real consumption, investment, and real returns of assets. We may ultimately learn from the work initiated by the "Ricardian discussion" that the "Ricardian world" offers like the Modigliani–Miller theorem a useful benchmark for any analysis of our real problems. It may well be that the new analysis gradually emerging yields insights into more significant mechanisms associated with debt-financed deficits than elaborated by "conventional analysis."

3.3 Some Recent Empirical Work on the Ricardian Theme

This section surveys the empirical evidence bearing on Barro's "Ricardo theorem." The initial round of empirical investigations could not reject Barro's thesis. Subsequent examinations by Summers and Kotlikoff, however, strengthened the doubt. The section is retained for completeness. Analytic arguments and counterarguments hardly settle the issue. They may establish some presumptions with varying weights. An uncertain incidence of future tax liabilities seems to be, for instance, a better approximation to reality than the matching of the distributions of current tax cuts and future tax liabilities. The fact of uncertainty appears clearly more acceptable than its denial or the postulated perfect matching. The approximate realization of such matching in the tax cuts effected on the basis of Kennedy or Reagan decisions would be, in my judgment, quite astonishing. The matching would have to be reflected in a corresponding matching of experienced tax reductions, additional savings, and resulting acquisitions of government bonds. Simple institutional facts (size of denomination relative to tax cut, access costs to capital markets) distort the pattern and most likely prevent an approximate matching between tax cuts and bond acquisitions, even with a maintained matching between tax cuts and savings. But the partial distortion of the matching need not be decisive per se. The nonmatching segment of taxpayers may be concentrated toward the lower end of the income distribution involving a smallish fraction of total tax cuts. Alternatively, these taxpayers may invest the accrued savings in one form or another of indirect claims on bonds. The financial intermediation involved in this case usually redistributes risk between the intermediary and the holder of its liabilities. The more or less indirect claims on bonds are thus not equivalent to bonds. A positive but smallish wealth effect could thus emerge. But an empirical assessment of the Ricardian thesis along these lines seems very costly and quite uncertain.

A study of another major implication bearing on bequest patterns may be more promising. The Ricardian theme implies that any tax cut relative to permanent government expenditures induces adjustments of bequest by the older generations in order to maintain the utility level of the subsequent generation. A similar effect occurs with changes in social security benefits (i.e., negative taxes) for the older generation. The studies actually executed so far (Feldstein 1978; Barro 1978) yielded conflicting results. A direct examination of bequest patterns linked to major tax-policy shifts could add some information. The Ricardian theme implies, however, in the context of our actual age distribution and conditional life expectation a somewhat loose relation between relative tax cuts and additional bequest. Some of the anticipated tax liabilities will still be borne by the "older" agents. A tighter relation should prevail between relative tax cuts and additional savings, however.

Asessments based on some of the crucial linkages emphasized by the Ricardian hypothesis require a large amount of rather specific information in order to produce approximately useful results. The operation of liquidity constraints offers a good example. There is good evidence for the relevant occurrence of such constraints for some segment under the wealth distribution. We know from various studies that there exist social groups which confront borrowing rates massively higher than the government's borrowing rates. But it is difficult and somewhat speculative to assess the relative significance of this fact without detailed additional cross-sectional data. Professional research quite sensibly attemped, under the circumstances, another route. Early investigations by Tanner (1970) and Kochin (1974) explored the implication bearing on the invariance of consumption expenditures with respect to government debt or debt-financed deficits. Buiter and Tobin (1978), among others, followed these efforts. The net result of this early round was hardly conclusive, with some diversity of results. Six more recent studies by Feldstein (1982), Kormendi (1983), Aschauer (1985), Plosser (1982), Boskin and Kotlikoff (1985) and Bernheim, Schleifer, and Summers (1985) are selected for closer examination.

3.3.1. Feldstein
Feldstein expresses the major implication of the Ricardian thesis in terms of

specific constraints on the coefficients in a regression. This regression relates consumers' expenditures (C)

$$C = \beta_0 + \beta_1 Y + \beta_2 W + \beta_3 SSW + \beta_4 G + \beta_5 T \\ + \beta_6 TR + \beta_7 D + \mu \qquad (7.9)$$

with the relevant variables under consideration, where Y is national income, W wealth, SSW measures social security wealth, G expresses government expenditures, T taxes, TR transfer payments, D total government debt, and μ is a random term. All variables are measured in real terms per capita. The Ricardian hypothesis implies the following patterns:

$$\beta_5 = 0, \; \beta_6 = 0, \; \beta_3 = 0 \text{ and } \beta_7 = -\beta_2.$$

The last condition assures that an increase in measured wealth due to government debt exerts no effect on real consumption. Feldstein considers, in addition, a special "fiscal impotence" hypothesis defined by the four conditions listed plus $\beta_4 = -1$. This hypothesis does not, however, represent the neoclassical position developed specifically by Barro. This problem will be discussed in a subsequent section. The rejection of $\beta_4 = -1$ yields, in particular, no evidence bearing on the Ricardian thesis.

Feldstein concludes an examination of 11 distinct estimations of the regression equation with the judgment that government spending and taxes "can have substantial effects on aggregate demand." He also concludes that "each of the implications of the pre-Ricardian equivalence hypothesis is contradicted by the date." This strong and unambiguous conclusion is somewhat puzzling when evaluated against the results obtained from the regression analysis. The reader may judge for himself with the aid of the following table 7.1. This table compares the frequency among the regression results with which the standard error of the coefficient estimate *se* exceeds or equals the coefficient estimate of *ce*, and the number of cases with a coefficient estimate at least double the corresponding standard error. The last condition – that is, $\beta_7 = -\beta_2$ – can only be judged on the basis of three regressions. Two cases confirm the hypothesis, and one case provides negative evidence. This pattern is really rather mixed and hardly offers a decisive rejection of the Ricardian thesis. The condition on transfer payments (i.e., $\beta_6 = 0$)

Table 7.1 Regression results

	se > ce	ce > 2se
β_5	7	2
β_6		7
β_3	10	

emerges as the clearest, but not particularly overwhelming, rejection. The other results bearing on the remaining three conditions seem actually more supportive with respect to the Ricardian thesis.

Several issues associated with the regression analysis obscure the interpretations and assessment of the results. The taxes used naturally refer to "non-lump-sum" taxes with their specific incentives and disincentives. Even a highly significant $\beta_5 < 0$ would be difficult to interpret under the circumstances. We also note that the error-structure problem explored by Plosser and Schwert and the issues associated with potential nonstationarity are neglected.

3.3.2. Kormendi

Kormendi recently offered an interesting paper exploring our subject. His discussion expands the role of government following the suggestions of Martin Bailey. The government sector is essentially recognized as a production sector supplying consumption and investment goods. It also operates with a "dissipation factor" representing the social cost of government production. A "consolidated explanation" of private-sector real consumption (excluding purchases of consumer durables) is developed according to the rationality concept of the neoclassical position. This means that household's information about their available resources or opportunities fully reflects the underlying social reality without any distortion of their perceptions. The resulting consumption function is represented by the regression

$$PC_t = a_0 + a_{11}Y_t + a_{12}Y_{t-1} + a_2GS_t + a_3W_t + a_4TR_t + u_t, \qquad (7.10)$$

when PC = personal consumption, Y = net national product, GS = government spending on goods and services, W = private real wealth, and TR = transfer payments. All variables are again in real terms. The "consolidated hypothesis" implies that $a_{11} > 0 < a_3$ and $-1 < a_2 < 0$. The magnitude of the latter coefficient reveals the nature of the government sector's production process and of its output. Kormendi emphasizes, moreover, that $a_4 > 0$ can be reconciled with the consolidated hypothesis. This pattern occurs in the case where transfer payments involve a redistribution from social groups with lower marginal propensity to groups with higher marginal propensity to consume.

The comparative robustness of the "consolidated explanation" yields, in Kormendi's judgment, some initial indications of the neoclassical hypothesis. This robustness is evaluated in accordance with the procedure developed by Plosser and Schwert (1978). The results are quite satisfactory. The estimates derived from the application of ordinary least squares to level data, from generalized least squares, and from first differences coincide very closely.

A second step of the examination enlarges the regression. This yields a "nested specification" subsuming both the standard version and the consolidated explanation;

$$\Delta PC_t = a_0 + a_{11}\Delta Y_t + a_{12}\Delta Y_{t-1} + a_2\Delta GS_t$$
$$+ a_3\Delta W_t + a_4\Delta TR_t + a_5\Delta TX_t + a_6\Delta RE_t + a_7\Delta GINT_t + u_t, \tag{7.11}$$

where TX = taxes, RE = retained earnings, and $GINT$ = interest payments made by the government. The alternative hypotheses imply the following patterns with respect to the crucial four coefficients:

standard version: $a_2 = 0, a_5 < 0, a_6 < 0, a_7 > 0,$
consolidated version: $a_2 < 0, a_5 = a_6 = a_7 = 0.$

The results are quite unambiguous. The standard version is clearly rejected. The estimates of a_5, a_6, and a_7 do not differ significantly from zero at standard levels. An F-test applied to the last three coefficients confirms the consolidated version. It should also be noted that the estimates of a_{11}, a_{12}, a_2, a_3, and a_4 coincide with estimates obtained from the examination of comparative robustness. The standard version implies, moreover, that $a_5 = - a_1 = (a_{11} + a_{12})$. This condition is also rejected.

The test of the net wealth position of government debt yields, in view of the discussion of uncertain future tax liabilites, a remarkably interesting result. The full discounting of future tax liabilities associated with current debt finance implies that the coefficient for government debt D in an extended regression including this variable must be zero. The standard version would assign, in contrast, a positive coefficient. Estimation based on a sample including the war years produces a highly significant *negative* value for the debt coefficient. The exclusion of the war years still yields a *negative* coefficient 1.6 standard errors from zero. The author's interpretation of the result is worth quoting:

> The real income stream deriving from government debt involves inflation risk and some default risk to holders of the debt. The future tax stream implied by the debt, on the other hand, involves that same inflation and default risk plus considerable additional risk as to both its intertemporal and cross-sectional incidence. Thus,. in rationally assessing the future tax consequences of government debt, the current certainty equivalent value of the future taxes may exceed the current certainty equivalent value of the income stream (which is simply the market value of the debt). In such a case, the net wealth of the private sector is adversely affected by government debt, implying a negative effect for ΔGB, (and a positive effect for ΔTX) on private consumption.

3.3.3. Aschauer

Aschauer's exploration also addresses, similarly to Feldstein and Kormendi, the implications of the neoclassical thesis bearing on households' consumption behavior. The present paper develops, however, a difference procedure. The author investigates the Ricardian equivalence proposition in the context of an intertemporal optimization framework. A rather standard separable utility function is maximized subject to a consolidated condition derived from combining the representative household's and the government's budget constraint. The integrated constraint reflects the household's full recognition of the real conditions determined by the government's fiscal operation. The argument of the utility function refers to "effective consumption" $C = C + \Theta G$, defined as the sum of private-sector consumption plus a component of government spending G that contribute to the household's consumption. The parameter Θ expresses the marginal rate substitution between the two components in effective consumption. With a quadratic utility function, constraint maximization yields an Euler equation

$$EC_t^* = \alpha + \beta C_{t-1}^*. \tag{7.12}$$

The coefficients are determined by the parameters of the utility function and the constraint. Upon translation into a stochastic context, the Euler equation coincides with Hall's (1981) formulation. The latter argued that in the context of a life cycle model, $\beta = 1$ and that consumption moves along a random walk.

Aschauer supplements the Euler equation with past values of the deficit D and estimates the regression

$$C_t = \alpha + \beta C_{t-1} + \gamma_1 D_{t-1} + \gamma_2 D_{t-2} + \gamma_3 D_{t-3} + \gamma_4 D_{t-4} + \mu_1. \tag{7.13}$$

This extension was motivated by the author's concern to evaluate the impact of fiscal policy. The neoclassical position incorporated in the underlying optimization schemes implies that all the γ-coefficients are zero. An OLS estimation of the augmented regression yields a clear contradiction of the neoclassical thesis. The deficit variable contributes significantly to the explanation of private consumption C. The sign pattern is significantly different from zero. Aschauer argues that this result "may be more apparent than real due to the fact that past taxes and deficits may help to predict current government spending." This information content of past deficits combined with the substitution relation between G and C conditions nonzero levels for the γ-coefficients.

The author develops this idea in two steps. First he decomposes effective consumption C^* in the (stochastic) Euler equation $EC^* = \alpha + \beta C_{t-1}^*$ and obtains

$$C_t = \alpha + \beta C_{t-1} + \beta \Theta G_{t-1} - \Theta G_t^0 + \mu_t, \tag{7.14}$$

where $G_t^0 = E_{t-1} G_t$. Secondly, he introduces a forecasting equation for G_t in order to relate G_t^0 with observations:

$$G_t = \gamma + \epsilon(L)G_{t-1} + w(L)D_{t-1} + v_t. \tag{7.15}$$

The last two expressions determine the system with the crucial properties to be estimated and evaluated. This system consists of the forecasting equation, eqn (7.15), and eqn (7.16):

$$C_t = \delta + \beta C_{t-1} + \eta(L)G_{t-1} + \mu(L)D_{t-1} + v_t. \tag{7.16}$$

The derivation of the system implies some cross relations linking η with μ and w. These cross relations offer the relevant test statements:

> (They) restrict the way in which past government expenditures and past government deficits may influence present consumption expenditure. In particular, if the Ricardian equivalence proposition does not hold, past values of the government deficit should have explanatory power for consumption expenditure apart from the role in forecasting government spending. Consequently, a finding that the data do not do violence (to the restrictions) yields some grounds on which to argue that to a first approximation, the joint assumption of rational expectations and Ricardian equivalence provides a plausible description.

The nature of the formulated hypothesis implies that the relation between constrained and unconstrained estimates determines the crucial test information. The log-likelihood ratio provides thus the relevant test statistic. It appears that the null hypothesis representing the neoclassical thesis cannot be rejected at a significance level lower than 24 percent. A test based on a forecasting equation for G with longer lags yields a significance level of 10 percent and another test imposing additional constraints shows a significance level of 25 percent for the likelihood statistic.

3.3.4. Provisional Comments

Kormendi and Aschauer manage to demonstrate that the neoclassical position represented by the Ricardian equivalence proposition cannot be so easily dismissed. The case for the conventional alternative, which assigns significance to financial decisions, is neither clear nor overwhelming. The evaluation centered on the patterns exhibited by consumption behavior so far remains unsettled and open. Advocates of the "conventional hypothesis" (like the author of this paper) are forced to admit that the neoclassical position deserves serious investigation. Further examination may affect both the conventional and the neoclassical thesis. Neither position may survive unscathed. The suggestions concerning the role of uncertainty and risk joined with Kormendi's estimate of the debt parameter may give a clue for possible future work. Such work should, in particular, also attend to a serious gap in the papers discussed above. The Ricardian proposition implies a tight relation between relative tax cuts, additional savings and acquisitions of government debt by households. According to this proposition the induced additional savings do not spill over beyond bond acquisition to consumer durables. The absence of any significant effect of the relevant fiscal policy variables on real consumption expressed by nondurables, services, and use-value of durables offers only very partial evidence. The regressions explored need be complemented with a similar regression addressed to the investment in consummer durables and possibly other assets typically held by house-holds that are not equivalent to government debt.

Some problems associated with Aschauer's paper need to be noted. The statistical work is based on level data. The error structure problem empha-sized by Plosser and Schwert may not be serious according to the value of the DW statistic. The problem posed by potentially nonstationary data remains and is not clear in its implications. Some more attention, as exemplified by Kormendi, to these troublesome issues would seem desirable. Aschauer's procedure offers, moreover, no sharply focused discriminating test between the neoclassical and the alternative thesis. The Euler equation supplemented with lagged deficits (i.e., eqn (7.13)) hardly represents the "conventional thesis." The weird pattern of coefficients for D_{t-1} and D_{t-2} contradicts the conventional thesis. The subsequent test based on eqns (7.15) and (7.16) with their cross parameter properties thus offers at best a test of the neoclassical proposition against an uninterpreted class represented by the augmented Euler equation *excluding* the conventional thesis.

3.3.5. Plosser

Plosser's examination of the Ricardian thesis addresses an entirely different dimension than the previous three papers. His paper investigates the implica-tion of the Ricardian hypothesis bearing on asset-market patterns. A temporal reallocation of taxes expressed by a corresponding accumulation or decumulation of debt does not affect asset prices and interest rates under the Ricardian hypothesis. The basic idea is implemented in the spirit of a neo-classic analysis. Market efficiency or rational expectation is combined with the expectations hypothesis of the term structure of interest rates. This analytic foundation implies a relation between the surprises in holding period yields of securities with different maturities and corresponding sur-prises in fiscal or monetary magnitudes:

$$H_{t+1} - EH_{t+1} = B[X_{t+1} - EX_{t+1}] + v_{t+1},$$

where H_{t+1} is a column vector of holding period returns from t to $t+1$ of bonds of various maturities, E refers to the expectational operator, B is a matrix conformable with the dimensions of the vectors H and X; the latter vector contains the relevant fiscal and monetary variables. These variables refer in this specific case to the debt monetized by the central bank, the government debt held by the public and government purchases of goods and services. v_{t+1} denotes a random vector.

The neoclassical position implies that an unexpected increase in government purchases raises interest rates and thus lowers holding period returns. This implication is compatible with Keynesian or monetarist analysis. The underlying analysis, however, attributes the result in each case to a somewhat different mechanism. The crucial difference between the neoclassical thesis and the alternative positions, however, surrounds the role of government debt. Surprises in this magnitude yield no consequences with respect to holding period returns under the Ricardian hypothesis. They should produce, in contrast, negatively related consequences under the alternative hypotheses. Lastly, surprises in the monetized portion of the public debt yield, according to Keynesian and (older) monetarist analysis, positively related surprises in holding period returns. Neoclassical analysis is not inherently inconsistent with a nonvanishing effect of monetary surprises. It remains, however, somewhat ambiguous on this point without further specifications bearing on expectations and shock structure. With some dominance of comparatively permanent shocks in the monetary variable, its surprises convey a useful signal value bearing on future inflation. This response mechanism would produce *negative* reactions in holding period returns to *positive* monetary surprises. These reactions would, moreover, increase with the maturity of the security under consideration.

In order to complete the analysis, two analytic building blocks are added. The forecasting equation

$$X_{t+1} = A(L)X_t + u_{t+1} \tag{7.17}$$

is introduced with $A(L)$ designating a matrix of polynomials in the lag operator L; u again refers to a random vector. This formulation advances implicitly an hypothesis about the structure of the process generating the observations of the X-vector. Lastly, an expression for EH_{t+1} is derived from the rational expectation theory of the term structure:

$$EH_{t+1} = R_{1t} + \phi,$$

where R_{1t} refers to a vector consisting only of the current one-period spot rate, and ϕ is a vector containing the marginal increments of liquidity premia associated with different maturities beyond the spot rate. Plosser also offers an alternative interpretation of ϕ based on the Sharp–Lintner capital-asset model. In this case ϕ would be equal to a β-vector multiplied by the difference between the expectation of a holding period yield for a market basket and the certain current spot rate R_{1t}.

The first step in the empiricial examination evaluates the joint hypothesis about market efficiency and the term structure. The implication that current surprises of holding period returns are independent of past observations on money, debt, and government purchases is tested with a suitable regression.

The results are quite unambiguous and support the joint hypothesis. A second step in the procedure explores the statistical results bearing on the matrix of coefficients B in eqn (7.16). Holding period returns for four different maturities are investigated. In two cases the coefficient estimate of the debt variable is less than its standard error. One coefficient estimate is significant at the 10 percent level, and the fourth coefficient estimate, slightly exceeding its standard error, occurs with a significance level above 10 percent. All coefficient estimates associated with the debt variable are positive. The signs are thus inconsistent with the "conventional analysis." The significance levels confirm, on the other hand, the null hypothesis expressed by the neoclassic thesis. Sign and significance level together yield a clear rejection of the "conventional hypothesis."

The coefficient estimates of the monetary variable also support some version of the neoclassic thesis. Their signs, with the exception of the security with the shortest maturity, are, however, consistent with the "conventional analysis." Only one out of four coefficients reaches a significance level of at most 10 percent. The sign and the confirmation of the null hypothesis obviously provide no support for the supplementary hypothesis bearing on the signal effect of monetary surprises in the context of a specific shock structure mentioned above. The coefficient estimates associated with government purchases provide some support for the occurrence of an effect. All estimates exhibit the sign implied by the hypothesis. Two of the four estimates are significant at the 5 percent level and one at the 10 percent level. The significance level for holding period returns on the longest maturity rises beyond 10 percent. We also note the significant estimates for the constant parameter in the regression. This confirms the occurrence of a liquidity premium or the operation of a non-vanishing β-factor on government securities.

The interpretation of the test deserves some attention. This issue may be usefully addressed with the aid of a somewhat more explicit characterization of the test procedure. The following pair of propositions control the test:

$$F \supset [ME \cdot EHTS \cdot NCH \supset T], F \supset [ME \cdot EHTS \cdot CH \supset -T].$$

F refers to a sentence presenting the hypothesis summarized in the forecasting equation; ME denotes a sentence advancing the market efficiency hypothesis; and $EHTS$ denotes a hypothesis about the term structure of interest rates; NCH and CH refer to the alternative hypotheses – that is, the neoclassical and the conventional. Lastly, T refers to the test statement about the B coefficients under the null hypothesis. The crucial point to be addressed here is the conditionality of the test relative to the untested hypothesis contained in F. The compelling force of any confirmation or disconfirmation of T depends decisively on the assumption made about F. Suppose F is true and $ME \cdot EHTS$ and T are confirmed. We can effectively discriminate under the circumstances and conclude that NCH is confirmed and CH disconfirmed. But suppose that F is false. The logical relations between the various sentences offer in this case no grounds to discriminate between *NCH* and *CH* on the basis of tests bearing on *T*. With the truth of *F* given, and *ME·EHTS* confirmed independently, the confirmation of *T must* disconfirm *CH* and *can* confirm *NCH* in order to satisfy the truth of the whole conditional proposition. Should *F*, on the other hand, be false, then the whole conditional is true irrespective of our decision about *NCH*, *CH* and *T*. The truth of the conditional imposes under the circumstances no constraint on confirmation or disconfirmation of *NCH* or *CH* relative to any given decision about *T*. The falsehood of *F* implies that the test is irrelevant and uninformative. It follows that in the absence of any information about *F* the results of the test cannot be assigned substantial weight.

One procedure designed to raise the informativeness of the test involves repetition with a variety of different forecasting equations. Plosser's paper moves in this direction. The test is repeated with a forecasting equation including current bond-market information. The results bearing on government purchases appear somewhat sharpened. The other results are essentially unchanged. We may conclude that Plosser's paper does not essentially modify the balance of evidence summarized above. It did, however, usefully direct our attention to an alternative dimension – the financial markets and the corresponding opportunities for systematic future examinations of the neoclassic thesis.

3.3.6. Bernheim–Shleifer–Summers and Boskin–Kotlikoff

Two papers recently appeared in the professional circuit that appear to shift the balance of evidence somewhat against the hypothesis of debt neutrality. Both papers move beyond the macro data applied to an examination of consumers' behavior. They exploit in very different ways some micropatterns systematically related to the relevant analysis. The first paper, by Bernheim, Schleifer, and Summers (1985), seems particularly noteworthy. It starts with the observation that most of the existing wealth was transmitted by the prior generation. We noted in a previous paragraph that an "accidental transfer" hypothesis without any bequest motive could explain the *occurrence* of bequests in a non-Ricardian world. This explanation would probably hold even with an availability of annuities. But it seems doubtful that this hypothesis can explain the order of magnitude of the bequests. The crucial contribution made by BSS (i.e., the three authors) emerges from the explicit construction of a detailed ("non-Ricardian") hypothesis explaining the occurrence of bequests that incorporates a bequest motive. This hypothesis, in spite of the acknowledged bequest motive, yields radically different implications from Barro's hypothesis. The explicit specification of this alternative bequest hypothesis offers opportunities for new and richer critcal evaluations with untapped data.

The "exchange motivated bequests" hypothesis involves a simple idea developed with a subtle analysis. The idea applies the basic REMM (resourceful, evaluating, maximizing man) model to the interactions between older and younger persons. The hypothesis thus rejects Barro's assumption that older persons are concerned about the future consumption opportunities of their descendants. Older generations accumulate wealth in tradeable (i.e., bequeathable) form in order to purchase services from the younger generation. The services bought by the prospect of bequests occur essentially in the form of attention extended by the younger to the older. An implicit exchange transaction of potential wealth for current attention determines the eventual wealth transfer from older to younger.

The authors structure their analysis with two sets of utility functions and a set of constraints describing wealth accumulations over time. The utility functions represent the agents in the interacting groups. The expression

$$\sum_{t=S}^{\infty} \beta^{t-s} P(\epsilon, t) U_t(C_t, a_t)$$ (7.18)

describes the utility function of the testator, where β is a discount factor, $P(s,t)$ is the probability of survival from the initial period s to period t and U_t is the instantaneous utility as a function of consumption C_t and the attention vector $a_t = (a_{1t} \ldots a_{nt})$. This attention vector describes the degree of attention extended to the testator by each of the N members of the set of "credible" beneficiaries addressed by the testator. The latter's utility increases with C_t and a_t. He is also assumed to have a finite deterministic life span T so that $P(s, T+1)=0$.

The utility function of the N beneficiaries is given by

$$\sum_{t=S}^{\infty} \beta_n^{t-s} U_{nt}(C_n, a_{nt}).$$ (7.19)

We need only comment here that BSS assume beneficiaries to live forever. This assumption simplifies matters with no loss in relevant substance. U_n has a positive derivative with respect to $C_{n,t}$ and a negative derivative with respect to $a_{n,t}$. Attention is valued quite differently by the two sides of the exchange.

Expression (7.20) and (7.21) introduce descriptions of wealth accumulations.

a. $W_{t+1} = (W_t - C_t - A_t)(1 + r_t) + A_t(1 + \rho_t),$ (7.20)

b. $B_t = W_t - C_t - A_t$

The first applies to testators, with W designating wealth, A the annuity investment made, r the market rate of interest, ρ_t the rate of return on A, and $B = \sum_n b_n$ the total sum of bequests; b_n is the component of B going to beneficiary n. Formulation (a) holds in the case where the testator survives, and (b) holds in the case of death during the period.

$$W_{n,t+1} = (W_{n,t} - C_t + b_{n,t}I(t-1))(1 + r_t).$$ (7.21)

Expression (7.21) supplies the condition for beneficiary n. $I(t)=1$ in the case where the testator dies during the period; otherwise it is zero.

The structure of the strategy game between testators and beneficiaries has now been defined. The testator invests in bequeathable wealth in order to induce attention from potential beneficiaries, and the latter compete with attention for bequests. BSS develop a clever and intricate argument to determine a (Nash) solution to this game. A general sense of the detailed argument will suffice here. The testator chooses an optimal plan $(C^*, a, b_1^*, \ldots, b_N)$ for consumption, attention, level, and distribution of bequests. Optimization proceeds subject to the constraints, including a feasibility condition. The latter imposes that the choice of $(a, b_1, \ldots, b_N)$ must be confined to a range assuring to beneficiaries at least a utility equal to nonparticipation in the game (i.e., $a_n = b_n = 0$). The beneficiaries may be interpreted to play a subgame conditioned on the vector $(b_1^*, \ldots, b_N^*)$. The testator can, of course, not impose his optimal choice of attention on beneficiaries. He thus faces a problem of selecting a bequest rule – that is, a vector function $b(H, B)$, where H denotes the history of the game and B the total level of bequests – that induces beneficiaries to supply a^* voluntarily in their own interests. BSS show the existence of a specific rule in situations with at least two beneficiaries. The rule does produce a Nash equilibrium solution (a^*, b^*). This equilibrium implies that the testator fully appropriates the surplus utility created by the exchange. The Ricardian equivalence theorem fails to be satisfied under this "exchange motivated bequests" hypothesis. Bequests do occur and they are motivated. They are, however, not motivated by the future welfare of descendants but by the purchase of current attention. A debt-financed deficit yields, in general, under the circumstances, no offsetting intergenerational transfers and personal saving. Opportunities are modified and real variables change.

As extensive empirical evaluation follows the analytic argument. The hypothesis implies that parents influence their children's behavior by holding wealth in bequeathable forms. It implies, in particular, that contacts between parents and children within families with bequeathable wealth are more extensive. The authors exploit the data from a longitudinal retirement history survey. They especially derive data on bequests b and contacts. A normalized measure V of contacts per child is constructed with the raw data. An OLS regression of V on b yields the "proper sign" but does not confirm the hypothesis. The authors trace this negative result to potential endogeneity of b. The hypothesis does imply that b and V are simultaneously and interactingly determined. A TSLS procedure thus corresponds better to the structure of the hypothesis. The results are dramatically different in this case. The null hypothesis of no effect of b on V can be rejected with high confidence. A special test assessing the exogeneity of b supports the choice of a TSLS procedure. Exogeneity of b can also be rejected wth substantial confidence.

The authors recognize that consistency of the empirical pattern with the hypothesis cannot exclude other possible explanations. They evaluate a variety of such alternatives in order to strengthen support for the hypothesis advanced. They consider thus the possibility that influences emanating from several omitted and personal dimensions are erroneously attributed to b. The effect of b on V survives this examination. Some alternative explanations of the observed correlation between V and b do not distinguish between wealth in bequeathable and in nonbequeathable forms. The hypothesis advanced assigns, in contrast, no significance to the latter. The statistical results again confirm the hypothesis under examination. The case for alternative hypotheses emphasizing the role of the cost of contacts imposed on children or of the parents' housing wealth fails similarly when confronted with relevant data. Other implications are also exploited in order to extend the range of relevant observations bearing on the hypothesis. Lastly, data on the comparatively low frequency of privately purchased annuities or of gifts offer some useful information. BSS discriminate, with their help, between the hypothesis considered, the "accidental bequest" hypothesis discussed in a previous section, the "bequests for their own sake" hypothesis, and the "intergenerational altruism" hypothesis. The authors' hypothesis also survives this last round of assessments. A careful reader of this paper may agree that the wide-ranging and imaginative empirical evaluation establishes a serious case on behalf of the hypothesis that bequests are a component of an exchange. The relevant and pervasive occurrence of such transactions is, moreover, inconsistent with the Ricardian thesis of debt neutrality.

A serious limitation of prior studies bearing on the Ricardian thesis is their concentration on macro data of consumption patterns. BSS substantially enriched our assessment by exploring a wider range of implications requiring micro data. Boskin and Kotlikoff (1985) pursue a similar course in an investigation that required a massive labor and computational input. Their examination addressed an important implication of the Ricardian hypothesis expressed by the intergenerational altruism model. Under this hypothesis consumption expenditures depend only on "collective resources" representing the real underlying situation. It implies, in particular, that consumption does not depend on the age distribution of the population. The analysis is based on a present value of family utility. This formulation involves a series of instantaneous utility functions specified for all descendants and their respective age groups. A description of wealth accumulation for both household and government serves as a constraint on the optimal choice for an intertemporal consumption pattern of the "infinitely living" family. The first-order condition determines an expression within the usual family of Euler equations relating consumption in adjacent periods. The problem, however, allows no tractable analytic solution describing consumption as a function of predetermined magnitudes. The authors thus pursue with great patience a different course. They solve a finite-period approximation to the infinite optimization problem. The approximation is chosen so as to lower changes in the optimal consumption pattern produced by extending the period to a negligible level. The data set used covers the period 1946–81. A dynamic programming approach is applied to compute the solutions for the relevant sample period. It should be noted that this optimal pattern $\bar{C}$ is derived in the context of stochastic uncertainty about future rates of return and earnings. The derivation, moreover, depends on a specific utility function and an age-weight assigned to age-group instantaneous utilities. The authors actually investigate combinations of parameters (of instantaneous utility and the discount factor) in order to find the selection that determines for $\bar{C}$ the closest fit (in terms of root mean squares) to the data.

The test is performed with a regression of actual consumption C on $\bar{C}$ and five age groups expressed in terms of their respective income shares. The hypothesis of intergenerational altruism,

$$C = \beta_0 + \beta_1 \bar{C} + \lambda_1 s_1 + \ldots \lambda_5 s_5 + \epsilon, \qquad (7.22)$$

implies that $\lambda_0 = \lambda_i = 0$ for $i=1, \ldots, 5$ and $\beta_1 = 1$. The statistical inference confirms the last condition but disconfirms the others. The pattern of λ-coefficients seems consistent with some life cycle hypothesis. The coefficient pattern estimated implies, in particular, that a redistribution of 10 percent of income from the younger to the older generation would raise consumption by 1 percent and lower the net national savings rate by 9 percent.

The authors' preliminary capital and labor-intensive investigation clearly disconfirms the Ricardian thesis couched in terms of an "intergenerational altruism" hypothesis. This disconfirmation must be substantially qualified, however. The test does not uniquely address this crucial hypothesis. It is mixed with an array of auxiliary hypotheses bearing on the choice of utility function, age-weight assignments, the specification of uncertainty, and other components. The disconfirmation could, of course, apply to the set of auxiliary hypotheses. This comment does not lower the value of a major piece of work developed by Boskin and Kotlikoff. Their examination does reenforce the results obtained by BSS, and further research involving variations in the choice of auxiliary hypotheses may confirm the rejection of the Ricardian thesis.

3.4 A Neoclassical Analysis of Government Expenditures

The Ricardian theme does not imply irrelevance of fiscal policy. Expenditures and taxes remain potent instruments shaping output, employment, and welfare. Barro (1981b, 1984) also initiated in this field the neoclassical explorations. The general analysis of fiscal policy uses the same market-clearing approach so extensively exploited in monetary analysis.

Barro's discussion of fiscal policy moves incisively beyond the sinkhole

theory of the government's operations. The private-sector output acquired
by the public sector forms the basis for the supply of public consumption
goods to households and productive input services to private producers.
"Public consumption" competes to some extent with private consumption.
A paramete, α, summarizes this fact. It expresses the marginal rate of substitution between public and private consumption. With $\alpha=1$, "public consumption" and "private consumption" substitute one for one. A vanishing α
– that is, $\alpha=0$ – reflects absence of any substitution between the two types of
consumption. With $0 < \alpha < 1$ a unit increase in "public consumption"
lowers private consumption by less than one unit.

The government's supply of productive services raises an input available
to private producers. Private-sector output thus expands in accordance with
the marginal productivity of this input in private production. A parameter β
reflects this marginal productivity. The parameter describes the increase in
private-sector output produced by a unit increase in government real
expenditures. Government real expenditures both fully reflect the public
sector's absorption of private output and its supply of goods and services to
the private sector. The government sector is made to behave as if it con-
tracted for goods and services produced by the private sector that are immediately made available to private households and producers. It is, moreover,
assumed that the government's input services do not affect the marginal product of labor and capital in the private production process.

The system used to analyze the impact of government expenditures and
(distortionary) taxes is confined to some basic elements expressed by two
equations:

$$C(\underline{r}, \underline{G_1}, \underline{\bar{G}}, \ldots) + I(\underline{r}, \ldots) + G_1 = Y(\underline{r}, \underset{+}{G_1}, \underset{+}{\bar{G}}, \ldots), \tag{7.23}$$

$$M = L(\underline{r} + \pi, \underset{+}{Y}, \underline{G_1}, \ldots). \quad P. \tag{7.24}$$

Equation (7.23) describes the market-clearing condition for the output
market. The various symbols have standard meanings: C = private real consumption, I = private-sector real investment, G_1 = current government real
expenditures, $\bar{G}$ = permanent government real expenditures anticipated for
a horizon beyond the current period, Y = real income, r = real rate of
interest, M = money stock, P = price level, and π = expected rate of inflation. The signs below the variables indicate the direction of response of the
dependent variable. The two distinct magnitudes for government real
expenditures are introduced in order to analyze the impact of transitory and
permanent changes in government expenditures. This analysis proceeds
initially under the assumption of lump-sum taxes. Distortionary taxes are
introduced at a later stage. The path of the money stock together with the
two government expenditure variables refer to the exogenous components in
the analysis. This implies that π is also held fixed in accordance with the path
of M.

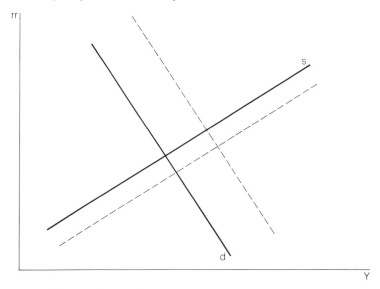

Figure 7.3   Effect of transitory increase of government expenditure on demand and supply.

We consider first the impact of a transitory increase of G_1. A simple diagram (figure 7.3) is used for this purpose. Line d represents the demand for output occurring on the left side of eqn (7.23). Line s marks the supply located on the right of the same equation. An increase in G_1 against a background of a constant permanent government expenditure implies that some expected future expenditures must fall to offset the temporary rise of G_1. Constancy of $\overline{G}$ means that the representative real opportunities expressing the household's real wealth remain unchanged. These real opportunities are defined by the difference between the present value of future real income and the present value of future government real expenditures.

A constant $\overline{G}$ implies that an increase in G_1 induces no wealth effect on demand or supply of output. This means, in particular, that $\Delta G_1 > 0$ shifts the demand and supply line in the graph for reasons other than changes in basic real opportunities. The net effect of the impact on output and real interest rates can be easily determined by comparison of the horizontal shifts of the two curves. The supply shifts to the right by an amount β per unit change in G_1, whereas demand shifts by an amount of $1 - \alpha$ in the same direction. Assuming that $\alpha + \beta < 1$, as Barro does, the increase of G_1 creates an excess demand of $1 - \alpha - \beta$ per unit increase at the initial real rate. The market-clearing condition thus forces a rise in the real rate of interest. The simultaneous shift of both curves to the right assures, moreover, that output also rises. We note immediately that we observe, in contrast to a Keynesian analysis, no multiplier effect. The diagram suggests that the increase in output per unit increase in G_1 is less than $1 - \alpha < 1$. The economy's response thus imposes a crowding-out effect on both private consumption and investment. Crowding out is, however, avoided with $\beta = 1$ and $\alpha = 0$.

The solution for r and Y can be inserted into the portfolio equation in order to determine the response of the price level. Before we consider this final result we need to examine the rationale of G_1 in money demand. G_1 operates in the nature of an in-kind transfer. It is thus interpreted to lower, relative to Y, the household's monetary transactions. The increase in G_1 thus reenforces the effect of a higher real rate of interest on real balances. The net result thus depends on the comparative strength of the income effect. The price level rises in response to a temporary increase in government expenditures, provided that the effect exerted by r and G_1 on real balances dominates the income effect. With a dominant income effect, prices fall.

A different pattern emerges under a permanent increase in government expenditures. This requires a simultaneous rise in G_1 and $\bar{G}$. We need to consider, therefore, the consequences of an increase in $\bar{G}$. Once again we evaluate the shifts in demand and supply of output. We note first that the immediate effects induced by G_1 expressed by α on household demand and β on production do not occur in this case. The increase in $\bar{G}$ with G_1 constant provides no additional goods or services in the current period. The current impact of $\bar{G}$ operates via wealth and labor effort. A unit increase in $\bar{G}$ lowers real opportunities of the private sector by one unit, holding r constant. This is modified by future α and β effects. The first effect provides additional resources to households, and the second raises the future income stream. Additional modification results from a higher labor supply produced by lower real wealth. This last modification raises real income by an amount a. The net wealth decline is thus $1 - \alpha - \beta - a$. Barro postulates at this stage a one-to-one relation between changes in real wealth and real consumption. This implies that the average propensity to consume with respect to wealth possesses a suitable positive derivative with respect to real wealth. The increase in $\bar{G}$ induces no direct effects on investment and G_1. The total direct-demand effect coincides therefore with the horizontal shift of the consumption function – that is, $-(1 - \alpha - \beta - a)$. We combine this shift in aggregate demand due to $\bar{G}$ with the shift due to G_1 (which is $1 - \alpha$) and obtain $\beta + a$ as the net shift in aggregate demand attributable to a *permanent* rise in government expenditures. This matches the positive horizontal shift on the supply side, which also equals $\beta + a$. It follows that a permanent expansion of government expenditures raises output with no effect on real rates of interest. The price level effect is algebraically larger than the response produced by a transitory increase in government expenditures. But the price effect still remains ambiguous and conditioned by the comparative strength of Y and G_1 in money demand. The dominance of Y implies a *fall* in the price level. Lastly, similar to the case of transitory expenditure increases, there occurs no multiplier effect. The expansion of output $\beta + a < 1$ is less than the unit increase in $G_1 + \bar{G}$. The resulting crowding out is, moreover, concentrated on private consumption.

The impact of tax policies is investigated in a similar vein. A flat-rate tax on income net of depreciation and exemption is introduced. This tax modifies the relevant margins for household and investor decisions. This modification implies that the after tax real rate of interest and the tax rate appear as arguments in the consumption and supply functions. It follows that an increase in the tax rate offset by expanded exemptions in order to satisfy the government's budget constraint lowers output and the real interest rate.

This analysis has been exposed by Barro to some empirical assessment. One evaluation (1984a) traces the broad contours of transitory expenditures. Such expenditures are essentially confined to war episodes and thus emerge for all practical purposes in the nature of military expenditures. The Vietnam episode can be disregarded, since the comparatively negligible magnitude of transitory spending (2 percent of GNP) is probably swamped by other influences on real GNP. In contrast, the two world wars and the Korean war episode are quite informative. Transitory spending loomed with substantial force. It is remarkable that aggregate output responded with a fraction of around 0.55 to 0.60 to transitory expenditures in all three cases. It is noteworthy, moreover, that crowding out operated dominantly on real investment. These observations appear quite consistent with the implication of Barro's analysis.

A more thorough statistical investigation addressed the relation between aggregate output on the one side and both transitory or permanent expenditures on the other side. The latter two variables were represented by some ingeniously complicated measures, which probably avoid nonstationary characteristics. The nonstationary character of output is attended to by the inclusion of a time trend. The results seem remarkably consistent with the implications bearing on the response pattern of output. Transitory expenditures induce a larger impact than permanent expenditures. But the case for even a most modest multiplier effect for transitory spending remains quite weak. Still, larger permanent expenditures do lift aggregate output permanently above the time trend, but at some cost of private real expenditures.

The results may be sensitive to the range of auxiliary hypotheses guiding the measurement procedures. Further investigations along this interesting approach need to be made in order to deepen the assessment of a neoclassical fiscal analysis. One particular issue needs our attention in this context. Nelson and Plosser (1982), followed by Stulz and Wasserfallen (1985), demonstrated with extensive tests that the hypothesis of a deterministic trend is overwhelmingly dominated by the hypothesis of a stochastic trend. A stochastic trend usually collapses the stationary component and radically modifies the result of regression analysis applied to it. One suspects that substituting a stochastic trend for the time trend and then regressing the resulting stationary component on transitory and permanent expenditures would substantially alter the outcome.

Some comments should still be addressed to the analysis. The contrast with Keynesian analysis should be noted first. Barro confirms that an essentially price-theoretical approach (Brunner, 1970) lowers the significance of interacting multiplying flows. The latter moves into center stage of the analysis once we proceed on the assumption of given price level or nominal wages. A "non-market-clearing" analysis typically converts fiscal actions into a multiplier effect on output. This effect is produced by variations induced in aggregate demand encountering unresponsive prices. Barro's neoclassical approach differs radically from the Keynesian tradition. Fiscal policy is analyzed in the context of full information and market clearing. This context would prevent any real effects of monetary shocks. This environment does not preclude temporary and permanent real responses to fiscal actions. These responses, however, depend crucially on the properties of output supply. The supply responses fully determine the output effect of permanent expenditure increases. We also note the emphasis on changing output composition produced by fiscal action associated with the "crowding out" of private consumption and investment. The difference in this respect between temporary and permanent fiscal action is also significant. This result cannot be reproduced within the standard IS/LM framework.

There remains a question bearing on the interpretation of this analysis. The full information market-clearing approach describes, in my judgment, a benchmark forming a "gravitational center" of economic processes approximating long-run aspects. Two important revisions would probably move us somewhat closer to reality in some sense without sacrificing Barro's basic price-theoretical thrust. The prevalence of incomplete information needs to be recognized, and a more general concept of market clearing needs to be used. This concept acknowledges that prices do not reflect all ongoing shocks. They will rationally reflect perceived permanent shocks but not (perceived) transitory shocks. There will be a market clearing under the circumstances relative to (perceived) permanent shocks but not with respect to *all* shocks. Some shock-absorbing buffers thus operate in the economy and distribute the output adjustment to shocks over time. This pattern would probably produce a more substantial difference between the effects of temporary and permanent expenditure changes.

A representative work of neoclassical analysis in the new mode was recently developed by Aschauer and Greenwood (1985). The analysis is built in a dynamic choice-theoretic context. A representative household optimizes over two periods subject to a constraint that incorporates tax parameters affecting labor income in either period and a tax parameter imposed on the second period's capital income. Market-clearing conditions are added for each period. These conditions reveal on the supply side the structure of production; that is, investment in the first period adds to output in the second period. The first-order optimality condition together with the market-clearing condition determines the system of equations used to examine the impact of fiscal policy. A budget constraint for the government sector with a "Ricardian thrust" assures a consistent pattern of fiscal action. Moreover, the government provides, similar to Barro's case, consumption goods to households and input services to private producers. The household's utility function depends, moreover, on total consumption available to the household, which is the sum of private consumption and the weighted government contribution with weight less than unity. This weight again represents the marginal rate of substitution between the two types of consumption.

The analytic structure is applied to an examination of tax policies, stabilization policy with the aid of adjustable tax parameters, expenditure policies, and optimal taxation. An increase in the second period's (flat) tax rate on labor income induces intertemporal substitutions that raise the first period's labor supply and investment, but lower the second period's labor supply. The welfare effect of this tax increase depends crucially on the occurrence of distortionary taxes. Welfare falls when first-period income is untaxed. Welfare rises, however, in the case where first-period income is already taxed. The new tax modifies to some extent the intertemporal distortion of the first tax.

The consequences of stabilization policy are explored under the assumption that the production process in the second period is subjected to random shocks. The larger their variance, the lower the representative household's welfare level. But a stabilization policy operating with a state-contingent tax parameter actually lowers the welfare level. However, uncertainty due to stabilization raises current consumption and decreases current work effort, output, and investment.

A temporary (unexpected) increase in first-period government expenditures (expressed by a linear combination of consumption and productive services) lowers welfare, provided the marginal product of government productive services and the marginal rate substitution between private and public consumption is less than unity. Work effort in both periods increases, whereas investment declines. Output rises in the first period and falls in the second period.

An anticipated increase in the second-period government expenditures *raises* first-period investment and work effort in both periods. The consequences of a *permanent* increase in government expenditures follow from combining the prior two cases. Work effort and output rise in both periods, and consumption declines.

Aschauer's (1985) elaborate analysis produces results somewhat similar to Barro's investigation. The argument also proceeds on the basis of full information and continuous full-market clearing. There is, however, no money and, thus, no price level in the model. The choice-theoretic foundation prevents simply adding a money demand equation. Money would have to be added to the utility function or embedded in a production or exchange constraint (Brunner, 1951). The usual homogeneity conditions can, however, be expected to be satisfied. Aschauer's results probably carry over to a monetary economy. Finally, an examination of the detailed structural knowledge required for stabilization and optimal tax policy reveals the dubious relation between such analysis and actual policy issues. This aspect will be reconsidered in the last section of the paper.

4 Deficits, Monetary Regimes, and Economic Activity
4.1 The Endogenous States of the Monetary Regime: Sargent and Wallace

The "stability problem" associated with deficit finance revealed an interrelation between fiscal and monetary regimes. This issue surfaced again in recent years, but in a modified context. Thomas Sargent and Neil Wallace (1982) approached the interrelation between the two regimes, or the financial coordination problem, with a concern directed to a very different issue. They question the long-run survival of an anti-inflationary monetary regime when confronted with persistent deficits sufficiently large to raise the real stock of government debt relative to real national product. The problem may be explored with the aid of the government's budget constraint:

$$\overset{\circ}{S} + \overset{\circ}{B} = G + TR - TA + iS, \tag{7.25}$$

where S denotes the stock of publicly held debt, B is the monetary base, G refers to nominal government expenditures on goods and services, TR designates transfer payments, and TA designates tax revenues; i should be interpreted as the average interest rate on outstanding debt. The budget equation can be translated into the following expression:

$$\overset{\circ}{s} = \overline{\text{def}} + \left[(rr-n) + \left(n - \frac{\Delta y}{y} \right) + \left(\pi - \frac{\Delta p}{p} \right) \right] s$$
$$- \left[(\pi+n) + \left(\frac{\Delta p}{p} - \pi \right) + \left(\frac{\Delta y}{y} - n \right) \right] b - \overset{\circ}{b}, \tag{7.26}$$

where s describes the ratio of real debt to real national income. b similarly represents the volume of base money per unit of nominal national income (i.e., it is the reciprocal of base velocity), $\overline{\text{def}}$ consists of the basic deficit ratio expressed as

$$\overline{\text{def}} = \frac{G + TR - TA}{Y}, \tag{7.27}$$

with Y indicating nominal national product. The other symbols are rr = real interest rate, n = normal rate of real growth, y = actual output, π = expected rate of inflation, and p is the price level.

Expression (7.26) may be considered as a differential equation in s. A stable process requires that the bracketed expression associated with s on the right side be negative. Actual real growth $\Delta y/y$ and actual inflation $\Delta p/p$ sufficiently large would produce a negative sign. But this state is purely transitory. Over the long run relevant for this investigation the sign would be determined by $rr - n$, the relation between the real rate and the normal growth rate. This relation appeared with a major role in traditional growth theory. It implicitly occurs also in the analysis surrounding infinite intertemporal budget constraints. The arguments bearing on the Ricardian thesis require, in particular, that $rr > n$. A real rate rr exceeding the normal real growth n is a necessary condition for the Ricardian thesis. Government debt would appear as net wealth under the opposite inequality. However, the inequality $rr < n$ raises subtle issues about its relevant occurrence in a steady-state context. A major problem is the reconciliation of finite assets values with $rr \leqslant n$. Such reconciliation could possibly be achieved in a model combining "intergenerational selfishness" with uncertainty of death (Blanchard, 1984). This combination would determine a discount rate exceeding the real rate of interest. The relevant long-run relations may now be written as

$$\overset{\circ}{s} = \overline{\text{def}} + (rr-n)s - (\pi+n)b. \tag{7.28}$$

We note that a steady-state condition also requires that $\overset{\circ}{b} = 0$. This expresses the fact that the price level is fully adjusted at any time to the prevailing volume of the monetary base, and b is fully adjusted to the ongoing inflation. Under the first state – that is, $rr > n$ – consistent with the Ricardian thesis, the debt–deficit process is unstable. For any initial value $\overset{\circ}{s} > 0$ the real debt ratio will persistently rise with the persistence of deficits $\overline{\text{def}}$ and low inflation. According to the Ricardian thesis, such a state does not persist. The temporal distribution of taxes implies that a stream of positive deficits over the nearer future will definitely be offset by higher taxes and negative deficts in the wider future. We should clearly recognize here the structure of the argument. A predetermined path of deficits $\overline{\text{def}}$ excluding "inflation taxes" proceeds in a "Ricardian World." The infinite intertemporal budget constraint thus imposes eventually an increase in taxes. But the predetermined characters of $\overline{\text{def}}$ and, implicitly, of ordinary taxes means that the inflation tax remains as the only possible adjustment to satisfy the infinite budget constraint. It thus follows that a noninflationary policy cannot be maintained over time in the context of a permanent deficit that is sufficiently large.

The infinite budget constraint reveals the nature of the problem. The single-period constraint

$$G_t + S_{t-1}(1 + i_{t-1}) = T_t + S_t + B_t - B_{t-1} \tag{7.29}$$

can be assembled into an intertemporal expression in terms of real magnitudes per unit of real income

$$\sum_{t=0}^{\infty} \left(\frac{1+n}{1+rr}\right)^{t} (g_t - t_t) + s_0 \frac{1+rr}{1+n} = \sum \left(\frac{1+n}{1+rr}\right)^{t} \frac{\Delta B_t}{B_t} \frac{1}{V}, \quad (7.30)$$

where V is the velocity of the monetary base. Once the left side is fixed at a substantial positive level, it follows that a very low growth of $\Delta B/B = \pi$ over an initial segment must be followed by larger monetary growth in the future.

The argument presented by Sargent and Wallace can be reconstructed along the following lines, using expression (7.28) above. The stock of real debt per unit of real income at time N satisfies

$$s(N) = s_0 + [\overline{\text{def}} - (\pi + n)b] \frac{\exp(rr-n)N}{rr-n}. \quad (7.31)$$

Under the assumption that $\overline{\text{def}} > (\pi + n)b$, the stock s grows monotonically with time N. Sargent and Wallace simply state that there exists ultimately a limit for s (somehow). The higher the levels reached by $s(N)$ the greater must be the subsequent inflation. This follows again from expression (7.29). Once an upper limit $\bar{s}$ is imposed with an unchanged $\overline{\text{def}}$, the inflation rate must adjust in accordance with

$$\bar{\pi} = \frac{\overline{\text{def}}}{b} + (rr - n)\frac{\bar{s}}{b} - n. \quad (7.32)$$

The positive relation between $\bar{\pi}$ and $\bar{s}$ is immediately obvious. A persistent accumulation of the real debt burden can ultimately always be terminated by sufficiently high levels of inflation.

Expression (7.32) can be used with two different interpretations according to the nature of the inequality betwen rr and n. With $rr > n$ it describes the inflation rate required to satisfy an imposed stock of relative real debt s. Alternatively, with $rr < n$ it determines the equilibrium stock s associated with any predetermined inflation rate; that is

$$s = \frac{\overline{\text{def}} - (\pi + n)b}{n - rr}. \quad (7.33)$$

In the first case fiscal and debt conditions dominate monetary policy, and in the second case monetary policy dominates the debt position.

The difference between the two states involving the nature of the adjustment to a constant real debt ratio s can be outlined in terms of figure 7.4.

Line 1 represents the component $\overline{\text{def}} + (rr - n)s$ of $\overset{\circ}{s}$, and line 2 the component $[-(\pi + n)]b$. Now consider the first state with $rr > n$ and an inflation rate π_0 below the inflation rate $\bar{\pi}$ required to hold s constant. This means that the vertical distance between line 1 and the π-axis exceeds the vertical distance between the π-axis and line 2. The rate of change of s is positive under the circumstances, and line 1 drifts higher. This drift continues so long as the basic deficit $\overline{\text{def}}$ is maintained and π_0 is less than $\bar{\pi}$ (eqn 7.32). In order to

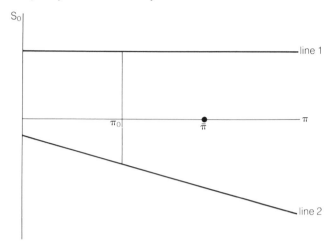

Figure 7.4   The difference between fiscal/debt conditions and monetary policy, involving adjustment to a constant real debt ratio S.

stabilize the real debt ratio s, the inflation rate must be raised to the required rate $\bar{\pi}$, which rises with s. The higher line 1 is allowed to drift up, the further out to the right shifts $\bar{\pi}$.

In the second state characterized by $rr_\bullet < n$, the real debt ratio s adjusts, in contrast, to any predetermined level π_0. Suppose the initial condition is again described by the graph. The real debt ratio s rises under the circumstances, and this *lowers* line 1 because $rr - n < 0$. This process persists until the vertical distance between line 1 and the π-axis coincides with the vertical distance between the π-axis and line 2.

Darby's (1984) rebuttal of the problem addressed by Sargent and Wallace concentrates essentially on the stability of the process and some observations supporting the required inequality. But the stability hardly removes the central issue brought to our attention by Sargent and Wallace. We are shown (table 7.2) the equilibrium real debt ratio associated with various basic deficit ratios under a stable process. The assumptions made with respect to π, b, rr, and n are listed below the table. A glance at the table indicates that deficits of the order experienced or still expected in the United States and Europe would eventually produce, even in the context of a stable process, a massive increase in the real debt ratio from the current US level of about 0.35. We should be reminded that this massive relative expansion of the government debt would occur in the context of a "non-Ricardian" world defined by $rr < n$.

Important real consequences emerge under the circumstances. Real rates of interest rise, and output is shifted from investment to consumption. Normal growth will consequently decline. The negative difference $rr - n$ may

Table 7.2   Real debt ratio for various deficit ratio s

def	s
0.01	0.40
0.05	2.40
0.1	4.90

$\pi = 0$, $b = 0.05$, $rr = 0.02$, $n = 0.04$

thus disappear, and the economy may move into an unstable debt accumulation process. The smaller (absolutely) the initial negative difference $rr - n$ and the larger the permanent deficit with the implicit equilibrium real debt ratio, the greater is the likelihood of a change in the sign of the crucial inequality.

The shift from $rr - n < 0$ to $rr - n > 0$ does not mean that the system necessarily assumes a "Ricardian property." The change in inequality is certainly consistent with such a property. It need not occur, however, because the inequality forms just a *necessary* condition for the Ricardian equivalence to occur. Persistence of a "non-Ricardian" world under the condition $rr > n$ aggravates, of course, the real consequences outlined above. These consequences especially induce the persistent rise of interest rates and the real debt burden. They eventually determine responses in the political arena that initiate an inflationary regime.

We should note that this argument is consistent with the monetarist and Keynesian analysis of the financial consequences associated with a budget deficit discussed in section 2.3. The "monetarist" framework used 12 years ago for this purpose can easily be applied to the current problem. The common argument contrasts, however, with the argument attributed above to Sargent and Wallace in order to obtain the same result. The infinite budget constraint is made to impose the *eventual* inflationary solution. The Sargent–Wallace analysis suffers, however, from a troublesome indefiniteness associated with the arguments centered on infinite intertemporal budget constraints. The latter only conveys to agents that taxes must be adjusted *some time at an indeterminate* future in order to obey the constraint. The economic or social mechanism eventually producing the shift from debt finance to inflation remains, moreover, quite obscure. A "Ricardian world" does not seem to provide such a mechanism. Sargent and Wallace suggest in passing the operation of limits of demand for securities. But such "limits" would be reflected in rising real interest rates and thus violate the "Ricardian pattern." The implicit indefiniteness in the world described by Sargent and Wallace means that agents are confronted with a substantial uncertainty with respect to timing, magnitude, and variance of the inflation tax.

This uncertainty is not recognized by the "Ricardian model." The resulting purchasing power risk associated with nominal bonds produces a risk premium represented by a covariance term (Baghat and Wakeman 1983) in the standard capital-asset pricing model. This risk premium is added to the basic (risk-free) real rate of interest to form the effective real rate. Considerations of uncertainty operating in the context of an infinite intertemporal budget constraint thus move the analysis beyond a "Ricardian world." The uncertain temporal reallocation of taxes produces real consequences affecting agents' real opportunities.

A cautionary note must be added. Once we abandon "non-lump-sum" taxes, the relevant real rate rr should be net of taxes on interest payments or receipts. Second, the relation between rr and n needs to be more carefully rephrased in order to avoid a relation between a risky return expressed by n – most especially once we acknowledge the relevance of a stochastic trend (Nelson and Plosser 1982; Stulz and Wasserfallen 1985), and a possibly riskless return to represent rr.

It was argued above that the stability of the debt process – that is, the sign of the difference $rr - n$ – does not address our crucial problem raised by Sargent and Wallace. The crucial problem is the long-run danger of permanent inflation at a potentially massive scale.

Table 7.3 covering both states summarizes the long-run inflation threat associated with persistent deficits. The inflation rate is computed under the condition that the real debt ratio is held constant either at 0.33 or 0.5. We notice that, irrespective of the stability conditions $rr - n$, the long-run inflation threat embedded in a permanent basic deficit of 5 percent of gross national product would move us to levels not yet experienced as a maintained phenomenon in the United States or Europe.

Table 7.3 Inflation rate for various levels of persistent deficits

$s = 0.33, \ b = 0.05$			
$0.06 = rr > n = 0.03$		$0.02 = rr < n = 0.03$	
def	π	def	π
0.01	39%	0.01	10%
0.05	139%	0.05	90%
0.10	239%	0.10	190%

$s = 0.5, \ b = 0.05$			
$0.06 = rr > n = 0.03$		$0.02 = rr < n = 0.03$	
def	π	def	π
0.01	50%	0.01	7%
0.05	150%	0.05	87%
0.10	250%	0.10	187%

4.2 The Endogenous State of the Monetary Regime: A Choice-Theoretic Analysis

The absence of any motivating force in the account presented by Sargent and Wallace explaining the eventual change in monetary regime directs our attention to McCallum's (1984) paper. The author adapts the model introduced by Sidrauski for his purpose. A representative agent maximizes the present value of current and future (instantaneous) utility over an infinite horizon. Instantaneous utility depends on real consumption and real money balances. Bonds, issued by the government, convey no direct utility to the agent. They do occur, however, in the agents' budget constraint. The agent is, moreover, visualized as a joint consuming-producing unit. A simple production technology is thus incorporated in the budget constraint. Maximization proceeds subject to the (infinite) set of these constraints. The first-order conditions yield restrictions on consumption c, real balances m, the stock of real capital k, the Lagrangian variable, and the usual inequality constraint bearing on the real rate of interest and the agent's bond holdings b. These conditions are supplemented with the government sector's budget constraint, which provides for finance of the deficit by means of money creation and bond issues. Consolidation of household and government constraint yields an income–expenditure statement in real terms.

A steady-state solution for all the relevant variables is easily satisfied under mixed bond–money financing. The steady-state condition requires that both money and bonds rise by equal percentages in this case. The deficit is, moreover, defined in the sense of the basic deficit exclusive of interest payments. Once the real deficit is fixed the associated percentage rise in nominal money balances determines the inflation rate. The optimality condition for real capital k yields the optimal stock by equating its marginal product with the exogenous utility rate of time preference. Insertion of the latter result into the consolidated constraint yields the optimal rate of consumption. The remaining first-order conditions determine real balances, Lagrangian multiplier and equality between the real rate of interest and the utility rate of time preference. The latter follows from the occurrence of a positive bond stock. Lastly, the magnitude of this stock is settled by the real version of the government's budget constraint.

The solution of the mixed finance case carries through without a hitch and also satisfies the transversatility conditions. Similarly, financing the deficit with money only poses no problem. The argument proceeds as above. This case implies, however, that the real rate of interest remains below the utility rate of time preference. A problem arises, however, when the deficit, as defined, is only financed by bond issues. The transversatile conditions are violated in this case. There exists no steady-state solution for bond-financed permanent deficit. We also note that the real version of the government budget constraint would imply a *negative* steady-state stock of bonds that cannot be reconciled with the model.

McCallum demonstrates that the problem is quite sensitive to the specification of the deficit to be held constant. The pattern changes once we move beyond the basic deficit and include the interest service on the outstanding debt. The transversatility condition is not violated for the stock of bonds once this extended deficit measure is held constant. This reflects the fact that the growth of real debt per capita does not explode as in the case of a constant "basic deficit" but actually converges to zero. The difference in this case is that the persistent increase in interest payments due to the rise in the stock of bonds is matched by corresponding increases in taxes. Last, McCallum establishes that a permanently noninflationary bond-financed deficit can occur, provided the growth rate of bonds is less than the utility rate of time preference. This implies that the basic deficit is negative and converges with time toward zero. The extended deficit remains, however, positive and converges to equality with the government's interest payments.

McCallum's analysis qualifies somewhat the central proposition advanced by Sargent and Wallace. A permanent deficit need not be inflationary and need not impose a change in the monetary regime. It depends partly on the nature of the policy rule specifying the permanent deficit. But McCallum's analysis still leaves unanswered a central issue in the Sargent–Wallace argument. We learn that a noninflationary bond-financed basic deficit is impossible. It is impossible because the steady-state system cannot produce that result. This answer does not attend to the question of why, in reality, initial attempts at a noninflationary finance of a basic deficit are eventually doomed. A similar problem involves the other result, suspending the Sargent–Wallace proposition. The analysis describes a world of certainty, perfect foresight, and nondistortionary taxes. The real variables are not affected by noninflationary finance under the circumstances. It was argued in an earlier section that the prevalence of distortionary taxes with uncertainty about the incidence of future taxes very likely modifies substantially this picture of a bond-financed permanent deficit. This case is reenforced by the remaining possibility that we live in a "non-Ricardian" world.

4.3 The Empirical Relevance of the Issue

More recent experiences (Israel, Brazil, Argentina) yield, however, more telling information than this preliminary and somewhat inconclusive evidence. The section is retained for completeness.

We still need to consider the relevance of the potential threat posed by a permanent large deficit to an anti-inflationary regime. The analysis offers by itself no evidence that an anti-inflationary policy executed in the present against a background of a permanent deficit policy cannot be maintained over the long run. A number of papers over the past years examined this issue. They investigated, in particular, whether persistent deficits eventually induced inflationary policies. Robert King and Charles Plosser (1985) offer for our purposes an excellent example of this literature. They first introduce some historical background and discuss the behavior characteristics of six different seignorage measures for the United States. They find that seignorage averaged over the period considered about three-tenths of 1 percent of gross national product. The various seignorage measures are also correlated for descriptive purposes with a range of important macro variables. The authors note here a correlation of 0.44 between the deficit and inflation over the postwar period.

> However, it is worthwhile to note that the correlation is essentially zero (0.02) for the 1929–52 period. By way of contrast, there appears to be a positive correlation between money creation and both real and nominal deficits in the 1929–52 period.

There is, in general, no evidence for a contemporaneous relation between deficit and money creation in the United States. The underlying analysis does not stress, however, any particular contemporaneous relation but essentially an *intertemporal dynamic relation*. "The empirical strategy, therefore, is to look for a dynamic relation between revenue from money creation and deficits." The crucial question is whether past deficits explain subsequent revenues from money creation. The statistical results show "that seignorage does not appear to make a significant contribution to predicting any of the other government policy variables." Even more noteworthy is that deficits do not help predict seignorage.

The study extends attention beyond the United States. Among the eight nations outside Latin America only Italy exhibits some significiant contemporaneous correlation between national income account deficits and money creation. The four Latin American nations included show, in contrast, some significant contemporaneous correlation between these magnitudes. An investigation of *dynamic intertemporal* interrelation confirms, however, the result obtained for the United States. Switzerland forms an exception. This is somewhat surprising and makes, against the background of Swiss financial institutions, little systematic sense.

The study demonstrates that we so far possess little systematic evidence about the dynamic link between current fiscal policy and future monetary policy. The problem may have barely confronted Western nations over most of the postwar period. But the experience of Italy, Israel (Fischer, 1984), and Argentina (Dutton, 1971), and more casual observations from other nations does suggest that we should not rely on the persistence of the monetary regime observed over the sample period in a radically different fiscal context. The dynamic link emphasized by Sargent and Wallace hardly emerges in contexts of the modest deficits dominantly prevailing in the United States and some other nations until recently. The issue has thus just been opened, and

King and Plosser offer a useful starting point for future explorations of the subject. But such explorations need to attend to a subtle but basic analytic issue. We encounter here a generalization of the problem faced in the old fiscalist debate. It is anything but clear how the relevant fiscal variable need be specified. In particular, it is not obvious that the official administrative deficit, the national income account deficit, or some real versions of these measures form the relevant magnitude for the analysis of our problem. Kotlikoff (1984) raised some searching questions about the standard measures of deficits. These questions extend to the analysis of any possible relation between budgetary operations and subsequent monetary regimes.

4.4 The Deficit and Economic Activity

Traditional Keynesian and neo-Keynesian analysis suffered no doubt that lower income taxes or higher government expenditures raise economic activity. The presumed permanent inefficiency of the economy could be expected to offer a leverage for fiscal policy to influence output and employment. Recent experience with large deficits expected to persist into an indefinite future generated in the public arena increasing doubt about their beneficial effects. Analysis based on "non-Ricardian" assumptions emphasized, of course, for a long time the negative long-term effects of permanent deficits. These effects operate via the asset market on capital accumulation and normal output. Public doubts concentrate, however, for a variety of reasons on the short-run effects associated with deficits. Voices emerged that argued that deficits actually exert a contractionary effect and lower output in the short run independent of further effects on normal output growth. Academia could hardly stay behind the new developments. The issue certainly deserves examination. Two papers are selected in order to probe the argument of "contractionary deficits" or "preserve fiscal policy."

Feldstein (1984a) recently explored the possibility of a "contractionary deficit." His analysis revives an argument widely used by Keynesians in the 1950s to explain in real terms a persistent inflationary drift. Prices are supposed to be asymmetrically responsive to positive and negative changes in demand. Allocative demand shocks are converted under the circumstances into a persistent inflationary drift. Sectors experiencing rising real demands raise prices by a substantial margin, whereas sectors exposed to shrinking real demand lower their prices, at most, quite modestly. This idea is exploited by placing fiscal policy within an environment of specifc interacting sectors. Feldstein initially presents a simple argument along the following line. Suppose income taxes are reduced. Consumption demand rises and investment falls. The latter follows from higher interest rates. Consumption goods prices rise, whereas investment goods prices remain unchanged. The increase in the price level against a constant velocity and money stock necessarily lowers the level of output. Lower taxes thus lower output.

This suggestive argument motivates a more general and explicit analysis based on the following summary structure:

$$X = C_h + C_g + I_h + I_g, \tag{7.34}$$

$$\Pi_c(C) \cdot C + \Pi_1(I) \cdot I = v(r + \pi) \cdot M, \tag{7.35}$$

$$C = C_h + C_g, \qquad I = I_h + I_g, \tag{7.36}$$

where X = real income, C = real total consumption composed of household consumption C_h and government consumption C_g, I = real total investment consisting of household investment I_h and government investment I_g, r = real rate of interest, π = expected rate of inflation, M = money stock, $\Pi_c(C)$ = price level of consumption goods as a function of C, $\Pi_1(I)$ = price level of investment goods as a function of I, and v = monetary velocity.

All variables in eqn (7.34) occur in real terms. The simple addition of the components C and I in order to sum up to real income will not hold, in general, for a multisector specification with variable relative prices. Feldstein therefore postulates units of C and I that uniformly assure unit prices in the initial position.

Expression (7.35) states a quantity equation. The left side represents nominal income and the right side nominal demand. The struture is completed by introducing a consumption function and an investment function:

$$C_h = \phi(X - T), I_h = \psi(r), \tag{7.37}$$

T refers to income taxes.

Expressions (7.34), (7.35), and (7.37) can be represented in a simple diagram. Line 1 in figure 7.5 describes eqn (7.34), and line 2 eqn (7.35). The signs of the slopes are immediatly established by inspection, and so are the directions of the shift induced by a reduction in taxes T. Both lines are shifted up, increasing the real rate of interest. The effect on real income remains ambiguous without additional constraints. Feldstein specifies three conditions sufficient to produce a shift of the intersection point to the northwest, as indicated in the graph. These conditions are (i) a low-interest elasticity of monetary velocity, (ii) a large-interest elasticity of investment, (iii) a high elasticity of Π with respect to C

The formal exercise certainly produces the desired perverse fiscal policy. Its relevance remains, however, quite doubtful. The analysis appears strangely regressive at this time. Important price-theoretical contributions are disregarded, and we revert to a peculiarly ancient Keynesian world. Analytically more serious is a basic logical flaw. Movements along line 1 and of shifts in its position hold prices constant at unity by construction. Movements along line 2 and shifts in its position modify price Π_c and Π_1. Any shift of line 1 along 2 thus modifies prices under the assumptions of unchanged prices. The same contradiction appears whenever line 2 is shifted along line 1. A change in T (or C_g, I_g) is thus analyzed within a framework exhibiting a flawed structure. This contradiction would seem to remove all significance from this attempt to establish a presumption for a "contractionary deficit."

Consider now an alternative procedure to move into a new world of fiscal policy analysis that reverses a long-accepted result of Keynesian analysis. Mankiw and Summers (1984) explored this possibility in the context of a slightly modified, but otherwise thoroughly standard, IS/LM analysis.

$$Y = C(Y - T, r) + I(Y, r) + G, \tag{7.38}$$

$$M = L(C, I, G, r). \tag{7.39}$$

The letters designating the relevant magnitudes assume their usual meanings. The modification applies to the money demand in eqn (7.39). Money demand depends separately on the three expenditure components. Mankiw and Summers essentially concentrate on consumption C as the relevant scale variable. The multiplier of income Y with respect fo T is immediately determined as

$$\frac{\partial Y}{\partial T} = \frac{C_Y[(L_C - L_I)I_r - L_r]}{\Delta}, \tag{7.40}$$

$$\text{where } \Delta = -[1 - C_Y - I_Y] \cdot [L_I \cdot I_r + L_C \cdot C_r + L_r]$$
$$- [I_r + C_r] \cdot [L_C \cdot C_Y + L_I \cdot I_Y] > 0.$$

The detailed structure of the positive denominator Δ need not concern us here. It follows that the standard result holds according to the necessary and sufficient condition

$$\frac{\partial Y}{\partial T} < 0 \text{ iff } L_C < L_I + \frac{L_r}{I_r}. \tag{7.41}$$

A necessary and sufficient condition for a "perverse response" can now be given as

$$\frac{\partial Y}{\partial T} > 0 \text{ iff } \epsilon(L, C) > \left[\epsilon(L, I) + \frac{\epsilon(L, r)}{\epsilon(I, r)} \right] \frac{C}{I},$$

where $\epsilon(y, x)$ denotes the elasticity of y with respect to x. The major portion of the paper offers a valiant attempt to present a case for the crucial inequality yielding a positive tax multiplier. The discussion assumes that $L_1 = L_g = 0$.

The authors first assess with some rough calculations the crucial inequality. They assemble for this purpose available estimates and income account data. The results confirm the condition. Similar calculations suggest, moreover, that the expenditure multiplier is little affected by the change in specification. With a value less than one it is hardly a "multiplier," however. The tax multiplier, in contrast, changes sign.

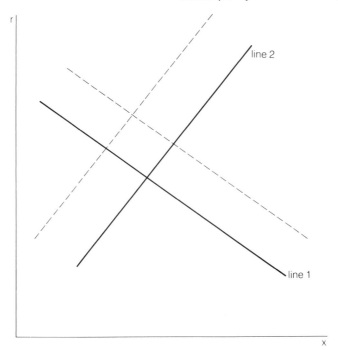

Figure 7.5   Illustration of equations 7.34, 7.35 and 7.37.

A survey of the literature indicates to the author the superiority of permanent income or wealth as a scale variable. The permanent-income hypothesis of consumption suggests, under the circumstances, that consumption would offer a good proxy for the scale variable. The choice of consumption is further supported in the eyes of the authors by the ownership distribution of money. Measures comparing the variability of velocity derived from a variety of scale variables, and the results obtained from money demand regressions appear to offer more significant evidence in this context. The first difference of a consumption velocity based on $M1$ exhibits the lowest variability. Similarly, the regressions assign, in general, a dominant weight to consumption compared to national income, disposable income and final sales, or total private spending as a scale variable.

The reservations about the traditional Keynesian tax policy are developed on the basis of a framework very close to that underlying the original fiscalist debate and judged to be unsatisfactory at the time by some Keynesian participants. Mankiw and Summers nevertheless raised a relevant point that may be robust beyond the simple IS/LM formulation used. An examination of the Brunner–Meltzer (1976) model reveals that the impact of a tax cut on income from human wealth is substantially attenuated by wealth and substitution effects on asset markets. A tax cut on income from nonhuman wealth produces a stronger response. The two tax cuts induce, moreover, opposite shifts between consumption and investment. These distinctions are glossed over by Mankiw and Summers and so are the substitution responses conditioned by distortionary taxes. Their explorations could be interpreted to mean that the short-run stabilization function of tax policies should be recognized as a questionable exercise. Comparatively much more important are long-run aspects of tax policies shaping the use and development of an economy's resources.

4.5 The Behavior of Deficits

With the beginning of this decade, fiscal policy and deficits became a major theme attracting public attention. Wall Street and the media assigned increasing importance to the deficit. There emerged a widening conviction that we had entered a new era characterized by large permanent deficits. This conviction essentially suggests that the nature of the process determining the behavior of deficits in the United States substantially changed by the end of the 1970s. Such a change would reflect the emergence of a new pattern in the political process controlling the deficit. The occurrence of a structural break in policy regime cannot be excluded a priori. But our impressions of the past four years offer no relevant evidence in support of the thesis. In order to judge our situation we need a theory about the process controlling the deficit. Guided by such a theory, suitable tests yield some evidence on the thesis asserting the recent emergence of a new fiscal regime in the United States.

For most of the postwar period there was little reason to address this issue. Macro analysis thus neglected to develop a theory about the behavior of deficits. Barro's (1981a, b; 1984a, b) prolific contributions attend in recent years also to this dimension of fiscal policy. The basic idea guiding the research emphasizes that tax rates are essentially adjusted to perceived permanent government expenditures. Their response to perceived temporary changes in government expenditures remains, under the circumstances, quite modest. Tax revenues thus behave much more smoothly over time than actual government expenditures. A first study by Barro derives the tax-smoothing behavior from the government's optimizing behavior addressed to the minimization of the excess burden imposed by taxes on the economy. Bond-financed deficits associated with temporary bulges in government expenditures are thus designed to minimize the social costs of taxation. The specific simple theory elaborated in Barro's first study (1981a) actually implies that optimal tax policy sets a constant tax rate over time. This view was recently contested by Feldstein (1984b). This argument emphasizes that we need to compare the social costs of changes in tax rates adjusted to finance transitory bulges in government expenditures with the social costs of smaller but permanent tax rate increases needed to finance the additional interest payments resulting from the prior bond financing. An incorporation of plausible parameter values into this analysis suggests that tax financing of temporary government expenditures is superior to debt financing, provided the economy's stock of real capital is smaller than its optimal magnitude. Feldstein emphasizes, moreover, that in the case of permanent expenditure there exists essentially no financial choice. One way or the other these expenditures are covered by taxes. This analysis seems to imply that the optimal stock of public debt is zero.

Feldstein's analysis obviously cannot provide the starting point for an empirical analysis of deficits and public debt even if we accept its relevance as a benchmark for a welfare analysis of budgetary operations. Any positive interpretation of the essentially normative analysis is, moreover, imme- diately disconfirmed by the facts. Lastly, an evaluation of the normative analysis as a benchmark for welfare statements lies beyond the range addressed in this paper. But its normative relevance does not preclude that intertemporal tax smoothing may offer a good basis for an analysis of deficit behavior. This smoothing pattern may be explained very differently from Barro's initial formulation that was questioned by Feldstein. It thus seems quite appropiate that Barro simply postulates a tax-smoothing pattern in his most recent examination. This hypothesis is actually formulated in its most rigid form as a constant tax rate. The basic idea is, however, consistent with some contingent flexibility of tax rates over time.

The hypothesis to be tested is constituted by two building blocks. The first introduces the tax-smoothing hypothesis, and the second combines it with the specification of deficit in terms of the budget constraint. The tax- smoothing hypothesis is applied to an intertemporal budget constraint in order to determine the expected constant tax rate. This constraint is

$$\int_0^\infty g(t)e^{-rt}\,dt + b(0) = \int_0^\infty \tau(t)y(t)e^{-rt}\,dt, \tag{7.42}$$

where $g(t)$ designates real government expenditures, b the inherited stock of real debt, τ the tax rate, and $y(t)$ the portion of income forming the tax base. Equation (7.42) immediately implies the condition for a constant tax rate:

$$\tau = \frac{\displaystyle\int_0^\infty g(t)e^{-rt}\,dt + b(0)}{\displaystyle\int_0^\infty y(t)e^{-rt}\,dt}. \tag{7.43}$$

This condition can be transformed to yield a statement relating the tax rate with permanent government expenditures g^* and permanent income y^*. These permanent levels perceived at the initial time $t = 0$ involve two assumptions. The first specifies a trend growth rate n for g and y such that the present value of g (or y) along the trend equals the present value of the actual future course of g (or y). We thus obtain

$$\int_0^\infty g(0) \cdot e^{-(r-n)t} \, dt = \int_0^\infty g(t) e^{-rt} \, dt \tag{7.44}$$

and a similar expression for y. Secondly, the permanent levels g^* (and y^*) are then defined by the condition

$$g^*(0) = (r - n) \int_0^\infty g(t) e^{-rt} \, dt,$$

$$y^*(0) = (r - n) \int_0^\infty y(t) e^{-rt} \, dt. \tag{7.45}$$

This condition establishes a relation between the present value of $g(t)$ (or $y(t)$) and its permanent level of g. A suitable replacement in expression (7.42) yields the desired relation between the average tax rate τ and the permanent magnitudes.

$$\tau = \frac{g^* + (r - n)b(0)}{y^*}. \tag{7.46}$$

The second building block invokes the budget constraint expressed in real terms

$$\frac{db}{dt} = g + rb - \tau y, \tag{7.47}$$

where b represents the stock of real debt. Replacing τ in (7.47) with the aid of (7.46) and rearranging terms yields the basic relation

$$\frac{db}{dt} = \left(1 - \frac{y}{y^*}\right)[g^* + (r - n)b] + (g - g^*) + nb. \tag{7.48}$$

The first term describes a cyclical effect. The deficit increases during recession and recedes during upswings. The effect of the business cycle on the deficit increases, moreover, with g^*. The second term – that is, $(r - n)b$ – within the bracket is negligible and can be disregarded. The second term indicates that temporary government expenditures affect the deficit one for one. Lastly, the third term reflects the financing of interest payments on outstanding debt made possible by the "normal growth" in debt corresponding to the trend growth of the economy. This item unvoidably occurs once we assume a constant tax rate. Otherwise the relative interest burden would fall and tax rates could not be constant.

Equation (7.48) describes the growth of real debt as of any path of the price level. It follows that multiplying both sides of eqn (7.48) by the price variable does not adequately render the growth of nominally valued debt B. The expression πB multiplying the inflation rate by the stock B must be added. We thus obtain

$$\frac{dB}{dt} = (n + \pi)B + \left(1 - \frac{y}{y*}\right)Pg* + P(g - g*). \tag{7.49}$$

One more term must be added, however. The structure of this last term depends on whether the debt variable is measured at market or at par value. In either case the dependent variable is modified over time whenever the average market rate of interest changes.

The underlying analysis ultimately yields the following regression:

$$\frac{B_t - B_{t-1}}{P_t Y_c} = a_0 \frac{B_{t-1}}{P_{t-1} Y_{t-1}} + a_1 \pi_1 \frac{B_{t-1}}{P_{t-1} Y_{t-1}} \tag{7.50}$$

$$+ a_2 \, \text{YVAR} + a_3 \, \text{GVAR} + a_4 \, \text{RVAR} + U_c.$$

YVAR refers either to $(1 - y/y*) (g*/y_t)$ or to an expression based on the unemployment rate related to the first by a modified "Okun's law." Either formulation reflects the cyclic influence on the deficit. GVAR expresses the temporary government expenditures, and RVAR the adjustment required to reflect the effect of changes in interest rates on market or par value of debt B. The hypothesis summarized by eqn (7.50) implies that

$$a_0 = n \quad \text{and} \quad a_1 = a_2 = a_3 = 1. \tag{7.51}$$

An extensive range of empirical examinations substantially confirms the component $a_1 = 1$ of the total hypothesis. The confirmation holds for the whole sample 1920–82, for the sample without the war, and subsamples 1920–40 or 1950–82. The coefficient a_3 on temporary government expenditures lies between 0.5 and 0.6 for the whole sample and drops to 0.22 whenever the war data are deleted. The results from the subsamples confirm this pattern. The largest estimate is 0.16. Two estimates out of 12 are (nonsignificantly) negative, and ten are smaller than their respective standard error. We observe here no confirmation of the hypothesis. All estimates of a_3 are very significantly below unity. The "cyclic coefficient" a_2, in contrast, is uniformly positive and highly significant for all estimation periods and choices of YVAR. The coefficient estimate, however, occurs systematically on the high side. It clusters around 1.5. This result is not consistent with the strict tax smoothing hypothesis. It reveals a measure of cyclical flexibility in tax rates. Lastly, the estimate of a_0 appears to be persistently too low as an estimate of the trend growth in real GNP.

The regression analysis so far yields no evidence that the current decade ushered in a new regime of budgetary processes. The observations on the deficit cast up by the four years 1980–83 are quite compatible with the patterns observed in past years. The estimated deficit traces the actual value quite well, and the residuals remain in the usual range. The regression even overpredicts the deficit for three out of four years. Barro's results also imply that realization of the CBO's baseline projections over the next five years would indicate a break in the structure of the process generating deficits. We would then actually have moved into a new policy regime. An unchanged policy regime would require substantial adjustments in expenditures and tax revenues in order to stay below the CBO projections.

The estimates of the coefficients associated with temporary government expenditures confront us with a serious and frequently occurring problem associated with the evaluation of hypotheses. Approximation errors in the measurement of specific variables may burden the statistical work with an uncertain interpretation. It is, in the present context, quite likely that the measurement of temporary government expenditures contains a substantial and variable error margin. But we know, of course, that measurement errors in the regressor bias the coefficient estimates toward zero. This problem is worsened by the fact that the sample period 1920–82 contains a single major observation for temporary government expenditures offered by World War II. Small values and little variation in this variable over most of the sample period combined with a potentially significant measurement error obscure the message of the data. A discriminating evaluation is not possible under the circumstances. It is very difficult to decide whether the results bearing on a_3 summarized above should be interpreted as a rejection of the hypothesis $(a_3 = 1)$ or can be reconciled with the hypothesis on the basis of the data problems indicated. A possible strategy to further explore the matter involves a search for data with more "action" and experimenting with different approaches to the measurement of theoretical entities as, for instance, in this case, the g^* variable. Barro (1985) examined these opportunities with another paper exploiting British data for the period 1730–1918. These data exhibit much more variation in temporary government expenditures produced by military spending. The statistical investigation deletes the cyclic component. No reliable data seem to be available for this magnitude. This omission may partly explain the serial correlations of the regression residual. The regression estimated was confined to the two terms

$$\frac{B_t - B_{t-1}}{P_t Y_t} = a_0 \frac{B_{t-1}}{P_{t-1} Y_{t-1}} + a_1 \hat{g}_t + w_t, \tag{7.52}$$

where $\hat{g}$ denotes temporary government expenditures, and w a random term. The first term in this formulation summarizes the first two terms of eqn (7.50). The hypothesis thus implies that α_0 is equal to the sum of trend growth n plus the average inflation rate over the sample period 1755–1918. The estimate $a_0 = 0.21$ coincides remarkably well with this sum. The estimate for a_1 moves, moreover, much closer to unity (i.e., $a_1 = 0.9$) than in the case of the United States. This estimate is two standard errors from unity. The

British data thus confirm the essential idea of the underlying hypothesis, but they do suggest some contingent tax adjustments.

The analysis of deficit behavior introduced a new dimension into macro-analysis. The public discussion erupting in recent years speculating about structural changes in our fiscal processes reveals the relevance of this emerging research. Barro deserves some credit for raising the issue in advance of the public arena's attention. The exploration of the "Ricardian theme" eventually led to an examination of deficits and public debt. We are hardly in a position at this stage to accept Barro's hypothesis with any sense of conviction. The evidence is still too unclear in this respect. But neither can we reject it. So far, it is "the only game in town."

5 Concluding Remarks

The professional discussion of fiscal policy has moved a long way over the past 20 years. The "great debate of the 1960s" centered on the role of fiscal policy expressed by the effect of expenditures and taxes on national income and economic activity. This discussion did modify the earlier position of the postwar period represented by the works referred to in section 2. There seemed also to ensue by the early 1970s a consensus that fiscal policy did probably produce permanent nominal effects and temporary real macro effects. There remained substantial controversy about magnitude and temporal patterns of the consequences. There also persisted a basic disagreement about the role of fiscal operations in a concept of stabilization policy. An activist exploitation of fiscal instruments for purposes of short-run stabilization was typically advocated by the Keynesians. This contrasts with a more classical conception advocated by scholars with a monetarist and neoclassical view. This view rejects short-run manipulations and advocates policies addressed to the establishment of an institutional framework, not to sequences of fiscal actions. Such an "institutional policy" should provide an essentially confined, and thus reliably predictable, pattern of fiscal operations. This issue will be considered in the last paragraphs.

The temptation to sneer at the empirical work executed at the time seems, on occasion, irresistible. It would indeed be pointless to reproduce such investigations today. It would also express some measure of incompetence relative to the state of current economic and statistical analysis. But this work had a function at the time and was not irrelevant with respect to a strong thrust embedded in the Keynesian message. It did contribute to modifying positions even when not explicitly acknowledged. Modigliani's presidential address to the American Economic Association (1977) had a different flavor than the Keynesian stories of the 1950s. We note on the other side at least some monetarists with a more explicit recognition of fiscal variables than before. An unpalatable fact found, however, little resonance at the time. The central (non-price-theoretic) emphasis assigned in Keynesian analysis to income–expenditure flows made it quite sensitive to the choice of "autonomous expenditures." This choice seems anything but settled. The meaning of traditional Keynesian theory, on an empirical level beyond formal classroom exercises, remains obscure.

More recent discussions of fiscal impact on the macro behavior of the economy may usefully lead us beyond this impasse. The market or coordination failure conception underlying the Keynesian approach naturally produced an analysis downplaying the role of prices with an emphasis on interacting income–expenditure flows. The classic tradition rejects the basic failure conception motivating Keynesian analysis. A framework emphasizing a system of ("multiplying") interacting flows is thus replaced with an essentially price-theoretical conception. This conception should not be identified, however, with a (total) market-clearing analysis. The price-theoretical approach developed by Barro includes, moreover, the important distinction between anticipated and unanticipated fiscal events or, most particularly, recognizes the differential impact of temporary and permanent fiscal actions. The multiplier effect essentially vanishes in this price-theoretical context. The consequences of fiscal events, moreover, depend crucially on the government sector's use of the goods and services acquired from the private sector. Once we abandon the sinkhole theory, new channels of influence are recognized. Barro's analysis shows, for instance, that the impact of government expenditures on goods and services depends significantly on their "supply-side effects." This differs radically from the "demand-side dominance" of Keynesian analysis. This analytic evolution, initially suggested by Martin Bailey, still needs further elaboration. The operation of the government sector involves more than a pure redirection of privately produced goods within the private sector. It should be recognized as a production sector absorbing inputs converted into an output. The difference in the incentive structure between private and public sectors implies an important difference between the production functions of the two sectors. We also need to consider to what extent these consequences associated with the government sector as a production sector bear more significantly on longer-term aspects of an economy.

The dimensions covered by fiscal policy were significantly extended with the introduction of the Ricardian theme. The "Ricardian equivalence theorem" defines a useful benchmark for our professional discussions. It obliges advocates of a more or less "conventional thesis" to specify the conditions responsible for the real consequences of the government's decisions about how to finance expenditures. The possible recognition of a pure debt effect on real variables, explicitly acknowleged by the "stability analysis" of the early 1970s, would hardly suffice today. The discussion unleashed over the years directed our attention to new mechanisms or channels of influence conveying real impulses from the government's financial decisions. The association of deficit finance with intergenerational transfers, the role of uncertainty and risk related with future tax liabilities, and the condition of intergenerational transfers linked with the function of bequests deserve critical exploration by the profession. We may yet convince ourselves that the government's "financial mix" does exert some real consequences but, to some extent, for reasons beyond the pure debt effect. We also note that the extension of fiscal analysis summarized above increasingly directs our attention to a range of influences modifying the division of total output between real consumption, household real capital, and real capital used in the production process. These channels condition normal output. Their operation may be more important than the immediate impact on total output.

The emergence of an apparently persistent deficit was bound to attract the profession's interest. Attempts to justify some public concern that "deficits are contractionary" are so far at best speculatively "interesting." More significant seems to be the attempt to explain the observable behavior of deficits. A useful explanation would offer a criterion for judging the occurrence of changes in fiscal regime. The issue raised by Sargent and Wallace also deserves serious further attention. It involves a basic question about the political role of monetary and fiscal institutions and the relevant deficit measure guiding policy. The problem arises whenever fiscal institutions dominate the monetary institutions over the longer horizon. Political economy analysis seems to support this assumption. It follows under the circumstances that a breakdown of the "Victorian rule" (Buchanan, 1985) ultimately determines an inflationary adjustment of monetary policy. The nature of the monetary regime ultimately depends on the prevailing fiscal regime. A noninflationary monetary regime thus requires for its survival a fiscal regime approximating a "Victorian rule." But the analysis of this issue remained somewhat incomplete. The economic and political mechanism creating the accommodation of monetary policy to a permanent deficit still requires some attention. The empirical relevance is also unresolved at this time. There exists so far little supportive evidence, but then we may have only entered the age of permanent deficits.

Finally, a basic issue of political economy should be faced. The contrasting conceptions of fiscal policy offered by the Keynesian vision and the classical tradition were characterized in a previous paragraph. The issue cannot be left unattended with the easy escape into "ideology." There is more involved that deserves the careful attention of the political economist.

Three substantive issues condition the policy conception: the basic coordination failure of a market economy, the information problem confronting policymakers, and the characteristic operation of political institutions. Some Keynesians emphasize that the basic coordination failure of market economies necessitates the intervention of the government in order to offset this failure. Such intervention exploits to a large extent the powers of fiscal policy. The coordination failure to be corrected with the aid of fiscal policy involves, moreover, both a short-run and a long-run dimension. The latter dominated the attention at the end of World War II with the projections of oversaving and secular stagnation. This "structural coordination failure" justifies a permanent large deficit to offset private oversaving. This portion of the Keynesian argument offers no basis for *activist* manipulation of fiscal policy or for a large government sector. Activist manipulation follows from an emphasis of a "dynamic coordination failure" that produces inefficient fluctuations in output and employment.

One strand of the issue thus depends on the substantive question of a long-run (structural) coordination problem. The view advanced by Keynesians in this respect forty years ago was thoroughly disconfirmed by the end of the 1950s. The issue remains, however, as we still encounter assertions that an economy may be trapped within a set of multiple "underemployment equilibria." The other strand, represented by the "dynamic coordination failure," constituting the case for an activist fiscal policy, involves three distinct substantive issues. We note first the idea that fluctuations in output and employment are inherently inefficient. The reviving interest in "real business cycle theories" warns us, however, that economic fluctuations are not necessarily inefficient. The analysis developed by Stulz and Wasserfallen (1985) demonstrates, moreover, that economic fluctuations may reflect the characteristics of financial regimes. But this cautionary note is really just a special case of the general information problem faced by policymakers. The activist argument implicitly assumes that policymakers do possess reliable and detailed knowledge about the dynamic properties of the economy. Such knowledge would certainly allow the pursuit of an effective fiscal intervention. But such knowledge, while necessary, is not a sufficient condition for socially successful fiscal activism. We still need to invoke a goodwill or public-interest theory or benevolent dictator view of government. The case for fiscal activism, at least for purposes of stabilization policy, thus involves two important empirical assumptions bearing on required information and the behavior of man in political contexts. The case for an "institutional policy" rests, in contrast, on the empirical proposition that the two crucial conditions postulated by advocates of activism do not hold in reality. We lack the needed *detailed* and *reliable* knowledge about the economy's dynamic structure. The range of analytic results and empirical positions covered in the survey demonstrates this state most explicitly. The consequences of this information problem are reenforced by the fact that self-interested behavior also permeates the political environment. There is little evidence that political agencies operate according to a generally recognized social welfare function. Fiscal activism produces, under the circumstances, more problems. We have no assurance that it will not *generate* truly inefficient fluctuations. These issues associated with the political economy of fiscal policy are wide open and far from settled at this stage. We may yet achieve some cognitive progress in this field once we recognize the substantive nature of the problems behind the ideological smoke.

References

Anderson, L.C. and J.L. Jordan. 1968. Monetary and fiscal actions: A test of their relative importance in economic stabilization. *Federal Reserve Bank of St. Louis Review* 50, 11–24.

Ando, A. and F. Modigliani. 1965. The relative stability of monetary velocity and the investment multiplier. *American Economic Review* 55, 696–728.

—— 1976. Impacts of fiscal actions on aggregate income and the monetarist controversy: Theory and evidence. In *Monetarism*, ed. J.L. Stein. Amsterdam: North-Holland.

Aschauer, D. 1985. Fiscal policy and aggregate demand. *American Economic Review* 75, 117–27.

—— and J. Greenwood. 1985. Macroeconomic effects of fiscal policy. In *The "New Monetary Economics," Fiscal Issues and Unemployment. Carnegie-Rochester Conference Series on Public Policy* 23, 91–138.

Baghat, S. and L.M. Wakeman. 1983. Non-diversifiable inflation risk and expected treasury bill returns. Working paper, University of Rochester, Rochester, New York.

Bailey, M.J. 1971. *National Income and the Price Level*. New York: McGraw-Hill.

Baltensperger, E. 1984. The public debt: Limits and effects. Working paper, University of Bern, Bern, Switzerland.

Barro, R.J. 1978. The impact of social security on private saving: Evidence from the US time series. *American Enterprise Institute*, 1–36.

—— 1981a. *Money, Expectations, and Business Cycles: Essays in Macroeconomics*. New York: Academic Press.

—— 1981b. Output effects of government purchases. *Journal of Political Economy* 89, 1,086–21.

—— 1984a. *Macroeconomics*. New York: Wiley.

—— 1984b. US deficits since World War I. Working paper, University of Rochester, Rochester, New York.

—— 1985. Government spending, interest rates, prices and budget deficits in the UK 1730–1918. Working Paper No. 1, Rochester Center for Economic Research, University of Rochester.

Barsky, R.B., N.G. Mankiw, and S.P. Zeldes. 1984. Ricardian consumers with Keynesian propensities. NBER Working Paper Series, No. 1400.

Bernheim, E.D., A. Schleifer, and L.H. Summers. 1985. Bequests as a means of payment. *Journal of Political Economy* 93, 1,045–76.

Blanchard, Olivier. 1984. Debt, deficits and finite horizons. NBER Working Paper Series.

Blinder, A.S. and R.M. Solow. 1974. *The Economics of Public Finance*. Washington, D.C.: Brookings Institute.

—— 1976. Does fiscal policy still matter? A reply. *Journal of Monetary Economics* 2, 501–10.

Bomhoff, E.J. 1983. *Monetary Uncertainty*. Amsterdam: North-Holland.

Boskin, M.J. and L.J. Kotlikoff. 1985. Public debt and US saving: A new test of the neutrality hypothesis. In *The "New Monetary Economics," Fiscal Issues and Unemployment. Carnegie-Rochester Conference Series on Public Policy* 23, 55–86.

Brunner, K. 1951. Inconsistency and indeterminacy in classical economics. *Econometrica*, 19, 152–73.

—— 1970. Ein neuformulierung der quantitatstheorie des geldes. *Kredit und Kapital.* 1–30.

—— 1971. Survey of selected issues in monetary theory. *Schweitzerische Zeitschrift für Volkswirtschaft und Statistik* 107 (1).

—— 1976. Inflation, money and the role of fiscal arrangements: An analytical framework for the inflation problem. In *The New Inflation and Monetary Policy*, ed. M. Monti. New York: Macmillan.

—— and A.H. Meltzer. 1972a. Money, debt and economic activity: An alternative approach. *Journal of Political Economy* 80, 951–77.

—— 1972b. A monetarist framework for aggregate analysis. In *Proceedings of the First Konstanzer Seminar on Monetary Theory and Monetary Policy*, ed. K. Brunner. Berlin: Dunker and Humblot.

—— 1976. An aggregative theory for a closed economy, and Reply. Monetarism: The principal issues: Areas of argument and the work remaining. In *Monetarism*, ed. J.L. Stein. Amsterdam: North-Holland.

Buchanan, J. 1985. Budgetary bias and post-Keynesian politics. In *Growth of Government*, ed. A. Lindbeck and J. Myrman.

Buiter, W. and J. Tobin. 1978. Debt neutrality: A brief review of doctrine and evidence. Manuscript.

Carlson, K. 1967. The federal budget and economic stabilization. *Federal Reserve Bank of St. Louis Review* 49, 5–12.

Chan, L.K.C. 1983. Uncertainty and the neutrality of government financing decisions. *Journal of Monetary Economics* 11, 351–72.

Christ, C.F. 1968. A simple macroeconomic model with a budget constraint. *Journal of Political Economy* 76, 53–67.

—— 1979. On fiscal and monetary policies and the government budget constraint. *American Economic Review* 69, 526–38.

Darby, M.R. 1984. Some pleasant monetarist arithmetic. *Federal Reserve Bank of Minneapolis Quarterly Review* 8, 15–20.

de Leeuw, F. and J. Kalchbrenner. 1969. Monetary and fiscal actions: A test of their relative importance in economic stabilization – A comment. *Federal Reserve Bank of St. Louis Review* 51, 6–11.

DePrano, M. and T. Mayer. 1965. Tests of the relative importance of autonomous expenditures and money. *American Economic Review* 55, 729–52.

Dutton, D.S. 1971. A model of self-generating inflation: The Argentine case. *Journal of Money, Credit, and Banking* 3, 245–62.

Evans, P. 1984. The effects on output of money growth and interest rate volatility in the United States. *Journal of Political Economy* 92, 204–22.

Feldstein, M. 1978. The impact of social security on private saving: Evidence from the US time series: A Reply. *American Enterprise Institute*, 37–47.

—— 1982. Government deficits and aggregate demand. *Journal of Monetary Economics* 9, 1–20.

—— 1984a. Can an increased budget deficit be contractionary? NBER Working Paper Series.

—— 1984b. Debt and taxes in the theory of public finance. NBER Working Paper Series.

Fischer, S. 1984. The economy of Israel. In *Monetary and Fiscal Policies and Their*

Applications. Carnegie-Rochester Conference Series on Public Policy 20, 7-52.

—— and R.C. Merton. 1984. Macroeconomics and finance: The role of the stock market. In Essays on Macroeconomic Implications of Financial and Labor Markets and Political Processes. *Carnegie-Rochester Conference Series on Public Policy* 21, 57-108.

Friedman, M. 1952. Price, income, and monetary changes in three wartime periods. *American Economic Review* 42, 612-25.

—— and D. Meiselman. 1963. The relative stability of monetary velocity and the investment multiplier in the United States, 1897-1958. In *Stabilization Policies*. Englewood Cliffs, NJ: Prentice-Hall.

—— 1965. Reply to Ando and Modigliani and to DePrano and Mayer. *American Economic Review* 55, 753-8.

—— and A. Schwartz. 1963. *A Monetary History of the United States 1867-1960*. Princeton: Princeton University Press.

Goldfeld, S.M. and A.S. Blinder. 1972. Some implications of endogenous stabilization policy. *Brookings Papers on Economic Activity* 3, 585-644.

Grenander, V. 1954. On the estimation of regression coefficients in the case of an autocorrelated disturbance. *Annals of Mathematical Statistics* 25, 252-72.

Hall, R.E. 1978. Stochastic implications of the life cycle – permanent income hypothesis: Theory and evidence. *Journal of Political Economy* 86, 971-87.

—— 1981. Intertemporal substitution in consumption. NBER Working Paper No. 720.

Hester, D.E. 1964. Keynes and the quantity theory: A comment on the Friedman – Meiselman CMC paper. *Review of Economics and Statistics* 45, 364-68.

Infante, E.F. and J.L. Stein. 1976. Does fiscal policy matter? *Journal of Monetary Economics* 2, 473-500.

Johnson, H.G. 1971. The Keynesian revolution and the monetary counter-revolution. *American Economic Review* 61, 1-14.

Keran, M. 1976. Monetary policy, balance of payments, and business cycles. *Federal Reserve Bank of St. Louis Review* 49, 7-17.

King, R.G. and C.I. Plosser. 1985. Money, deficits and inflation. In *Understanding Monetary Regimes. Carnegie-Rochester Conference Series on Public Policy* 22, 147-96.

Kochin, L. 1974. Are future taxes anticipated by customers? *Journal of Money, Credit, and Banking* 6, 385-94.

Kormendi, R.C. 1983. Government debt, government spending and private sector behavior. *American Economic Review* 73, 954-1,010.

Kotlikoff, L.J. 1984. Taxation and savings: A neo-classical perspective. *Journal of Economic Literature* 22,4.

Lucas, R.E. 1984. Money in a theory of finance. In *Essays on Macroeconomic Implications of Financial and Labor Markets and Political Processes. Carnegie-Rochester Conference Series on Public Policy* 21, 9-45.

Mankiw, N.G. and L.H. Summers. 1984. Are tax cuts really expansionary? NBER Working Paper Series.

Mascaro, A. and A.H. Meltzer. 1983. Long- and short-term interest rates in a risky world. *Journal of Monetary Economics* 12, 485-518.

McCallum, B.T. 1981. Monetarist principals and the money stock growth rule. *American Economic Review* 71, 134-8.

—— 1984. Are bond-financed deficits inflationary? A Ricardian analysis. *Journal of Political Economy* 92, 123-35.

Meese, R.A. and K.J. Singleton. 1982. On unit roots and the empirical modelling of exchange rates. *Journal of Finance* 57, 1,029–35.

Meltzer, A.H. 1981. Keynes' general theory: A different perspective. *Journal of Economic Literature* 19, 34–64.

—— and S.F. Richard. 1985. Why the social security system is in crisis. Unpublished manuscript.

Miller, M.H. and C.W. Upton. 1974. *Macroeconomics: A Neoclassical Introduction*. Homewood, Ill.:Richard D. Irwin.

Modigliani, F.I. 1977. The monetarist controversy or, should we foresake stabilization policies? *American Economic Review* 67, 1–19.

Nelson, C.R. and C.I. Plosser. 1982. Trends and random walks in macroeconomic time series. *Journal of Monetary Economics* 10, 139–62.

Plosser, C.I. 1982. Government financing decisions and asset returns. *Journal of Monetary Economics* 9, 315–52.

—— 1984. Money in a theory of finance. In *Essays on Macroeconomic Implications of Financial and Labor Markets and Political Processes. Carnegie–Rochester Conference Series on Public Policy* 21, 47–55.

—— and G.W. Schwert. 1978. Money, income and sunspots: Measuring economic relationships and the effects of differencing. *Journal of Monetary Economics* 4, 637–60.

Policies to Combat Depressions. 1956. A conference of the Universities – National Bureau Committee for Economic Research. Princeton: Princeton University Press.

Sargent, T.J. and N. Wallace. 1982. Some unpleasant monetarist arithmetic. *Federal Reserve Bank of Minneapolis Quarterly Review* 6, 1–17.

Seltzer, L.H. 1945. Is a rise in interest rates desirable or inevitable? *American Economic Review* 35, 831–50.

Silber, W.L. 1970. Fiscal policy in IS-LM analysis: A correction. *Journal of Money, Credit, and Banking* 2, 461–72.

Stulz, R.M. and W. Wasserfallen. 1985. Macroeconomic time series, business cycles and macroeconomic policies. In *Understanding Monetary Regimes. Carnegie-Rochester Conference Series on Public Policy* 22, 9–53.

Supplement to Review of Economics and Statistics. 1963. A Conference of the Universities – National Bureau Committee for Economic Research. Conference on Monetary Theory.

Tanner, J.E. 1970. Empirical evidence on the short-run real balance effect in Canada. *Journal of Money, Credit, and Banking* 2, 473–85.

Tinbergen, J. 1952. *On the Theory of Economic Policy*. Amsterdam: North-Holland.

Tobin, J. 1980. *Asset Accumulation and Economic Activity: Reflections on Contemporary Macroeconomic Theory*. Chicago: University of Chicago Press.

—— 1981. The monetarist counter-revolution today – An appraisal. *Economic Journal* 91, 29–42.

Wasserfallen, W. 1985. Makro ökonomische Unterschuger mit Rationalen Erwartungen: Empirische Analysen fur die Schweitz. Habilitation thesis accepted by University of Bern. To be published.

Weil, P. 1984. Love thy children: Reflections on the Barro debt neutrality theorem. Harvard University Working Paper.

8

Variability of Prices, Output and Money under Fixed and Fluctuating Exchange Rates: An Empirical Study of Monetary Regimes in Japan and the United States

Allan H. Meltzer

1 Introduction

The closing of the gold window at the US Treasury, announced in mid-August 1971, formally ended the Bretton Woods system of fixed but adjustable exchange rates. In Japan, the shift in regime and measures accompanying the shift are known as the "Nixon shock." The shock initially increased uncertainty in Japan, and elsewhere. Negotiations to reestablish fixed exchange rates at new parities eventually produced a new agreement that soon collapsed. In March 1973, major countries abandoned efforts to restore a fixed exchange rate regime.

The shift from fixed to fluctuating exchange rate changes the rules and procedures for issuing and withdrawing money, so it is a change in monetary regime. Changes in monetary regime change the ways in which shocks are transmitted through the economy and, to a degree, the type of shocks that

This paper appeared in *Bank of Japan Monetary and Economic Studies* 3. Tokyo: Institute for Monetary and Economic Studies, 1986, pp. 1–46. Reprinted with permission. The paper reports on a study completed while the author was a Visiting Scholar from Abroad at the Bank of Japan during the winter of 1984–5. The author is grateful to Dr. Yoshio Suzuki of the Institute for Monetary and Economic Studies and the Bank for their hospitality; Yoshiaki Shikano for providing cheerful assistance and helpful suggestions; and other helpful comments received from Kazumi Asako, Fumio Hayashi, Akiyoshi Horiuchi, Thomas Mayer, Charles Plosser, Juro Teranishi and Toshihisa Toyoda. The author is also grateful to the cooperation of Edward Bomhoff and Clemens Kool of Erasmus University, Rotterdam. Earlier versions were presented at the Bank of Japan and at Kobe, Hitotsubashi and Tokyo Universities. The final draft reflects the comments and suggestions of many participants at these seminars.

occur. As is well-known, a system of fluctuating exchange rates can transfer the effect of monetary shocks, coming from abroad, from the domestic money stock and the prices of domestic goods to the exchange rate. Fluctuating exchange rates give greater freedom to countries wishing to pursue independent monetary policies and provide more opportunity to control money. This freedom may be used to increase the stability of domestic prices, but it has been used also to produce relatively high and variable rates of money growth and inflation.

Theoretical analysis of fixed and fluctuating exchange rates considers the opportunities under each system. The classic statement of the benefits of fluctuating exchange rates is Friedman (1953). Critics of fluctuating rates usually allege that exchange rate fluctuations increase risk and inhibit trade. The classic statement of this case is Keynes's *Tract* (1971, pp. 87–94), although he limited the argument to seasonal fluctuations. A more recent statement by Kindleberger (1969) is less restricted. Kindleberger takes for granted that uncertainty about exchange rates increases uncertainty about prices and output and inhibits trade. See also McKinnon (1984).

A central issue in these discussions is the degree to which institutional arrangements – specifically the choice of monetary rules or regimes – damps or perhaps augments fluctuations. Analysis of the comparative merits of fixed and fluctuating exchange rates shows that the choice depends on such features as the relative size of the economy or the share of imports in consumption. Many early studies used a deterministic framework. Later work, allowing for some unforeseen shocks, has not yielded firmer or less conditional conclusions. Fischer (1977), and Flood (1979) list factors such as the slope of the Phillips curve, the response of spending to interest rates, the size of real balance effects and other factors that are likely to differ between countries. Further, the choice of an optimal monetary rule depends on the type of shocks that occur. For example, if there are frequent shocks to the growth rate of real output, a rule seeking price stability cannot be implemented successfully by keeping expected money growth constant. On the other hand, constant expected money growth is more appropriate if most shocks are a result of unanticipated changes in money.

Recent theoretical work carried out in the framework of the so-called Lucas supply function presumes that the dominant cause of fluctuations in output and prices is a monetary shock to aggregate demand. Initially, people misperceive the shock as a change in relative demand. The confusion of aggregative and relative demand does not persist. As soon as people learn that the stock of money has changed, output and prices (or rates of inflation) return to the expected values. In the language of this paper, the shock is a transitory shock to the level of output.

Little is known currently about the persistence of shocks. Recent studies by Bomhoff (1982, 1983) separate shocks empirically according to expected persistence and effects on levels or growth rates. Meltzer (1984), using

Bomhoff's procedure to compare the persistence of shocks to money, prices and output experienced under different monetary regimes, found substantial differences between the types of shocks and the variability of output, prices and money during different monetary regimes in the United States during this century. In the six regimes of the past century, transitory shocks were found to be less important than permanent shocks as a cause of disturbances.

Shocks differ by source as well as persistence. Analysis of the source of shocks and the interrelation between shocks to output, prices and money contributes to the discussion of the causes of fluctuations in economic activity and prices. Two alternative positions are well-known. One emphasizes the role of sudden changes in money or its growth rate as a main cause of fluctuations. The other assigns greater weight to real shocks affecting tastes, productivity or the degree of optimism and pessimism. Recent work by Kydland and Prescott (1983) and by Long and Plosser (1983) has revived interest in real theories of the business cycle. Work by Nelson and Plosser (1982) and by Stulz and Wasserfallen (1985) has revived interest in the view that postwar business cycles are mainly the result of random shocks – in their analyses, changes in the stochastic trend of output. The present paper attempts to contribute to these discussions in two ways. First, the paper presents measures of the size and degree of persistence of shocks to levels and growth rates obtained from univariate time series analysis. Then the paper considers the interrelations between shocks by estimating the effect of past real and nominal shocks on current shocks and by considering the extent to which current, unanticipated changes are unexplained and apparently unrelated to past shocks.

In a fixed exchange rate regime, current shocks to money are, at least partly, the result of current and past changes in prices and output at home and abroad. Current and past changes in prices and output reflect current and past changes in technology but also reflect current and past changes in money. This interacting set of relations is complicated further by the presence of anticipations about future monetary (or other) policies and about future effects of past changes in money and technology. A change in monetary regime to fluctuating exchange rates alters these relations, in principle, by eliminating the commitment to allow the money stock, or its growth rate, to be influenced by past real and monetary shocks. Anticipations about the future money stock and its influence on prices and output are revised, the extent of the revision depending on the degree to which the announced change in regime is followed by a change in the behavior of the central bank.

One cannot expect to resolve the long-standing issues about the comparative merits of monetary standards by considering a single country or a few countries during a short period of time. Previous work, Meltzer (1984), documents the substantial decline in variability of actual and forecast values of output, prices and money in the United States after the Second World War and shows that the variance of forecast errors declined more than proportionally to the decline in measured variability.[1]

This study narrows the time period to the postwar years but extends my earlier study in two ways. First, by using data for the US and Japan, we can begin to overcome one major issue about empirical studies – the extent to which the results are applicable beyond a particular sample. Second, the use of two major countries permits analysis of the degree to which shocks are interrelated and, also, the way in which the interrelations changed following the shift in regime from fixed to fluctuating exchange rates in 1971.

Section 2 orients the study by considering issues about the choice of monetary regime and the relation of this choice to the type of shocks and their consequences for the economy. Section 3 discusses the procedure used to separate shocks, the choice of data and some related issues. Section 4 compares the variability of output, prices and money and the distribution of variability by type of shocks in Japan and the United States under fixed and fluctuating exchange rates. Section 5 considers the interrelation of shocks. A conclusion completes the paper by summarizing the main findings.

2 The Choice of Monetary Standard

Choice of the monetary standard affects both the way in which a country receives and responds to shocks or impulses and the social cost of maintaining a payments system. Commodity money increases storage cost, but, according to proponents, commodity money reduces costs of monitoring, reduces the private and social costs of variable inflation and contributes to long-term price stability. Different monetary standards also change the type of risks that an economy bears and the ways in which they are borne.

Proper choice of the monetary standard can reduce cost and risk. From the perspective of the typical risk averse consumer who seeks to maximize the utility of consumption, the optimal choice of a standard reduces these costs to their minimum. The minimum risk in any society is the risk inherent in nature, trading and (other) institutional arrangements. Monetary arrangements cannot prevent real shocks to productivity or prevent changes in the policies of other countries or changes in non-monetary policies. But monetary arrangements can dampen (or not amplify) the domestic effects of shocks or impulses by preventing or reducing the monetary consequences of real shocks; policies of exchange rate control will differ from policies of money stock control in this respect.[2] Further, monetary arrangements can

---

[1]Forecasting methods are described in Bomhoff (1983) and are discussed below. DeLong and Summers (1984) also document the decline in variability and discuss reasons for the decline.

[2]The difference in the policies of the Bank of Japan preceding and following the first and second oil shocks of the 1970s provides an example of the ways in which different policy rules or procedures augment or reduce the impact of unavoidable shocks to the domestic economy.

affect the confidence the public has in the stability of future nominal values and, thus, work to stabilize the demand for money.

Shocks affect expectations and thus affect the size of future shocks to the same or other variables. One reason is that people may misperceive the persistence of shocks. Suppose a transitory shock is believed to be permanent, or conversely. Expected values will reflect the belief, and errors of forecast will reflect the misperception. Gradually, people correct the error or misperception and adjust their forecasts. The speed of learning depends on the amount of noise in the system, so if noise is relatively high, forecasts based on all available information can make errors in the same direction. Also, expectations are interrelated. An increase in expected money growth has implications for the expected exchange rate, the expected rate of inflation and other variables. A change in monetary regime affects the expected response to an unanticipated change in money growth or an unanticipated change in productivity.

A risk averse consumer is concerned about the choice of monetary regime. Greater stability of international values encourages diversification over a wider mix of assets and lowers risk and lowers the cost of hedging risks. Greater long-term stability of expected domestic and international prices lowers the risk that savings held in nominal assets will depreciate or appreciate over time. Unanticipated appreciation means that people, looking back, could have consumed more earlier without reducing consumption during retirement. Unanticipated currency depreciation lowers the real value of pensions and bequests denominated in the depreciating currency. In practice, risks of loss from currency appreciation or depreciation are not – and possibly cannot be – fully diversified, so concern for losses of this kind may lead risk averse consumers to reduce consumption during working years, lowering utility. The effect of hyperinflation on the real value of pensions in Germany and elsewhere during the twenties is well-known. Other less dramatic examples have occurred in countries experiencing high rates of inflation in the recent and more distant past. Greater uncertainty about future values also imposes an excess burden by raising the equilibrium rate of return to capital, reducing the capital stock and future consumption. Losses of this kind cannot be eliminated, but losses can be reduced by choosing a monetary regime that increases stability.

Some of the issues involved in the choice of monetary regime can be summarized by considering the case for a world money. A single currency, available for the world or for major trading countries, issued under conditions that maintained expected price stability over long periods of time, would reduce costs arising from internal and external price fluctuations and different rates of inflation. This is the key insight of the proponents of a world central bank or a world money. A problem with most proposals for a world money is that they often give little regard to the risks of future inflation or deflation. A world money reduces the cost of exchanging currencies and the cost of acquiring information about the monetary policies of many countries. General use of a single world currency restricts opportunities for societies to avoid the costs of inflation or deflation. To capture the gain to society from a world money, the public may be required to accept the social costs of inflation and variable nominal values.

Considerations of a world money brings out the societal gain from the introduction of a common medium of exchange and the social costs arising from fluctuations in the standard of value.[3] The nature of these costs can be developed by supposing that all countries adopt compatible monetary arrangements of the type recommended on several occasions, for example, Meltzer (1985). Under the proposed arrangement, each country commits its monetary authority to a path for money growth that adapts gradually to changes in the growth of real output and the growth of monetary velocity by setting the growth of money equal to the difference between the three-year moving average rates of growth of real output and velocity. On average, a policy of this kind limits the size of price fluctuations and contributes to expectations of domestic price stability. The international character of the policy – the fact that it is adopted by several large countries – contributes to the stability of exchange rates. Thus, the proposal contributes to the stability of prices of domestic and internationally traded goods in a way that cannot be achieved either by a single country, acting alone, that seeks domestic price stability or by a group of countries acting together to fix exchange rates. A single country can, at best, reduce fluctuations in domestic prices and thus limit the effects of these fluctuations on real variables. A fixed exchange rate can, at best, stabilize exchange rates. The proposed agreement to seek price stability can achieve as much domestic price stability as a single country acting alone and, in addition, can remove one source of fluctuations in exchange rates.

Unanticipated changes in technology, changes in the age composition of the population and other real shocks would continue to produce fluctuations in prices, output and exchange rates. Under the proposed arrangement, or others, fluctuations cannot be eliminated entirely. The choice of monetary regime or monetary standard can, at most, reduce the cost of such shocks by damping rather than augmenting the initial effects and by reducing errors in anticipations.

In principle, activist policies – including activist rules for policy as described by McCallum (1984) – do not minimize the cost of fluctuations if policymakers and the public cannot distinguish promptly between transitory and permanent changes or between changes in level and changes in growth rate. Transitory changes in level are self-reversing. If transitory changes are unanticipated, monetary policy can do nothing to prevent or offset these changes.

---

[3]Some of these issues are treated more explicitly in Brunner and Meltzer (1971), but that analysis does not consider the choice of monetary regimes.

The choice of monetary standard can, however, affect the cost of unforeseen changes by reducing the frequency of monetary changes or by limiting their size. Some argue that the central bank can use monetary changes to offset some effects of real shocks or changes in anticipations. Many economists urged discretionary changes in money at the time of the 1970s oil shocks. They reasoned that the permanent increase in the price level lowered aggregate demand by reducing real money balances, so they called for an increase in money to restore the level of real balances and reduce the social cost of adjusting to the shock. Costs may be raised, not lowered, if the one-time change in money is perceived by the public as a change in the rate of money growth. If the public believes that money growth is higher, they shift from money to real assets and, in other ways, anticipate a change in the rate of inflation.

Examples of this kind bring out some of the issues in the choice of monetary standards or monetary regimes. There are, as always, two types of errors that we can describe as excessive activism and excessive passivity. The former occurs when a policy regime introduces more variability than it removes. The latter occurs when a policy regime fails to reduce variability that can be offset. Examples of excessive activism are the use of monetary or interest rate changes to offset transitory changes and the effect on expectations if people perceive changes in level as changes in rates of change. An example of excessive passivity is a failure to adjust the growth rate of money when a change in the growth rate of output has been identified. The Bretton Woods system encouraged excessive passivity by countries outside the United States. By failing to adjust their exchange rates or change the monetary regime, they paid the cost of higher and more variable inflation and, later, the costs of disinflating.

This section emphasizes that the choice of a policy regime that reduces risk or uncertainty depends on the type of shocks that occur. Shocks may be real or nominal, permanent or transitory, changes in level or in growth rate. The choice of monetary regime and other institutional arrangements is a way of affecting the distribution between the categories and the level of risk that society bears.

3 Empirical Procedures

The statistical procedure used in the paper has two parts. The first computes the size of shocks – unanticipated changes – in each of a series of variables treated separately. Shocks are measured by taking deviations from forecasts made using the multi-state Kalman filter developed by Harrison and Stevens (1976) and implemented by Kool (1983) and Bomhoff (1983). The second procedure analyzes the relationship between shocks using vector autoregressions, VAR.

The multi-state Kalman filter uses a set of filter models to analyze data and a Bayesian learning process to revise the weights on the different models.[4] There are, in fact, two learning processes. Estimates of the underlying variability change as errors of forecast rise and fall. Each period, the program revises the conditional variance of the forecast for the next period. In addition, the program revises the probabilities assigned to the types of errors that occur. These revisions change the weights assigned to the types of errors that are anticipated: permanent and transitory errors in the level of the series and permanent changes in the growth rate of the series. (Permanent changes in level are transitory changes in growth rate.) Changes in weights affect the length of the lag in response and the weight that is placed on recent observations relative to data from the more distant past. The greater the probability assigned to transitory changes, the more weight is assigned to observations in the distant past and the slower is the optimal adjustment to new information. As more weight is assigned to permanent changes in level, or permanent changes in rates of change, optimal forecasts rely more on recent observations. In the limit, if all variability is transitory, the optimal response to an error is not to adjust, whereas if all variability is perceived as permanent, complete adjustment of expectations to new information is optimal.

In practice, weights on the particular components are adjusted according to the general success of the forecasting scheme in the recent past and its reliability in the two most recent quarters. Two quarters are the minimum period required to decide that a particular change is not entirely transitory, but the lag in adjustment increases when a permanent change occurs after a long series of transitory changes.

The forecasting model used in the study consists of equations (8.1) to (8.3) where ϵ_t, γ_t and ρ_t are, respectively, transitory shocks to the level of a series, permanent shocks to the level and permanent shocks to the growth rate.

$$X_t = \bar{X}_t + \epsilon_t \qquad\qquad \epsilon_t \sim N(0, \sigma_\epsilon^2) \qquad\qquad (8.1)$$

$$\bar{X}_t = \bar{X}_{t-1} + \hat{X}_t + \gamma_t \qquad \gamma_t \sim N(0, \sigma_\gamma^2) \qquad\qquad (8.2)$$

$$\hat{X}_t = \hat{X}_{t-1} + \rho_t \qquad\qquad \rho_t \sim N(0, \sigma_\rho^2) \qquad\qquad (8.3)$$

Combining the three equations, we have

$$X_t = \hat{X}_{t-1} + \bar{X}_{t-1} + \epsilon_t + \gamma_t + \rho_t \qquad\qquad (8.4)$$

where X is the logarithm of the observed value of output, price level or money stock. The expected value of X_t at the start of period t, denoted EX_t, is

---

[4]A more complete discussion is in Bomhoff (1983, ch. 4) and Kool (1983). The author relies on their discussions.

$$EX_t = \bar{X}_{t-1} + \hat{X}_{t-1} \tag{8.5}$$

The shocks, ϵ_t, γ_t, ρ_t are serially uncorrelated, mutually independent disturbance terms with zero means and the variances σ^2 shown in each equation.

People do not know the underlying level, $\bar{X}_t$, or the permanent growth rate $\hat{X}_t$. They observe only X_t and use the model to infer these values from the information on X_t available at the time forecasts are made. Shocks cannot be observed separately so, as shown in (8.5), the expected value and hence the forecast of X_t depends on beliefs about the underlying level and permanent growth rate of X. Consequently, the forecast of k periods in the future, made at the beginning of period t, is

$$_tEX_{t+k} = \bar{X}_{t-1} + k\hat{X}_{t-1}$$

Relatively high variance of the permanent growth rate indicates that values in the distant future are relatively uncertain. Relatively high transitory variance implies that uncertainty about values in the distant future is not much greater than uncertainty about near-term values.

Following Kool (1983), we can exploit the equivalence between eqns (8.1) to (8.3) and the familiar ARIMA (0,2,2), shown in (8.6).

$$\Delta^2 X_t = (1 - Q_1 B - Q_2 B^2)a_t$$
$$a_t \sim N(0, \sigma^2_a) \tag{8.6}$$

Differences in the values of Q_1 and Q_2 place different weights on transitory changes in level, permanent changes in level and permanent changes in rate of change. For example $Q_1 = Q_2 = 0$ implies that $\Delta^2 X_t$ depends only on the permanent rate of growth estimated from the last two values of X.

One advantage of the multi-state Kalman filter is that it adjusts to changes in the underlying stochastic process, if such changes occur. A change in monetary regime from control of money to fixed exchange rates may change the underlying stochastic process from one in which most errors are transitory changes in level (ϵ) – that arise from imperfect control – to processes in which either money growth or the level of the money stock is a random walk. The Kalman filter can decide, based on the quality of forecasts, that the process is dominated by white noise; in this case most weight is given to ϵ. Or, if the lowest forecast errors are obtained on the assumption that the process is a random walk in the level or growth rate of the series, most weight is placed on γ or ρ.

In the actual data analysis, the weights on the transitory and permanent components adjust each period, based on Bayesian learning. The program computes prior probabilities for each type of shock each period. Shocks are divided into normal and outlier observations, with the sum of the three normal shocks taking 95 percent of the prior probabilities. Initially, one-third of the weight is assigned to ϵ, γ and ρ respectively, so the initial priors are $31\frac{1}{3}$ percent for each normal shock and $1\frac{2}{3}$ percent for each outlier.

Table 8.1 Forecast accuracy

Series	Period quarterly	Kalman filter		Random walk	
		Mean absolute error (×100)	Standard error of estimate (×100)	Mean absolute error (×100)	Standard error of estimate (×100)
Japan					
Nominal GDP	1957/1–1983/4	1.18	1.62	2.95	3.38
Deflator	1957/1–1983/4	0.68	0.94	1.35	1.74
Real GDP	1957/1–1983/4	1.07	1.47	1.79	2.24
M_1	1957/1–1983/4	1.52	1.95	3.41	3.91
V_1	1957/1–1983/4	2.07	2.58	1.82	2.38
United States					
Nominal GNP	1890/1–1984/2	2.59	4.15	3.06	4.09
Monetary base	1947/1–1984/2	0.36	0.47	1.31	1.51
Base velocity	1947/1–1984/2	0.97	1.26	0.96	1.24

The data are also used to revise the variance of the forecast error. The assumptions used for these computations and for the computations of the weights assigned to each type of shock are more fully described in Kool (1983).

An indication of the comparative forecasting accuracy of the multi-state Kalman filter is given by the data in table 8.1. All series are natural logarithms of variables. Comparisons are to forecasts using a random walk.

The mean absolute errors and the standard errors of estimate for the Kalman filters are typically lower than the forecast errors from the random walk model. The principal exceptions are the velocity measures where the multi-state Kalman filter is not more accurate than the random walk. The Kalman filter uses only data for periods prior to the forecast, however, so forecasts are closer to "true" forecasts than the forecasts from the random walk.[5]

Although the forecasts using the Kalman filters compare favorably to forecasts obtained by alternative methods, they are not fully efficient. A multi-variate version of the multi-state Kalman filter is not available, so information in related series is neglected. To take account of this inefficiency, and to investigate the interdependence of shocks, forecast errors obtained using the multi-state Kalman filter are analyzed using vector autoregressions (VAR). The VAR relate the shocks estimated from the univariate Kalman filters, so they suggest the degree to which the measured shocks are either interdependent or dependent on past shocks to other varia-

---

[5]The Kalman filter forecasts differ from true forecasts because they do not make allowance for the lag in compiling and publishing data.

bles. The VAR are estimated using the program developed by Doan and Litterman (1981). In this program, each shock (forecast error) in period t, $X_{1t} - {}_{t-1}EX_{1t}$, depends on lagged value of specified shocks, where expected values are formed at the start of the period. The procedure is equivalent to a series of linear regressions that investigates first (say) the dependence of forecast errors for the money stock on lagged forecast errors for money, prices and output, then the dependence of forecast errors for prices on prior forecast errors for money, prices and output and, finally, the dependence of forecast errors for output on lagged forecast errors for the three variables. By estimating the relation between lagged shocks and current shocks, the VAR take into account some of the information in the quantity equation that is ignored in the univariate estimates.[6] Specifically, let m_t, y_t, and p_t be forecast errors for logs of money, real output and prices, computed as the difference between the (log) measured value for period t and the expected value for t constructed at the start of the period using the Kalman filter. Then the VAR system consists of three equations of the form

$$m_t = b_0 + b_1(L)m_t + b_2(L)y_t + b_3(L)p_t$$

where the $b_i(L)$ are polynomials in the lag operator.

Standard data sources are used for Japan. These are seasonally adjusted quarterly data for nominal and real gross domestic product (GDP), the price deflator, the consumer price index and the stock of money as reported by the International Monetary Fund. Monetary velocity is computed as the ratio of nominal GDP to money. M_1 is used throughout. The Bank of Japan projects M_2 + CDs and assigns greater importance to this measure of money. See, Suzuki (1984). For the entire period, however, Ishida (1984) using Divisia estimates shows that M_1 has been less influenced by deregulation and other changes, so it is a more homogeneous product for the period as a whole.

US data are from a larger project analyzing the shocks to the US economy under various monetary systems since 1890. See Meltzer (1984). Quarterly data for output and prices from 1890 to 1980 are from Gordon (1982). Monetary data for early periods are from Friedman and Schwartz (1963) with the exception of data for the monetary base (adjusted for changes in required reserve ratios). These data for recent years are from the Federal Reserve Bank of St. Louis and are available as quarterly data from 1947 to middle 1984.[7] All data are seasonally adjusted. The Kalman filter estimates start at

---

[6]The VAR do not completely exploit the restriction in the quantity equation, however. In general, if the errors are m_t, v_t, y_t and p_t, $m_t + v_t$ will differ from $y_t + p_t$. The reason is that there is no way to restrict the sums. Each of the measured errors of forecast consists of a "true" shock and the misperception of the shock (measurement error) by the Kalman filter. If "true" shocks could be measured, estimates would be consistent with the quantity equation, and measurement error would be zero. The author is grateful to Kazumi Asako for insisting on this point.

[7]Friedman, Schwartz and Gordon use standard sources for the period analyzed here, but the models depend to some degree on earlier data.

the beginning of each data series, so the forecast errors for the US are based on much longer series. Initial conditions, including initial assumptions about the probability distribution of shocks, have little influence on the US and greater influence on forecast errors at the start of the Japanese data. The same is true of the underlying variances of the series. Initial values of the underlying variances are based on the first ten observations, as explained by Kool (1983). The different lengths of the US and Japanese data series imply a larger influence of the initial estimates of the underlying variance for Japan during the early quarters of the fixed exchange rate period.

Comparison of fixed and fluctuating exchange rate periods requires choice of a date on which the regime changed. There are several candidates. The two most appealing are third quarter 1971, when the United States closed the gold window, and first quarter 1973, when the Smithsonian agreement broke down and the shift to fluctuating rates was recognized as a permanent change. I chose third quarter 1971 as the end of the fixed exchange rate system. Estimated variances and distributions of shocks into permanent and transitory are not very sensitive to the choice. Where interpretation depends on the choice of date, I report estimates also for fluctuating rates beginning second quarter 1973.

The multi-state Kalman filter treats the data as a continuous time series. An alternative procedure would analyze each regime separately. The alternative would remove the influence of a prior regime from the forecasts of the subsequent regime. A shift in regime would be analyzed as a break in forecast patterns, but forecasts would depend considerably more on somewhat arbitrary initial conditions assumed for the underlying variances and the probabilities assigned to particular shocks at the start of the new regime. The procedure used carries these (probability) weights from one regime to the next and revises the weights as new information arrives.

By treating the time series as a single series, a new regime affects the forecast error and its computation initially only by the immediate change in behavior. These initial effects are not negligible during the period studied. For Japan, there are large "outlier" shocks to several variables in third and fourth quarter 1971 and in first quarter 1973. The procedure allows people to acquire information about any change in variance gradually and to revise the weights assigned to particular shocks as they find that forecast errors increase. This procedure has greater intuitive appeal as a model of learning about the consequences of a change in regime than the use of new, arbitrarily chosen, values for the underlying variances and the prior probabilities with each change in regime.

4 Forecast Errors and Types of Shocks

Popular discussion and some academic work take for granted that the shift from fixed to fluctuating exchange rates was followed by an increase in variability of prices and output. Kindleberger (1969) is a strong statement of this view, but a related view can be found in McKinnon (1984) and Fukao (1984). The basis for some of these claims appears to be the observed variability of exchange rates. Evidence that exchange rate variability or uncertainty about future exchange rates has affected output or prices is harder to find.

This section presents measures of the variance of actual values and forecast errors for Japan and the United States under fixed and fluctuating exchange rates. Under the fluctuating rate regime, many central banks announce targets or projections of future money growth. Cukierman and Meltzer (1986) show that these announcements add to the information used to form rational expectations even if the announcements are not completely credible. Since announcements affect expectations and therefore alter forecasts, I treat the period in which announcements are made as a separate subperiod of the fluctuating rate regime. There are, then, three regimes: fixed exchange rates, and fluctuating exchange rates with and without preannounced monetary growth.

Column 1 of table 8.2 shows the computed variance for the fixed and fluctuating exchange rate regimes. Forecasts are for levels of the variable, and forecast errors are computed from levels, so variances of the levels are shown for comparison. Column 2 gives the variance of forecast errors for the two regimes and for the period of announced projections. Forecasts are obtained using the multi-state Kalman filter, described above. Column 3 is the ratio of the forecast error variance to the actual variance (times 100).

The shift from a fixed to fluctuating exchange rate regime was followed by a relatively large *decline* in the variance of real and nominal output (GDP),

Table 8.2   Actual variances and forecast error variances (×100) Japan 1957–1983

Period	Nominal GDP (1)	(2)	(3)	Price Deflator (1)	(2)	(3)	Real GDP (1)	(2)	(3)
1	40.350	0.051	0.13	3.673	0.014	0.38	19.741	0.036	0.18
2	12.568	0.015	0.12	4.517	0.007	0.15	2.254	0.012	0.53
3		0.003			0.004			0.002	
	M_1			V_1			CPI		
1	49.627	0.037	0.07	0.727	0.079	10.87	4.656	0.010	0.21
2	10.191	0.046	0.45	0.228	0.064	28.07	7.769	0.014	0.18
3		0.048			0.056			0.004	

Column (1) Variance log actual value × 100
       (2) Forecast error variance × 100
       (3) Ratio of (2) to (1) × 100

Period 1 1957/2–1971/3
       2 1971/4–1983/4
       3 1978/3–1983/4

the variance of money and velocity. The measured variances of the two price levels rose. The decline is most striking for real output; the variance is approximately one-ninth of its previous value following the shift in monetary regime.

Variances of forecast errors also declined for most variables other than the money stock following the change in regime. One possible reason for the decline is that the change contributed to the stability and predictability of the Japanese economy. Increased stability lowered the variability of the demand for money (or velocity) and possibly the covariance of money and velocity also. Use of monetary announcements was followed by a further reduction in forecast error variance for prices, real output and velocity. The latter finding is consistent with the hypothesis that the announcements contain information useful for forecasting prices, output and the demand for money.

Alternative explanations come to mind readily. One alternative was suggested earlier. The decline in actual and forecast variances may be unrelated to the change in monetary regimes. The period may have been more stable and easier to forecast despite the change in regime. This explanation seems implausible given the two oil shocks, the international debt problem, the prolonged and deep recessions of the mid-seventies and early eighties. A second alternative is that the decline in the growth of output in Japan reduced the measured or actual variance of the level of output. This explanation is less relevant for the variance of nominal GDP and less relevant also to the variance of forecast errors. Forecast values for each period include an estimate of the maintained growth rate that is revised quarterly, as shown in eqns (8.3) and (8.4).[8]

The variance of forecast errors for the money stock, M_1, did not decline following the introduction of monetary announcements and rose following the shift from fixed to fluctuating exchange rates. This suggests that variability of output and prices can be further reduced by improving monetary control to reduce variability.

The variability of money is a sufficient but not a necessary condition for variability of output or prices. The increase in measured variability of money may reflect transitory changes that the public correctly ignores. Or, the public may treat large shocks as outliers to which they assign low weight when deciding on the level of spending. In effect, the public acts on the belief that the central bank will not consistently deviate from its expected or announced growth path in one direction or another, so they assign low weight to large errors of forecast for money. In Japan, there is some evidence that credibility

---

[8]Errors of forecasting the growth rate declined also in Japan. Using equations (8.2) and (8.3), it is seen that the measured or actual growth rate is $\bar{X}_t - \bar{X}_{t-1} = \hat{X}_{t-1} + \gamma_t + \rho_t$, and the forecast error is the sum $\gamma_t + \rho_t$, the transitory and permanent errors in growth rate. Table 8.3, 8.4, 8.6 and 8.7 present these data for Japan and the US.

has been relatively high in recent years. The Bank of Japan announces projected money growth for M_2 + CDs. Deviations of growth of M_2 + CDs from projection, computed quarterly, have a mean absolute error of approximately 1.3 percent for the period of projections, 1978/3 to 1983/4.[9,10]

The Kalman filter computes prior and posterior probabilities for the normal and outlier values of the three shocks, ϵ, γ, and ρ. Table 8.3 shows the percentage distribution of posterior probabilites by type of shock. The six columns show the normal and outlier values of transitory (ϵ), permanent level (γ) and permanent growth (ρ) shocks. There is considerable uniformity in the distribution of the shocks across regimes, but there are some differences also. Money and the price deflator show a relatively larger proportion of "outlier" shocks to the growth rate under the fluctuating exchange regime. Transitory shocks to velocity and real output declined following the regime change. Several variables show relatively large "outliers" in the column labeled permanent changes in level under the fluctuating rate regime. Many of these shocks occur at the time of major events. The outlier shocks to money growth are in 1971/3, 1971/4, 1972/4 and 1973/1, the times of the so-called Nixon shock, the revaluation of the yen and the end of the Smithsonian agreement. For the price deflator, there are outlier shocks to the rate of change at the time of the oil embargo, the rise in oil prices and President Carter's introduction of domestic credit controls affecting the purchase of consumer durables many of which are imported from Japan.

The so-called Lucas supply curve, Lucas (1973), is commonly used to study the relation between shocks to prices and output. This model relies on confusion between relative and absolute price levels as a source of disturbance in the economy. The reasoning is that people are unable to distinguish between relative and absolute price changes at the time they occur. If price level changes are mistaken for changes in the relative price of particular goods or services, output expands. Later, people learn and correct their error. Inflation or prices and real values return to their underlying stationary position.

Shocks in models based on Lucas (1973) have mainly transitory changes in output and inflation. Bomhoff (1983) and Brunner, Cukierman and Meltzer (1983) consider permanent as well as transitory shocks. The data in table 8.3 are a measure of the relative importance of the various shocks. For real

---

[9]The Bank of Japan announces its target for the four quarters ending in quarter $t + 1$ at the end of quater t. At the time of announcement they know complete data for growth in quarters $t - 1$ and $t - 2$. The error in their projection is measured here as the actual minus projected growth for quarters t and $t + 1$.

[10]Column 3 of table 8.2 is a measure of goodness of fit. One minus the ratio divided by 100 is approximately the R^2 for predicted and actual values. The increase in column (3) for real GDP is similar to a decline in the correlation from 0.998 to 0.995.

Table 8.3 Posterior probabilities by period (in percent) Japan

	Normal			Outlier		
Period	Transitory	Permanent level	Permanent growth	Transitory	Permanent level	Permanent growth
			Nominal GDP			
1	21.1	47.3	28.7	0.3	1.8	0.7
2	23.3	51.9	17.7	0.1	6.8	0.1
3	15.8	57.0	19.8	a	7.3	a
			Price deflator			
1	14.9	38.8	42.4	0.3	1.6	2.0
2	3.6	30.3	52.0	0.4	2.9	10.9
3	3.6	21.6	62.3	0.8	0.2	11.4
			Real GDP			
1	25.4	46.8	23.9	0.4	2.4	1.0
2	16.8	48.0	28.5	a	6.0	0.5
3	14.7	48.4	31.0	a	5.1	0.6
			M_1			
1	13.8	22.0	60.6	0.3	1.4	1.9
2	13.5	19.6	58.3	a	1.8	6.7
3	13.6	22.4	55.9	a	2.9	5.1
			V_1			
1	28.8	37.2	29.4	1.1	2.8	0.6
2	14.4	43.4	32.9	0.1	6.3	3.0
3	9.4	46.5	34.5	a	8.0	1.5
			CPI			
1	27.5	17.9	48.6	0.4	2.7	2.9
2	17.5	17.4	59.5	a	5.1	0.4
3	6.5	12.1	78.4	a	2.4	0.6

Periods 1 1957/2–1971/3
         2 1971/4–1983/4
         3 1978/3–1983/4
a = 0.05 or less

GDP, the percentage of transitory shocks declines from approximately 25 percent under the fixed rate regime to less than 15 percent in period 3, the regime of fluctuating rates and monetary announcements. Transitory shocks to the price deflator increase in relative magnitude following the shift to fluctuating rates, but the percentage of shocks to the rate of price change, relevant for the Lucas' type model, declines. This is shown in column 2 of table 8.3 (or by the sum of columns 2 and 5). (Recall that permanent shocks to the price level are transitory shocks to the rate of price change.) In all periods, permanent shocks to the rate of price change are most frequent. Permanent shocks to the growth rate appear to be the dominant reason for uncertainty about future values of prices and money.

The percentages in table 8.3 can be used to allocate the forecast error variances in table 8.2 according to the frequency with which each particular type of shock occurred under each regime. To allocate the variance of the forecast error, I multiplied the probabilities in table 8.3 by the variances in column 2 of table 8.2. The products shown in table 8.4 are estimates of ϵ, γ and ρ in eqns (8.1) to (8.3). Normal and outlier shocks are combined. The sum of the three columns in table 8.4 is (100 times) the forecast error variance shown in column 2, of table 8.2.

Table 8.4 shows declines in transitory and permanent error variances for prices and output following the changes in monetary regime. If we use

Table 8.4 Allocation of error variance by period ($\times$10,000) Japan

Period	Transitory	Level	Growth
		Nominal GDP	
1	1.10	2.50	1.49
2	0.34	0.87	0.26
3	0.05	0.20	0.06
		Price deflator	
1	0.20	0.54	0.60
2	0.02	0.22	0.42
3	0.01	0.08	0.27
		Real GDP	
1	0.92	1.75	0.89
2	0.21	0.68	0.37
3	0.03	0.12	0.07
		M_1	
1	0.52	0.87	2.33
2	0.62	0.99	3.02
3	0.66	1.23	2.96
		V_1	
1	2.36	3.15	2.35
2	0.93	3.17	2.29
3	0.52	3.07	2.02
		CPI	
1	0.26	0.19	0.49
2	0.25	0.32	0.86
3	0.02	0.05	0.28

Periods 1 1957/2–1971/3
2 1971/4–1983/4
3 1978/3–1983/4

forecast error variances as measures of uncertainty, there is no sign that the fluctuating exchange rate regime increased either short-term or long-term uncertainty about the level of prices or output in Japan or their rates of change. On the contrary, more reliable forecasts of short- and long-term levels of output and prices became available following both changes in regime. Transitory variation in the price level and GDP almost vanished. Longer-term uncertainty depends on the value of ρ. The decline in ρ under fluctuating rates – shown by the lower variance of forecast errors assigned to permanent changes in growth – is a measure of the reduced uncertainty about future levels (and rates of change) of prices and output. Since lower uncertainty increases the welfare of risk averse consumers, these data suggest that welfare increased in Japan following the change in regime.

The monetary data show less change. One possibility, considered below, is that the variability of money reflects unforeseen changes undertaken by the central bank to offset changes in velocity. A successful policy of offsetting shocks to the demand for money, or monetary velocity, is consistent with the decline in the variability of forecast error variance for nominal GDP and the reduced size of transitory fluctuations in velocity. An alternative explanation is that forecast variances for real output and prices are unaffected by the increased monetary uncertainty because output markets ignore part of the variability in monetary and financial variables.

Short-term variability of velocity forecasts declined following the deregulation of financial markets. Short-term shifts in the demand for money appear to be smaller. More stable expectations of prices or inflation have not reduced the variability of forecasts of the permanent component of velocity, however.[11]

The shift from fixed to fluctuating exchange rates and the use of monetary announcements has much less effect on forecast errors in the United States. Measured variability of money and output declined following the change in monetary regime, but errors on forecast remain about the same. The use of announcements has much less effect on forecasts of US nominal output than in Japan. As a result of the greater decline in forecast error variance, Japan now has a lower variance of forecast errors for output than the US. For prices and money, forecast error variance remains lower in the United States, but the difference for prices is much smaller. Table 8.5 shows the US data. Note that the time periods are not identical.[12]

---

[11]The use of univariate procedures creates a problem here. Velocity is measured as the ratio of nominal output to money. No restrictions are imposed to keep the variance of velocity equal to the sum of the variances of M and GDP minus twice their covariance.

[12]Computations for 1957–71, using quarterly data were used to check whether results are sensitive to the choice of period. No major differences were found for the variances or the posterior probabilities for the US. Great weight should not be placed on these comparisons. First, the differences are typically not significantly different from zero. Second, as previously

Table 8.5 .Actual and forecast variances ($\times 100$) US

Period	(1)	(2)	(3)	(1)	(2)	(3)
		Nominal GNP			M_1	
1	12.3	0.013	0.0010	3.0	0.005	0.0017
2	7.2	0.013	0.0018	2.8	0.009	0.0032
2A		0.014				
		Deflator			M_2	
1	2.0	0.002	0.0010	9.8	0.003	0.0003
2	3.5	0.002	0.0006	4.3	0.004	0.0009
		Real GNP			V_1	
1	4.4	0.011	0.0025		0.014	
2	0.7	0.014	0.0200		0.011	
		Monetary base			Base velocity	
1	4.1	0.002	0.0005	2.5	0.014	0.056
2	4.5	0.002	0.0004	0.3	0.016	0.533
2A	8.0	0.003	0.0000	0.6	0.020	0.333
2B		0.004			0.024	

Period 1   1951/2–1971/3
        2   1971/4–1980/4
        2A 1971/4–1984/2
        2B 1976/1–1984/2

Column (1) Actual variance log level $\times$ 100
        (2) Variance forecast error $\times$ 100
        (3) Ratio forecast to actual variance $\times$ 100

Once again, we find that the actual variance of real and nominal output and the variance of money and base velocity were lower during the fluctuating rate regime. The variance of the deflator was higher in the US, as in Japan, in part a reflection of the oil shocks of the seventies. Variances of forecast errors remained about the same. It is difficult to find support here for the belief that fluctuating exchange rates hamper trade by increasing variability or uncertainty.

The posterior probabilities are expressed as percentages in table 8.6. The table shows the proportion of the shocks in each regime classified as normal and outlier values of ϵ, γ and ρ. There are noticeable differences between the fixed and fluctuating exchange rate periods. Unlike the comparable data for Japan, shown in table 8.3, the relative size of "outliers" declined for most variables. Velocities of the base and M_1 and the level of the monetary base

noted, the variances of M, V and GDP are measured independently, so the sums of the variances may not add to twice the covariance. Using the estimates in table 8.2 and 8.8 suggests, however, that the latter difference is typically not large.

Table 8.6 Posterior probabilities by period (in percent) US

Period	Transitory	Normal level	Growth	Transitory	Outlier level	Growth
			Nominal GNP			
1	0.2	8.9	81.9	0.1	1.1	7.8
2A	1.9	57.1	35.2	a	4.6	1.2
			Deflator			
1	1.0	57.6	38.0	a	1.8	1.7
2	0.2	60.9	35.7	a	2.2	1.1
			Real GNP			
1	1.1	23.8	66.4	a	5.0	3.5
2	3.7	33.3	57.8	a	3.5	1.6
			M_1			
1	0.8	23.0	66.7	a	0.9	8.6
2	a	14.0	79.9	a	0.2	5.8
			V_1			
1	0.7	14.3	72.7	0.2	0.4	11.7
2	0.2	16.9	69.5	a	1.5	12.0
			Monetary base			
1	6.7	18.6	66.6	0.2	1.6	6.3
2A	36.3	13.0	41.4	0.1	4.8	4.3
2B	36.2	12.4	39.4	0.1	6.7	5.2
			Base velocity			
1	7.0	47.3	37.8	0.1	6.9	0.9
2A	0.9	37.1	53.0	a	7.7	1.2
2B	1.1	40.7	45.8	a	10.5	1.8

Period 1 1951/2–1971/3   2A 1971/4–1984/2
     2 1971/4–1980/4   2B 1976/1–1984/2
a = 0.05 or less

are the exceptions. After the Federal Reserve began announcing monetary targets, there was a further increase in outlier shocks to the monetary base and base velocity. Some of these outliers occur when credit controls were introduced in the spring of 1980. Some reflect other periods of sudden change in US monetary policy. The policy shifts appear to increase uncertainty about the longer-term values of money and velocity. Although the shifts eventually lowered expected inflation, increased uncertainty about monetary policy has the effect of raising the real cost of the change.

Studies by Nelson and Plosser (1982) and by Stulz and Wasserfallen (1985), using time series analysis, find that the use of stochastic trends in place of deterministic trends reduces the size of cyclical fluctuations. The fluctuations commonly called business cycles appear to be dominated by changes in stochastic trend. Cyclical components – transitory changes in the growth rate – appear to be relatively small.

The multi-state Kalman filter does not fully support these findings for the United States and Japan. Shocks to real growth, ρ, are changes in the stochastic trend, and permanent shocks to the level of output, γ, include the transitory shocks to the growth rate of output usually called business cycles. For the US, table 8.7 shows that about one-third of all shocks to real output are normal and outlier shocks to the permanent level of output (γ) in both regimes. For Japan, table 8.4 shows that more than half of the shocks to real output are normal and outlier changes in the permanent level of output. For prices, the Japanese and US data differ in the opposite direction. More of the shocks in the US are to the price level; more of the shocks in Japan are to the rate of price change. For money, data for both countries show that the variance of the stochastic growth rate dominates cyclical fluctuations.

Table 8.7 gives the details of the allocation of the shocks by type of shock for the US. Data for the base show that the increased variance of forecast errors, shown in table 8.5, is mainly an increase in the transitory component of the log level of the base, ϵ, but there are no offsetting declines in other components. The variance of transitory shocks to the level of the base increased much more than the variance of γ, and ρ, following the change in regimes.

The large increase in the transitory variance of the monetary base shown in table 8.7 may indicate the use of monetary policy to offset fluctuations in base velocity or the demand for money. Table 8.8 finds little support for this interpretation. The simple correlation between contemporaneous shocks to money and velocity is typically close to zero for the US and slightly higher and positive in Japan under fluctuating exchange rates. A positive value suggests that the covariance is positive. Positive covariance implies that monetary control procedures augment shocks to output or prices by increasing variability of aggregate demand.[13]

Earlier, we considered two explanations of the finding that the variance of forecast errors for nominal GDP declined without a corresponding decline in the variance of forecast errors for measures of money and velocity. One explanation is rejected if we accept as meaningful the positive or low negative covariance between errors to money and velocity. The alternative explanation is that the economy damps shocks and variability coming from the monetary system.[14] The real sector, on this explanation, works to stabilize the economy in the face of relatively large shocks and uncertainty coming from the monetary sector. This finding, if correct, does not imply that mone-

---

[13]A positive value is also found for the contemporaneous correlation of shocks to the base and base velocity. The negative covariance of shocks to M_2 and V_2 suggests that monetary changes contributed to some reduction in the variance of nominal output shocks under fixed exchange rates.

[14]The statement in the text should not suggest causality. The shocks coming from the monetary system may start as productivity shocks and feedback to output after affecting money. Some of these interactions are studied below.

Table 8.7   Allocation of error variance by period ($\times 10{,}000$) US

Period	Transitory	Level	Growth
		Nominal GNP	
1	[a]	0.13	1.19
2A	0.03	0.87	0.51
		Deflator	
1	[a]	0.14	0.09
2	[a]	0.13	0.08
		Real GNP	
1	0.01	0.32	0.78
2	0.05	0.51	0.82
		M_1	
1	[a]	0.12	0.37
2	[a]	0.12	0.74
		V_1	
1	0.11	0.42	0.92
2	0.63	0.15	0.28
		Monetary base	
1	0.01	0.03	0.13
2A	0.11	0.05	0.13
2B	0.13	0.07	0.17
		Base velocity	
1	0.10	0.78	0.55
2A	0.02	0.89	1.07
2B	0.03	1.24	1.15

Period 1 1957/1–1971/3   2A 1971/4–1984/2
       2 1971/4–1980/4   2B 1976/1–1984/2
[a] = 0.05 or less

Table 8.8   Correlation of shocks

US	1951/2–1971/3	1957/2–1971/3	1971/4–1980/4	1976/1–1984/2
M_1 and V_1	−0.02	−0.01	−0.09	−0.10
p and y	+0.08	+0.08	−0.08	
M_2 and V_2	−0.20	−0.20	+0.01	
Base and VB	+0.01		+0.12[b]	−0.09
Japan		1957/2–1971/3	1971/4–1983/4	1978/3–1983/4
M_1 and V_1		0.02	0.15	0.16
p and y		0.04	−0.37	0.10
Japan and US[a]		1957/2–1971/3	1971/4–1980/4	
real output		0	0.52	
M_1		0.37	0	
V_1		0.03	0	
nominal output		0	0.05	
deflator		0	0	

[a] Current and two lag values of US variable, correlation is square root of R^2 adjusted for degrees of freedom.
[b] −0.07 for 1971/4 to 1984/2.
Symbols p = price deflator, y = real output, M = money stock, V = monetary velocity.

tary variability is costless. Consumption, investment and asset allocation decisions are subject to increased uncertainty and there may be costs associated with the arrangements that buffer monetary shocks.

If both expectations and actual values adjust slowly to changes in money, monetary shocks are not fully reflected as shocks to current prices and nominal output. Output and expected output (or prices) may adjust slowly to the changes in money reflected in the monetary shocks. Slow adjustment of price expectations is consistent with most studies of prices, but partial or slow adjustment of output is not. Nevertheless, the data here suggest that some of the monetary variability may be ignored. On this interpretation, some of the shocks to money or velocity would be (uncorrelated) random errors of forecast in our data. Below, we investigate this hypothesis more thoroughly.

Shocks to the price level and real output, p and y in table 8.8, have low contemporaneous correlation. A strong, positive correlation would suggest the presence of a Lucas-type Phillips curve between the levels of prices and output. The strongest relation is negative, for Japan, under fluctuating exchange rates. A negative relation is also found for the US during this period. A plausible explanation is that the correlation reflects the influence of the two oil shocks in the 1970s. Below, we investigate this relation in greater detail.

Table 8.8 also takes a first glance at the relation between shocks in the two countries. Shocks to Japanese magnitudes are assumed to depend on current and lagged values of shocks to the same variable for the US as noted at the bottom of the table. The data shown are obtained from values of R^2, adjusted for degrees of freedom. When the adjusted R^2 is negative, the correlation is set to zero. The data tell nothing about the sign of the relation.

For most variables, there is no evidence of any relation between US and Japanese shocks. The exceptions are the money stock under the fixed rate regime and real output under fluctuating rates. The latter may reflect, at least in part, the oil shocks common to all countries.

One relation, notable for its absence, is a relation between velocities in Japan and the United States under fluctuating exchange rates. McKinnon (1984) claims that currency substitution increases instability under fluctuating exchange rates. Currency substitution implies a relation between the demands for currencies, yen and dollars, in this case. Table 8.8 shows no effect of shocks to the demand for dollars, or US monetary velocity, on yen velocity or conversely.

Evidence from simple correlations, or from correlations between a small number of current and lagged values is at best suggestive. The finding of very few shocks to Japan from current or past shocks to the same US variables neglects more complex interactions. The following section attempts a more complete analysis.

5   Interaction Between Shocks

The variables considered in this paper are part of an interactive system in which unanticipated changes or shocks to one variable affect anticipations for the particular variable and others. Shocks to one variable may also induce shocks to another variable or to the same variable at a later date. Interaction between shocks can occur even in a fully rational world for several reasons. Two are most important here, but a third possible source of relations should be noted. First, there are costs of learning about changes in money, output, prices and other variables. Costs of learning affect the speed of adjustment of assets and output and may make price setting a rational alternative to price taking as suggested in Meltzer (1982). Second, people cannot identify shocks as permanent or transitory or as shocks to levels or rates of change at the time they occur. Shocks may be misperceived initially. While people learn, additional unanticipated changes can perturb the system as part of the adjustment to revised information. (Brunner, Cukierman and Meltzer, 1983). Third, the estimates from the univariate multi-state Kalman filters are not constrained by the quantity equation, as noted earlier. Inconsistencies from this source may distort the relations presented here.

The size of the shocks or unanticipated changes for Japan and the United States, reported in tables 8.2 and 8.5, includes both endogenous responses to current and past values of shocks to other variables and autonomous changes. Economic theory has built on these interrelations from its earliest days. The price–specie flow theory is one example of a theory that can be interpreted as a relation between current unanticipated changes in money, prices and output and prior unanticipated changes in money, prices and output. A main point of this theory is that monetary (gold) changes are induced by changes in the balance of trade or by capital flows arising from changes in opportunities or changes in anticipations about future values. The theory can be viewed as a dynamic theory relating past unanticipated changes to current anticipations and unanticipated changes. The price–specie flow theory is, of course, only one hypothesis, among many, relating current and past unanticipated changes of the variables analyzed here.

This section uses vector autoregressions (VAR) to study the relation between unanticipated changes in money, velocity, output and prices in Japan and the US. The study is restricted to the relation between the shocks – the degree to which a shock to one variable for one country is, at least in part, the result of unforeseen *prior* changes in the level of that variable or in the levels of other variables at home or abroad. Shocks to one variable also affect anticipations, and changes in anticipation have consequences for current and future forecasts. These influences on anticipations are ignored except as they affect errors of forecast. To the extent that anticipations are estimated correctly, forecast values correctly measure any permanent influence of lagged shocks. There are then no relations between shocks, and the procedures used here would find none. A finding of no relation between shocks does not imply that there is no effect of variability. The effect would be given by the revised anticipated values but would be neglected here.

The aim of this section is to study the relation between shocks or impulses as a step toward a better understanding of the comparative effects of alternative monetary regimes (or institutional arrangements) on variability and uncertainty. Several hypotheses are tested. Four are of particular interest. First, economists have long maintained that the transmission of shocks depends on the type of monetary regime. A shift from fixed to floating exchange rates is likely to be followed by a change in the stochastic process governing the money stock and the price level. If unanticipated changes in money and prices affect output, the stochastic process governing output may change also.[15] Countries are better able to control money under fluctuating rates if they choose to exercise control, but one of the costs of increased monetary control is increased variability of the exchange rate. Second, the fluctuating rate regime reduces variability coming from abroad, particularly variability transmitted through the monetary system. The previous section shows that variability has declined in Japan. This section considers the hypothesis that the decline is a consequence of improved monetary control. Third, McKinnon (1984) argues that currency substitution between countries is a leading cause of exchange rate fluctuations. We test for a relation between velocity shocks for Japan and the US, for the effect of exchange rate changes on velocity, and the effect of monetary and velocity shocks on exchange rate changes. Fourth, by removing most of the influence of past foreign and domestic shocks in several different ways, we investigate the extent to which shocks to money and output appear to reach an irreducible minimum for particular periods under the policy and other institutional arrangements of that period.

All of the tables below report on results for specific lag lengths. Usually, estimates were made for four, six and eight lags and occasionally for 12 lags. Since one purpose of the investigation is to find how much variance can be reduced under particular regimes, the standard error of estimate was used as a main criterion for choice of lag length to be reported. We are interested, also, in the relation between shocks. The F-statistics and significance levels were used as a second criterion. This criterion is much less robust. A particular set of lagged shocks may pass the usual test for significance at (say) lag

---

[15]Sims (1980) pioneered in the use of VAR systems in economics and recommended the use of VAR methods for identification. Although he divides his sample and tests for the differences between samples, he ignores the effect of regime change and most of the effect of foreign shocks on domestic variables.

four but not at lag six or lag eight. For example, lagged monetary shocks may have a relatively strong effect on output shocks at lags one to four, while by lag eight the effect is attributed to shocks to foreign GNP or foreign money. One further caveat should be mentioned. Coefficients have different signs in some regressions at different lags. The sum of the coefficients shown in the tables may be low either because effects are small or because coefficients of opposite sign have been summed.

Table 8.9 shows the interrelation of domestic shocks in Japan under fixed and fluctuating exchange rates. The largest difference between the two periods is in the equation for price shocks. Following the shift to fluctuating exchange rates, past shocks to money and output have larger and more reliable effects on price shocks; past price shocks have smaller and slightly less reliable effects. There is a much weaker response of money to output shocks under fluctuating rates, and the reciprocal shock from lagged money shocks to output is smaller in magnitude. Under the fluctuating exchange regime, shocks to money appear to be independent of domestic shocks or, at least, shocks to the variables specified here. Further, shocks to real output appear to be unrelated to any of the lagged shocks under fixed exchange rates, and price shocks and output shocks have no significant interaction. Following the regime change, these shocks are more closely related through dynamic interaction. The results are qualitatively unchanged if we date the start of fluctuating exchange rates at second quarter 1973.[16]

The price shock equation under fluctuating rates has the significant positive effect of past output shocks on price shocks implied by the Phillips curve. The output equation shows a negative relation between the same variables when price shocks are the lagged variable. The coefficients have approximately the same magnitude in the two equations under fluctuating exchange rates. For 1973–84, the absolute values of both coefficients increase, but they remain approximately equal in absolute value. This suggests continuing dynamic interaction that damps gradually rather than the one-way relation specified by Phillips curves.

To investigate the effects of longer lags and, later, the interaction between US and Japanese shocks, we consider a system consisting of nominal output and money. Table 8.10 shows the relations between shocks to nominal output and money in the US and Japan under different monetary regimes at eight and 12 lags.

At the longer lag, there is a relatively strong influence of past money shocks on nominal GDP shocks under fixed exchange rates for the US and Japan and under fluctuating exchange rates for Japan. There is no evidence of any influence of lagged shocks to GDP and money on money shocks in

---

[16]Revisions of tables 8.9 and 8.10 with fluctuating rates starting in second quarter 1973 are available from the author on request.

Table 8.9   Interrelation of domestic shocks VAR for Japan

Dependent variable ·	Variable	Sum of lag coefficients	F-statistic	Significance level	$\bar{R}^2$	SEE	DW
		Fixed exchange regime, 4 lags 1958/2–1971/3					
yJ	M1J	1.00	1.70	0.17	0	1.94	2.07
	yJ	−0.34	1.02	0.40			
	pJ	−0.54	0.34	0.85			
pJ	M1J	0.26	0.64	0.63	0.18	0.96	2.22
	yJ	0.45	1.65	0.18			
	pJ	−1.27*	3.55	0.01			
M1J	M1J	−0.55	0.89	0.48	0.19	1.75	1.93
	yJ	−0.72*	2.50	0.05			
	pJ	−0.41	1.22	0.32			
		Fluctuating exchange regime, 4 lags 1971/4–1983/4					
yJ	M1J	−0.01	1.30	0.28	0.17	1.00	2.14
	yJ	−0.23	0.27	0.89			
	pJ	−0.72*	2.87	0.04			
pJ	M1J	0.17*	3.26	0.02	0.47	0.59	1.71
	yJ	0.69*	6.12	a			
	pJ	0.36**	2.27	0.08			
M1J	M1J	−0.80	1.35	0.27	0	2.24	2.03
	yJ	−0.12	0.58	0.68			
	pJ	−0.48	0.24	0.91			

All variables are shocks (unanticipated changes)
Symbols: yJ = real GDP,   pJ = price deflator,   M1J = money stock
*   significance level 0.05 or less
** significance level 0.05 to 0.15
a = 0.05 or less.

Japan; the relation is principally one way. This finding is surprising given the controls on interest rates and the determination of the government and the Bank of Japan to keep nominal lending rates low. See Suzuki (1980). Policies of this kind typically lead the central bank to expand and contract money when there are positive and negative shocks to aggregate demand respectively. There is no evidence here that this happened in Japan. The effect of real output shocks on monetary shocks is negative in table 8.9, and there is no evidence of a positive influence of nominal GDP shocks on money in table 8.10.

In contrast, the US under fixed exchange rates appears to have permitted GNP shocks and past shocks to money to persist with effects on nominal GNP and money in subsequent periods. This is consistent with the very hesitant adjustment of short-term market rates by the Federal Reserve. Under the fluctuating exchange rate regime, the pattern of response appears to have changed. Past shocks to money and GNP appear to have no reliable information. These data suggest that, following the shift to fluctuating

Table 8.10   Interrelation of domestic shocks VAR for Japan and US

Dependent variable	Variable	Sum of lag coefficients	F-statistic	Significance level	$\bar{R}^2$	SEE	DW
Japan: Fixed exchange regime, 12 lags 1960/2–1971/3							
GDPJ	M1J	1.34*	2.21	0.05	0.39	1.61	1.30
	GDPJ	−0.57**	1.92	0.09			
M1J	M1J	−0.30	1.04	0.45	0.16	1.71	2.23
	GDPJ	−1.01	1.30	0.29			
Japan: Fluctuating exchange regime, 12 lags 1971/4–1983/4							
GDPJ	M1J	1.69*	2.85	0.01	0.45	0.90	2.18
	GDPJ	−0.10*	2.77	0.02			
M1J	M1J	−4.06	1.20	0.34	0.02	2.14	1.88
	GDPJ	−1.04	0.59	0.83			
US: Fixed exchange regime, 8 lags 1951/2–1971/3							
GNPUS	M1US	1.50**	1.57	0.15	0.22	1.02	2.05
	GNPUS	2.12*	3.35	a			
M1US	M1US	1.90*	2.30	0.03	0.26	0.60	2.01
	GNPUS	0.12*	2.97	0.01			
US: Fluctuating exchange regime, 8 lags 1971/4–1980/4							
GNPUS	M1US	5.85	0.74	0.66	0	1.18	2.19
	GNPUS	−2.02	0.64	0.73			
M1US	M1US	−0.64	0.93	0.51	0.32	0.77	2.08
	GNPUS	−0.69	1.13	0.38			

All variables are shocks to nominal values. GDPJ is the shock to nominal GDP for Japan: GNPUS is the shock to nominal GNP for US, and M1US is the shock to nominal money for the US.

Other symbols and notation are defined in table 8.9.

exchange rates, the unanticipated changes in money and GNP estimated by the Kalman filter, contain no information about future shocks. This finding is, of course, contrary to the conclusions reached by Barro (1978) using a different method of estimating unanticipated changes.[17]

The data in table 8.10 suggest that the decline in the variability of output in Japan is, at least in part, a consequence of the change in monetary regime. The influence of past monetary shocks on GDP shocks has declined and, with it, the variability of GDP has declined, reducing uncertainty and increasing welfare. The variability of Japan's nominal GDP fell from 2.25, the square root of the forecast error variance for the fixed exchange rate period shown in table 8.2 (in the same units), to 1.22 under fluctuating rates. Removing the effect of prior monetary shocks reduces variability to 1.61 under fixed rates and 0.90 under fluctuating rates. If we use these measures

---

[17]The difference may also result from differences in the choice of lags or from differences between nominal GNP shocks and Barro's use of real output to measure unanticipated changes in output.

as estimates of the effect of changes in regime and in techniques of monetary management, it appears that the shift to fluctuating rates was followed by a reduction of nearly 50 percent in the standard error of forecast. A further reduction in variability of 25 percent (from 1.22 to 0.9) was achieved by improved domestic monetary control.

VAR for Japan and the US as a system, in table 8.11, modify some of these findings and reinforce others. Under the fixed exchange regime, shocks to money have no reliable effects on GNP shocks in the US as they did in table 8.10. However table 8.11 shows a stronger and more reliable relation between past shocks to money (the monetary base) and shocks to GNP under fluctuating exchange rates.

The VAR for Japan show considerable influence of past US shocks on the shocks to Japan's money stock and GDP under fixed exchange rates. In contrast to table 8.10, shocks to the Japanese money stock under fixed exchange rates are no longer purely random movements; they are strongly affected by shocks to the US money stock. Nominal GNP shocks in the US are mainly the result of an autoregressive process. The shocks to nominal US GNP affect the US money stock, the Japanese money stock and the Japanese GDP directly and through the monetary system. The most reliable effects run from shocks to the US money stock to shocks to Japan's money stock and then to Japan's GDP. The effects of past money shocks on US GNP, visible in table 8.10, are too unreliable to be accepted as significant. Interaction, between nominal shocks in the two countries under fixed exchange rates, is summarized by the following schema. Lagged effects of a variable on itself are omitted. A solid line denotes a single asterisk in table 8.11, and a broken line shows the weaker interactions shown by a double asterisk.

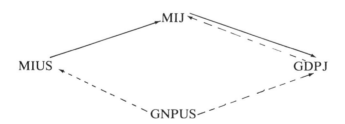

Some observers suggest that, under fluctuating exchange rates, the Bank of Japan intervenes to affect the exchange rate. See Fukao (1984). Table 8.11 shows a negative effect of shocks to the US base on M1J. The response loses statistical significance, however, if we date the start of fluctuating exchange rates in second quarter 1973. For the shorter period, shocks to the Japanese money stock fluctuate randomly and have a relatively large quarterly forecast error. Estimates for the period 1973 to 1984 are given in table 8.12. This table also shows estimates for the same period that include the change in the exchange rate, denoted DEXJ, as an additional variable.

Under the fluctuating exchange regime, shocks to the monetary base, and for the period beginning in second quarter 1973, shocks to money in Japan appear to be independent of other shocks in the system. These measures of money fluctuate randomly in response to shifting policies. Shocks to the base are followed by shocks to US GNP, and shocks to the money stock in Japan are followed by shocks to Japanese GDP. Using a solid line to denote a single asterisk in table 8.12 and a broken line to denote the weaker interactions represented by a double asterisk, we have the following schema.

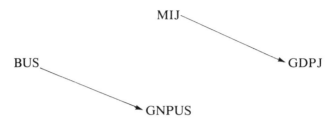

The regressions reported in table 8.12 are consistent with a monetary theory of business fluctuations in which unanticipated changes in money (or the monetary base) are followed by unanticipated changes in nominal GNP under fluctuating exchange rates. They are inconsistent with a theory in which real shocks to GNP are interrelated and independent of prior monetary shocks or in which monetary shocks are mainly the result of prior shocks to nominal (or real) output. These findings are, at best suggestive, since they are based on findings for two countries during one relatively brief period.

Table 8.12 introduces the change in the yen–dollar exchange rate as an impulse. If the exchange rate is approximately a random walk, the change in the exchange rate is approximately white noise, comparable to the forecast errors of the other variables. The regressions reported in table 8.12 test whether the change in the exchange rate is affected by past shocks to money and output and whether unanticipated movements of the exchange rate produce shocks to money and output.

Past shocks to money and output appear to have little effect on changes in the exchange rate, and there is little evidence of a systematic effect of past changes in the exchange rate on any of the nominal values in the table. The standard error of DEXJ shows that the variability of the exchange rate is relatively large, but I find no evidence of a systematic effect of the variability on other variables.

McKinnon (1984) emphasizes the effect of currency substitution on exchange rates and economic fluctuations. To study these effects, I used a bivariate system consisting of velocity shocks for US and Japan under fixed and fluctuating exchange rates. The only persistent relations found are between lagged and current values of velocity within a country. There is no significant interaction between VJ and VB or VM at four, six, eight, ten or

Table 8.11   Interrelation of domestic and foreign shocks VAR for Japan and US as a system

Dependent variable	Variable	Sum of lag coefficients	F-statistic	Significance level	$\bar{R}^2$	SEE	DW
		Fixed exchange regime, 8 lags 1959/2–1971/3					
GDPJ	M1J	0.73*	2.67	0.04	0.30	1.83	2.00
	GDPJ	0.01**	2.04	0.10			
	M1US	1.49	0.85	0.57			
	GNPUS	−0.03**	1.86	0.13			
M1J	M1J	0.84	1.66	0.18	0.59	1.15	1.78
	GDPJ	−0.22**	2.41	0.06			
	M1US	1.90*	3.46	0.01			
	GNPUS	0.88**	2.01	0.10			
GNPUS	M1J	0.58	0.60	0.77	0.34	0.84	2.04
	GDPJ	−0.19	1.00	0.46			
	M1US	3.84	1.71	0.17			
	GNPUS	−3.35**	2.07	0.10			
M1US	M1J	−0.22	1.06	0.43	0.54	0.56	2.12
	GDPJ	−0.32	1.53	0.22			
	M1US	−1.08	0.72	0.67			
	GNPUS	−1.68**	2.40	0.06			
		Fluctuating exchange regime, 6 lags 1971/3–1983/4					
GDPJ	M1J	0.21*	2.46	0.05	0.38	0.95	1.81
	GDPJ	0.40	1.62	0.18			
	BUS	0.10	1.55	0.20			
	GNPUS	0.58*	2.44	0.05			
M1J	M1J	0.12	0.62	0.72	0.22	1.90	1.80
	GDPJ	−0.44**	1.84	0.13			
	BUS	−2.58*	2.52	0.05			
	GNPUS	1.69	1.64	0.18			
GNPUS	M1J	−0.59	0.85	0.54	0.18	1.08	2.08
	GDPJ	−0.55	0.86	0.54			
	BUS	4.08*	3.98	0.01			
	GNPUS	−0.70	1.29	0.30			
BUS	M1J	a	0.70	0.65	0	0.62	1.94
	GDPJ	0.25	0.45	0.84			
	BUS	0.33	0.90	0.51			
	GNPUS	−0.57	0.36	0.90			

BUS is the US monetary base.
Other symbols are defined in tables 8.9 and 8.10.

12 lags. An objection to this procedure is that central banks may smooth some of the shocks, so the partial effects may be obscured. Table 8.13 considers the interaction between shocks to money and velocity in Japan and US under fixed and fluctuating exchange rates. For fluctuating exchange rate regime, the change in the exchange rate, DEXJ, is included.

There is no evidence of a relation between VJ and VB under either fixed or fluctuating exchange rates. Unanticipated shifts in relative demands for currency have neither large nor reliable effects on velocity. There is, however,

Table 8.12   Interrelation of domestic and foreign shocks VAR for Japan and the US as a system

Dependent variable	Variable	Sum of lag coefficients	F-statistic	Significance level	$\bar{R}^2$	SEE	DW
		Fluctuating exchange regime, 6 lags, 1973/2–1983/4					
GDPJ	M1J	0.17**	2.51	0.07	0.26	0.93	2.02
	GDPJ	0.40	1.25	0.34			
	BUS	−1.21	0.69	0.66			
	GNPUS	1.45	1.64	0.21			
M1J	M1J	0.19	0.15	0.99	0.03	1.87	1.97
	GDPJ	−0.33	0.73	0.64			
	BUS	−0.24	1.55	0.23			
	GNPUS	0.85	1.40	0.28			
GNPUS	M1J	−0.71	0.85	0.55	0.26	1.07	2.03
	GDPJ	−0.80	1.18	0.37			
	BUS	3.99*	3.99	0.02			
	GNPUS	−1.15	1.74	0.18			
BUS	M1J	0.01	0.69	0.66	0	0.69	1.86
	GDPJ	−0.05	0.67	0.68			
	BUS	1.18	1.12	0.40			
	GNPUS	−1.15	0.92	0.51			
		Including changes in exchange rate, 4 lags, 1973/2–1983/4					
GDPJ	M1J	−0.08*	3.06	0.04	0	1.09	1.98
	GDPJ	0.12	1.07	0.40			
	BUS	−0.21	0.46	0.76			
	GNPUS	0.29	0.76	0.56			
	DEXJ	0.08	0.46	0.77			
M1J	M1J	−0.14	1.54	0.23	0	1.92	2.06
	GDPJ	−0.63	0.63	0.64			
	BUS	1.77	1.01	0.43			
	GNPUS	0.26	0.90	0.48			
	DEXJ	0.01	1.16	0.36			
GNPUS	M1J	−0.31	1.12	0.38	0.29	1.05	2.21
	GDPJ	−0.52	0.67	0.62			
	BUS	0.60*	3.76	0.02			
	GNPUS	−0.56	0.96	0.45			
	DEXJ	0.05	1.25	0.32			
BUS	M1J	0.11	0.27	0.89	0	0.68	1.84
	GDPJ	a	0.36	0.83			
	BUS	−0.57	0.60	0.66			
	GNPUS	0.05	0.33	0.85			
	DEXJ	0.01	0.45	0.77			
DEXJ	M1J	−0.73	0.21	0.93	0.13	10.97	2.18
	GDPJ	−1.28	0.19	0.94			
	BUS	4.63	1.49	0.25			
	GNPUS	−3.13	1.49	0.25			
	DEXJ	0.46	1.61	0.21			

DEXJ is first difference of yen per dollar. Other symbols are defined in tables 8.9, 8.10 and 8.11.

Table 8.13   Interrelation of money and velocity shocks under fixed and fluctuating exchange rates

Dependent variable	Variable	Sum of lag coefficients	F-statistic	Significance level	$\bar{R}^2$	SEE	DW
		Fixed exchange regime, 4 lags 1958/2–1971/3					
VJ	VJ	0.01	1.05	0.40	0.12	2.60	2.06
	M1J	0.83*	2.76	0.04			
	VB	0.63	0.74	0.57			
	BUS	−2.64**	1.82	0.15			
M1J	VJ	−0.59	1.66	0.18	0.10	1.84	1.93
	M1J	−1.09**	2.01	0.11			
	VB	−0.14	0.62	0.65			
	BUS	0.91	0.69	0.60			
VB	VJ	−0.17	1.68	0.18	0.28	0.98	1.84
	M1J	−0.26	1.37	0.26			
	VB	−1.20*	2.77	0.04			
	BUS	1.17	1.16	0.34			
BUS	VJ	−0.04*	4.58	a	0.17	0.39	1.81
	M1J	a**	1.83	0.14			
	VB	0.15	0.79	0.54			
	BUS	0.09*	2.67	0.05			
		Fluctuating exchange regime, 4 lags 1971/3–1983/4					
VJ	VJ	−0.02	1.56	0.22	0.13	2.28	1.74
	M1J	0.14*	2.74	0.05			
	VB	−0.39	1.61	0.20			
	BUS	0.48**	2.09	0.11			
	DEXJ	0.01	0.51	0.73			
M1J	VJ	−0.39**	2.21	0.10	0.26	1.86	1.93
	M1J	−0.97*	3.06	0.04			
	VB	0.86**	2.39	0.08			
	BUS	0.16*	4.48	0.01			
	DEXJ	−0.02	0.94	0.46			
VB	VJ	−0.57	1.12	0.37	0.03	1.43	2.17
	M1J	−0.75	0.64	0.64			
	VB	−0.64	0.78	0.55			
	BUS	0.99	0.36	0.84			
	DEXJ	−0.04	0.97	0.44			
BUS	VJ	−0.24	0.71	0.59		0.56	2.05
	M1J	−0.46	0.91	0.48			
	VB	0.20	1.15	0.36			
	BUS	0.18	0.94	0.46			
	DEXJ	0.02*	2.91	0.04			
DEXJ	VJ	−7.80**	2.00	0.12	0.06	11.33	1.84
	M1J	−9.95	1.63	0.20			
	VB	−2.36	0.59	0.67			
	BUS	−12.40	1.46	0.24			
	DEXJ	0.05	1.68	0.18			

VJ and VB are shocks to monetary velocity and base velocity in the US and Japan respectively. All other symbols are defined in previous tables of this section.

an effect of shocks to the demand for yen (relative to GDP) on changes in the yen–dollar exchange rate. The four lag coefficients are all negative, and the coefficient is largest at lag two. The negative sign implies that, after five quarters, a 1 percent shock to VJ that raises the demand for yen relative to GDP (reducing velocity) depreciates the yen–dollar exchange rate by approximately 3 percent of its mean value.[18] This effect is perverse and may be spurious. It does not recur in the money–output system reported in table 8.12 or at other lags that I have considered.

Central banks engage in smoothing operations that are intended to offset changes in exchange rates. One interpretation of intervention is that a central bank, or central banks acting together, introduces unanticipated changes in money. Such changes appear to have no reliable effect on the change in exchange rates. Tables 8.12 and 8.13 suggest that the changes in exchange rate have a relatively large standard error, but the size of quarterly changes is independent of monetary and other shocks. Again, this does not imply that the shocks have no effect. The effect on expected values has not been studied.

Some of these findings are altered for the period beginning second quarter 1973 examined in table 8.12. There is, again, no evidence of a reliable systematic effect of exchange rate changes on the shocks to money and velocity in the two countries. Shocks to the US monetary base have a larger (positive) effect on shocks to M1J, but the effect is no longer significant using four lags.[19] The main change in the shorter period is in the DEXJ equation. Shocks to the US monetary base and US base velocity show significant negative effect on DEXJ at the 0.01 and 0.03 levels of significance. These findings suggest that unanticipated increases in US nominal GNP were followed within a year by an unanticipated depreciation of the dollar against the yen. This result is sensible only if the shocks to money and velocity raise prices much more than real values.

A major reason for activist, discretionary monetary policies is that central banks seek to offset shifts in the demand for money. Variability is introduced into the stock of money to reduce variability in demand. Earlier, we found no evidence of a negative relation between shocks to money and velocity. Table 8.13 pursues the issue by testing for effects of unanticipated lagged changes in velocity on current monetary shocks. A negative coefficient for velocity in the equations for BUS or M1J would support the hypothesis that central banks offset past shocks with a lag.

For Japan, the coefficients are negative under both fixed and fluctuating exchange rates and weakly significant under fluctuating exchange rates.

---

[18]The mean value for the period is approximately 260 with standard deviation of quarterly changes approximately 40.

[19]BUS has a weakly significant effect on M1J if six lags are used. The output summarized in this paragraph is available from the author on request.

There is some evidence that monetary operations contributed to the decline in the variability of velocity in Japan. For the US, the coefficient of VB is positive, but not significant, in both the fixed and fluctuating exchange regimes. Federal Reserve efforts to offset shocks appear to have increased variability of money and other variables at home and abroad without smoothing shocks to the demand for money at home.

Past shocks to money are followed by unanticipated positive changes in velocity. For Japan, the effects are statistically significant under fixed and fluctuating exchange rates. For the US, the responses are positive also, but they are not statistically significant. These findings are consistent with the findings in table 8.12 showing a positive response of nominal GNP to monetary shocks.

The US is generally thought to have pursued solely domestic goals under fixed exchange rates. A surprising finding in table 8.13 is the negative effect of VJ on the US monetary base during the fixed rate regime. The sum of the coefficients is small, because there are offsetting negative and positive coefficients. The initial effects of an increase in VJ lowered the unanticipated change in the monetary base but was followed after a year by an increase in BUS. The F-statistic suggests that the response was more reliable than any of the other variables in the equation.

One explanation of the response is that positive productivity shocks to output in Japan raised output and velocity. The increase in output was followed by an increase in exports from Japan to the US. Under fixed exchange rates, the rise in Japan's trade balance, and the decline in the US trade balance, should raise Japan's money stock and lower the US money stock. VJ has the expected negative effect on the US, but the effect on money in Japan is relatively weak, and the sum of the coefficients is negative, contrary to the hypothesis. An alternative explanation is that the productivity shock raised the return to capital in Japan and produced a capital flow toward Japan. The Federal Reserve's policy of targeting interest rates would lead to an increase in the base following an unanticipated change, not the observed decrease. A third alternative is that the shocks to money in Japan are to the demand for money. Increases in the demand for money lower velocity and raise interest rates. To increase the US base, the rise in interest rates must affect US and world interest rates. If this, in fact, occurred, the Federal Reserve policy procedures would produce a negative shock to the base. This reasoning assigns a larger effect to changes in the demand for money in Japan than seems consistent with the relative sizes of Japan and the US at the time.

Table 8.13 again suggests that the relations between shocks and the transmission of impulses differed under the fixed and fluctuating rate regimes. If these differences are meaningful, studies that investigate these relations, and tests of "causality" that ignore differences between regimes are likely to reach incorrect conclusions.

6 Conclusion

This study considers the types of shocks, or unanticipated changes, that affected the US and Japan under fixed and fluctuating exchange rates. A multi-state Kalman filter uses Bayesian prior probabilities to separate errors into permanent changes in level, permanent changes in growth rate and transitory changes in level. Forecasts are made for one period ahead using the prior probabilities to weight past permanent and transitory changes. The program treats each series as a univariate time series. Vector autoregression is used, subsequently, to study the relation between shocks. The study is empirical; the only theoretical restriction imposed on the data is the quantity equation, and it is used only to compute monetary velocity.

One principal finding about shocks, or unanticipated changes, is that most shocks are classified by the statistical procedure as either permanent changes in level or permanent changes in the rate of change. This finding reinforces some of the conclusions reached by Nelson and Plosser (1982) and by Stulz and Wasserfallen (1985) using different methods and data. Unlike the well-known Lucas model of the Phillips curve, transitory changes in prices (or other variables) appear to be a relatively minor source of uncertainty. Unlike Stulz and Wasserfallen, who found that shocks are dominated by changes in stochastic growth rates, both transitory and permanent changes in growth rates appear to be important. Transitory changes in growth rate (or permanent changes in level) include the type of shocks that are called business cycles.

A second main finding concerns the effect of a change in regime. The shift from the fixed to fluctuating exchange rates is treated as a change in monetary regime. The paper explores the effect of the regime change on variability and uncertainty about future prices and output. Although much has been written about the instability arising from the fluctuating rate system, I find that, for Japan, the measured variability of money, velocity, real and nominal output is lower under fluctuating rates than under fixed rates and that, for the United States, measured variability of nominal and real output declined also. For Japan, the variance of forecast errors, obtained using the Kalman filter, declined markedly under fluctuating rates.

Additional reductions of forecast error variance for output and prices were found following the decision by the Bank of Japan to announce projections of monetary growth. These announcements, if credible, increase information about money growth and reduce uncertainty. Reductions in the variability of output and prices lower the risks faced by consumers and investors and raise welfare. Announcements of monetary targets by the Federal Reserve were not, as in Japan, followed by a reduction in uncertainty. Variability of output and base money increased slightly.

Vector autoregression was used to study the interaction between unanticipated changes in money and output in the US and Japan and changes in the dollar–yen exchange rate. A related effort considered the interrelation of unanticipated changes in money and velocity for the two countries and changes in the exchange rate. The variability of exchange rate changes is relatively large, but I found no systematic relation between prior changes in the exchange rate and subsequent unanticipated changes in money, in velocity or in nominal output. This does not imply that changes in exchange rate, or in other variables, are inconsequential. Such changes may affect anticipations. However, the findings here are consistent with the hypothesis that most of the changes are absorbed within the financial sector and do not introduce additional unforeseen changes in output or the demand for money.

These findings suggest that the financial system damps the influence of changes in exchange rates on output and prices. Further, I have found no evidence of the importance of currency substitution stressed by McKinnon (1984). Tests of McKinnon's hypothesis as a relation between unanticipated changes in the demands for money in Japan and the US produce null results.

The output of the multi-state Kalman filter permits investigation of a type of Phillips curve. For Japan and the United States, there is no evidence of the positive relation between contemporaneous unanticipated changes in the level of prices and unanticipated changes in the level of output. For Japan, under fixed exchange rates, lagged shocks to real output are unrelated to price shocks and lagged shocks to the price level are unrelated to output shocks. Under fluctuating exchange rates, we find a significant negative effect of past price shocks on unanticipated output and a significant positive effect of the same magnitude in the opposite direction. These findings suggest that, in Japan, there was no reliable Phillips curve between shocks under the fixed exchange regime. Under fluctuating rates the pattern is one of dynamic interdependence between unanticipated changes rather than the structural relation that Phillips curve studies seek to isolate.[20]

The two-step procedure used here is open to the criticism that the computation of unanticipated changes using the Kalman filter ignores information in related series. The use of VAR to analyze these shocks provides some evidence of the extent of the inefficiency.[21] Comparing the lowest standard errors of estimate from any VAR to the standard error of forecast shows that reductions range from zero to 40 percent. The smallest reductions are for the monetary base and base velocity in the US and for real GDP in Japan under fluctuating exchange rates; the largest reduction is for the money stock in Japan under fixed exchange rates. For Japan, the average

---

[20]The relation is studied in levels, but the conclusion drawn is unlikely to be affected. If transitory shocks to levels are small, as is often the case, the errors in the price level equation are similar to the errors in the rate of price change equation.

[21]The VAR most likely overstate the inefficiency because they estimate relations for the whole sample period using information that would not be available at the time.

reduction in the estimated standard errors for prices, money, real and nominal output and velocity is approximately 18 percent in both regimes. For the US, the average reductions for the variables considered – monetary base, base velocity, money stock and nominal output – are approximately 20 percent in the fixed rate regime and 7 percent in the fluctuating rate regime. These estimates overstate the inefficiency. The reason is that standard errors of forecast from the Kalman filter are relatively small, so the absolute size of reductions is relatively small. The percentage reduction of the standard errors is comparable to a partial correlation coefficient. Further, the average reductions achieved with the VAR are not from a single system, so all of the reductions are not obtained simultaneously.

The larger part of the errors of forecast appears to be unrelated to past values of the variables considered. This suggests that many of the fluctuations called business cycles have relatively large, random components that are not likely to be predicted. For the present, these errors are treated as variability arising from nature, trading processes and institutional arrangements. Some of the errors are monetary, others real. If we use the standard errors of estimate, or the minimum values just discussed, as measures of the minimum values of these shocks under the prevailing regimes, the minimum values of shocks to real GDP and money in Japan appear to be between 1 and 2 percent after removing the estimated effects of past money and price shocks on output and of past output and price shocks on money. Under fixed rates, real shocks were somewhat larger than monetary shocks in Japan. Under fluctuating rates, monetary shocks have been larger. Velocity is subject to the largest relative errors of forecast, and most of the variability remained after removing effects of lagged shocks to money. Efforts to adjust money by forecasting quarterly values of the demand for money (or velocity) are not likely to minimize the risks that consumers bear. Table 8.14 shows these data.

One reducible source of variability and uncertainty is the error in forecasts of the money stock. Forecast errors for money and the monetary base appear

Table 8.14   Japan: Standard errors of estimate (in percent)

	Money	Velocity	Real GDP	Price
	Fixed rates			
From Kalman filter*	1.92	2.81	1.90	1.18
From VAR	1.75[c]	2.60[a]	1.94[b]	0.96[b]
	Fluctuating rates			
From Kalman filter*	2.14	2.53	1.10	0.84
From VAR	1.86[a]	2.28[a]	1.00[b]	0.59[b]

* The square root in percent of the forecast error variance (divided by 100) in table 8.2
[a] From table 8.13
[b] From table 8.9
[c] From table 8.11

to be followed, after a lag, by forecast errors in nominal output in the US and Japan. Under fluctuating rates, there appears little if any feedback to the base or money. Variability of the base and money appear to be entirely random fluctuations that can be reduced by improved monetary procedures.

The implication of this last finding is that institutional changes that produce more stable money or money growth would reduce variability and uncertainty. If both countries adopted independent, compatible monetary policies to achieve domestic price stability, the findings here suggest that shocks to output would be reduced. Although I have not investigated the effects of shocks on expectations, it seems likely that more stable monetary growth in both countries would contribute to more stable exchange rate expectations and more stable exchange rates as well.

The results reported here are subject to a number of limitations. Only a small number of variables have been considered. Interest rates and fiscal shocks have been ignored. Procedures are entirely empirical and are dependent to an unknown degree on the use of a particular forecasting technique and a particular statistical hypothesis. Many further estimates and tests will be required to explore the properties of the procedure and the robustness of the results.

References

Barro, R. J. 1978. Unanticipated money growth, output and the price level in the US. *Journal of Political Economy* 86, 549–80.

Bomhoff, E.J. 1982. Predicting the price level in a world that changes all the time. *Carnegie-Rochester Conferece Series on Public Policy* 17, 7–56.

——— 1983. *Monetary Uncertainty*. Amsterdam: North-Holland.

Brunner, K., A. Cukierman and A.H. Meltzer. 1983. Money and economic activity, inventories and business cycles. *Journal of Monetary Economics* 11, 281–320.

——— and A.H. Meltzer. 1971. The uses of money: Money in the theory of an exchange economy. *American Economic Review*, December.

Cukierman, A. and A.H. Meltzer. 1986. A theory of ambiguity, credibility and inflation under discretion and asymmetric information. *Econometrica* 54, 1099–128.

DeLong, J.B. and L.H. Summers. 1984. The changing cyclical variability of economic activity in the United States. NBER Working Paper, 1450, September.

Doan, T.A. and R.B. Litterman. 1981. *User's Manual RATS, Version 4.1*, Minneapolis: VAR Econometrics.

Fischer, S. 1977. Stability and exchange rate systems in a monetarist model of the balance of payments. In *The Political Economy of Monetary Reform*, ed. R. Aliber. New York: Allanheld, 59–73.

Flood, R.P. 1979. Capital mobility and the choice of exchange rate system. *International Economic Review* 20, 405–16.

Friedman, M. 1953. The case for flexible exchange rates. In *Essays in Positive Economics*, ed. M. Friedman. Chicago, 157–203.

—— and A.J. Schwartz. 1963. *A Monetary History of the United States, 1867–1960.* Princeton: Princeton University Press for the National Bureau.

Fukao, M. 1984. Monetary policy under a floating rate system. Research Bureau. Economic Planning Agency (Japan), March (unpublished.)

Gordon, R.J. 1982. Price inertia and policy ineffectiveness in the United States, 1890–1980. *Journal of Political Economy* 90, 1,087–117.

Harrison, P.J. and C.F. Stevens. 1976. Bayesian forecasting. *Journal of the Royal Statistical Society*, Series B 38, 205–47.

Ishida, K. 1984. Divisia monetary aggregates and demand for money: A Japanese case. *Bank of Japan Monetary and Economic Studies* 2, 49–80.

Keynes, J.M. 1971. *A Tract on Monetary Reform (1923)*, Vol. IV of the *Collected Writings of John Maynard Keynes*, Macmillan and St. Martin's Press for the Royal Economic Society.

Kindleberger, C. 1969. The case for fixed exchange rates, 1969. *The International Adjustment Mechanism*, Federal Reserve Bank of Boston, Conference Series 2, October, 93–108.

Kool, C.J.M. 1983. Forecasts with multi-state Kalman filters. Appendix 1 to Bomhoff (1983).

Kydland, F. and E.C. Prescott. 1983. Time to build and the persistence of unemployment. *Econometrica*.

Long, J.B. and C.I. Plosser. 1983. Real business cycles. *Journal of Political Economy* 91, 39–69.

Lucas, R.E. Jr. 1973. Some international evidence on output inflation tradeoffs. *American Economic Review* 63, 326–35.

McCallum, B. 1984. Monetarist rules in the light of recent experience. *American Economic Review* 74, 388–91.

McKinnon, R. 1984. *An International Standard for Monetary Stabilization.* Washington: Institute for International Economics.

Meltzer, A.H. 1982. Rational expectations, risk, uncertainty and market responses. In *Crises in the Economic and Financial Structure*, ed. P. Wachtel. Lexington Books.

—— 1984. Some evidence on the comparative uncertainty experienced under different monetary regimes. In *Alternative Monetary Regimes*, ed. C.D. Campbell and W.R. Dougan. Baltimore: Johns Hopkins, 122–53.

—— 1985. Rules for price-stability: An overview and comparison. In *Price Stability and Public Policy*, Federal Reserve Bank of Kansas City: 207–20.

Nelson, C.R. and C.I. Plosser. 1982. Trends and random walks in macroeconomic time series. *Journal of Monetary Economics* 10, 139–62.

Sims, C.A. 1980. Macroeconomics and reality. *Econometrica* 48, 1–48.

Stulz, R.M. and W. Wasserfallen. 1985. Macroeconomic time series, business cycles and macroeconomic policies. *Carnegie-Rochester Conference Series on Public Policy* 22, 19–54.

Suzuki, Y. 1980. *Money and Banking in Contemporary Japan.* Yale University.

—— 1984. Financial innovation and monetary policy in Japan. *Bank of Japan Monetary and Economic Studies* 2, 1–48.

Index

Compiled by Jackie McDermott